The New

BECOMING VEGETARIAN

THE ESSENTIAL GUIDE TO A HEALTHY VEGETARIAN DIET

Vesanto Melina, MS, RD
Brenda Davis, RD

Healthy Living Publications
Summertown, Tennessee

Cover Art: Jennifer Blume (www.jenniferblume.com)
Cover Design: Warren Jefferson
Editors: Joanne Stepaniak, Cynthia Holzapfel

Published in the United States by
Healthy Living Publications
an imprint of Book Publishing Company
P.O. Box 99
Summertown, TN 38483
1-888-260-8458

12 11 10 09 08 07 06   9 8 7 6 5 4

Printed in the United States

ISBN 1-57067-144-3

Illustration on page 120 courtesy of the Kansas Wheat Commission.

Melina, Vesanto, 1942-
  New becoming vegetarian : the essential guide to a healthy vegetarian diet / Vesanto Melina, Brenda Davis.
    p. cm.
Includes bibliographical references and index.
  ISBN 1-57067-144-3
  1. Vegetarianism. I. Davis, Brenda, 1959- II. Title.
  RM236.M44 2003
  613.2 62—dc21
                                    2003007593

Printed on recycled paper

The Book Publishing Co. is committed to preserving ancient forests and natural resources. We have elected to print this title at VictorGraphics on Williamsburg Recycled Offset, which is 30% postconsumer recycled and processed chlorine free. As a result of our paper choice, we have saved the following natural resources:

32 trees
1,517 lbs of solid waste
13,763 gallons of water
2,981 lbs pounds of greenhouse gases
5,535 kw hours of electricity

BOOK
PUBLISHING
COMPANY

We are a member of Green Press Initiative. For more information about Green Press Initiative visit: www.greenpressinitiative.org

To our children,

Xoph (Chris) and Kavyo;
Leena and Cory.

May your life be a reflection
of what you believe,
in the deepest recesses
of your heart and soul.

TABLE OF CONTENTS

List of Tables, Figures, and Other Charts

Acknowledgments

To everyone who contributed time, attention, and energy to this project, we offer our heartfelt appreciation.

Sincere gratitude to those who made this book possible: Our editors Cynthia Holzapfel and Joanne Stepaniak for their care and expertise, to our publisher Bob Holzapfel, and to Warren Jefferson and Gwynelle Dismukes at Book Publishing Company for their work in making this book come to life. It is a pleasure and a privilege to work with so many gifted individuals who share our vision. Your remarkable experience of the vegetarian way of life over decades on The Farm is a huge inspiration for our work. A special thank you, as well, goes to artist Jennifer Blume for the beautiful art that graces the cover of this edition.

Love and gratefulness to our families and close friends: Cory Davis (Brenda's son), for many hours of diligent recipe testing, careful record keeping, and amazing presentation of the foods prepared. Also many thanks to Cory for his daily offerings of beautifully prepared lunches, fresh-squeezed juices, and back rubs and hugs. Paul Davis (Brenda's husband) for endless support, review of various sections, and valuable assistance with charts. Leena Davis, for her advice, understanding, and encouragement. Vesanto's wonderful community at Windsong, a source of learning and wisdom about living in harmony and about vegetarian diplomacy. Vesanto's son Chris and daughter Kavyo; for the time, love, and thoughts we share. Shirley and Al Hunting, our "other home" in Seattle. Victoria Harrison, RD, coauthor in the first version of *Becoming Vegetarian* (and now living in Hong Kong) for valued friendship and work that persists in this edition.

Deepest appreciation to our cherished advisors and those sharing many hours of invaluable insight: Stephen Walsh for his thoughtful review of chapters 1, 2, 3, and 7 and insights on vitamin B_{12}; Dr. Paul Appleby for articles and careful research; Dr. Mark and Virginia Messina, Dr. Reed Mangels, and Dr. Suzanne Havala who have written such carefully researched materials on vegetarian nutrition and who continue to be an inspiration.

Special thanks to those who contributed to specific chapters, and/or provided thoughtful reviews and suggestions: Kathleen Quinn RD, Sue Firus RD, and other staff at Dial-a-Dietitian; Debbie Reid; staff at Health Canada; Dr. Thomas Barnard, medical expert and author; Dilip Barnam, president, Triangle Vegetarian Society of North Carolina; Dr. Michael Klaper, director of the Vegan Health Study; Ketti Goudey MS, RD; writers Greg McIntyre and Valerie McIntyre; Paul Pomeroy; and Syd Baumel of www.aquarianonline.com.

Warm acknowledgement to those who gave of their time and energy to support this project: John Robbins, Howard Lyman, Dr. Susan Barr, Maureen Butler, Robert Sawatzky, Jenise Sidebotham, Ralph Perkins, Vanessa Clarke of the U.K. Vegan Society, and Deborah Pageau.

Thanks to those who created delicious recipes and allowed their use in this book: Joseph Forest; John Borders and his wonderful family—Cindy, Mattie, David, and Jack; Francis and Carol Sue Janes of Seattle's outstanding Café Ambrosia; Ron Pickarski; Joanne Stepaniak; Victoria Harrison; Yves Potvin; and Yves Veggie Cuisine.

Special thanks to artist Dave Brousseau for his work on the Vegetarian Food Pyramid.

Introduction

In 1994, when *Becoming Vegetarian* was first released, there were not many books about vegetarian nutrition by registered dietitians. For decades, dietitians had been less than enthusiastic about vegetarian diets, as had the medical community as a whole. Vegetarian diets were often categorized as fad diets and were considered risky, especially for infants, children, and pregnant women. However, the tables were beginning to turn. Studies not only established the safety of vegetarian diets, but also demonstrated clear and consistent health advantages, particularly where disease risk reduction was concerned. To quote Dr. Mervyn Hardinge, a pioneer of vegetarian nutrition who took part in Harvard University's early human dietary studies on plant protein: "Attitudes toward vegetarian diets have progressed from ridicule and skepticism to condescending tolerance, to gradual and sometimes grudging acceptance, and finally to acclaim."

Becoming Vegetarian has added momentum to this shifting paradigm. It has also helped to bridge the gap between the scientific community and grassroots vegetarian organizations, as both welcomed this book as a complete and reliable guide to vegetarian nutrition. The book quickly became a national bestseller in Canada, then was published in the United States, translated into French and Portuguese, and distributed in eleven countries. With over 120,000 copies in print, it is considered a classic.

Becoming Vegetarian has been, and continues to be, an amazing journey for the authors. While Victoria Harrison was not actively involved in the revised edition (she is now living in Hong Kong), her beautiful, loving energy remains sprinkled throughout its pages. For both of us, Vesanto and Brenda, *Becoming Vegetarian* was the beginning of adventurous writing and speaking careers that have taken us across Canada and as far afield as Honolulu, Martinique, Oxford, and Brussels. We have addressed thousands of health professionals at dietetic and medical conferences, including the annual conventions of the American

Dietetic Association and Dietitians of Canada. It is an immense privilege to be a part of this movement of reason and compassion, and a great honor to be connected to many amazing and inspirational people.

As dietitians, we were trained to educate consumers about food choices based on personal health. *Becoming Vegetarian* is about nutrition, and providing optimal nutrition at every stage of the life cycle. But its ultimate message goes beyond personal health. It is about recognizing the profound connection between our food choices and life all around us. The food we choose impacts the lives of those who had a hand in getting that food to our table. Our choices affect vast numbers of animals that are part of our food system; they impact wildlife that may lose habitat due to our abuse of land and water. What we eat has consequences for our rivers, oceans, soil, and air. Becoming vegetarian softens our ecological footprint—perhaps more than any other single choice we can make. As people become conscious about these connections, the shift toward a plant-based diet simply happens.

Our goal in writing *Becoming Vegetarian* was to assist people in the task of designing vegetarian diets that are practically foolproof. If vegetarian diets are to be accepted by the mainstream population, it will be because people feel absolutely certain that these diets are safe, adequate, and even optimal for themselves and for their children. Our dream is that all those who choose a vegetarian diet succeed brilliantly. In this vision, we include near-vegetarians, lacto-ovo vegetarians, and vegans. Our message is meant for those who are just beginning a dietary shift and for those who wish to fine-tune a diet followed for many years.

You may be wondering why a whole new version of *Becoming Vegetarian* was necessary. Whereas the first edition broke fresh ground, in the decade since, the amount of scientific research in this field has increased exponentially. Scientists have collaborated to forge new recommendations for our intakes of vitamins, minerals, protein, and fats. Vegetarian and especially vegan foods have become among the fastest-growing categories in the grocery trade. Mainstream supermarkets now stock a tremendous selection of delicious veggie "meats," tofu, and nondairy beverages; sales of many of these products have tripled over the last four years. All of these advancements needed to be communicated in practical terms to consumers. It was time to revise *Becoming Vegetarian*.

How is this edition different than the original? The new *Becoming Vegetarian* is seasoned with experience. It digs deeper; it questions harder. Much of what was considered mere speculation ten years ago is now accepted fact. We speak with greater confidence and provide more thorough guidance for readers. Several issues that were not dealt with in the original book are addressed in the new edition. For example, we have included chapters on whole grains, fruits and vegetables, weight management, and the prime of life. Our recipes have been updated and include contributions from outstanding chefs around North America.

Becoming Vegetarian was written for you. It is our hope that it will provide you with all the information you need to construct an exceptional diet, one that will nourish your body and soul. May you move forward with confidence and conviction in your journey toward a gentler, kinder, and healthier world.

Vesanto Melina and Brenda Davis

Chapter 1

Why Be Vegetarian?

Why be vegetarian? Over five million Americans would each have a unique answer. Vegetarians dance to their own music. They have the courage to challenge accepted practices, even those respected as tradition. A good number of vegetarians are health enthusiasts, most have a very big heart when it comes to animals, and many are deeply committed to protecting the environment. It is practically impossible to pick a vegetarian out of a crowd. While some appear to be counterculture types, others are construction workers, movie stars, businesspeople, hockey players, marathon runners, or grandmas and grandpas. Vegetarians are of various ages and from every walk of life. When we tell others we are vegetarian, their typical response is, "I don't eat much meat either." Being vegetarian is considered a very good thing, something to which many people aspire.

Types of Vegetarians

A vegetarian is defined as someone who does not eat meat, poultry, or fish. In contrast, those who include both plants and animals in their diet are called omnivores or nonvegetarians. The two most common types of vegetarians are lacto-ovo and vegan.

Lacto-Ovo Vegetarian

Lacto-ovo vegetarians avoid all animal flesh but do use eggs (ovo) and dairy products (lacto). Some people are simply lacto-vegetarians, using dairy products but not eggs, and others are ovo-vegetarians, using eggs but not dairy products.

Vegan (pronounced vee-gun or vee-gan)

Vegans avoid all products of animal origin, including eggs, dairy foods, gelatin (made from the bones and connective tissue of animals), and honey (the product of bees). Vegans avoid animal products not only in their diet but in every aspect of their lives. They typically shun leather goods, wool and silk, tallow soaps, and other products made with animal ingredients.

Variations on "Vegetarian"

Within the two main categories of vegetarian there are many variations, depending on the motivation, experiences, and unique needs of the individual. When people become vegetarian in an effort to achieve better health, there may be some flexibility in their use of animal products. However, when the choice is made on the basis of ethics or religion, there is a greater tendency toward complete adherence to the diet.

When people first become vegetarian, many rely heavily on dairy foods and eggs. As their knowledge and experience of vegetarian issues grow, they often begin to replace these animal products with protein-rich plant foods such as soy products, legumes, nuts, and seeds. This natural progression gets easier with each passing year. Convenient and delicious vegetarian options have multiplied dramatically in the marketplace in recent years. Mainstream grocery stores feature an impressive selection of nondairy milks, veggie "meats," tofu, and other vegetarian favorites. This trend away from the use of animal products is reflected in recent figures comparing the number of vegans to lacto–ovo vegetarians. Ten years ago it was estimated that 5 to 10 percent of all vegetarians were vegan and 90 to 95 percent were lacto-ovo vegetarian, whereas recent surveys show that 25 to 40 percent of all vegetarians are vegan.

While many vegetarians do not quite fit the definition of vegan, they are very close. Some avoid all obvious dairy products and eggs but are not concerned about traces of animal products in prepared foods. Others eat the occasional pizza slice or ice-cream cone but do not consume these products on a regular basis. This rapidly growing subsection of the vegetarian population is much closer in its dietary practices and nutritional intakes to vegans than to lacto-ovo vegetarians; thus, people following this type of diet are often called *near-vegans*.

We might expect that there is little room for diversity among vegans and near-vegans, but this is clearly not the case. Within the vegan/near-vegan category are many variations, among the most popular of which are health movements, such as macrobiotics, natural hygiene, living- and raw-food consumers, and fruitarians. All of these systems promote dietary regimes based on simple, whole foods. In most cases, processed foods, refined sugars, and concentrated fats are shunned, and, in many cases, nutritional supplements may be avoided as well. These diets are low in total fat, saturated fat, trans-fatty acids, cholesterol, and refined carbohydrates, minimizing potentially damaging dietary components. They also are rich in protective dietary constituents, such as fiber, phytochemicals (protective chemicals naturally present in plants), and several vitamins and minerals (including folate; vitamins A, C, and K; potassium; and magnesium). However, these regimes can be considerably more restrictive than those vegan diets that include the full spectrum of plant foods along with necessary supplements or fortified foods. Such diets may lack vitamin B_{12} and may be deficient in vitamin D. They also may provide insufficient protein, carbohydrate, fat, vitamins, and minerals, and too much fiber, to meet the needs of infants and young children.

Beyond the two main categories, lacto-ovo vegetarian and vegan, are people who call themselves vegetarian but do not qualify according to accepted definitions. These near-vegetarians comprise two to three times the number of those who never eat flesh foods. The explanation, it seems, is that many who eliminate red meat but still include poultry or fish consider themselves vegetarian. In addition, some who eat only a little meat, poultry, or fish often regard themselves as vegetarian. The term sometimes used to describe these folks is *semi-vegetarian,* although a more appropriate term is *near-vegetarian.*

DECIDING FACTORS: THE MOTIVATION FOR BECOMING VEGETARIAN

The road to a vegetarian lifestyle is paved with love—for our fellow beings, for the planet, and for ourselves. It matters far less what draws us to this path, or how far along the path we have come, than the fact that we are heading in a direction that leads to a kinder, more compassionate world.

Sometimes it is a single reason that motivates an individual to embark on this journey. With time and experience, other reasons often are adopted and the conviction to continue is strengthened. The four primary reasons people give for choosing a vegetarian or vegan diet are

1. **to support personal health and healing**
2. **to promote reverence for life**
3. **to protect the environment**
4. **to uphold religious or philosophical principles**

Let's briefly consider each of these reasons and their relative significance as deciding factors.

Supporting Personal Health and Healing

Health is the most commonly cited reason for becoming vegetarian. Most people now recognize that vegetarian diets are not only a healthy choice, but are likely to protect us against disease. The potential health advantages of vegetarian diets include

➤ *Less obesity*. Vegetarians are leaner than nonvegetarians. This often translates into better overall health.

➤ *Reduced risk of chronic disease*. Vegetarians have less heart disease, hypertension, type 2 diabetes, and certain forms of cancer than nonvegetarians. There also is some evidence that vegetarians enjoy protection against renal, kidney, and diverticular disease and rheumatoid arthritis.

➤ *Improved longevity*. Vegetarians live an estimated seven to nine years longer than nonvegetarians. While many people poke fun at vegetarians, saying "It just feels longer," the reality is that vegetarians tend to be healthier in their senior years.

➤ *Reduced risk of foodborne diseases*. Risk of contracting E coli 0157:H7, Salmonella, Listeria, Campylobacter, and other foodborne pathogens is significantly lower for vegetarians.

➤ *Lower intakes of environmental contaminants*. Exposure to heavy metals, DDT, PCBs, and other such contaminants is generally reduced in vegetarian diets, as these substances accumulate as we move up the food chain.

➤ *Nutrient intakes that are closer to current nutrition recommendations*. When compared with nonvegetarian diets, vegetarian diets provide a balance of protein, carbohydrate, and fat that is closer to current recommendations. Plant-based diets are also lower in saturated fat, cholesterol, animal protein, and possibly trans-fatty acids, and higher in vitamins C and E, provitamin A carotenoids (the plant form of vitamin A), folate, fiber, magnesium, and phytochemicals.

Promoting Reverence for Life

When people make choices that support their own health and well-being, the benefits extend far beyond the individual to other living beings and indeed to the planet as a whole. This is because of the intimate and powerful connection that links all beings. For a growing number of people, becoming vegetarian is a strong statement against violence and cruelty toward animals. Every year in North America close to ten billion animals (not including fish) are slaughtered for food. While many people imagine the lives of these animals as they are described in storybooks, the truth is a stark contrast. The concerns about the lives and deaths of food animals today can be briefly described as follows:

➤ *Food animals are raised inhumanely.* As our population increases, and our demands for food escalate, incidences of overcrowding, confinement, isolation, and brutality become commonplace. Food animals often are subjected to surgeries, mutilations, and amputations without anesthetics. Crowding and isolation rob these animals of the opportunity to engage in normal social behavior, often driving them insane.

➤ *Food animals are transported to slaughter in appalling conditions.* Many food animals experience extreme trauma during transport, often going without food or water for extended periods of time. As a result, millions of animals die each year en route to slaughter.

➤ *Food animals are slaughtered inhumanely.* Laws and regulations regarding the "humane slaughter" of food animals are in place to ensure that these animals are rendered unconscious by an approved, humane method before being shackled, hoisted, and bled. Unfortunately, a concern with profit means that as the speed of the production line increases, so do violations of humane slaughter laws and regulations. Stunning methods often are unreliable, and animals improperly stunned become terrified, frequently fighting for their lives. These animals are sometimes beaten, or worse, dismembered, skinned, or boiled alive.

WHAT IS THE FOOD CHAIN?

The food chain is the order in which various organisms consume others. Microorganisms and plants are at the bottom of the food chain, then herbivores, followed by small omnivores and carnivores, building to larger ones, then to large fish, large cats, and at the very top of the food chain are humans. Eating higher on the food chain has a couple of major disadvantages. First, it requires tremendous resources, as eating plants directly requires far less land, water, and fossil fuels than eating animals that have eaten the plants. Second, the higher we eat on the food chain, the more contaminants we ingest. This is because large animals that people eat consume far more of the contaminated plants than we could consume directly. These contaminants are then passed on to people when they consume these animals.

➤ *Animals have rights.* Animals are not inanimate objects, but thinking, feeling creatures who deserve to be treated with respect and compassion. While most people treat their pets with love and kindness, many fail to recognize that "food" animals are just as intelligent as "companion" animals, and they feel pain every bit as much as pets or people do. Indeed, whether an animal is a pet or a food is not always determined by their species, but rather by the human beings who "own" them. Animals that are pets in one culture may be used as food sources in other cultures. To assume that our treatment of food animals is of no moral consequence is absurd. The words of one of the greatest philosophers of all times, Nobel Peace Prize winner, Dr. Albert Schweitzer, truly give us pause for thought:

> *The thinking man must oppose all cruel customs no matter how deeply rooted in tradition and surrounded by a halo. When we have a choice, we must avoid bringing torment and injury into the life of another, even the lowliest creature; to do so is to renounce our manhood and shoulder a guilt which nothing justifies.*

Protect the Environment

People are beginning to realize that we cannot continue to consume the earth's resources at the current rate if there is to be any hope for future generations. The choice to become vegetarian is a way of reducing our ecological footprint, and is probably the most effective step any individual can take toward this goal. Albert Einstein once said, "Nothing will benefit human health and increase the chances for survival of life on earth as much as the evolution to a vegetarian diet." We have much evidence to suggest that this man knew what he was talking about. Choosing a vegetarian diet can help protect the environment in many ways.

➤ *It assists in the preservation of water resources.* Animal agriculture demands tremendous amounts of fresh water. It is estimated that almost 50 percent of all water consumed in the United States is used for raising livestock. While water requirements vary according to location and the amount of irrigation required to grow animal feed, on average it takes about 100 times more water to produce a pound of beef than it does to produce a pound of wheat. It takes less water to produce the food that a vegan needs for one year than to produce the food that a meat eater needs for a month.

➤ *It helps prevent water pollution.* According to the Environmental Protection Agency (EPA), agriculture is the biggest polluter of America's water systems. It is responsible for 70 percent of waterway pollution, its damage exceeding that of sewage treatment plants, urban storm sewers, and pollution from contaminants in air. The major offenders are livestock-feeding operations. Manure, traditionally used as a natural fertilizer to enrich soil, generally is not returned from immense feedlots to distant farmland. Animals produce about 130 times more manure than humans (e.g., animals produce 130 pounds of manure for every pound that humans produce). This waste is not processed through a sewage system or treatment plant and all too often ends up poisoning rivers, causing severe oxygen depletion in the estuaries, and devastating fish populations. Livestock manure is a breeding ground for dangerous pathogens such as E coli, Giardia, and Pfiesteria, which cause sickness and death in people living in regions where factory farms are concentrated. Furthermore, waste from North America's 9 billion chickens and 150 million other farmed animals is permeated with hormones that propel the bird "from egg to fryer in thirty-nine days" and other similar unnatural feats.

➤ *It helps preserve the planet's most valuable ecosystems.* Tropical rain forests are ecological treasures, housing half of the world's plant and animal species. These precious resources are being destroyed at an alarming rate. According to the Rainforest Action Network, two-thirds of the rain forests in Central America have been cleared primarily for the purpose of raising cheap beef to stock American fast-food establishments. They estimate that for every fast-food burger made from rain forest beef, fifty-five square feet (almost seventeen square meters) of tropical rain forest has been cleared. With the trees go twenty to thirty different plant species, one hundred different insect species, plus dozens of birds, mammals, and reptile species.

➤ *It provides powerful protection against desertification.* Overgrazing is considered the primary reason more land around the world is turning into desert. In the western United States, 70 percent of the land is used for grazing livestock. When land is overgrazed, the soil is compacted, decreasing its ability to absorb water. When heavy rains fall, topsoil is carried away. Six inches (fifteen centimeters) of topsoil are needed to grow healthy crops. It takes approximately three thousand years for nature to produce this amount of topsoil. Every twenty-eight years in the United States, every fourteen years in developing countries, and every seven years in China, one inch of topsoil is lost as the result of current intensive farming practices. At this rate, it is estimated that there are as few as forty-five years of farmable soil left on the planet.

> ➤ *It may help protect against catastrophic environmental changes.* Intensive animal agriculture is a significant factor in global warming, increasing all major global warming gases: carbon dioxide, methane, nitrous oxides, and chlorofluorocarbons. Carbon dioxide emissions come largely from fossil fuels. Raising livestock requires huge amounts of fossil fuels—for shipping feed, heating shelters (often large buildings), transporting animals to slaughter, and trucking the products to meat-packing plants and stores. According to Worldwatch Institute, 15 to 20 percent of all methane emissions come directly from livestock. In addition, the chemical fertilizers used to produce food for grain-fed animals are important contributors to nitrous oxides. Finally, the increased refrigeration necessary to preserve animal products releases chlorofluorocarbons in the atmosphere.

> ➤ *It reduces consumption of the earth's dwindling resources.* It is estimated that if every inhabitant on this planet used as many resources to produce his or her food as each American does, we would need three planet earths to sustain the current population. Unfortunately, that is the very direction we are heading. Between 1990 and 1995, China's grain consumption increased by 40 million tons. Of this total, 33 million tons were consumed as animal fodder and 7 million tons as food for humans. China's cultural dietary practices, like those of many other developing countries, are rapidly changing from an emphasis on plant foods to animal foods. Tragically, more and more of the world's resources are used for raising livestock to provide food for the wealthy, while one in every six people goes hungry every day. Today, our planet is home to nearly 1 billion pigs, 1.3 billion cows, 1.8 billion sheep and goats, and 13.5 billion chickens—more than two chickens for each man, woman, and child. We have altered vast ecosystems and devoted massive resources to support this inefficient way of eating. The world's cattle alone consume a quantity of food equal to the caloric needs of 8.7 billion people—more than the entire human population on earth.

Uphold Religious or Philosophical Principles

Some individuals choose a vegetarian or near-vegetarian diet in keeping with their religion or the philosophy of a particular movement. Major world religions that promote vegetarian or vegan diets, to varying degrees, as part of their basic teaching include Buddhism, Jainism, Taoism, Hinduism, and Seventh-day Adventists (a branch of Christianity). In addition, many religions that do not explicitly promote plant-based diets have subgroups that promote vegetarian lifestyles. Good examples are the Christian Vegetarian Association, Doukhobors, Jewish Vegetarians of North America, the Muslim Vegan/Vegetarian Society, and some Sufis.

Although many people become vegetarian as a result of their religious persuasion, the reasons why any given faith would promote a vegetarian diet tend to include one or more of those outlined in the preceding three sections. For example, the Eastern religions base their dietary choice on principles of compassion for all living beings, while the Seventh-day Adventists promote vegetarianism on the basis of its benefits to human health.

VEGETARIANISM STANDS THE TEST OF TIME

Vegetarianism has been a dietary option since the dawn of recorded time. Its origins remain somewhat of a mystery, although the mythologies of many cultures tell of a beginning without violence, where people lived off the plants of the earth. One of the most widely recognized records is from the biblical scriptures in the book of Genesis where Adam and Eve are told what they are permitted to eat:

> *And God said, behold, I have given you every herb-bearing seed, which is upon the face of all the earth, and every tree, in which is the fruit of a tree yielding seed; to you it shall be for meat.* –Genesis 1:29

Throughout history, vegetarianism has been a part of cultures worldwide. Many of the world's greatest philosophers and intellectuals refused meat when such a choice was contrary to dictates of the ruling class.

Pythagoras, who evidently brought these concepts from the East, is often considered "the father of vegetarianism" in the West. Until the late nineteenth century, when the word "vegetarian" was coined, people who lived on a meat-less diet were referred to as Pythagoreans. Pythagoras, born around 580 B.C., was credited with the discovery of the Pythagorean theorem, many other mathematical and geometrical findings, the idea of planetary motion, and the speculation that the earth moves around the sun. He also founded a society that pursued wisdom, believed in reincarnation, and practiced meditation. Among the Pythagoreans, materialism and meat eating were taboo. Contrary to the general view of the time, women were considered equal to men. Pythagoras also believed that one's maximum philosophical potential could be reached only when the body was an efficient instrument. Thus, a strict exercise regime including gymnastics, running, and wrestling was practiced.

Following Pythagoras, many influential thinkers through the centuries promoted a vegetarian diet. The following insightful quotes provide a glimpse of a small selection of these extraordinary human beings:

But for the sake of some little mouthful of flesh we deprive a soul of the sun and light, and of that proportion of life and time it had been born into the world to enjoy.
—Plutarch (A.D. 46–120)

Not to hurt our humble brethren is our first duty to them, but to stop there is not enough. We have a higher mission—to be of service to them wherever they require it.
—St. Francis of Assisi (1182–1226)

Fast all day, kill cows at night, here prayers, there blood—does this please God?
—Kabir, Islamic mystic and poet (1440–1518)

I have from an early age abjured the use of meat, and the time will come when men such as I will look on the murder of animals as they now look on the murder of men.
—Leonardo da Vinci (1452–1519)

What is it that should trace the insuperable line?... The question is not, Can they reason? nor Can they talk? but, Can they suffer? —Jeremy Bentham (1748–1832)

Non-violence leads to the highest ethics, which is the goal of all evolution. Until we stop harming all other living beings, we are still savages.
—Thomas Edison (1847–1931)

We consume the carcasses of creatures of like appetites, passions and organs with our own, and fill the slaughterhouses daily with screams of pain and fear.
—Robert Louis Stevenson (1850–1894)

Flesh foods are not the best nourishment for human beings and were not the food of our primitive ancestors. There is nothing necessary or desirable for human nutrition to be found in meats or flesh foods which is not found in and derived from plant foods.
—Dr. J. H. Kellogg (1852–1943)

The greatness of a nation and its moral progress can be judged by the way its animals are treated.
—Mahatma Gandhi (1869–1948)

Until we have the courage to recognize cruelty for what it is—whether its victim is human or animal—we cannot expect things to be much better in this world. We cannot have peace among men whose hearts delight in killing any living creature. By every act that glorifies or even tolerates such moronic delight in killing we set back the progress of humanity.
—Rachel Carson (1907–1964)

Among the most colorful characters of the historical advocates of vegetarianism was George Bernard Shaw (1856–1950). When Shaw decided to eliminate meat from his diet, it was so contrary to his culture that his physician was alarmed. He cautioned the young Shaw that if he continued to insist on this meat-free diet, he would surely die of malnutrition in short order. Shaw replied that he would sooner die than consume a "corpse." One can appreciate the irony of the situation when, as he approached his eighty-fifth year, Shaw proclaimed:

> *The average age (life expectancy) of a meat eater is 63. I am on the verge of 85 and still work as hard as ever. I have lived quite long enough and I am trying to die; but I simply cannot do it. A single beef steak would finish me; but I cannot bring myself to swallow it. I am oppressed with a dread of living forever. That is the only disadvantage of vegetarianism.*

Many courageous individuals throughout history have taken a strong stand against the use of animals for human consumption. However, one of the greatest influences on the vegetarian movement of today was the group of about 140 dedicated individuals in England who banded together for discussion and support. The result was the modern world's first vegetarian society in 1847, which was soon followed by similar societies in Europe and the United States.

Alternatives Go Mainstream

Among twentieth-century vegetarians, a small and growing core felt the need to avoid all animal products, and, as a result, the word *vegan* was added to our vocabulary in 1944. The late 1960s and early 1970s launched a new era for vegetarianism. Peace-loving "counterculture" groups sprang up with a message of ecology and natural living. To many people, vegetarianism became linked with the hippie movement. Health professionals often viewed the vegetarian diet as a dangerous fad that could lead to nutritional deficiencies, while nutritional research explored whether or not these views were well-founded.

In 1971, Frances Moore Lappé's book *Diet for a Small Planet* gave a tremendous boost to the vegetarian cause. Her three-million-copy best-seller, which expressed the author's love for humanity and our planet and exposed the inefficiency of feeding mountains of grain to livestock, drew many toward a plant-based diet. John Robbins further strengthened the vegetarian movement with *Diet for a New America* (1987), *May All Be Fed* (1992), and *The Food Revolution* (2001). Robbins's genial writing style appeals to mainstream audiences, while addressing the hard-hitting connection between our dietary choices and the environment, world hunger, and diseases of affluence. He also is a strong advocate for animal rights, which profoundly touches people as an idea whose time has come.

During the last decades of the twentieth century, health professionals increasingly recognized the potential advantages of vegetarian diets. After research at Harvard University, Loma Linda University in California, Kingston Hospital in London, and other highly respected centers established the nutritional adequacy of plant-based diets, the emphasis gradually shifted to their health benefits. Large studies were launched by Dr. Colin Campbell of Cornell University (the China Study), by Oxford's Dr. Tim Key, Dr. M. Thorogood, Paul Appleby, and others (the Oxford Vegetarian Study), by international groups (the EPIC study), and Seventh-day Adventist research teams (the Adventist Mortality Study and the Adventist Health Study).

In prestigious medical journals, Dr. Dean Ornish presented evidence that we can actually reverse coronary artery disease through a combination of a vegetarian diet and lifestyle changes. This alternative to painful surgery and medications with dreadful side effects held such appeal that Ornish became a regular on the cover of popular magazines and a sought-after guest on talk shows such as *Oprah*. Health care systems began to recognize that billions of dollars, as well as lives, could be saved by a dietary shift. The Physicians' Committee for Responsible Medicine (PCRM), headed by Dr. Neal Barnard, began research on the benefits of diets that are free of animal products for various conditions such as diabetes, menstrual pain, PMS, and obesity. Outspoken physicians, including Michael Klaper, Benjamin Spock, Thomas Barnard, John McDougall, and Caldwell Esselstyn, went public with a message urging a shift toward a vegetarian diet.

The American Dietetic Association, in its position papers on vegetarian nutrition, took a strong stand regarding the adequacy of both vegetarian and vegan diets, stating that such diets could meet our nutritional needs at every stage of the life cycle. Prominent nutrition experts, including Suzanne Havala-Hobbs, PhD, Reed Mangels, PhD, Mark Messina, PhD, Virginia Messina, MPh, Winston Craig, PhD, and Joan Sabate, PhD, with faculty members at Loma Linda University, wrote books and scientific articles on vegetarian nutrition to support the understanding of health professionals. The International Congresses on Vegetarian Nutrition, held every five years, have attracted scientists from more than thirty-six countries around the globe.

Tentatively, then with enthusiasm, Americans explored new vegetarian foods as they appeared in the marketplace. Tofu was transformed from the object of jokes into a superfood. In a footnote to the U.S. Food Guide Pyramid, the *Dietary Guidelines for Americans 2000* identified fortified soymilk as an acceptable alternative to cow's milk. *The Manual of Clinical Dietetics* (2000) went further and included calcium-set tofu, fortified soyfoods and juices, certain greens, beans, almond butter, and tahini in the "Milk and Milk Alternatives" food group. Culinary magazines featured colorful spreads of nutritional giants such as broccoli, kale, garlic, papayas, and blueberries. Veggie "meats" captured a solid share of refrigerator space in supermarkets across the nation. While vegetarians welcomed these easy-to-use products, most of the buyers were non-vegetarians. *Food Processing* magazine listed vegetarian items in the hottest categories for the future.

The Continuing Survey of Food Intake for 1994 to 1996 reported that 2.6 percent of Americans describe themselves as vegetarians. Significantly more (4.2 percent) chose vegetarian fare instead of meat, fish, or poultry at mealtimes, though not necessarily calling themselves vegetarian. In Canada, a 2002 survey showed 4 percent of adults to be vegetarian in name and practice. Depending on the wording of questions, various polls indicate between 20 and 46 percent of North Americans are cutting back on, or eliminating, red meat.

THE FUTURE IS BRIGHT!

Today we see people of every age and from every walk of life choosing to become vegetarian. An even greater segment of the population is moving in that direction and increasingly incorporating plant foods into more meals. While one in four Americans eat fast foods every day, some franchises now feature veggie burgers. Restaurant menus include one or more "heart healthy" vegetarian options. The server and chef are likely to understand the word vegan. Each July, hundreds of people spend a week at the Vegetarian Summerfest in Johnstown, Pennsylvania, and thousands flock to daylong food festivals in Boston, Charlottesville, Los Angeles, Louisville, Seattle, and many other urban centers in the United States and Canada, such as Toronto and Vancouver.

Whether we are near-vegetarian or entirely avoid animal products, there are common bonds in the caring we express through our dietary choices. For some of us, our caring is centered on creating vibrant good health in our loved ones and ourselves. For others, our caring is inspired by a respect for animals. For still others, our caring centers on planet earth and the environment. Yet for all, our choice of a vegetarian meal is a way to make a statement, to vote consistently in a way that really counts.

The vegetarian alternative offers hope for a brighter future. There is little doubt that the shift toward plant-based diets is gaining momentum and there's no indication it's going to slow down anytime soon. The positive impact of these trends is potentially enormous.

OTHER RESOURCES

These websites are doorways to a world of resources:

www.vrg.org	Vegetarian Resource Group
www.ivu.org	International Vegetarian Union
www.vegdining.com	For your restaurant and travel needs
www.pcrm.org	Physicians Committee for Responsible Medicine

For scientific references for this chapter, see
http://www.nutrispeak.com/bvreferences.htm

Chapter 2

MAXIMIZING THE VEGETARIAN ADVANTAGE

There was a time when people believed that meat and milk were the foundation of a healthy diet. Nutrition education resources emphasized that meat was necessary for high-quality protein and iron, and dairy products were essential for building and maintaining strong bones. People were thoroughly convinced that without these animal products, otherwise healthy individuals would become weak and sickly, children would not grow properly, and athletes could not achieve their potential. Vegetarians were looked upon as heretics and often ridiculed for their unconventional views. Vegetarian diets were considered risky, if not downright dangerous, for children and pregnant or lactating women.

This prevailing attitude did not come about by chance. In the early 1900s, U.S. food policies were directed toward eliminating deficiency diseases (diseases caused by nutrient deficits). The food supplies of the less fortunate often were meager and the variety was limited. For these undernourished people, adding meat and milk to the diet made a big difference. In addition, early feeding studies showed that children, especially those who were small for their age, grew faster with more animal products. As a result, these foods were granted special status. Federal governments offered large subsidies to farmers in an effort to increase production. They also supported intensive marketing initiatives and massive nutrition education campaigns to insure increased consumption. Diseases of nutritional deficiency rapidly diminished, and the interests of animal agriculture became deeply entrenched in the economy. It appeared as though the job of improving the health of the nation through nutrition had been brilliantly accomplished.

However, by the middle of the twentieth century, a less favorable health picture emerged. While deficiency diseases were no longer the threat they had once been, heart disease, cancer, type 2 diabetes, and obesity had begun to rise ominously.

BEYOND A REASONABLE DOUBT

Authorities were baffled; scientists could uncover no bacteria or virus on which to blame the surge in these devastating conditions. Scientists began to ponder the possibility of an environmental influence, and it was not long before diet became a primary suspect. For the second half of the twentieth century, researchers studied the dietary and lifestyle patterns of various populations and their relative risk of various diseases. They set up clinical trials to compare the effects of dietary changes on groups of individuals and examined specific foods and nutrients in an effort to determine their effects on health. In 1990, the World Health Organization (WHO) commissioned a panel of nutrition experts from around the world to sift through the existing research and assess the strength of the evidence linking diet to disease. The resulting technical report, *Diet, Nutrition, and the Prevention of Chronic Diseases*, was strong and clear in its conclusion:

> *Medical and scientific research has established clear links between dietary factors and the risk of developing coronary artery disease, hypertension, stroke, several cancers, osteoporosis, diabetes, and other chronic diseases. This knowledge is now sufficiently strong to enable governments to assess national eating patterns, identify risks and then protect their populations through policies that make healthy food choices the easy choices.*

With regard to specific dietary patterns, the panel stated:

> *The population nutrient intakes recommended in this report translate into a diet that is low in fat, and especially saturated fat, and high in complex starchy carbohydrates. Such a diet is characterized by frequent consumption of vegetables, fruits, cereals and legumes, and contrasts sharply with current diets drawing substantial amounts of energy from whole-milk dairy products, fatty meats, and refined sugars.*

Over the next decade, evidence linking diet to chronic disease continued to mount, prompting numerous health organizations to develop dietary guidelines and recommendations urging a shift toward plant-based diets. What was truly remarkable was how consistent these diverse groups were in their public health messages. In 1999, five of the top health organizations in the United States (the National Institutes of Health, the American Dietetic Association, the American Pediatric Society, the American Cancer Society, and the American Heart Association) joined forces to develop and endorse one set of dietary guidelines. By unifying their message, these organizations hoped to present a stronger voice, one that would alter food choices, ultimately reducing rates of chronic disease. The key message: **Choose most of what you eat from plant sources.** More specifically, the group recommended that people choose a diet rich in grain products, vegetables, and fruits, one that is low in fat, saturated fat, and cholesterol, and moderate in sugar, salt, and alcohol, if used. Richard J. Deckelbaum, MD, coauthor of their report and professor of pediatrics and nutrition at Columbia University in New York City, explains one of the most salient points that came out of their work:

> *The good news is that we don't need one diet to prevent heart disease, another to decrease cancer risk, and yet another to prevent obesity and diabetes. A single healthy diet cuts across disease categories to lower the risk of many chronic conditions.*

Today, governments, health organizations, and nutrition authorities are acutely aware of the health benefits of plant-based diets, and their nutrition education materials consistently reflect this knowledge. However, while people are strongly encouraged to increase the amount of plant foods they eat, there is an obvious hesitation to tell people to cut back on their intake of animal products. Instead, we are told to eat less saturated fat and cholesterol. One might wonder why, when animal products are the primary sources of these potentially damaging dietary components, there would be any reluctance to urge the public to eat less of them. Marion Nestle, chair of the Department of Nutrition and Food Studies at New York University, provides a thought-provoking explanation in her exceptional exposé, *Food Politics.*

> *The meat industry can live with euphemistic advice to consume diets "low in satu-rated fat." It is only when that term gets translated into food sources—"animal fat" or "eat less meat"—that industry groups are galvanized into action, and nutrition scientists and educators become uncomfortable and advise "moderation."*

There is no denying the political and economic links between governments and agricultural industries. To further complicate matters, health organizations and nutrition authorities are frequently engaged by these industries as allies or partners in wellness initiatives. The end result is a message that is, at best, diluted, and, more often, seriously compromised. Fortunately, the population is becoming increasingly savvy when it comes to matters of health and nutrition. Efforts to hide the potentially deleterious effects of high-fat meat and dairy products behind more complex nutrition concepts, such as saturated fat and cholesterol, are becoming futile. The World Health Organization, in their latest report, *Diet, Nutrition and the Prevention of Chronic Diseases (2003),* urges consumers to empower themselves to create health-supporting lifestyles and communities. Their concluding sentence reads: "Beyond the rhetoric, this epidemic can be halted—the demand for action must come from those affected. The solution is in our hands."

THE HEALTH OF VEGETARIANS

With plant-based diets being so highly valued as protectors against chronic disease, one might imagine all vegetarians dancing until dawn on their ninetieth birthday. While there is little question that vegetarians enjoy some advantages where chronic disease is concerned, quantifying this advantage is no simple task. First, it is important to understand that becoming vegetarian is no guarantee of a healthful diet. In fact, it is possible to completely blow it as a vegetarian. Think about it. Coconut cream pie, hot-fudge sundaes, jam-filled doughnuts, potato chips, and soda pop all fit the definition of vegetarian foods. And when it comes to comparing vegetarians to nonvegetarians in scientific studies, we find certain limitations that affect the research findings.

➤ *Vegetarians are not consistently defined.* In some studies, the participants are actually near-vegetarians who eat meat less than once a week, rather than true vegetarians. Some have been meat eaters for sixty years and vegetarian for only two years. These individuals would rarely experience the same level of protection afforded to someone who has been a long-term vegetarian, yet they are sometimes lumped into the same category.

➤ *People's reasons for being vegetarian can place them at different ends of the health spectrum.* Some have adopted a plant-based diet in response to recent, devastating news from their cardiologist or oncologist. Thus, people with serious illnesses may be grouped with long-term health and fitness enthusiasts.

➤ *Specific food choices are not always considered.* There is tremendous diversity of food choices among individuals, whether vegetarian or nonvegetarian. Some vegetarians are raw-food vegans, while others are junk-food junkies.

Simply comparing vegetarians and nonvegetarians is of limited value if specific dietary choices are not considered.

➤ *Other lifestyle factors are not always taken into account.* Numerous factors, apart from diet, can affect health. If smoking habits, exercise level, and response to stress are not considered, it becomes difficult to determine what proportion of the risk reduction is due to diet and how much is due to nondietary factors.

➤ *Studies are often too small to accurately reflect the general vegetarian population.* While interesting insights may be gained by observing just a few vegetarians or vegans, these studies do not provide the final answers.

Keeping this in mind, our knowledge regarding the health consequences of vegetarian diets has expanded enormously over the past few decades. As a result, the primary research focus has shifted away from the question "Are vegetarian diets safe?" to "How much protection can vegetarian diets afford?" Even our most conservative nutrition organizations, which, for many years, categorized vegetarian eating patterns as fad diets, now recognize their safety and potential benefits. The 2003 American Dietetic Association and Dietitians of Canada position paper on vegetarian diets provides an excellent reflection of the current view: "It is the position of the American Dietetic Association and Dietitians of Canada that appropriately planned vegetarian diets are healthful, nutritionally adequate, and provide health benefits in the prevention and treatment of certain diseases."

Today, there is little question that well-constructed vegetarian and vegan diets can provide completely adequate nutrition at every stage of life and foster excellent health. While vegetarian diets have been charged with increasing risk of deficiency diseases, what many people fail to realize is that there is at least as much potential for malnutrition (i.e., faulty nutrition) with animal-centered diets as with vegetarian diets, perhaps more. According to the State of the World 2000 (Worldwatch Institute), there are three kinds of malnutrition:

1. **Hunger**—a deficiency of calories and protein. Hunger affects some 1.2 billion people worldwide. In countries with the greatest hunger problems, more than 50 percent of the population are underweight.

2. **Overconsumption**—an excess of calories, often accompanied by deficiency of vitamins and minerals. Overconsumption also affects 1.2 billion people worldwide. In countries with the greatest amount of overeating, more than 50 percent of the population are overweight.

3. **Micronutrient deficiency**—a deficiency of vitamins and minerals. This form of malnutrition affects two billion people worldwide and

overlaps with both hunger and overconsumption. It is the result of insufficient variety in the diet, and/or excess fat and sugar, crowding out foods that would otherwise contribute essential nutrients.

Technically, hunger (malnutrition due to limited protein and calories) need occur only with insufficient access to food. In Western vegetarian populations, hunger is uncommon. It can occur, for example, in rare instances when infants and children are fed extremely low-fat, high-fiber diets, or when calories are restricted to achieve a model-thin slimness. Micronutrient deficiencies can occur among vegetarians when good sources of iron or vitamin B_{12} are not included in the diet, or when the diet is based on junk foods or refined carbohydrates and lacks vegetables, fruits, legumes, whole grains, nuts, and seeds.

Two types of malnutrition are widespread among nonvegetarians: *overconsumption* and *micronutrient deficiencies*. Overconsumption dramatically increases risk for numerous chronic diseases and is the fastest-growing form of malnutrition in the world. It is most commonly seen in diets centered on animal foods, processed foods, and fast foods. These diets are low in fiber and high in fat, cholesterol, sugar, and salt. In such diets, micronutrient deficiencies are associated with lack of variety (e.g., burgers and fries) or with too much refined food, especially high-fat, high-sugar items that squeeze out valuable whole grains, vegetables, fruits, and legumes.

Both vegetarian and nonvegetarian eating patterns have the potential to nourish a population, if appropriately planned—or to be risky, if not.

Overall Health and Longevity of Vegetarians

Vegetarians tend to be a very healthy group of people. Death rates from chronic diseases in vegetarians are about half that of the general population. Some of the advantage can be attributed to nondietary lifestyle factors. Fewer vegetarians smoke or abuse alcohol, and a higher percentage are very physically active. When vegetarians are compared with similar health-conscious nonvegetarians (i.e., those with comparable smoking, drinking, and exercise habits, and who eat plenty of vegetables, fruits, and whole grains), their advantage decreases, yet they still hold an edge. This suggests that avoiding flesh foods brings its own health benefits.

Scientific studies consistently show that vegetarians are slimmer than nonvegetarians. Within the Seventh-day Adventist (SDA) community, vegetarians are not only leaner than their meat-eating counterparts, but the relative degree of overweight was found to increase with the frequency of meat consumption. In the United Kingdom and Europe, vegetarians have also been found to be slimmer than nonvegetarians. These differences are noted for men and women, and in all age groups. When meat eaters, fish eaters, lacto-ovo vegetarians, and vegans are compared, those who had been vegan for at least five years were the leanest, and meat eaters the most overweight. Overall, vegetarians are about 5 percent leaner than nonvegetarians, and vegans are about 5 percent leaner than lacto-ovo vegetarians. This seemingly small variation leads to remarkable differences in the incidence of obesity. Rates of obesity among meat-eaters are approximately double that of vegetarians and triple that of vegans. Why are vegetarians at such an advantage when it comes to healthy body weights? Researchers suggest that at least some of the advantage stems from the reduced total and animal fat intakes, and increased vegetables and fiber. It also is possible that the advantage is not exclusively due to diet, but may reflect increased levels of activity in the vegetarian population.

Vegetarians also enjoy greater longevity than nonvegetarians. In the Adventist Health Study, vegetarian men where found to live an average of 9 years longer and vegetarian women 6.6 years longer than the general population. When compared to similar, health-conscious Adventist nonvegetarians, vegetarians lived one and one-half to two years longer.

Rates of Specific Diseases

Let's have a look at the rates of disease in vegetarians compared with nonvegetarians. We will examine the two major killers—heart disease and cancer—and zero in on how vegetarians can maximize the advantage they currently enjoy. We also will consider other major diseases for which there is significant evidence of benefit from vegetarian diets, including diabetes, kidney disease, gastrointestinal diseases, gallstones, rheumatoid arthritis, and dementia.

Heart Disease

Heart disease reigns as the number one killer in North America, accounting for about 40 percent of all deaths. For many people, a heart attack is their first warning of heart disease, and for one in four of these people, it will be their last. Those who survive are often told that they will need coronary bypass surgery to make a detour around the blocked part of the coronary artery, or an angioplasty to widen narrowed arteries. Many assume that surgery will take care of the problem and they can simply go on with life, being a little more careful not to stress their weak ticker. Unfortunately, they'd be dead wrong. While it is tempting to think that surgery is the answer, 20 to 40 percent of patients who are given angioplasty develop another blockage within six months of the procedure, and 40 percent of bypass surgery patients experience closure of their graft within ten years. Heart disease is rarely a disease of chance; it is more commonly a disease of choice—a product of diet and lifestyle. Unless we make changes in our day-to-day activities and eating habits, the disease will continue its damage, eventually taking our lives. The good news is we have the information and technology necessary to prevent it and, in some cases, to reverse it.

Where do vegetarians stand?

Vegetarians have a solid advantage over nonvegetarians when it comes to heart disease. On average, death rates from heart disease in vegetarian men are less than half those of the general population, with somewhat smaller differences seen in women. As with other diseases, some of the benefits are due to differences in lifestyle choices, apart from diet. However, significant advantages remain, even after these factors are taken into consideration.

The largest study ever done comparing the heart disease rates in vegetarians with similar, health-conscious nonvegetarians was a collaborative study in the United Kingdom. It pooled the results of five large prospective studies (studies that follow large groups of people for long periods of time) with a combined total of 76,000 participants. On average, death from heart disease was 31 percent lower among vegetarian men compared to nonvegetarian men, and 20 percent lower among vegetarian women compared to nonvegetarian women. These figures also took into account body mass index (BMI, a measure of body fatness), alcohol use, education level, exercise level, and, in most studies, smoking. Death rates for vegetarians were also lower than for near-vegetarians who ate meat less than once per week.

Examining these studies independently provides further insight. In the Heidelberg Study, after eleven years of follow-up, heart disease risk was nearly 75 percent less for vegetarians and approximately 50 percent less for near-vegetarians relative to the general population. The Oxford Vegetarian Study, after almost eighteen years of follow-up, found 58 percent less risk in vegetarians compared with the general population, and 14 percent less risk in vegetarians compared to nonvegetarians making similar lifestyle choices. In the Health Food Shoppers Study, after almost nineteen years of follow-up, vegetarians had 53 percent less risk compared to the general population, and 15 percent less risk compared to nonvegetarians with a healthy lifestyle. The Adventist Health Study compares health and death rates of a group of health-conscious people with differing dietary patterns (about 40 percent of the population studied were vegetarian). Vegetarian men enjoyed 37 percent less risk compared with similar nonvegetarian men. This study also found that risk increased with more beef in the diet. Those eating beef up to three times a week had almost twice the risk of heart disease compared to vegetarians. Those eating beef more than three times a week had well over double the risk. Among the most interesting findings of this study was that nuts reduced the risk of heart disease more than any other food studied. People who eat nuts four or five times a week cut their risk in half, compared with those who eat only one serving of nuts or less a week. The earlier Adventist Mortality Study compared heart disease rates in men who were vegan, lacto-ovo vegetarian, and nonvegetarian. Vegetarians had 60 percent less risk, and vegans 80 percent less risk, compared with similar nonvegetarians. However, the collaborative study did not note such a profound advantage for vegans. In fact, in this larger combined analysis, vegans had 26 percent less risk compared with 34 percent in lacto-ovo vegetarians. This is a surprise, because based on blood cholesterol levels we would expect vegans to have significantly less heart disease than lacto-ovo vegetarians. However, we can offer some possible explanations for this finding.

Why are vegetarians at an advantage?

What is it that protects vegetarians from heart disease? Some assume that vegetarians gain an advantage simply because they are more health conscious—they smoke less, exercise more, and are leaner. While it is true that vegetarians tend to lead healthier lifestyles, the vegetarian diet itself has been shown to reduce risk by about 15 to 25 percent, independent of other factors. So what is it about vegetarian eating patterns that provides this advantage? Examining the various risk factors for heart disease sheds a lot of light on this question.

Heart disease risk factors

Heart disease is rarely the result of a single frailty or stroke of bad luck. Most often, many factors combine to put someone in the danger zone. There are two categories of risk factors—major or "classic" risk factors and contributing or "novel" risk factors.

Major risk factors have been proven to significantly increase risk. They include factors that are diet-related (shown in table 2.1), factors we cannot change (family history, gender, and age), and factors, apart from diet, that we can change (smoking, physical activity, and stress).

Contributing factors are those for which there is some evidence, but exactly how they act and how much of an impact they have has not yet been determined. These are shown in tables 2.2 and 2.3. Table 2.3 features risk factors that may be higher for vegetarians.

The tables explain how each factor affects risk and the extent of its impact (when known), compare the risk of vegetarians and nonvegetarians for each factor, and list specific foods and dietary components that affect risk.

The information in the tables provides valuable insight into our original question, "Why are vegetarians at an advantage?" Vegetarian diets contain significantly less of the dietary constituents that contribute to heart disease, while being more concentrated in those that offer protection. However, there are a few protective constituents that are reduced in many vegetarian diets, as shown in table 2.3. These may, to some degree, counteract the benefits of the vegetarian diet, diminishing its potential for protection. These may explain why vegans in the collaborative study had higher rates of heart disease than would

| TABLE 2.1 | MAJOR DIET-RELATED RISK FACTORS FOR HEART DISEASE (HD) |

High total cholesterol (TC) and low-density lipoprotein (LDL) levels

- ➤ LDL carries cholesterol to your arteries where it forms plaques. LDL is the main part of TC.
- ➤ For every 1% increase in TC, HD risk increases by 2–3%.

Vegetarian advantage:	TC levels are approximately 14% lower in V* and 35% lower in vegans than in NV*.
Risk increased by:	Saturated fat, cholesterol, trans-fatty acids, and animal protein.
Risk decreased by:	Soluble fiber, plant protein (especially soy protein), plant sterols and stanols, several phytochemicals (see table 2.2), and mono- and polyunsaturated fats replacing saturated fats.

Hypertension/high blood pressure (BP)

- ➤ High BP raises the heart's workload and increases risk for HD and stroke.

Vegetarian advantage:	Vegetarians have lower BP (5–10 mm Hg less) than NV. Hypertension rates in V are one-third to one-half that of NV.
Risk increased by:	Excess fat and calories, overweight, and excess sodium in some people.
Risk decreased by:	High-fiber intakes, plentiful potassium, magnesium, phytochemicals, and omega-3 fatty acids.

Obesity and overweight

- ➤ Excess weight puts strain on the heart, increases BP, TC, and triglyceride levels, lowers HDL levels, and elevates risk of diabetes.

Vegetarian advantage:	Rates of obesity are two to three times greater among NV than V.
Risk increased by:	Overconsumption, excessive intakes of fat and refined carbohydrates.
Risk decreased by:	High-fiber diets, moderate food intake.

Diabetes

- ➤ High blood sugar can raise cholesterol levels, increasing risk of heart disease. Even with good blood sugar control, risk is higher. People with diabetes have two to three times more HD than nondiabetics.

Vegetarian advantage:	Studies report lower rates of diabetes among V. SDA research suggests rates of less than half those of the general population.
Risk increased by:	Excess calories leading to overweight, meat, saturated fat, trans-fatty acids, refined carbohydrates.
Risk decreased by:	Fiber, magnesium, whole plant foods.

* V = Vegetarians; NV = Nonvegetarians

TABLE 2.2   CONTRIBUTING DIET-RELATED RISK FACTORS FOR HEART DISEASE (HD)

High triglycerides (TG)

➤ High TG can lead to smaller, denser LDL particles, which are more likely to trigger the obstructions in the blood vessels that lead to heart attacks and strokes (as opposed to lighter, fluffy LDL).

Vegetarian advantage:	Several studies show similar TG levels in V* and NV*, although a recent study showed vegan TG levels to be almost 20% lower than NV.
Risk increased by:	High saturated fat, high cholesterol, refined carbohydrates, simple sugars, alcohol.
Risk decreased by:	Omega-3 fatty acids, soy protein, fiber, replacing saturated fats with mono- and polyunsaturated fats.

Low levels of high-density lipoprotein (HDL)

➤ HDL carries cholesterol from your bloodstream to your liver where it is broken down and then excreted. HDL reduces the oxidation of LDL cholesterol.

Vegetarian advantage:	Higher levels are protective. Some vegetarians have lower HDL levels; however, it is thought to be because they have less cholesterol to be removed from the body.
Risk increased by:	Trans-fatty acids, refined carbohydrates.
Risk decreased by:	Weight loss.
Risk possibly decreased by:	Joint action of soy protein and isoflavones, fish, monounsaturated fats, and moderate alcohol consumption. **Note:** Risk is most profoundly reduced by exercise.

High Lipoprotein (a) (Lp[a])

➤ Lp(a) is an LDL particle with an abnormal protein called (a) attached. A high level of Lp(a) may trigger plaque formation and increase HD by up to three times.

Vegetarian advantage:	Some evidence suggests that V eating whole foods diets have lower levels of Lp(a) than V eating processed foods or NV.
Risk increased by:	Trans-fatty acids, possibly processed food, high-fat, low-fiber diets, possibly powdered soymilk from soy protein isolates.
Risk possibly decreased by:	Low-fat, whole food, vegetarian diets.

Elevated C-reactive protein (CRP)

➤ CRP is a body protein that is elevated when there is inflammation of blood vessels and plaque buildup. Increased CRP may indicate low-grade inflammation and higher risk of cardiovascular disease (CVD) and sudden cardiac death.

Vegetarian advantage:	Studies have shown reduced CRP levels in whole food vegan diets, although information is limited.
Risk increased by:	Low magnesium levels, high-fat, processed food diets.
Risk possibly decreased by:	Whole food vegan diets, antioxidants, certain phytochemicals, fruits, vegetables rich in salicylic acid.
	Note: Bacterial or viral infections such as Chlamydia pneumoniae and Helicobacter pylori, smoking, environmental pollution, and lack of exercise may increase CRP.

Iron overload

➤ Too much iron can act as a pro-oxidant, increasing oxidation of LDL cholesterol and damaging body tissues.
➤ We don't yet know if risk is increased with moderately elevated iron levels.

Vegetarian advantage:	About 12% of the NV population has one gene for enhanced iron absorption and one in 250 have two such genes, markedly increasing their risk for heart disease. Vegetarians have lower levels of iron stores and possibly of oxidative damage from excess iron.
Risk increased by:	High intakes of iron, especially heme iron (present in meat, poultry, and fish).
Risk decreased by:	Vegetarian diets.

Oxidized LDL cholesterol

➤ When LDL becomes oxidized, it is extremely damaging to blood vessels. It is a major contributor to plaque formation.

Vegetarian advantage:	Vegetarians, especially vegans, have higher levels of antioxidants and lower levels of lipid oxidation products in their tissues than nonvegetarians.
Risk increased by:	Saturated fat, cholesterol, pro-oxidants such as damaged fats and excess iron.
Risk decreased by:	Antioxidant nutrients (vitamins C and E, carotenoids, selenium) primarily in foods; phytochemicals.

* V = Vegetarians; NV = Nonvegetarians

TABLE 2.3	CONTRIBUTING RISK FACTORS THAT ARE POTENTIALLY HIGHER FOR VEGETARIANS

Elevated blood-clotting factors

➤ Heart attacks and strokes are caused by a blood clot resulting in a blockage in blood vessels. When the artery lining is injured, the tendency to clot increases. Platelet aggregation is the process by which platelets stick together at the site of injury within blood vessels and is the first step in clot formation.

Vegetarian advantage:	Vegetarians have reduced levels of several clotting factors, including fibrinogen and factor VII, providing protection against heart disease. However, several studies have noted elevated levels of platelet aggregation, which may reduce the protective effect of vegetarian diets.
Risk increased by:	High-fat diets, saturated fat, and trans-fatty acids.
Risk decreased by:	Omega-3 fatty acids, polyunsaturated fat, taurine, soluble fiber, and certain phytochemicals.

Elevated total homocysteine (tHcy)

➤ High levels of tHcy damage the walls of the arteries, causing plaques to form. Homocysteine is a breakdown product of the amino acid (aa) methionine (a sulfur-containing aa that is highest in animal products). Three B-vitamins are needed to reduce tHcy levels—folate, B_6, and B_{12}. For every 1% increase in tHcy, heart disease risk increases by 1%.

Vegetarian advantage:	Close to a dozen studies have shown higher tHcy levels in vegetarians, with the highest levels found in vegans. This is thought to be related to vegetarians and vegans not insuring adequate intakes of vitamins B_{12} (and perhaps B_6). Homocysteine levels are normalized with supplemental B_{12}.
Risk increased by:	Low levels of folate and vitamins B_6 and B_{12}.
Risk decreased by:	Dietary and supplemental folate and vitamins B_6 and B_{12}.
	Note: High intakes of methionine have not been associated with increased tHcy levels.

have been expected based on their blood cholesterol levels. If vegetarians are to maximize their risk reduction, they must be aware of these components and include adequate dietary sources.

Potentially damaging dietary components

The dietary components that have been most consistently associated with promoting heart disease include

Saturated fat. Animal products such as meat and dairy are the main sources of saturated fat in the diet. Tropical fats are also loaded with saturated fat, but because we eat relatively little of these fats, they don't contribute much to our overall saturated fat intake. Other plant foods are generally low in saturated fat (see page 173 for percentages of saturated fats in a variety of foods). Compared to nonvegetarians, lacto-ovo vegetarians eat about one-third less saturated fat and vegans about half as much.

Trans-fatty acids. Ninety percent of our trans-fatty acids come from hydrogenated and partially hydrogenated fats in processed foods, such as packaged cookies, crackers, snack foods, hydrogenated margarine, shortening, and deep-fried foods. The other 10 percent comes from meat and milk. (Trans-fatty acids are naturally produced in animals.) Several studies suggest that vegetarians consume less trans-fatty acids than nonvegetarians, while vegans consume even smaller quantities. (For more on trans-fatty acids, see page 159.)

Cholesterol. Cholesterol is found only in animal foods and is particularly concentrated in organ meats and eggs. Even high-fat plants—such as nuts, seeds, avocados, and olives—are cholesterol free. Lacto-ovo vegetarians vary in the amount of cholesterol they eat, but it is generally less than nonvegetarians (unless they eat a lot of eggs). Vegan diets are completely cholesterol free.

Refined carbohydrates. This category includes both complex carbohydrates (found in white bread, white rice, and baked goods made with white flour) and simple carbohydrates (found in white sugar, brown sugar, syrups, soda pop, and candy). Intakes of refined carbohydrates can be high in any diet, although there is some evidence that vegetarians, especially vegans, consume more whole grains.

Oxidative stressors. Oxidative stressors (components that react with certain types of reactive oxygen molecules causing damage to body tissues called *free-radical damage*) include oxidized fats, peroxides, environmental contaminants, and heme iron. Oxidized fats and peroxides are found in fats and oils that have been damaged by heat, light, or oxygen (e.g., excessive cooking temperatures or poor storage). Environmental contaminants tend to become more concentrated as animals eat contaminated plants and larger animals eat smaller contaminated animals, resulting in the highest concentrations in animal products. Heme iron is present exclusively in meat, fish, and poultry. Thus, vegetarians, and especially vegans, consume fewer oxidative stressors than nonvegetarians.

Animal protein. Animal protein is concentrated in meat, poultry, fish, and dairy products, with lean meats, poultry, and fish being especially rich sources. Compared with nonvegetarians, lacto-ovo vegetarians consume much less animal protein, while vegans consume no animal protein at all.

Potentially protective dietary components

The dietary components that have been found to offer the most powerful protection against heart disease are the following:

Fiber (especially soluble fiber). Fiber is found only in plant foods. Legumes, berries, dried fruits, bran cereals, and whole grains are especially high in fiber. Excellent sources of soluble fiber (the type of fiber that becomes gummy in water) include legumes, flaxseeds, oat bran, and pectin-rich fruits. Vegetarians consume about two to three times as much fiber as nonvegetarians, with vegans having the highest intakes.

Omega-3 fatty acids. There are several different omega-3 fatty acids (one of the two families of polyunsaturated fats; see pages 162 to 164). The most significant are alpha-linolenic acid (ALA) and two very important longer-chain fatty acids, eicosapentaenoic acid (EPA) and docosahexaenoic acid (DHA).

All of these seem to be protective for heart health, although the longer-chain EPA and DHA seem most effective. Fortunately, we can convert ALA to EPA and DHA in our bodies. ALA is found in flaxseeds and flaxseed oil (our richest sources), hempseeds and hempseed oil, canola oil, walnuts and walnut oil, butternuts, soybeans and soyfoods, and green leafy plants. EPA and DHA are found mainly in fish and seafood. EPA also is present in most seaweed (in very small quantities), and DHA is found in some microalgae and eggs (especially omega-3-rich varieties).

Both vegetarian and nonvegetarian diets tend to be low in omega-3 fatty acids. Vegetarian diets contain very little EPA and DHA. However, in recent years, DHA from microalgae has become available in supplement form. (See chapter 7 for more information on these omega-3 fatty acids.)

Folate, vitamin B$_6$, and vitamin B$_{12}$. The most concentrated sources of folate are legumes, vegetables (especially leafy greens), fruits (especially citrus fruits), nutritional yeast, sunflower seeds, and whole and folate-enriched grains and grain products. Vitamin B$_6$ is widely distributed throughout the food supply and is plentiful in whole grains, legumes, and many plant foods. Vitamin B$_{12}$ is found in all animal foods and in vitamin B$_{12}$–fortified foods. Plant foods are not reliable sources of vitamin B$_{12}$ unless fortified. Vegetarian diets contain approximately double the folate of nonvegetarian diets, similar amounts of vitamin B$_6$, and lower levels of vitamin B$_{12}$. Vegan diets are especially low in B$_{12}$, unless they include fortified foods or supplements.

Phytochemicals. Phytochemicals are naturally occurring plant chemicals that give flavor, texture, odor, and the full spectrum of colors to plants. They help regulate growth and defend against attacks by insects or fungi. There are thousands of different phytochemicals, each with unique properties, and many have been shown to be highly protective to human health.

Vegetables and fruits are our primary sources of phytochemicals. Blueberries and other berries, kale and other greens, and garlic are especially rich sources. Legumes, whole grains, nuts, seeds, herbs, and spices also provide an impressive array of these protective plant components. Since these occur only in plants, vegetarian diets are richer in phytochemicals than nonvegetarian diets.

Antioxidant nutrients. Vitamins C and E, carotenoids, and selenium are known as "antioxidant nutrients" (nutrients that help to protect us and our food supply from the ravages of oxidative stressors or free radicals). Vitamin C is found almost exclusively in plant foods, especially in fruits and vegetables. The most concentrated sources of vitamin E are vegetable oils, nuts, seeds, wheat germ, avocado, and sweet potatoes. Our richest sources of carotenoids are deep orange and yellow vegetables and fruits. Selenium is found in both plant and sea foods and is high in nuts (especially Brazil nuts), seeds, and grains.

Compared with nonvegetarians, vegetarians (especially vegans) have higher tissue levels of many antioxidants: vitamins C, E, and carotenoids. Intakes of vitamins C and carotenoids are close to double those of the general population. Tissue levels of selenium are similar for vegetarians and nonvegetarians.

Monounsaturated and polyunsaturated fats. Monounsaturated fats are plentiful in nuts and nut oils (except for walnuts), olives and olive oil, avocados, and high-oleic sunflower and safflower oil. The primary sources of polyunsaturated fats are vegetable oils (sunflower, safflower, corn, soy, and grapeseed), grains, seeds, and walnuts. Vegetarian diets tend to be higher in unsaturated fats, especially polyunsaturated fats.

Plant protein (especially soy protein). Concentrated sources of soy protein include tofu, tempeh, veggie "meats," textured vegetable protein, soy nuts, edamame (green soybeans), soymilk, and soy yogurt. Legumes provide abundant protein, while other plant foods, chiefly whole grains, nuts, seeds, and many vegetables, also are good sources. Vegetarian diets are naturally rich in plant protein and often in soy protein, as numerous popular vegetarian products are soy based.

Plant sterols and stanols. These naturally occurring plant compounds, similar in structure to cholesterol, block cholesterol absorption from the gut. Fruits, vegetables, nuts, seeds, cereals, and legumes contain small amounts of these compounds. More concentrated sources are new margarines on the market that have added sterols and stanols. Vegetarian diets are naturally higher in plant sterols and stanols than nonvegetarian diets.

Salicylic acid. It is common knowledge that taking aspirin may protect the heart. This is because aspirin contains acetylsalicylic acid, which is converted to salicylic acid in our bodies. Salicylic acid is an anti-inflammatory and appears to reduce the chronic inflammation involved in heart disease. Salicylic acid also is present in some plants, helping them to resist infection. It is found in varying amounts in all fruits, vegetables, herbs, and spices. While the amounts of salicylic acid in foods are not as high as in aspirin, they are high enough to boost blood levels significantly. However, if you've been advised to take a baby aspirin every day, don't stop because you are eating more fruits and vegetables (unless advised by your doctor). Studies have found that vegetarians have greater intakes and blood levels of salicylic acid than nonvegetarians.

Maximizing the vegetarian advantage

Well-planned vegetarian diets offer highly effective protection against heart disease. For the best results, the diet must be centered on whole plant foods, including a wide variety of legumes, vegetables, whole grains, fruits, nuts, and seeds. Processed foods containing hydrogenated or partially hydrogenated fats and deep-fried foods are best avoided. Refined carbohydrates, such as white flour products and white rice, and animal products, such as cheese and eggs, if used, should be limited. However, it has become evident that even if you are doing all of these things, your protection against heart disease could still be thwarted by ignoring a couple of crucial dietary factors.

Vegetarian diets in the treatment of heart disease

Are vegetarian diets an effective alternative, or complement, to drugs and surgery? Although studies designed to answer this question are limited in number and small in size, their results are encouraging. In 1990, physician and clinical researcher Dean Ornish demonstrated that a very low-fat vegetarian diet (10 percent or less calories from fat) and lifestyle changes (stress management, aerobic exercise, and group therapy) could not only slow the progression of atherosclerosis, but significantly reverse it. After one year, 82 percent of the experimental group participants experienced regression of their disease, while in the control group the disease continued to progress. The control group followed a "heart healthy" diet commonly prescribed by physicians that provided less than 30 percent of calories from fat and less than 200 mg of cholesterol a day. Over the next four years, people in the experimental group continued to reverse their arterial damage, while those in the control group became steadily worse and had twice as many cardiac events. In 1999, cardiologist Caldwell Esselstyn reported on a twelve-year study of eleven patients following a very low-fat vegan diet coupled with cholesterol-lowering medication. Approximately 70 percent experienced reversal of their disease. In the eight years prior to the study, these patients experienced a total of forty-eight cardiac events (e.g., heart attacks and angina), while in over a decade of the trial, only one noncompliant patient experienced an event.

This might lead us to assume that very low-fat vegetarian diets are "as good as it gets" when it comes to the prevention and treatment of heart disease. However, there is also compelling evidence to support that higher-fat plant-based diets, such as Mediterranean-style diets, can be extraordinarily protective and potentially useful in the treatment of heart disease. These diets are centered on relatively unprocessed plant foods and include about 30 to 35 percent of calories as fat, mostly from olive oil. They typically include small amounts of animal products. One of the largest studies to examine the potential benefits of this type of diet was the Lyon Heart Study, which compared the effects of a Mediterranean-style diet with those of an American "heart healthy," 30-percent fat diet (605 participants; 302 on the Mediterranean diet, 303 on the "heart healthy" diet). After two and one-half years on a Mediterranean-style diet, patients had an unprecedented 76 percent lower risk of dying of a heart attack or stroke when compared with patients on the "heart healthy" diet. The study was originally planned to last five years. However, the ethics and safety committee stopped the study in half that time to allow control-group participants equal access to the Mediterranean-style diet that had proven to be so effective.

CAUTION:
DON'T UNDERMINE THOSE ADVANTAGES!

For maximum protection against heart disease, vegetarians must ensure their diets include reliable sources of **vitamin B_{12}** and **omega-3 fatty acids**.

Some vegetarians, and especially vegans, have diets low in vitamin B_{12}. This is both unfortunate and completely unnecessary. It is unfortunate because a lack of this essential vitamin has numerous negative health consequences, including a significant rise in homocysteine levels, increasing risk of heart disease. It is unnecessary because it is easy for vegetarians and vegans to ensure sufficient vitamin B_{12} intakes with fortified foods or supplements. **It is extremely important that vegetarians, who make such positive diet and lifestyle choices, do not undermine these benefits by ignoring their need for vitamin B_{12}.** (See chapter 8 for more information on achieving excellent vitamin B_{12} status.)

Long-chain omega-3 fatty acids—EPA and DHA—can help reduce blood pressure, triglyceride levels, platelet aggregation, inflammation, and cardiac arrhythmias. Long-chain omega-3 fatty acids come mainly from fish. **Vegetarians can improve levels of EPA by consuming sufficient quantities of ALA, the form of omega-3 fatty acids in flaxseeds, walnuts, and other plant foods, or by consuming direct sources of DHA (DHA-rich eggs or supplements).** (See chapter 7 for more information on improving omega-3 fatty acid status.)

These studies strongly suggest that it is something other than a lack of fat in the very low-fat vegetarian diets or the presence of olive oil in the Mediterranean diet that is responsible for their health benefits. Perhaps the effects are due more to the vegetables, fruits, legumes, and whole grains, which serve as the foundation of these diets, and the abundance of plant protein, fiber, phytochemicals, vitamins, and minerals—all components in foods that are protective to health. Neither eating pattern is high in saturated fat, trans-fatty acids, cholesterol, or animal protein—food components that seem to contribute to heart disease.

The question of fat and heart disease was also looked at in the Nurses' Health Study and Health Professionals Follow-Up Study (more than 80,000 people were followed for several years). Researchers found that rates of heart attacks and deaths from heart disease were more strongly related to types of fats in the diet than total fat intake. They estimated that replacing 5 percent of total calories from saturated fat with unsaturated fat would reduce the risk of heart attacks and death from heart disease by about 40 percent. (This is the equivalent of replacing 3 ounces/85 grams of cheddar cheese with 2 ounces/57 grams of mixed dry-roasted nuts on a 2,400 calorie diet.) Researchers also found that replacing only 2 percent of total calories from trans-fatty acids with unsaturated fats would reduce risk by an astounding 50 percent. Two percent of fat as trans-fatty acids would typically be less than 5 grams; this is the amount in 2 ounces (57 grams) of microwave popcorn or a medium order of fries.

It is possible that well-constructed vegetarian diets, which contain sufficient vitamin B_{12} and omega-3 fatty acids, and include moderate amounts of healthful fats from whole plant foods such as nuts, seeds, olives, and avocados, could have even more impressive results than very low-fat vegetarian diets or traditional, higher-fat Mediterranean diets.

The implications for both the prevention and treatment of coronary artery disease are enormous. Well-planned vegetarian diets have one major advantage over drugs and surgery—the side effects are pleasant. You can anticipate some weight loss, a drop in blood pressure, better blood sugar control, improved regularity, and possibly even improvements in immune-inflammatory conditions such as arthritis. A vegetarian diet sure beats stomachaches, diarrhea, flushing, nausea, liver damage, cataracts, and gallstones, which many people experience on cholesterol-lowering drugs, or a slow, painful recovery from open-heart surgery.

Cancer

Cancer is the second leading cause of death in the developed world. It strikes one out of every two American men and one out of every three American women at some point during their lifetime, with 80 percent of the cases appearing in people over the age of fifty-five. Of all the chronic diseases, cancer is the most dreaded and perhaps the least well understood. Many people believe it is a random killer, like an infectious disease. It is not. The American Cancer Society estimates that 75 percent of all cancers are the product of our environment and lifestyle. Experts estimate that as many as 30 to 40 percent of all cancers are caused by diet. When we look at specific cancers, the figure can be substantially higher. An estimated 66 to 75 percent of cancers of the stomach, colon, and rectum are preventable by diet, as are 50 to 75 percent of esophageal cancers, 33 to 66 percent of liver cancers, and 33 to 50 percent of cancers of the mouth, throat, nose, pancreas, and breast. Every year, over ten million people worldwide develop some form of cancer and over six million die of the disease. Thus, it is estimated that three to four million cases of cancer could be avoided each year if people made better food choices. Although we are beginning to understand the links between diet and certain forms of cancer, there are many questions yet unanswered. While it doesn't appear that scientists will discover a cure for cancer anytime soon, we are gaining ground in prevention and treatment. Being a vegetarian may just provide the edge that is needed.

Where do vegetarians stand?

Vegetarians experience lower death rates from cancer, compared with the general population, although it is unclear how much of the difference is due to diet and how much to other positive lifestyle choices. Some, but not all, studies have found less risk of cancer among vegetarians when compared with similar health-conscious nonvegetarians.

Among the most useful information we have comes from the largest long-term study to date comparing disease rates of vegetarians and nonvegetarians, the Adventist Health Study (U.S.). After adjusting the data for age, gender, and smoking, vegetarians had an 88 percent lower risk of colon cancer than nonvegetarians, and 54 percent lower risk of prostate cancer. In the Heidelberg Study (Germany), cancer in vegetarians was only 48 percent for men and 74 percent for women, compared to the general population, and those who had been vegetarian for over twenty years had about 50 percent fewer deaths from cancer. The greatest advantages were seen for cancers of the gastrointestinal system and stomach.

In the Health Food Shoppers Study (U.K.), cancer death rates were about 70 percent of the cancer death rates in the general population. In this study, cancer rates did not differ significantly between vegetarian health food shoppers and similar nonvegetarian health food shoppers. In the Oxford Vegetarian Study (U.K.), death rates from cancer in vegetarians were 61 percent those of nonvegetarians. Although differences were not significant when vegetarians were compared to nonvegetarians with a healthy lifestyle, rates were about 11 percent lower in the vegetarian group.

Why are vegetarians at an advantage?

Is it the lack of meat or the abundance of vegetables and fruits that gives vegetarians the edge? While it is tempting to assume one simple answer, the reality is that both are likely responsible, along with many related factors. Vegetarian diets can affect metabolism and general physiology in a favorable way, reducing our cancer risk. For example, vegetarians have reduced fecal excretion of cholesterol, its by-products, and bile acids. High excretion of these constituents is linked to increased cancer risk. Vegetarians have lower levels of secondary bile acids, which are possible tumor promoters. In addition, vegetarians have remarkably different bacterial flora and less cancer-causing substances in their bowels. There is some evidence that vegetarian females are exposed to less estrogen over the course of a lifetime and their overall balance of sex hormones is protective, compared with nonvegetarians.

Thousands of scientific studies have explored the relationship between diet and cancer, giving us some solid clues as to which factors play the greatest roles in promoting cancer and which provide the most powerful protection. In 1997, the World Cancer Research Fund (WCRF) and the American Institute of Cancer Research (AICR) commissioned a panel of experts from twenty countries to examine the available evidence on the diet and cancer connection. The resulting 670-page document, *Food, Nutrition and the Prevention of Cancer: A Global Perspective*, provides the most comprehensive analysis of this research to date. The panel, in their discussion of the issue of vegetarian diets and cancer, summarizes their findings as follows:

> *In conclusion, various studies have shown that groups following lacto-ovo, lacto-vegetarian, and vegan diets have decreased incidence of cancers at several specific sites. Plausible biological mechanisms have been identified by which vegetarian diets may specifically reduce the risk of cancers of the colon, breast, and prostate. Any effect of vegetarian diets is likely to be due not only to the exclusion of meat (which has been judged by the panel to increase the risk probably of colorectal cancer and possibly of cancers of the pancreas, prostate, kidney and breast), but also due to the inclusion of a larger number and wider range of plant foods containing an extensive variety of potential cancer-preventive substances.*

When people think about diet and cancer, the first things that generally come to mind are possible carcinogens lurking in the food supply. Yet few are aware of the powerful protectors provided by plant-based diets. The evidence for the many ways in which they reduce cancer risk is both strong and consistent. Let's take a closer look at the dietary components that have been shown to promote cancer and those that appear to be most protective.

Dietary components that may promote cancer

The dietary components that have been most consistently associated with increased cancer risk are

Alcohol. There is no doubt that alcohol increases the risk of cancer, especially cancers of the mouth, esophagus, and surrounding areas, and cancer of the liver. There is also substantial evidence that alcohol increases cancers of the colon and rectum (colorectal cancers) and breast cancer. The evidence against alcohol is consistent for all types of alcoholic beverages. The WCRF/AICR panel recommends against alcohol consumption. They add that if alcohol is consumed, it should be limited to less than two drinks per day for men and one for women. Alcohol consumption among vegetarians has been shown to be lower than in the general population.

Total fat, saturated/animal fat. For many years, experts thought that eating too much fat was a huge contributor to cancer. Today, we understand that while high-fat diets may increase risk for some cancers—such as endometrial, colorectal, and hormone-related cancers (breast and prostate)—it is the type of fat that seems to play an even bigger role. For breast cancer, some research suggests that too many calories may be a greater culprit than too much fat. There is reasonable evidence that diets high in saturated and animal fat increase the risk of lung, colorectal, endometrial, ovarian, and hormone-related cancers. In a recent study of 6,689 women, diets high in animal fat increased risk of ovarian cancer by 70 percent, compared with diets low in animal fat. Another study of 906 women in China found an almost fivefold increased risk of ovarian cancer in those consuming high amounts of animal fat. The WCRF/AICR panel recommends that fatty foods be limited, particularly those of animal origin. Vegetarian intakes of total fat are slightly lower than the general population, while intakes of saturated fat and animal fat are substantially lower than the general population.

Meat. A century ago Todd Ferrier (a health writer and philosopher) wrote: "There is a growing consensus of opinion among the eminent Medical Faculty that the great increase in cancerous growths may be traced to the effete products taken into the system with flesh foods." While we now know that there are many causes of cancer, these physicians just may have been on to something. Today we have solid evidence that meat, especially red meat, increases the risk of colorectal cancer. There is some evidence that suggests it may also increase the risk of cancers of the prostate and kidney. While most of the available evidence implicates only red meat in colon cancer, the Adventist Health Study suggests that white meat (poultry and fish) may also be suspect. Compared with vegetarians, people eating red meat at least once a week had a 37 percent increase in risk, and those eating red meat more than once a week had an 86 percent increase. Surprisingly, those eating white meat less than once a week had a 50 percent increase, while those eating it more than once a week had a 200 percent increase in risk. The WCRF/AICR panel recommends that red meat (beef, lamb, and pork), if eaten at all, should be limited to less than 3 ounces (80 grams) daily. Of course, vegetarians consume no meat.

Grilled (broiled) and barbecued meats, poultry, and fish, and fried foods. Evidence is rapidly mounting that grilling, broiling, and other high-temperature cooking of meats, poultry, and fish increases risk of cancer, particularly colorectal cancer. Frying foods also appears to increase cancer risk. Grilling (broiling) and barbecuing generate two major groups of carcinogens—heterocyclic amines and polyaromatic hydrocarbons. The more intense the heat, the greater their production. Heterocyclic amines and polyaromatic hydrocarbons enter cells, damage DNA, and can trigger the cancer process. The WCRF/AICR panel recommends that charred food be avoided. They suggest that those who eat meat, poultry, and fish should minimize the use of direct flame and avoid burning meat juices. Vegetarians do not eat grilled meat, poultry, or fish, but may consume some grilled or fried foods.

Smoked and cured meats, poultry, and fish. These foods may increase risk of colorectal cancer. Some studies also suggest that stomach cancer risk could be increased by cured flesh foods, and cancer of the pancreas by both cured and smoked flesh foods. A recent Chinese study of 189 participants found that intake of smoked foods more than doubled the risk of stomach cancer. A Finnish study found that the intake of smoked and salted fish increased risk of colon cancer by more than two and one-half times (comparing those who ate the most smoked and salted fish with those who ate the least). Cured and smoked foods (such as bacon) are our largest dietary sources of nitrites and preformed N-nitroso compounds (nitrites can also be converted to nitroso compounds in our stomach), which are recognized carcinogens. Vegetarians consume no smoked or cured meats.

Cholesterol. Evidence is growing for a link between cholesterol intake and risk of cancers of the lung, pancreas, and endometrium. More than half the research that has studied cholesterol and both lung and pancreatic cancers found increased risk with high cholesterol intakes. Almost all the research on endometrial cancer has confirmed that higher intakes of cholesterol, which is present only in animal products, increase risk. Lacto-ovo vegetarians tend to consume less cholesterol than the general population, while vegans consume none.

Trans-fatty acids. Few studies have examined the impact of trans-fatty acids on cancer risk. However, one recent study showed a very strong positive association with breast cancer. Researchers in Europe investigated the relationship between trans-fatty acids and breast cancer in 698 postmenopausal women. A high intake of trans-fatty acids (as determined by tissue concentrations) was associated with a 40 percent increase in risk, even when age, BMI (body mass index, an estimate of body fatness based on the ratio of your size to your weight), use of hormone supplements, and socioeconomic status were taken into account. Further research is needed before any specific recommendations can be made regarding trans-fatty acid intakes and cancer risk. Trans-fatty acid intakes appear to be somewhat lower in the vegetarian population than in the general population.

Refined grains. Studies indicate that refined grains may increase risk of cancers of the whole gastrointestinal system—from the mouth to the rectum. There is some indication that vegetarians eat fewer refined grains than non-vegetarians.

Dairy products. A number of studies suggest that milk and dairy products may increase risk of prostate, breast, and kidney cancer. Higher intakes of dairy products have been associated with increased levels of insulin-like growth factor 1 or IGF-1, a hormone important to the growth and function of many organs. Elevated levels of IGF-1 have been associated with an increased risk of prostate, breast, and other cancers. This association raises the possibility that dairy products could increase cancer risk by raising levels of IGF-1 in the bloodstream. While research is leaning in this direction, further studies will be needed to determine whether milk consumption is a contributing factor in cancer. It is important to note that several studies suggest that milk, or perhaps calcium and calcium-rich foods in general, may protect against colon cancer. The amount of dairy products eaten by lacto-ovo vegetarians varies tremendously, as it does in the general population, while vegans consume no dairy products at all. For more information on dairy products and alternative calcium sources, see chapter 4.

Food additives, pesticides, DDT, PCBs, hormone residues, and other chemical contaminants in foods. While most people assume that food additives and contaminants are among the greatest contributors to cancer risk, the evidence is weak, at best. This may be because it's difficult to find groups of people that have not been exposed to additives, pesticides, and contaminants, at least to some degree, to act as a control group! Some food contaminants are highly toxic in large doses and have been found to be carcinogenic. Although there are few studies on people, there is some evidence that DDT residues may increase risk of breast cancer and PCBs may increase risk of bladder cancer. Some studies also have found increased risk in farm workers with direct exposure to these substances. There is little convincing evidence that food additives, such as colors and preservatives, are significant cancer-causing agents, although there is some question regarding saccharin, cyclamates, and aspartame. Certain chemical residues are known to accumulate in the fat of animals and humans, becoming more concentrated as larger animals eat contaminated plants and smaller animals. Fish and seafood can be high in such pollutants (especially PCBs, dioxin, and DDT) due to the dumping of environmental contaminants in rivers, lakes, and oceans.

In general, while commercially grown, sprayed fruits and vegetables contribute significantly to our overall intake of pesticides, we have strong evidence that our consumption of these foods is highly protective. The WCRF/AICR panel suggests that when additives, contaminants, and residues are properly regulated, the exposure risk is minimal; however, unregulated or improper use may increase cancer risk. It makes sense to attempt to limit our exposure by making organic choices that support a clean and healthy environment. Levels of chemical contaminants in tissues of vegetarians may be somewhat lower than nonvegetarians, while levels in vegans may be substantially reduced.

Dietary factors that may protect against cancer

The dietary components that have been found to offer the most powerful protection against cancer are

Vegetables and Fruits. There is substantial evidence that diets high in fruits and particularly vegetables lower the risk of cancer. High intakes of fruits and vegetables appear to protect against cancers of the mouth and surrounding areas, esophagus, stomach, and colorectum. In some cases, cancer risk is reduced by 50 to 60 percent when those eating high amounts of vegetables and fruits are compared with those eating few vegetables and fruits. There are many components of vegetables and fruits that are thought to be protective. Antioxidant vitamins and minerals, fiber, and phytochemicals all play a part in warding off cancer.

The WCRF/AICR panel estimates that 20 percent of all cancers could be avoided if people increased their vegetable and fruit intake to at least five servings a day, even if no other dietary changes were made. The panel recommends an intake of five to ten servings of vegetables and fruits per day or 7 to 14 percent of calories. This recommendation does not include starchy vegetables and fruits, such as tubers and plantains. Vegetarians consistently consume higher amounts of vegetables and fruits than the general population. Whereas the day's vegetable intake for many North Americans consists of a side of fries with ketchup, it's not unusual for vegetarians to eat 4 cups (1 L) of salad at a meal.

Fiber. Fiber is nature's broom, and among its greatest tasks is keeping the colon healthy; so it comes as no surprise that people who eat lots of fiber have lower rates of colorectal cancers. Based on the results of thirteen large studies, it was estimated that the risk of colorectal cancers in the United States could be cut by about one-third if people were to increase their intakes of fiber from foods by 13 grams (the amount in 1 cup/250 ml each of oatmeal and lentil soup). There also is evidence that fiber cuts risk of cancers of the stomach, pancreas, and breast. A large Swedish study found that the more fiber people ate (mainly cereal fiber), the less likely they were to develop stomach cancer. People who ate the most cereal fiber had less than one-third the risk of those with the lowest intakes. The combined results from twelve studies showed that eating more fiber reduced the risk of breast cancer. Most American health authorities recommend eating 20 to 35 grams of fiber per day, which is about double the current intakes. Many experts suggest that optimal intakes are even higher: 40 to 50 grams per day or more. Vegetarians average about 30 to 50 grams of fiber per day.

Phytochemicals. Phytochemicals (chemicals naturally occurring in plants) appear to provide powerful protection against all forms of cancer. However, the research is in such early stages that we have few details about which phytochemicals are most effective, which cancers they act against, and how much of any plant food we need for maximum protection. The cancers for which we have the most data regarding the protective effects of phytochemicals are the hormone-related cancers and cancers of the stomach and bladder. Phytochemicals block tumor formation and growth by

➤ reducing cancer cell proliferation (multiplication of cancer cells);

➤ supporting enzyme systems that make cancer-causing agents ineffective and promote their excretion;

➤ reducing oxidative damage to tissues and to DNA;

➤ acting like antibiotics by killing bacteria that are associated with certain cancers (for example, by destroying Helicobacter pylori, a bacterium associated with stomach cancer);

➤ blocking the cancer-promoting action of estrogens, which might help reduce hormone-related cancers.

Foods that are particularly high in these cancer-blocking phytochemicals are cruciferous vegetables (broccoli, cauliflower, kale, collards, cabbage, turnips, Brussels sprouts, kohlrabi, mustard greens, and turnip greens), umbelliferous vegetables (carrots, parsley, celery, dill, fennel), tomatoes and tomato products, allium vegetables (garlic and onions), berries (especially blueberries), grapes, plums, citrus fruits, certain herbs (turmeric and ginger), and soyfoods.

Although we don't have enough information to recommend specific amounts of phytochemical-rich foods, it's clear that eating more plant foods (vegetables, fruits, whole grains, legumes, nuts, and seeds) will reduce our risk of cancer. There is no doubt that vegetarian diets have higher phytochemical concentrations compared with standard American diets.

Vitamins. There is convincing evidence that folate and foods containing vitamin C and carotenoids reduce cancer risk, and some evidence that vitamin E is protective as well. Vitamin C may protect against numerous cancers, including much of the gastrointestinal system, the lungs, pancreas, and cervix. Carotenoids seem to protect against lung cancer and possibly colon cancer, while folate appears effective against colorectal cancers. Much of the evidence for these vitamins suggests that they provide the greatest protection when they come from foods rather than supplements, although there is some evidence that vitamin C, folate, and vitamin E could be beneficial even in supplement form. There is no evidence that supplements of beta-carotene are protective. In fact, two large trials reported that participants who took synthetic beta-carotene were 18 percent and 28 percent more likely to develop lung cancer than those not taking the supplements. The explanation may be that a wide spectrum of carotenoids is needed to afford protection, and isolating a single carotenoid may interfere with the protective effects of the others. At this point, we don't have enough evidence to advise using specific doses of vitamins to reduce risk of cancer. However, everyone should attempt to eat plentiful food sources of vitamin C, carotenoids, folate, and vitamin E, as these are all significantly higher in vegetarian diets compared to nonvegetarian diets.

Minerals. Two minerals—selenium and calcium—have been shown to possibly reduce cancer risk, at least for some types of the disease. Low selenium intakes appear to be associated with increased risk of several different cancers. Selenium serves as a cofactor for various enzymes, some acting as antioxidants and others as detoxifiers of carcinogenic substances. Several studies have shown that cancer risk declines with higher intakes of selenium from foods, although some work indicates a protective role for selenium supplements as well. While the evidence is compelling, further studies are needed before specific recommendations regarding selenium supplementation for cancer prevention or treatment can be made. What we do know is that it makes good sense to meet the recommended intakes for selenium. Great plant sources of selenium include Brazil nuts and other nuts and seeds, whole grains, dairy products, and egg yolks. The calcium story is a little confusing, as it appears to decrease risk of colon cancer, while possibly increasing risk of prostate cancer. Thus, it would make sense to insure adequate calcium intakes without being excessive. Intakes of selenium and calcium in vegetarians are similar to that of the general population, although calcium intakes often are reduced in vegans.

Whole grains. There is little doubt that whole grains protect people against cancer, especially cancers of the gastrointestinal system (stomach cancer, in particular) and hormone-related cancers. Whole grains are rich in fiber and fermentable carbohydrates, as well as antioxidants, trace minerals, and phytochemicals—all protective against cancer. Vegetarians tend to eat more whole grains than the general population.

How these protectors work

Protective substances in our diets can block or suppress the development of cancer in a number of ways at different stages. They can prevent carcinogens from entering the cells and damaging DNA. They can support enzyme systems that make carcinogens ineffective. They also can stop the out-of-control multiplication of cells.

Maximizing the vegetarian advantage

Making wise food choices can go a long way toward improving our odds of avoiding cancer and possibly even beating the disease if we are afflicted. We can begin by keeping food intake moderate, consuming just enough calories to support a healthy body weight. We can balance our calories coming in with our energy going out by getting sufficient exercise. Next, we need to make a variety of whole plant foods the foundation of our diet. If anything gets "supersized," it should be vegetables and fruits. Processed foods—especially those made with white flour and added fat, sugar, and salt—should be limited. If animal products are used, it is best to stick to low-fat or nonfat choices. There is simply no doubt about it—building our diet around whole plant foods is our best line of defense against cancer.

For more detailed information about diet and cancer, read the excellent book *Healthy Eating for Life to Prevent and Treat Cancer* by The Physicians Committee for Responsible Medicine with Vesanto Melina (Wiley and Sons; New York, NY).

EFFECTS OF VEGETARIAN DIETS ON OTHER DISEASES

When we consider the profound effects vegetarian diets can have on the risk for and treatment of heart disease and cancer, it is no surprise that plant foods can decrease our risk of other chronic diseases, too. Let's briefly review a few of the diseases for which the evidence is most compelling.

Type 2 Diabetes

A disease of diet and lifestyle, type 2 diabetes is sweeping North America and rising to epidemic proportions. It is estimated that 80 to 97 percent of all type 2 diabetes is induced by the overconsumption of food (leading to overweight) and insufficient activity. Risk of diabetes is approximately double for those who are moderately overweight (with a body mass index above 25) and triple for those who are obese (with a body mass index above 30). So pervasive is this connection that the new term diabesity has been coined to describe the type of diabetes brought on by overweight. Most alarming is the rise in type 2 diabetes in children and teens. Until recently, the disorder was known as adult-onset diabetes because it occurred mostly in people over fifty years of age. Today, it is estimated that approximately one-third of all newly diagnosed diabetes in children and teens in North America is type 2.

While excess body fat plays a strong role in this disease, the way the fat is distributed is perhaps even more significant. Weight concentrated around the abdomen and in the upper part of the body (apple shaped) increases risk far more than weight that settles around the legs and hips (pear shaped). In addition, fat accumulated in and around vital organs (visceral fat) is far more damaging than fat that accumulates close to the skin's surface.

The lowest rates of type 2 diabetes occur in populations consuming whole foods and plant-based diets. Some experts believe that is mostly due to their lower body weights, although very high-fiber diets themselves may be protective. When populations such as these adopt high-fat, low-fiber diets, diabetes risk quickly escalates. If they return to a whole food, plant-based diet, the incidence of diabetes is again reduced.

Studies show that vegetarians are less likely to develop type 2 diabetes. In the Adventist Health Study, rates of type 2 diabetes were 53 percent lower for male vegetarians and 55 percent lower in female vegetarians than in nonvegetarians. People aged fifty to sixty-nine showed the greatest difference in diabetes rates, with 76 percent less diabetes in vegetarians.

Many dietary factors can help to explain the vegetarian advantage. Vegetarians generally are leaner than nonvegetarians. They tend to have significantly higher fiber intakes and lower intakes of saturated fat, both of which may improve insulin sensitivity. There also is some evidence to suggest that the absence of meat, especially processed meat, may provide additional benefits.

We can maximize our protection against type 2 diabetes, or improve its outcome if we already have this condition, by eating just enough calories to achieve and maintain a healthy body weight. A wide variety of unprocessed plant foods should form the foundation of our diet. Legumes ought to be included in our meals every day, as they are tremendously helpful in controlling blood sugar levels. Fruits should be the primary source of simple sugars, as they offer far more nutritional value and have significantly less effect on blood sugar than refined simple sugars.

Healthy fats should be included, with the best sources being nuts, seeds, olives, and avocados. These foods are high in calories, so quantities must be moderate. Adequate intakes of omega-3 fatty acids are especially important for people with diabetes (aim for at least 2.2 grams of alpha-linolenic acid per 1,000 calories; just under a teaspoon of flaxseed oil or an ounce of walnuts). People with diabetes may wish to include a direct source of DHA (see pages 163 to 167 for more information). Whole grains are a far better choice than refined white flour products.

For a much more comprehensive look at type 2 diabetes and its management, *Defeating Diabetes* by Brenda Davis and Dr. Tom Barnard is a "must read" (Book Publishing Company; Summertown, TN).

Gallstones

There is solid evidence that gallstones are much less common in people eating plant-based diets than in those eating typical high-fat, animal-centered, North American–style diets. One study of over 600 nonvegetarian and 130 vegetarian women aged forty to sixty-nine years found that nonvegetarians had two and one-half times the risk of developing gallstones, compared to vegetarians. Even after age and body weight were taken into consideration, risk was still double that of vegetarians. Researchers suspect that the advantage enjoyed by vegetarians is due primarily to the lower rates of obesity; reduced intakes of saturated fat, cholesterol, and refined sugars; and the increased consumption of fiber. We can maximize our protection by not overeating, limiting our intakes of saturated fat and cholesterol from eggs and dairy products, including plenty of whole plant foods in our diet, and limiting use of refined, processed foods.

Kidney Disease and Stones

Research shows vegetarians to be at lower risk for kidney disease and kidney stones than nonvegetarians. Vegetarian diets, once considered inappropriate for people with renal disease, recently have been shown to be useful in the treatment of the disease, in some cases significantly improving kidney function. The protection enjoyed by vegetarians is thought to be due to several factors.

➤ Vegetarians consume less protein, especially animal protein. High-protein diets, especially those rich in animal protein, increase glomerular filtration rate (GFR) and have a negative impact on kidney function in other ways. One study found that plant protein produced less protein in the urine and less kidney damage than animal protein, independent of total protein intake. Another study compared a vegan diet with the low-protein diets that are used in the treatment of kidney disease and found similar benefits to GFR and a slower progression of the disease. In addition, the vegan diet lowered cholesterol levels and blood pressure, while the conventional diets did not.

➤ Vegetarians consume significantly less saturated fat and cholesterol. High intakes of saturated fat and cholesterol increase blood cholesterol levels and increase damage to blood vessels in the kidneys.

➤ Vegetarians have higher intakes and tissue levels of antioxidants, which help to reduce LDL cholesterol oxidation and preserve kidney function.

➤ Vegetarians have a reduced risk of diabetes. Diabetes is the leading cause of kidney disease in North America. It can cause severe damage to the kidney's blood vessels.

➤ Vegetarians have only one-third to one-half as much hypertension. High blood pressure is the second leading cause of chronic kidney failure in North America. Severe hypertension can cause kidney damage very quickly, while mild hypertension can cause problems over many years.

We can protect our kidneys by keeping protein intake moderate, relying primarily on plant foods as protein sources, and maintaining a healthy body weight. Our diet should be built around vegetables, fruits, and other antioxidant-rich foods. Processed foods containing added fat, sugar, and salt should be limited.

Gastrointestinal Diseases

Since fiber, which is found only in plant foods, is so supportive of intestinal health, it's no surprise that vegetarians have fewer gastrointestinal disorders than nonvegetarians, and specifically less constipation and diverticulitis. While such disorders were exceedingly rare 100 years ago, they now affect an estimated 30 to 40 percent of people over the age of fifty. One study showed that diverticulitis was 50 percent lower in vegetarian adults age forty-five to fifty-nine, compared with nonvegetarians. The much higher fiber intakes of vegetarians and vegans compared with nonvegetarians is the most likely explanation for this advantage; however, other dietary factors may also play a role. A number of studies have found links between meat consumption and diverticulosis. One study, conducted in Taiwan, noted a twenty-five-fold difference between the most frequent and least frequent consumers of meat products. A Greek study found a fiftyfold difference in risk between people who ate a lot of vegetables but rarely consumed meat and those who rarely ate vegetables and frequently consumed meat. Meat's potent damaging effect may be related to its promotion of bacteria that produce a toxic metabolite, which can weaken the walls of the intestine. Too much fat also seems to increase risk. We can minimize risk of gastrointestinal diseases, such as diverticulosis and constipation, by eating mainly whole plant foods: plenty of legumes, whole grains, vegetables, and fruits. Processed foods prepared with refined grains should not be dietary staples.

Rheumatoid Arthritis

Vegetarian diets may be valuable in both the prevention and treatment of rheumatoid arthritis. In the Adventist Health Study (almost 35,000 participants), vegetarians enjoyed a 50 percent reduction in rheumatoid arthritis compared to nonvegetarians. Although there are only a few studies looking at the effects of vegetarian or vegan diets on people who have rheumatoid arthritis, the results are quite compelling. One study of twenty-four participants found considerable relief from symptoms of rheumatoid arthritis with a 10 percent-fat vegan diet for four weeks. Four studies used a period of fasting followed by at least three months on a vegetarian diet. Participants showed significant long-term improvements in joint swelling, pain, morning stiffness, grip strength, and other indicators of overall health. While there are a number of possible explanations for these benefits, experts believe that they may be related to improved intestinal flora (bacteria in the intestines) on vegetarian or vegan diets. People with rheumatoid arthritis have been found to have more antibodies to specific bacteria compared with people without the disease. Plant-based diets appear to alter intestinal flora and the body's response to the bacteria in a positive way. While these results are encouraging, the studies are not large enough to draw any firm conclusions. However, people with rheumatoid arthritis may want to experiment on themselves using a vegetarian or vegan diet. For those wishing to attempt the more aggressive regime of fasting followed by a vegetarian diet, medical supervision is advised.

NUTRITION RECOMMENDATIONS TO PREVENT CHRONIC DISEASE

Evidence supporting the beneficial effects of vegetarian diets in both the prevention and treatment of the vast majority of chronic diseases has never been more clearly recognized or embraced. The current view on vegetarian diets is well reflected by the words of author, biologist, and nutrition researcher Marion Nestle:

> There's no question that largely vegetarian diets are as healthy as you can get. The evidence is so strong and overwhelming and produced over such a long period of time that it's no longer debatable.

It is reassuring that being vegetarian can bring such powerful health advantages. However, if we are to enjoy the benefits to their fullest, we must construct our diets with some thought, being mindful of the valuable lessons learned so far. The following guidelines are designed to assist you in this endeavor.

1. **Focus the diet on a wide variety of plant foods**. Plant foods should form the foundation of our diet. Include a wide variety of vegetables, fruits, legumes, whole grains, nuts, and seeds. Select minimally processed foods whenever possible.

2. **Eat seven or more servings of vegetables and fruits per day**. Vegetables and fruits are extraordinarily dense in nutrients and phytochemicals. Include them with every meal. Aim for a wide variety of colorful vegetables and fruits. While the usual recommendations are five to ten servings per day, evidence suggests that eating more servings may provide greater benefits. (Note that a serving is a small quantity, such as ½ cup. It's easy to eat two or three times that amount—and it won't make you fat.)

3. **Select whole grain products, and limit refined starches and sugars**. Whole grains contribute significant amounts of protein, vitamins, minerals, fiber, and phytochemicals. Refined starches (found in white flour products)

and sugars (such as white or brown sugar) are stripped of the greatest portion of these protective dietary components.

4. **Make plant foods our primary protein sources**. Our best sources of protein are legumes and products made from legumes (for example, tofu, tempeh, falafel, and hummus). These protein-rich foods are low in saturated fats, contain no cholesterol, and are free of trans-fatty acids. They also are rich sources of vitamins, minerals, and fiber.

5. **Keep total fat intake moderate, and select healthful fat sources**. While total fat intake may be less important than the type of fat, it is recommended that fat consumption be moderate. Nuts, seeds, soybeans, avocados, olives, and other whole plant foods provide the healthiest types of fat. As an added bonus, the fat in these foods is packaged with many protective components. Nuts, seeds, and soybeans are excellent sources of several trace minerals such as zinc and selenium. If using concentrated fats and oils, select those rich in monounsaturated fats (olive oil) and/or omega-3 fatty acids (flaxseed, walnut, or soybean oil).

6. **Include a reliable source of omega-3 fatty acids in the daily diet**. Plant foods that are rich in omega-3 fatty acids include flaxseeds and flaxseed oil, hempseeds and hempseed oil, canola oil, and walnuts. Be sure they are fresh when purchased, and store them in the refrigerator or freezer. Long-chain omega-3 fatty acids can also be obtained from microalgae supplements. (See page 166.)

7. **Limit intake of saturated fat, cholesterol, and trans-fatty acids**. Saturated fat and cholesterol are concentrated in animal foods. Trans-fatty acids are found primarily in processed foods. These are our least desirable fat sources. Our main sources of saturated fat are animal products and, to a lesser extent, tropical oils. Animal products are our only source of cholesterol. If you use animal products, such as dairy, select those that are low in fat. Trans-fatty acids are found primarily in processed foods containing hydrogenated fats and, to a lesser extent, in animal products. If using processed foods, select those that avoid or minimize the use of hydrogenated fats.

8. **Use salty foods in moderation**. Too much salt can contribute to hypertension (in some people), osteoporosis, and some forms of cancer. Moderate your intake of salty foods, and minimize the use of salt in cooking and at the table. Heavily salted foods include salty snack foods, many commercially prepared foods (such as soups, canned pasta products, frozen

entrées, packaged pasta, and rice mixes), pickles, and condiments. Tamari, soy sauce, and miso are high in salt, too.

9. **Limit use of smoked, charred, and cured foods**. These methods of food preparation and preservation, especially with animal products, increase our exposure to carcinogens and therefore should be minimized.

10. **Use plant foods grown without the use of pesticides whenever possible**. Select foods that have been grown without pesticides or with minimal use of pesticides. Look for certified organic products.

11. **Alcohol, if consumed, should be used in moderation**. Frequent use of alcohol can take the place of more nutritious foods and also can contribute to degenerative diseases. If consumed, limit alcoholic beverages to two drinks a day for men and one for women.

12. **Avoid being underweight or overweight, and get regular physical exercise**. Both overweight and underweight can increase the risk of disease. The safest way to maintain a healthy body weight is to eat a varied, balanced diet and to exercise regularly.

For scientific references for this chapter, see
http://www.nutrispeak.com/bvreferences.htm

Chapter 3

POWER FROM PLANTS

LEGUMES, NUTS, AND SEEDS

For many, the words *protein* and *meat* are almost interchangeable. People assume that meat is our primary source of protein and iron and that it is essential for building and maintaining strong muscles. There is a common belief that animal products outrank plant foods in their value to human health. This seed is planted very early by parents, schoolteachers, and popular TV shows. When people ask "What's for dinner?" they usually are referring to the type of meat that will be served, rather than seemingly inconsequential side dishes, such as broccoli or rice. The notion that beef, fish, or poultry must be the dominant theme of our meals is powerful and deeply ingrained. This focus on meats often makes people defensive when the "V" word is uttered. It is a stretch for most people to accept that life can be every bit as good, and our bodies every bit as strong, without consuming a single piece of animal flesh. Four common myths underlie these misconceptions. In this chapter, we will shatter these myths and provide you with the tools needed to set the record straight.

Myth #1:   **We need meat to get enough protein.**

Myth #2:   **Plant protein lacks essential amino acids and is poor quality.**

Myth #3:   **Vegetarians must carefully complement plant proteins at every meal.**

Myth #4:   **Most vegetarians end up with iron-deficiency anemia.**

None of these statements is true. Each is based on misconceptions from a bygone era. In fact, *no nutrient essential to human life is found in meat that also is not found in diets composed entirely of plant foods.* As we look at the diets of vegetarian and nonvegetarian animals, including humans, we see that every one of the nutrients used to build animal and human bodies is derived from plants and microorganisms. Protein and iron required for the muscles, blood, and bones of large, powerful herbivores such as elephants are derived from plant foods. Even vitamin B_{12}, a nutrient present in animal foods, actually originates from the bacteria and other microorganisms that grow in animals, in soil, and on plants. Vegetarians can easily ensure their diets include these and other required nutrients. At the same time, there are several myths in circulation that paint an unrealistically rosy picture of vegetarian diets—as if choosing a "virtuous" eating pattern allows one to ignore the need for some planning!

Myth #5:   All vegetarian diets provide more than enough protein.

Myth #6:   Eating any combination of plant foods will provide you the recommended amounts of zinc and other trace minerals.

Whether you are beginning to cut down on the amount of meat in your diet or have made a complete shift from meat, fish, poultry, and other animal products, it's important to examine the facts about our needs for protein, iron, and zinc. In this chapter, we'll help you chart a course, avoid problems, and find simple ways to meet your and your family's nutrient needs. In the process, you'll learn to harness the power of plant foods.

PROTEIN IN VEGETARIAN DIETS

Myth #1:   We need meat to get enough protein.

We begin with protein, the essential part of all plant and animal cells (including those in humans), and the myth that we need meat to get enough protein.

Vegetarians are often asked: Where will you get your protein? For a variety of reasons, this concern has been overemphasized. As you will recall from chapter 2, meat and other animal products gained special status in the first half of the twentieth century as necessary protein sources when deficiency diseases were our primary nutritional concerns. Farmers were granted subsidies for raising animals for food, and nutrition education materials emphasized the value of animal foods as the primary protein sources in our diets. As a result, the consumption of animal products increased, with protein intakes averaging 50 to 100 percent higher than recommended amounts. Contrary to what many people believe, excessive protein intakes do not lead to bigger muscles. (A big belly is more likely!) According to the World Health Organization (WHO) Technical Report 797: "There are no known advantages from increasing the proportion of energy derived from protein, and high intakes may have harmful effects in promoting excessive losses of body calcium and perhaps in accelerating age-related decline in renal function."

Protein is essential to build and repair cells throughout our bodies, transport oxygen (as part of the hemoglobin molecule in blood), make protective anti-bodies, and regulate the balance of water and acids, thus allowing our systems to function smoothly. These proteins are built from a "pool" of amino acids dis-tributed in the fluids throughout our bodies. The amino acids originate from the proteins in our diets. Several concepts are central to understanding why we don't need meat. (In fact, we would do ourselves a favor by relying on plant protein.)

1. **All of the amino acids we require either originate from plant foods or can be built in our bodies from other amino acids.** Our cells use an amino acid such as methionine to build a muscle fiber, and, for this purpose, a methio-nine molecule from a hamburger is no different than a methionine molecule from a soybean. In fact, the amino acids in animal products can be traced back to their plant origins.

2. **Too much protein is not good for you.** We require a certain minimum of dietary protein and specific amino acids. However, excess dietary protein, particularly animal protein, can contribute to heart disease, stroke, colorectal cancer, and osteoporosis, and it puts extra stress on the kidneys and liver. After fulfilling the necessary building, repair, and maintenance functions, extra pro-tein becomes a burden on the body. Some can be used as fuel, but it is not a clean-burning fuel like carbohydrate. Certain waste products (urea) must be eliminated, and this is where the stress comes in.

3. **In meat-centered diets, mounds of saturated fat and cholesterol accompany the bulk of this protein.** With meat, *three* distinct components are linked to increased blood cholesterol and risk of coronary artery disease: dietary cholesterol, animal protein, and saturated fat. Plant foods are entirely free of cholesterol and animal protein, and most are low in saturated fat (with the exception of tropical oils).

4. **Protein-rich plant foods bring us unique benefits not found in meat.** They provide protective phytochemicals found only in plant foods, including the isoflavones present in soy. Beans have a unique ability to level our blood

sugar because their protein is combined with fiber. Beans are rich in magnesium. Compared to meat, beans, peas, and lentils are lower in sulfur amino acids, resulting in less excretion of calcium and thereby helping us retain the calcium in our bones. Many beans and, to an even greater extent, calcium-set tofu actually *contribute* dietary calcium, whereas meat does not.

More is not always better; this is true of protein and particularly animal protein. In fact, the somewhat lower, yet adequate, protein levels in vegetarian diets are proving to be a health advantage. The quantity of protein in well-designed vegetarian diets is the golden mean, and meets recommended intakes at all ages. Even elite athletes can satisfy their protein needs without eating a single piece of meat.

Recommended Protein Intakes

How much protein do we need for good health? The exact amount depends on our age, body size, and, to some extent, on the composition of our diet. Protein needs are greater than average for many athletes (especially while building muscle mass) and for people recovering from certain illnesses. Scientists have established recommended intakes that include a considerable margin of safety, because people differ metabolically and proteins differ in composition and digestibility. For most individuals, these recommendations are well in excess of real needs.

Recommended protein intakes assume that people are getting enough total calories. If calories are insufficient (for reasons of poverty, illness, extreme weight-loss diets, anorexia nervosa, or unusually high levels of energy output), protein will be used as a fuel rather than being spared for its roles as a building material and regulator of cell function. While protein is not our preferred fuel, our bodies will use it when necessary to keep our systems going!

Because protein is used to build cells, from our toenails to the hair on our heads, our needs are greatly increased during times of growth. Recommended intakes during pregnancy, lactation, and infancy through adolescence are shown on pages 217 and 235.

Recommended protein intakes on the basis of body weight

The recommended dietary allowance (RDA) for protein is 0.8 grams of protein per kilogram of body weight (g/kg). This applies to nonvegetarians and vegetarians alike. The RDA includes a safety margin to cover individual variation in protein requirements.

Recommended Minimum Protein Intakes

Weight (lb)	Weight (kg)	Recommended protein (g)
110	50	40
132	60	48
155	70	56
176	80	64
198	90	72

To determine your weight in kilograms, divide your weight in pounds by 2.2. Examples of recommended protein intakes at different weights are shown here. For vegetarians, the recommendation assumes a diet that includes a variety of plant foods: legumes, grains, nuts and seeds, vegetables, and fruits, as in the Vegetarian Food Guide (page 191-203).

Some experts suggest that recommended protein intakes should be increased 15 to 20 percent for vegetarians over six years of age to compensate for the lower digestibility of some whole plant foods. This increased protein recommendation is suggested for those who get most of their protein from whole plant foods: legumes, whole grains, nuts, seeds, and vegetables. Higher intakes are thought to be unnecessary for those who rely on soy products, such as tofu and soymilk, or dairy products and eggs in addition to a variety of plant foods. Here is an easy way to estimate these slightly higher recommendations for vegetarians:

> *Easy estimate of protein needs:*
> **1 gram of protein per kilogram of body weight**

Using either the guideline of 0.8 gram per kilogram or 1 gram per kilogram, it is not difficult to meet and exceed protein recommendations with a diet that is mainly or entirely plant based. Menus 3 and 4 in this chapter (pages 72 and 73) show how to nourish even those whose protein needs are particularly high.

The protein RDA for children of different ages, whether vegetarian or not, are shown in table 3.1. These are set at 1.1 grams of protein per kilogram of body weight (g/kg) for ages one through three and 0.95 g/kg for ages four through eight and nine through thirteen. We show a "Reference Body Weight" in kilograms for a child in each age group as an example, and provide the total protein in grams needed by a child of this weight. According to the Institute of Medicine's 2002 Dietary Reference Intakes, the same RDAs apply to vegetarian, vegan, and nonvegetarian children.

Some experts are more cautious and advise that youngsters on vegan diets or diets based primarily on whole plant foods should include an extra margin of safety to compensate for the lower digestibility of some of these foods. Suggested safety margins are approximately 30 percent for children ages one

TABLE 3.1	PROTEIN RDAs FOR CHILDREN				
Age (years)	Reference Body Weight (kg)	Protein RDA (g/kg weight)	Suggested Protein for This Weight (g per day)	Protein with Safety Margin per Kilogram (g/kg body weight)	Protein with Safety Margin for This Weight (g per day)
1–3	12	1.1	13	1.1 + 30% = 1.4	17
4–8	20	0.95	19	0.95 + 20% = 1.1	22
9–13	36	0.95	34	0.95 + 15% = 1.1	40

through three, tapering to 15 percent by adolescence. According to these more conservative guidelines, the recommended protein with safety margin per kilogram and per body weight are shown in the two columns to the right in table 3.1. *These intakes, including the safety margin, are easily achieved in children's diets.*

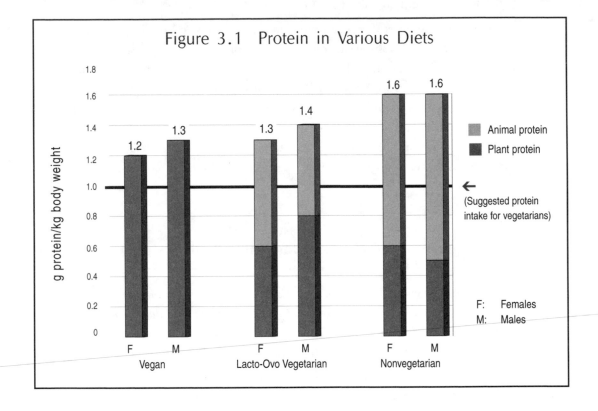

Figure 3.1   Protein in Various Diets

Scientific research has supported the adequacy of protein intake from plant-based diets since the classic study by Hardinge and Stare in the 1950s. Figure 3.1 compares intakes of total protein, including plant and animal protein, for adult vegans, lacto-ovo vegetarians, and nonvegetarians. On this chart, protein intakes are expressed as grams per kilogram of body weight, with the total shown at the top of each bar. When we compare the average intake of each group to one gram per kilogram of body weight (the darkened line across the middle of the chart), we see that all groups easily meet and exceed this amount. For nonvegetarians, approximately two-thirds of the protein was of animal origin (light portion of bar), and one-third of the protein was from plant sources (dark portion of bar). This ratio reflects a pattern similar to the overall protein intake of people in North America, Europe, Australia, New Zealand, and developed countries in other parts of the world.

Protein for vegetarian athletes

There is no separate protein RDA for athletes, as the scientific review committee that established the RDAs found "a lack of compelling evidence" that those doing resistance or endurance exercise have higher protein needs. For most people who engage in regular exercise, the easy estimate of 1 gram of protein per kilogram of body weight is plenty.

Yet, if muscle is being built, more protein may be appropriate. The American Dietetic Association, Dietitians of Canada, and the American College of Sports Medicine, in their joint position paper, "Nutrition and Athletic Performance" (December 2000), advise endurance athletes to get about 1.2 to 1.8 grams of protein per kilogram of body weight. For a brief period of time during the early stages of training, when muscle mass is increasing and protein needs are highest, athletes may aim for as much as 2 to 2.3 grams of protein per kilogram of body weight. Even these increased requirements can be met easily using plant-based diets. This is particularly true since people who are doing a great deal of exercise also consume considerably more calories. The greater amounts of grains, beans, nut butters, tofu, and other soyfoods that are eaten by top vegetarian athletes automatically result in much higher protein intakes. It isn't difficult to meet requirements of competitive athletes who eat big portions of Scrambled Tofu, Hot Tofu with Cool Greens, and Shepherd's Pie (see recipe list on page 307). The most common challenge is learning simple and practical ways to prepare protein-rich foods, such as the shakes and smoothies on pages 315 to 317 and the entrées on pages 338 to 347. It can take ingenuity to get high-protein vegetarian foods at sports events and while traveling—but it can be done. For more information on nutrition for vegetarian athletes, see pages 56 to 57 and the reference materials listed there.

Recommended protein intake as a percentage of total calories

Another way to look at protein recommendations is to consider the percentage of our total caloric intake from each of the three nutrients that provide calories: protein, carbohydrate, and fat. Carbohydrate and protein provide approximately four calories per gram, whereas fat, a highly concentrated form of energy, provides nine calories per gram. The box on this page shows the best way to divide dietary calories among protein, fat, and carbohydrates for those four years of age and older. This distribution is based on reports from the World Health Organization's Study Group and from the Institute of Medicine.

Recommended Distribution of Calories		
Protein	**Fat**	**Carbohydrate**
10–20%	15–35%	50–70%

Health experts suggest that a range of 20 to 25 percent of total calories from fat may be best for most of us to help prevent chronic disease. Optimal protein intake should be in the range of 12 to 15 percent of calories. For more details on children's diets, see chapter 10.

ACTION TIPS FOR VEGETARIAN ATHLETES

Can vegetarian diets support peak performance in athletes? Both vegetarian and nonvegetarian diets have the potential to enhance performance, when they are appropriately designed. However, well-constructed vegetarian diets may offer the upper hand where endurance sports are concerned. The following information will assist vegetarian athletes in achieving their maximum potential.

Energy (calories). Energy needs of athletes vary considerably depending on body size, body composition, gender, training, and typical activity pattern. For recreational athletes, caloric needs generally increase only slightly. However, for competitive athletes, caloric needs can shoot up markedly. Physical activity boosts energy expenditure and metabolic rate. Reports suggest that vegetarian diets may further increase energy needs by up to 10 to 15 percent. Thus, vegetarian athletes who are struggling with energy levels or finding it difficult to maintain their body weight will need to include plenty of energy-dense, vegetarian options in their diets, such as tofu, nuts, seeds, and blender drinks.

Carbohydrates, Protein, and Fat. It is recommended that most athletes distribute their caloric intake among protein, fat, and carbohydrates as shown above. The suggested distribution of calories for the general public is shown on page 55.

Recommended Distribution of Calories for Athletes

	Protein	Fat	Carbohydrates
Most Athletes	12-15%	<30%	60-65%
Endurance Athletes	12-15%	<25%	65-70%

High-carbohydrate diets are important for athletes, as they allow for maximum glycogen stores, helping to improve energy reserves. Increased carbohydrate intakes can also help reduce muscle fatigue. Protein needs are increased in athletes, as described above. It is important that athletes do not go overboard on fat restriction (no less than 15 percent of calories), as sufficient fat makes it easier to meet energy needs. In addition, fat is important for nutrient absorption and for maintaining fats within muscles at an optimal level.

Vitamins and Minerals. Although requirements for vitamins and minerals are generally increased in athletes, needs usually can be met simply by greater food intakes. Vegetarian athletes need to take special care to ensure sufficient intakes of these vitamins and minerals:

Vitamin B$_{12}$. Use fortified foods, supplements, or appropriate amounts of dairy products and eggs (see chapter 8).

Vitamin D. Ensure sufficient sunshine and/or fortified foods (see chapter 4).

Iron. Iron deficiency is common among athletes, especially endurance athletes. Female runners are at the highest risk. It is wise to monitor iron status by having occasional laboratory tests. Insure ample intake of iron-rich foods such as legumes, seeds, nuts, and fortified veggie meats. Maximize iron enhancers and limit inhibitors (see pages 80 to 81).

Zinc. Zinc needs increase with intense exercise, as it is necessary for metabolism and is lost in perspiration. To ensure sufficient intakes, include plenty of legumes, nuts, seeds, and whole grains in your diet (see pages 87 to 88).

Calcium. Do not assume weight-bearing exercise will rule out osteoporosis. While exercise is very important as a protective measure, osteoporosis is a growing problem in athletes, especially in girls and women who have limited their caloric intake to achieve very low body weights. For young female athletes whose periods are either sporadic or have stopped, 1,500 mg of calcium per day is recommended. For most people, this means using plenty of fortified soymilk, rice milk, or dairy products, preferably along with a supplement.

Fluids. Keep well hydrated. A sedentary person living in a cool climate loses about one and one-half quarts of fluid each day. An athlete can lose two to four quarts in an hour of heavy activity, especially in warm climates. If these fluids are not replaced soon, performance suffers. Water is the preferred fluid, although sports drinks are recommended for endurance events lasting longer than one hour.

Supplements. Well-planned vegetarian diets can provide all of the nutrients necessary for athletes. As with any diet, multivitamin and mineral supplements can help ensure that your requirements for certain harder-to-get nutrients are met. For those with lower energy intakes or eating poorly, these supplements are potentially quite beneficial. For additional information on supplements and sports nutrition for vegetarians, see the following resources:

Becoming Vegan by B. Davis and V. Melina (Book Publishing Company; Summertown, TN)

The Vegetarian Sports Nutrition Guide by L. Dorfman (Wiley and Sons; New York, NY)

The Veggie Sports Association: www.veggie.org/main/vegetarian.shtml

Do Typical Vegetarian Diets Provide Enough Protein?

The Harvard University research in the 1950s established that protein intakes of lacto-ovo vegetarians and of vegans meet and exceed recommended intakes (figure 3.1). Since that time, *studies in the United States, Great Britain, Australia, New Zealand, Canada, and various parts of Europe repeatedly confirmed that vegetarian diets provide more than enough protein.*

There are occasional cases of marginal protein intakes, for example, vegan women whose caloric intake is particularly low. But these are cases of consuming insufficient food and are not characteristic of vegan or vegetarian diets in general. Other examples of insufficient dietary protein (and iron and zinc) occur with the "fries and granola bars" vegetarians or those who try to live on pasta and bagels. Some of these people might eventually decide they must be the wrong blood type to be vegetarian or that being vegetarian just doesn't work for them. In fact, the problem is not their blood type at all. They simply didn't keep their fridge stocked with protein-rich bean salads or tasty marinated tofu slices from the deli. They never learned how to make something quick, easy, and delicious with lentils, such as the recipe on page 347. They didn't realize that a banana, a cup of soymilk, and a handful of strawberries make a fine shake, providing 10 grams of protein. It has become increasingly easier to meet our protein needs, because we now have vegetarian convenience foods in mainstream supermarkets, veggie dogs at ballgames, and restaurants that offer meatless, heart-healthy entrées. It's simple for anyone—whether a restaurant diner, a gourmet cook, or a novice in the kitchen—to get enough protein. It just takes a little know-how.

Protein in Plant Foods

Here are examples of the protein available in some common vegetarian foods:

- ✓ 1 cup (250 ml) of cooked lentils or beans (black, cranberry, garbanzo, navy, kidney, pinto) provides 14 to 18 grams of protein
- ✓ 1 cup (250 ml) of cooked soybeans provides 28 grams of protein
- ✓ ½ cup (125 ml) of peanuts provides 17 grams of protein

For purposes of comparison, note that a "quarter pounder" (113 gram) hamburger patty has 19 grams of protein, and a chicken leg has 15 grams. In addition to protein, all of these foods provide the minerals iron and zinc. (Also see table 3.5.)

Protein is present in most plant foods, with the notable exceptions of sugar, fats, and oils. Many of us are unaware of the substantial amounts of protein contributed by the plant foods in our diets. Figure 3.1 shows that plant protein provides at least half of our recommended protein intake, even for nonvegetarians. Although we generally think of meat and other animal products as concentrated sources of protein, an assortment of plant foods provides us with an excellent balance of protein, fat, and carbohydrate. Table 3.2 shows the percentage of calories from protein, fat, and carbohydrate in some common foods. When we compare these with the recommended distribution for our total

TABLE 3.2				PERCENT OF CALORIES FROM PROTEIN, FAT, AND CARBOHYDRATE IN FOODS			
	Protein	Fat	Carbohydrate		Protein	Fat	Carbohydrate
Legumes: Beans, Peas, Lentils, and Soyfoods				**Vegetables**			
Anasazi, black, lima, mung, pinto, red, or white beans; black-eyed or split peas	23–27%	2–4%	70–73%	Broccoli	34%	9%	57%
				Carrots, yams, baked potatoes	8%	1-3%	89-91%
Garbanzo beans (chickpeas)	21%	14%	65%	Kale	22%	11%	67%
Kidney beans	28%	1%	71%	Mushrooms	32–50%	0–6%	50–62%
Lentils	30%	3%	67%	Salad greens	31%	11%	58%
Peanuts	15%	71%	14%	Spinach	40%	11%	49%
Soybeans	33%	39%	28%	**Fruits**			
Soy protein isolate	91%	9%	0%	Apples	1%	5%	94%
Tofu, firm	40%	49%	11%	Dates, figs, raisins	3–4%	1–2%	94–96%
Veggie "meats," low fat	69–85%	1–4%	14–30%	Melons	5–9%	2–11%	82–93%
Veggie "meats," higher fat	56–75%	7–17%	18–28%	Oranges	7%	2%	91%
Nuts, Seeds, and Their Butters				Raspberries, strawberries	7%	9–10%	83–84%
Almonds	14%	73%	13%	**Animal Products**			
Cashews	11%	68%	21%	Beef, lean ground	37%	63%	0%
Hazelnuts (filberts)	9%	81%	10%	Beef, regular ground	33%	67%	0%
Pumpkin or sunflower seeds	17%	71%	12%	Cheddar cheese, medium	25%	74%	1%
Sesame butter (tahini)	11%	75%	14%	Codfish	92%	8%	0%
Grains				Cow's milk, 2%	27%	35%	38%
Amaranth	16%	15%	69%	Eggs	32%	65%	3%
Barley, corn, rice	9%	4–7%	84–87%	Salmon, sockeye	52%	48%	0%
Millet	11%	7%	82%	**Other Foods**			
Oatmeal	17%	16%	67%	Sugar	0%	0%	100%
Quinoa	13%	15%	72%	Oil	0%	100%	0%
Rye	18%	8%	74%	**Recommended Distribution**	**10–20%**	**15–35%***	**50–70%**
Wheat	15%	5%	80%				
Recommended Distribution	**10–20%**	**15–35%***	**50–70%**	*For more details on recommended intakes, see chapter 7.			

diet, shown on page 55 and at the bottom of table 3.2, it becomes clear that a heavy reliance on animal foods can easily lead to excessive protein and fat.

Legumes: Beans, Peas, Lentils, and Soyfoods

It's important for vegetarians to become acquainted with these protein power-houses and to find their special favorites. While soyfoods are excellent, convenient sources of protein, they are not "essential foods" for vegetarians. Within the legume group are numerous foods, each with distinctive appeal and nutritional advantages. We can choose among them to suit our own unique needs and preferences. For those who are keeping an eye on their weight, lentils, split peas, and most beans are extremely low in fat while high in protein, iron, zinc, and fiber. A lentil or bean soup or stew fills us up and gives us staying power between meals. During the growing years, youngsters can benefit from tofu and

nut butters, which contain healthful, unsaturated plant oils. Athletes appreciate that soy has a protein quality (i.e., combination of amino acids) comparable to the Amino Acid Scoring Pattern (table 3.3). Veggie "meats"—burgers, dogs, slices, and other meat alternatives—make life easier for many busy people. These high-protein, plant-based foods are shaped into familiar ground round, patties, croquettes, and links, yet they are free of animal protein, sat-

> ## WHAT ARE LEGUMES?
>
> Legumes are plants that have their seeds arranged in pods. When removed from the pods, these seeds are the familiar beans (Anasazi, black, cranberry, garbanzo, great Northern, kidney, lima, mung, navy, pinto, red, soy, white), lentils, and peas. Legumes are the protein powerhouses of the plant kingdom. As you can see in table 3.2, they have approximately twice the protein content of cereal grains. The percentage of calories from protein in lentils, kidney beans, soybeans, and tofu is in the same general range as regular ground beef, cheddar cheese, cow's milk, and eggs. Though their nutritional profile resembles nuts, peanuts are legumes (beans) as well. They grow in pods underground and are called groundnuts in Africa.

urated fat, and cholesterol, and most are low in fat. Some brands are fortified with iron, zinc, and vitamin B_{12}. See table 3.5 for the iron, zinc, and protein content of a variety of foods.

Calcium-set tofu and fortified soymilk are ideal for building strong bones, as they provide several minerals that support bone health, along with protein (an important component of bone) and isoflavones. Tofu will absorb the flavors of other ingredients in a dish, making it an extremely versatile food. White beans and black turtle beans are significant sources of calcium, too. Helping to prevent chronic disease and maintain good health, legumes fit well with today's nutritional recommendations. For people with diabetes, heart disease patients, and those who want to reduce their risk of these diseases, legumes have been shown to lower blood cholesterol levels and help equalize blood sugar.

North American farmers are major producers of about twenty types of legumes, and we can directly support our agricultural economy when we use these foods. Adding legumes to our diet can take us on a world food tour, as there are countless tasty dishes from around the globe that include them. Perhaps we have a favorite recipe for pea or lentil soup, enjoy chili at a Mexican restaurant, or acquired a taste for Middle Eastern or East Indian dishes while traveling. Preparing ethnic foods at home is a wonderful way to begin incorporating more legumes into our diets. See chapter 14 for recipe ideas to get you started.

Nuts and Seeds

Recent research on nuts and seeds has brought us new appreciation of the nutritional benefits of these often-neglected foods. Here's an example. People who ate nuts five times a week cut their risk of heart disease in half compared to those with similar lifestyles who ate nuts once a week or less. As shown in table 3.2, about 75 percent of calories in nuts are provided by fat. Yet instead of the saturated fat and cholesterol found in animal products, much of this fat is healthful monounsaturated fat or, in the case of walnuts and flaxseeds, essential omega-3 fatty acids. Nuts contain fiber and protective phytochemicals (such as resveratrol, saponins, phytates, and plant sterols), which can help to protect us against heart disease.

Nuts and seeds are rich in vitamin E. Without them, people's diets tend to be low in this fat-soluble vitamin, which stabilizes cell membranes and acts as an antioxidant. In addition to iron, certain nuts are good sources of one or more minerals. A single Brazil nut provides our quota of selenium for the day. Almonds and sesame seeds (and the sesame seed butter called *tahini*) provide calcium and make wonderful spreads for toast and sandwiches. Cashews are rich in zinc. For a nut, cashews are particularly high in carbohydrate and will thicken when ground in a blender with water and then heated, forming a lovely cream sauce or gravy. Seeds also are high in zinc Seed butters make a flavorful base for salad dressings and can replace all or part of the oil to provide a highly nutritious addition to salads. Not only do nuts provide us with valuable nutrients, their plant oils also help us to absorb minerals, fat-soluble vitamins, and phytochemicals.

In most food guides, nuts and seeds are included with protein-rich foods, such as legumes and meat, though their percentage of calories from protein is somewhat lower. When we eliminate meat, eggs, and high-fat dairy products from our diets, our intake of fat drops substantially. Consequently, nuts and seeds have a very special place in vegetarian diets. For growing children and others with high energy needs, these high-calorie foods balance the low fat levels of most other plant foods. Even in weight-loss diets, small amounts of nuts and seeds are now being included as the ideal form of fat.

Are nuts and seeds fatty foods to be avoided? That idea came about when peanuts and other salty, roasted nuts were an added burden of fat in the diet, eaten as a TV snack with beer after a big steak dinner. (Actually, nuts were the most healthful part of that whole scenario!) Instead, nuts and seeds are our very best sources of dietary fat because of the type of fat they contain and the protein and other nutritional benefits they possess. So sprinkle them on salads and casseroles; use them as the basis for creamy sauces, dressings, and smoothies; enjoy them in desserts and trail mixes; and spread their butters on your toast.

Grains

Wheat, oats, millet, and rice are not often regarded as significant protein foods, yet grains provide almost half of the world's protein. Certain grains, such as South American amaranth and quinoa, have amino acid patterns similar to those found in animal products (for more information about quinoa, see figure 3.2 on page 67.) As you can see in table 3.2, the percentage of calories from protein in the grains is in the neighborhood of 10 to 15 percent—the precise quantity recommended by health experts as a desired goal for our overall diet. As a bonus, grains are low in fat and provide iron, zinc, B vitamins, and fiber. (To find out more about the health benefits of grains, see chapter 5.) For a delicious way to introduce more of these nourishing foods into your diet, try the creamy and soothing Whole Grain Cereal recipes on pages 312 and 313.

Vegetables and Fruits

For many people, the amount of protein in their diets from vegetables is minimal, often only what is found in fries and ketchup! However, as our diets become more plant-centered, the presence of vegetables, and their protein, is more significant. This is especially true for raw foodists, whose portions of greens and other veggies can be immense! Observe that some vegetables derive 30 to 40 percent of their calories from protein (table 3.2).

Fruits are very high in water, which provides 85 to 90 percent of their weight. Of the calories present, most come from the natural sugars that make them so enjoyable. In oranges, berries, and melons, an average of 7 percent of calories comes from protein, as shown in table 3.2; other fruits, such as apples, contain less.

Protein Quality

It's clear that the plant kingdom offers us some potent protein providers. However, here's another myth that you may have heard:

Myth: Plant protein lacks essential amino acids and is poor quality.

Let's consider the indispensable amino acids that are the building blocks of protein and the digestibility of protein in different foods. Which amino acids must be present in dietary protein to meet our needs? Our protein building blocks are twenty-two different amino acids. Of these, nine must be supplied ready-made from the protein in the foods we eat. These nine are known as indispensable amino acids (IAAs), formerly known as essential amino acids.

Though they are present in animal products too, every one of the IAAs actually originates from plants. Animals get theirs from plants, either directly or indirectly from a plant-eating animal farther down the food chain. These IAAs are listed in table 3.3. All the other amino acids we need can be formed in our bodies from the IAAs and other dietary components. Each protein that we build, which may be hundreds of amino acids in length, has an exact sequence, combination, and arrangement of these twenty-two building blocks, and this determines whether this protein will function as insulin, a growth hormone, an enzyme, or another vital worker in the body.

Clearly, to build the proteins our bodies require, we need adequate amounts of the raw materials (IAAs). Yet, for several decades in the mid–twentieth century, we got on the wrong track about how much of these building blocks we need. The reasons behind this are understandable. When protein quality was first studied in controlled laboratory situations, single foods were used as the sole protein source. The research focused on how well a food would support growth, generally in baby rats. Compared to humans, young rats grow very quickly; for example, they double their birth weight in six days. Rats need a specific pattern of indispensable amino acids, including large amounts of the sulfur-containing amino acids (cysteine and methionine), to grow quickly and build proteins for the fur that covers their bodies. For example, rats need 50 percent more methionine than humans do. Lacking fur, humans thrive on far less. In fact, when we consume excessive amounts of cysteine and methionine, these sulfur amino acids can make us excrete too much calcium in the urine.

When a single animal or plant foods was given one at a time as the only food available to the animal, it was found that animal proteins, being more concentrated in total protein and in the sulfur-containing amino acids, were well suited to the needs of rats. The scientists conducting the animal studies designated the proteins from plants as "incomplete proteins," because, when used as the sole protein source, they were less suited to the fast growth of furry little rodents.

LEGUMES, SOYFOODS, NUTS, AND SEEDS: POWER FOODS

Myth: All vegetarian diets provide more than enough protein.

Vegetarians occasionally head down the wrong dietary path when they believe they can eat any combination of plant foods and get enough protein. While it is not at all difficult to get ample protein entirely from whole plant foods, there are ways of blowing it—for example, if their main food choices are chips, sweets, and vegetarian junk foods, or if their total caloric intake is insufficient. The reality for vegetarians is that legumes, soyfoods, nuts, and seeds are important keys to success in meeting recommended protein intakes.

THE BASICS OF AMINO ACIDS

What quantities of these indispensable amino acids must be present? As we gained an understanding of human protein requirements, a new way to measure the value of various proteins came to be accepted. This is the amino acid scoring pattern, along with the protein RDA, that was presented in 2002 by the Food and Nutrition Board/Institute of Medicine (FNB/IOM). This scoring pattern, shown in table 3.3, is based on human needs above age two and illustrates the relative amounts of the IAAs (in milligrams) that we require per gram of "ideal" food protein. We can use the scoring pattern as a gauge to measure the IAAs in specific foods and in our overall diets.

TABLE 3.3 IAA SCORING PATTERN	
Indispensable Amino Acid (IAA)	**Requirement (mg per g of protein)**
Tryptophan	7
Histidine	18
Total Sulfur Amino Acids (Methionine + Cysteine)*	25
Isoleucine	25
Threonine	27
Valine	32
Lysine	51
Total Phenylalanine + Tyrosine*	47
Leucine	55

To evaluate a particular protein, there are three steps. First, the amount of each IAA in one gram of food protein is determined. Second, these amounts are corrected for digestibility by multiplying them by a number representing their "true digestibility." Third, for each IAA—and especially for the IAA in shortest supply—the product is compared to the concentration of that IAA in the amino acid scoring pattern. This results in a score with a very cumbersome name—the protein digestibility-corrected amino acid score (PDCAAS). If one gram of food protein provides enough of each IAA to meet the standard, then the protein is given a score of 1 (or 100 percent). As way of illustrating this, table 3.4 shows calculations for soy protein. Next to the name of each IAA is the amount, in milligrams, present in one gram of soy protein. In the middle column, this number is multiplied by the digestibility factor for soy protein, which is 92 percent. (Note that there can be some variability in digestibility between amino acids.)

Reading across for each IAA, compare the digestibility-corrected amount in soy protein (middle column) with the corresponding figure in the Amino Acid Scoring Pattern (right column). As you can see, by following the bold row in table 3.4, the amount of methionine plus cysteine, corrected for digestibility, matches the amino acid scoring pattern (25 mg per gram of protein). Amounts for all other IAAs exceed the scoring pattern. Thus, soy protein meets the scoring pattern and has a PDCAAS of 1 (100 percent). In practical terms, this means that if we consume enough soy protein to exactly meet our recommended protein intake (0.8 gram soy protein per kilogram of our body weight), and no other dietary protein at all, this soy protein will provide all the IAAs we need. We wouldn't need to eat any other

TABLE 3.4	COMPARISON OF IAAs IN SOY PROTEIN WITH SCORING PATTERN		
IAA	**IAA in Soy Protein**	**IAA x 92%**	**IAA Scoring Pattern**
	(mg/g protein)		
Tryptophan	16	15	7
Histidine	29	27	18
Methionine + Cysteine*	**27**	**25**	**25**
Isoleucine	50	46	25
Threonine	41	38	27
Valine	50	46	32
Lysine	66	61	51
Phenylalanine + Tyrosine*	82	75	47
Leucine	76	70	55

*(Some of our requirement for the IAA methionine can be filled by cysteine, and some of our requirement for the IAA phenylalanine can be filled by tyrosine. Thus, these two are listed in addition to the IAAs.)

dietary protein at all. Milk and eggs also have scores of 1 (100 percent); beef has a score of 0.92 (92 percent). This example illustrates the PDCAAS scoring system. In reality, most foods have PDCAAS scores of less than 1. Generally, soy products are rated between 90 to 100 percent, with soy protein isolates having particularly high scores (depending on the manufacturing process used). This means that if you require 60 grams of protein per day and your sole source of protein is soyfoods with a PDCAAS score of 0.9 (90 percent), you would need to add about 10 percent more of this food to ensure that you get the recommended quantity of every essential amino acid. Note that for infants, the scoring pattern is based on the amino acid composition of breast milk.

The conclusions from these animal studies have limited relevance for two obvious reasons:

1. Humans are not big versions of baby rats. The protein and amino acid needs of growing rats are far different from those of humans at any age.

2. Humans do not live on any single food. Research using single foods as protein sources, rather than combinations that would be freely chosen by humans, provides little practical information about what works best for people.

We now recognize that a varied diet of plant foods suits human protein needs very well. By using animal studies, the value of plant protein had been underestimated.

Theoretically, it's possible to meet our protein needs from a "mono diet"; that is, a diet in which most of the protein comes from one food, and plenty of it. In human feeding experiments, such as the five-week Michigan State University Bread Study, adults were able to maintain their protein requirements with 90 to 95 percent of their dietary protein from wheat and the remainder from fruits and vegetables. But who would want to do this for long? Even more important, in order to function, our bodies require at least thirteen vitamins, more than seventeen minerals, plus carbohydrate, essential fatty acids, water, and fiber. To get these, we need variety in our diets. In practice, meeting our needs for all the indispensable amino acids (along with everything else) is better accomplished with a variety of plant foods.

Digestibility of Protein

The extent to which we digest and absorb proteins varies from one food to another and changes depending on how the food is prepared or processed. For example, cooked soybeans are far more digestible than raw beans and, as the Chinese discovered centuries ago, tofu is better still. Soy protein isolate, which is used to make veggie "meats" and is sold as a sports supplement, is highly digestible (though, as with any high-protein food, it doesn't agree with everyone). Sprouting or germinating beans before they are cooked may increase their digestibility. Cooking or processing certain foods can be nutritionally advantageous, by increasing the amount of protein as well as minerals and phytochemicals, such as lycopene, that we absorb from them.

The digestibility of proteins in tofu, soy protein isolate powder, meat alternatives, and refined grains is in the same general range as those in eggs, dairy products, and meat. Recent research published by the FNB/IOM indicates "that true digestibility exceeds 90 percent for many common foods, such as milk, cereals, soy, and other legumes." Many of the "convenience" vegetarian foods, soyfoods, and grain products also provide plenty of easily digested, top-quality protein. Proteins in whole grains, some legumes, and vegetables tend to be somewhat less digestible. At the same time, these "whole" plant foods have such a tremendous range of health benefits—including an abundance of fiber, phytochemicals, trace minerals, and vitamins—that they are a highly important part of our diets. The reduced digestibility of many plant proteins simply means that the protein requirements of vegans and people on whole food diets may be increased by around 10 to 15 percent. This is accomplished by using the guideline of one gram of protein per kilogram of body weight. These levels are easily reached as long calories are sufficient and protein-free items, such as sugar and fat, are limited. See menus 2, 3, and 4 on pages 71 to 73 for 2,000-calorie and 2,800-calorie vegetarian menus that provide plenty of protein.

Do Plant Foods Lack Certain Essential Amino Acids?

There has been a widely held misconception that plant proteins "lack something" or are missing essential amino acids when compared with animal proteins. This has led many people to undervalue plant protein. The "ideal" scoring pattern from tables 3.3 and 3.4 is illustrated in chart form in figure 3.2 on the next page. Amounts of each IAA, named in the key, are stated in milligrams of amino acid per gram of dietary protein. When we look at the relative amounts of IAAs in the protein of tofu, eggs, wheat, broccoli, and quinoa, we can see that the patterns for tofu and eggs meet and exceed the scoring pattern. The pattern for eggs has long been held as the "gold standard" for protein quality. The amino acid patterns for wheat, broccoli, and quinoa compare very favorably with the scoring pattern.

The Concept of the Limiting Amino Acid

As you can see, the patterns of IAAs differ from food to food. When we compare the IAAs in any food to the amino acid scoring pattern, one amino acid may be present in relatively small amounts. For example, wheat is a little short in lysine. In this situation, lysine is called the "limiting amino acid" in wheat. In theory, intake of that food could simply be increased to provide higher-

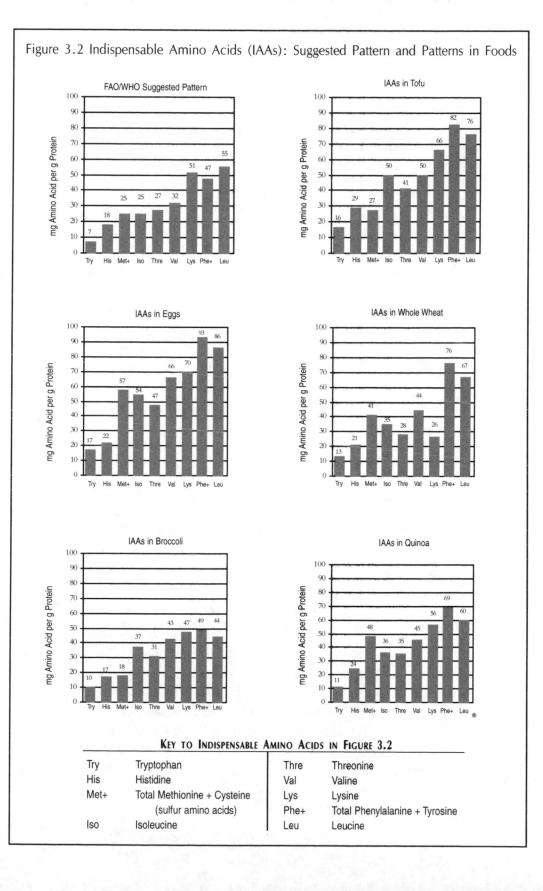

Figure 3.2 Indispensable Amino Acids (IAAs): Suggested Pattern and Patterns in Foods

KEY TO INDISPENSABLE AMINO ACIDS IN FIGURE 3.2

Try	Tryptophan		Thre	Threonine
His	Histidine		Val	Valine
Met+	Total Methionine + Cysteine		Lys	Lysine
	(sulfur amino acids)		Phe+	Total Phenylalanine + Tyrosine
Iso	Isoleucine		Leu	Leucine

than–recommended amounts of protein and, in the process, enough lysine. In practice, this is of great importance only when the total quantity of protein in the diet is barely adequate, as is true for some children in developing countries for whom wheat or rice is the main dietary staple and few legumes or green vegetables are available to balance the pattern.

Meeting All Amino Acid Requirements with Plant Foods

When people have access to a variety and abundance of plant foods, as we fortunate people do, we must use a different perspective. Every food has strengths and weaknesses in its amino acid pattern when compared with human requirements, and these naturally complement each other. During the process of digestion, dietary protein is broken down to form a common "pool" of amino acids in muscle and other body tissues that can be drawn on over the course of the day. For example, soybeans, pinto beans, other legumes, and many other foods in vegetarian diets contribute relatively large amounts of lysine. Though we may not think of broccoli as a protein provider, its scoring pattern has more lysine than wheat. The variety of amino acids in vegetables can be important for vegetarians who dine on immense salads and colorful entrees from their gardens. When we choose a diverse selection of plant foods, we automatically end up with the entire range of amino acids necessary to meet our protein-building needs.

Protein Complementation Update

In the early 1970s, the notion of protein complementation became widely accepted as the basis for planning vegetarian meals. This theory stressed the need for including specific quantities of grains and legumes (or nuts and seeds) at the same meal. Some people were left with the impression that they needed to spend hours with a scale and calculator in hand before getting dinner ready.

Myth: Vegetarians must complement plant proteins at every meal.

Research has established that all whole plant foods contribute IAAs to varying degrees, and commonly eaten combinations provide an assortment of the amino acids we need. A variety of foods can be eaten over the course of a day, because complementary proteins do not need to be consumed at the same meal. Here is what the World Health Organization Study Group says about our evolving understanding: "Progressively, it was realized that even in totally vegetarian diets containing a diversity of foods, plant sources tended to complement each other in amino acid supply. If the energy needs of the child or adult are met by these diets, then so are the protein needs."

The belief that plant foods lack indispensable amino acids is outdated and inaccurate. We do not have to carefully combine grains with legumes at every meal. In practice, we can simply follow the Vegetarian Food Guide (page 193). For young children, see the guides on pages 225 and 234 (chapter 10). These will help meet needs for all minerals and vitamins as well as the indispensable amino acids. *Beyond this, planned complementation of plant foods is not necessary.*

It's nice to know that we don't have to worry about it, but the fact is that people generally like to eat combinations of grains with legumes, in which the amino acid patterns naturally complement each other. Ethnic dishes based on centuries-old combinations of grains and legumes, or grains and nuts, are increasingly popular and available. We enjoy pea soup with a freshly baked, crusty loaf of bread; baked beans with aromatic cornbread; chili with tortillas; hummus with pita bread; and scrambled tofu with toast. Many of these include vegetables that further enrich the combination. At home and around the world, delicious, flavorful meals such as these provide a complete range of the necessary amino acids in more than adequate quantities.

Protein in Various Menus

Over the next several pages, we provide four 2,000-calorie menus that represent different points on a continuum. At one end of the continuum is Menu 1, for a nonvegetarian who eats a varied diet that includes meat, yet has adopted a number of "healthy eating" guidelines. Menu 2 is typical of many vegetarians who have substituted dairy products and eggs for meat, poultry, and fish. Next is Menu 3, for a vegetarian who has integrated legumes, veggie "meats," and nuts into the diet and is keeping the overall fat content low. Last on the continuum is Menu 4, for a vegan. Although it provides more protein, iron, and zinc than is necessary, this menu illustrates how nutrient-rich a plant-based diet can be. Each menu is accompanied by comments and a nutritional analysis showing the protein, iron, zinc, calcium, fiber, vitamin B_{12}, and balance of protein, fat, and carbohydrate for the day. There also are adaptations that bring the menus up to 2,800 calories for a larger or more active person. For more information on the fiber provided by each menu, see page 130, and on the fats present, see pages 158 to 165. There is a focus on healthful choices in all of the menus, and though desserts and snacks are included, these, too, make a nutritious contribution.

Plant sources of protein, consumed throughout the day, make a tremendous difference in sustaining our energy levels, because they release calories gradually. As we will see in the next sections, legumes, whole grains, and seeds are among our richest sources of iron and zinc.

MENU 1: NONVEGETARIAN (2,000 CALORIES)

Breakfast	Protein (g)	Iron (mg)	Zinc (mg)
Orange juice, ¾ cup (185 ml)	1.3	0.2	0.1
Cornflakes, 1 cup (250 ml)	1.8	8.7	0.2
Milk, 2%, 1 cup (250 ml)	8.0	0	0.4
Toast, whole wheat, 1 slice	2.7	0.9	0.6
Butter, 1 pat (5 g)	0	0	0
Jam, 1 tbsp. (15 ml)	0	0	0
Noncaloric beverage	0	0	0
Breakfast total (471 calories)	**13.8**	**9.8**	**1.3**
Lunch			
Roast beef sandwich:			
Bread, white, 2 slices	4.9	1.8	0.4
Beef, round lean, 2 oz. (57 g)	16.4	1.1	2.7
Margarine, 1 tsp. (5 ml)	0	0	0
Mayonnaise, 1 tsp. (5 ml)	0	0	0
Lettuce, 1 leaf	0.1	0.1	0
Carrot sticks, 1 carrot	1.0	0	0.2
Low-fat fruit yogurt, ¾ cup (185 ml)	7.0	0	0.6
Apple, 1	0.3	0.3	0.1
Noncaloric beverage	0	0	0
Lunch total (600 calories)	**29.7**	**3.3**	**4.0**
Supper			
Chicken, roasted, 3.5 oz. (100 g)	29.5	1.1	1.0
Potatoes, scalloped, ½ cup (125 ml)	3.5	0.7	0.5
Green peas, ½ cup (125 ml)	4.1	1.3	0.8
Dinner roll, white, 1	2.4	0.9	0.2
Butter, 2 pats (10 g)	0.1	0	0
Noncaloric beverage	0	0	0
Supper total (519 calories)	**39.6**	**4.0**	**2.5**
Snack or Dessert			
Cherry cheesecake, ¹⁄₁₂ pie (5 oz./142 g)	7.1	1.8	0.6
Snacks/dessert total (410 calories)	**7.1**	**1.8**	**0.6**
Total for day (2,000 calories)	**90.2**	**18.9**	**8.4**

Percentage of calories:	Protein	Fat	Carbohydrate
	18%	33%	49%

Nutrient: Recommended amount	Amount in menu
Iron: women 18 mg; men 8 mg	18.9 mg
Zinc: women 8 mg; men 11 mg	8.4 mg
Calcium (age 19–50): 1,000 mg	839 mg
Vitamin B$_{12}$: 2.4 mcg	3.1 mcg
Fiber: 30–62 g	19 g

Comments on Menu 1:

Our nonvegetarian has made some note-worthy efforts in the direction of healthy eating. She or he

✓ uses lean meats, keeps portions small, and avoids the skin on chicken;

✓ chooses low-fat milk and yogurt;

✓ strives to eat the recommended number of servings from each food group;

✓ avoids "junk" foods.

Of the 90 grams of protein in this menu, one-half (45.9 g) comes from beef and chicken and one-half from the other foods on the menu. Twelve percent of the iron comes from beef and chicken, and, because dairy products don't contribute iron, the rest is from plant foods. In this menu, animal products are important contributors of zinc: 44 percent comes from the meats, another 21 percent from dairy, and the remaining one-third comes from plant foods. Zinc intakes are borderline or low in the diets of many people and we see this situation reflected here. Though the menu includes 1 cup (250 ml) of milk, plus the equivalent of a second cup in the yogurt, scalloped potatoes, and cheesecake, the total calcium is lower than the recommended amount; little calcium comes from nondairy sources, such as those listed on page 99. The fiber intake is significantly lower than recommended, though higher than is typical of refined diets in developed countries.

We can increase the calories in this menu to 2,800 by adding an extra slice of toast with butter and jam; one-half of an extra sandwich; 2 ounces (57 grams) of chicken; a large muffin; and 1 cup (250 ml) of juice. This brings the protein to 126 grams.

MENU 2: LACTO-OVO VEGETARIAN (2,000 CALORIES)

Breakfast	Protein (g)	Iron (mg)	Zinc (mg)
Orange juice, ¾ cup (185 ml)	1.3	0.2	0.1
Multigrain cooked or dry cereal, 1 cup (250 ml)	6.1	1.6	1.2
Milk, 2%, 1 cup (250 ml)	8.0	0	0.4
Toast, whole wheat, 1 slice	2.7	0.9	0.6
Butter, 1 pat (5 g)	0	0	0
Jam, 1 tbsp. (15 ml)	0	0	0
Noncaloric beverage	0	0	0
Breakfast total (559 calories)	**18.1**	**2.7**	**2.3**

Lunch			
Egg salad sandwich:			
Bread, whole wheat, 2 slices	5.4	1.9	1.1
Hard boiled egg, 1 extra large	7.3	0.8	0.6
Margarine, 2 tsp. (10 ml)	0.1	0	0
Mayonnaise, 2 tsp. (10 ml)	0	0	0
Lettuce, 1 leaf	0.1	0.1	0
Carrot sticks, 1 carrot	1.0	0	0.2
Apple, 1	0.3	0.3	0.1
Noncaloric beverage	0	0	0
Lunch total (478 calories)	**14.2**	**3.1**	**2.0**

Supper			
Vegetarian cheese lasagne, 8 oz. (225 g)	16.6	2.5	1.9
Green salad, 1½ cups (375 ml)	2.7	2.0	0.6
Italian dressing, 1 tbsp. (15 ml)	0	0	0
Garlic bread w/ butter, 1 slice (1.5 oz./43 g)	5.0	3.6	0.3
Noncaloric beverage	0	0	0
Supper total (638 calories)	**24.3**	**8.1**	**2.8**

Snack or Dessert			
Cherry pie, ⅛ pie (4 oz./115 g)	2.5	0.6	0.2
Snacks or dessert total (325 calories)	**2.5**	**0.6**	**0.2**

Total for day (2,000 calories)	**59.1**	**14.5**	**7.3**

Percentage of calories:	Protein	Fat	Carbohydrate
	12%	37%	51%

Nutrient: Recommended amount	Amount in menu
Iron: women 32 mg; men 14.4 mg*	14.5 mg
Zinc: women 8 mg; men 11 mg	7.3 mg
Calcium (age 19–50): 1,000 mg	827 mg
Vitamin B$_{12}$: 2.4 mcg	1.9 mcg
Fiber: 30–62 g	24 g

Recommended iron intakes for vegetarians are 1.8 times those of nonvegetarians.

Comments on Menu 2:

This vegetarian has found it easy to replace meat, fish, and poultry with eggs and dairy products, and also enjoys easy-to-prepare homemade foods, such as grilled cheese sandwiches, egg dishes, and Italian entrées. Getting enough protein is simple; however, the fat content can mount up with some of these selections. In this menu, intakes of iron (for a woman), zinc (for a man), calcium, vitamin B$_{12}$, and fiber are a little below recommended levels. The addition of some legumes, soyfoods, nuts, and seeds would contribute more minerals and fiber, along with a bit more protein. For example, replacing butter on the toast with one tablespoon (15 ml) of almond butter would add 2.4 grams of protein, 0.6 mg of iron, and 0.5 mg of zinc. Delicious nuts and nut butters have many health benefits and can easily replace animal products that are high in cholesterol and saturated fats.

It also would be beneficial to include more vitamin B$_{12}$. Exchanging the egg salad in the sandwich for a B$_{12}$-fortified veggie "meat" (along with lettuce and slices of tomato) is one way. Tofu can be added to the lasagne or used to replace some or all of the cheese, increasing the amount of iron and zinc. When calcium-set tofu is used, the calcium is increased even more. These small changes to the lunch and supper choices would reduce the saturated fat and cholesterol.

We can increase the calories in this menu to 2,800 by adding an extra slice of toast with butter and jam; one-half of an extra sandwich; 2 ounces (57 grams) more lasagne; a large muffin; and ½ cup (125 ml) of juice. This brings the protein to 81 grams.

MENU 3: LACTO-OVO VEGETARIAN WITH MORE LEGUMES (2,000 CALORIES)

Breakfast	Protein (g)	Iron (mg)	Zinc (mg)
Calcium-fortified orange juice, ¾ cup (185 ml)	0.8	0.2	0.1
Cream of Wheat cereal, 1 cup (250 ml)	4.3	12.0	0.4
Milk, ½ cup (125 ml)	4.0	0.1	0.5
Toast, whole wheat, 1 slice	2.7	0.9	0.6
Almond butter, 1 tbsp. (15 ml)	2.4	0.6	0.5
Jam, 1 tbsp. (15 ml)	0	0.1	0
Noncaloric beverage	0	0	0
Breakfast total (524 calories)	**14.2**	**13.9**	**2.1**
Lunch			
Hummus, ¾ cup (185 ml)	14.8	4.6	3.4
Pita bread, whole wheat, 1	6.3	2.0	1.0
Cherry tomatoes, 5	0.7	0.4	0.1
Carrot sticks, 1 carrot	1.0	0	0.2
Oat bran muffin, 2 oz. (57 g)	4.0	2.4	1.0
Noncaloric beverage	0	0	0
Lunch total (688 calories)	**26.8**	**9.4**	**5.7**
Supper			
Spaghetti, whole wheat, 1½ cups (375 ml)	11.2	2.2	1.7
Chunky Red Lentil Tomato Sauce (page 340), 1⅔ cups (420 ml)	14.4	4.8	0.9
Red Star Vegetarian Support Formula nutritional yeast, 1 tsp. (5 ml)	1.0	0.1	0.4
Mixed salad with kale, 2½ cups (625 ml)	4.7	3.2	0.9
Liquid Gold Dressing (page 329), 1 tbsp. (15 ml)	2.0	0.4	0.7
Noncaloric beverage	0	0	0
Supper total (671 calories)	**33.3**	**10.7**	**4.6**
Snack or Dessert			
Nonfat frozen yogurt, 3¼ oz. (92 g)	3.5	0	0.7
Snacks/dessert total (117 calories)	**3.5**	**0**	**0.7**
Total for day (2,000 calories)	**77.8**	**34.0**	**13.1**

Percentage of calories:	Protein	Fat	Carbohydrate
	15%	21%	64%

Nutrient: Recommended amount	Amount in menu
Iron: women 32 mg; men 14.4 mg*	34 mg
Zinc: women 8 mg; men 11 mg	13.1 mg
Calcium (age 19–50): 1,000 mg	1,260 mg
Vitamin B$_{12}$: 2.4 mcg	3.5 mcg
Fiber: 30–62 g	55 g

*Recommended iron intakes for vegetarians are 1.8 times those of nonvegetarians.

Comments on Menu 3:

This vegetarian is using some dairy products, but also is including other calcium-rich foods: fortified orange juice, almond butter, beans, broccoli, kale, and on some days, fortified soymilk instead of cow's milk. (Read the labels on packaged products to check their nutrient content.) Using some fortified foods means that the diet can be nutrient rich while the fat intake stays relatively low (21 percent of calories from fat.) The fat in this menu comes from healthful sources, such as sesame tahini and olive oil in the hummus, flaxseed oil in the Liquid Gold Dressing, and almond butter (for more on fats, see chapter 7). This menu contains plenty of whole grain products which contribute zinc, selenium, chromium, magnesium, fiber, and phytochemicals. Chickpeas (in the hummus) and lentils add minerals, protein, and fiber. Red Star brand nutritional yeast, in the dressing and sprinkled on the pasta, provides most of the vitamin B$_{12}$ (see chapter 8).

This menu is almost entirely plant-based and can easily be made vegan by using fortified soymilk and soy yogurt. The protein is high enough to meet the needs of growing teens and athletes.

We can increase the calories in this menu to 2,800 by adding an extra slice of toast with butter and jam, an extra pita bread, and an additional ¼ cup (60 ml) of hummus; increasing the tomato sauce and pasta each by ½ cup (125 ml); and including one more muffin. This brings the protein to 108 grams. This is far more than most people need; however, it illustrates how easily it could be accomplished.

MENU 4: VEGAN (2,000 CALORIES)

Breakfast	Protein (g)	Iron (mg)	Zinc (mg)
Blueberries, 1 cup (250 ml)	1.0	0.2	0.2
Basic Whole Grain Cereal, 1 cup (250 ml) (page 312)	5.7	1.8	1.2
Wheat germ, 2 tbsp. (30 ml)	1.7	0.4	0.9
Fortified soymilk, 1 cup (250 ml)	7.0	1.8	0.6
Toast, whole wheat, 1 slice	2.7	0.9	0.6
Sesame tahini, ½ tbsp. (7 ml)	1.3	0.3	0.4
Blackstrap molasses, 1 tsp. (5 ml)	0	1.2	0.1
Noncaloric beverage	0	0	0
Breakfast total (586 calories)	**19.4**	**6.6**	**4.0**

Lunch			
Lentil soup, 1½ cups (375 ml)	11.7	4.0	1.6
Brown rice cakes, 3	2.2	0.4	0.8
Carrot sticks, 1 carrot	1.0	0	0.2
Celery sticks, 1 stalk	0.5	0.2	0.1
Trail mix: pumpkin seeds, raisins, dried cranberries, apricots, ¼ cup (60 ml)	1.3	0.8	0.5
Apple juice, 1 cup (250 ml)	0.6	0.8	0.1
Noncaloric beverage	0	0	0
Lunch total (558 calories)	**17.3**	**6.2**	**3.3**

Supper			
Hot Tofu, 1 serving (page 338)	33.9	6.0-18.0	3.3
Go-for-the-Green Salad), 3 cups (750 ml) (page 328)	3.5	2.0	0.8
Flaxseed oil, 2 tsp. (10 ml)	0	0	0
Lemon juice, wine vinegar, and herbs	0.1	0.1	0
Steamed asparagus, 10 spears	3.1	1.1	0.6
Whole wheat roll, 1	2.5	0.7	0.6
Noncaloric beverage	0	0	0
Supper total (683 calories)	**43.1**	**9.9–21.9**	**5.3**

Snack or Dessert			
Chocolate Mint Nut Bars, 2 (page 352)	2.8	0.7	0.4
Snacks/dessert total (173 calories)	**2.8**	**0.7**	0.4

Total for day (2,000 calories)	82.6	23.4–35.4	13.0

Percentage of calories:	Protein	Fat	Carbohydrate
	16%	28%	56%

Nutrient: Recommended amount	Amount in menu
Iron: women 32 mg; men 14.4 mg*	23.4-35.4 mg
Zinc: women 8 mg; men 11 mg	13 mg
Calcium (age 19–50): 1,000 mg	768-1,707 mg
Vitamin B$_{12}$: 2.4 mcg	4.9 mcg
Fiber: 30–62 g	42 g

Recommended iron intakes for vegetarians are 1.8 times those of nonvegetarians.

Comments on Menu 4:

This vegan tries to use plenty of whole foods while keeping things simple. A batch of Basic Whole Grain Cereal (page 312) lasts for several days, making a great breakfast or an occasional evening snack. Thin layers of tahini and blackstrap molasses taste wonderful on toast and also provide calcium. At work, lentil, pea, or bean soups can be purchased from a nearby restaurant, or brought from home. Nuts and seeds and their butters provide highly nutritious plant oils, minerals, and protective phytochemicals; they are used as a spread for toast, in the trail mix, and in the dessert square. The delicious and filling tofu dish (made with calcium-set tofu) and salad at supper provide a wealth of protein and minerals.

A range is provided for iron and calcium because the amount of these and other minerals, such as zinc, can vary considerably from one brand to another. So check the labels on tofu, fortified cereals, veggie "meats," and other foods. In this menu, vitamin B$_{12}$ comes from fortified soymilk and nutritional yeast. The main sources of zinc are tofu, lentils, wheat germ, whole grains, soymilk, seed butter (tahini), pumpkin seeds, and asparagus. See chapter 7 for a discussion of fats in this menu.

We can increase the calories in this menu to 2,800 by adding an extra slice of toast with butter and jam along with an additional ½ cup (125 ml) of whole grain breakfast cereal; increasing the soup by ½ cup (125 ml); adding a little more salad dressing and a roll at supper; and including a vegan sports bar. This brings the protein to 100 grams, which is more than enough for a growing teenage boy or most athletes.

IRON IN VEGETARIAN DIETS

Once you've convinced your family, friends, and colleagues that vegetarians can get enough protein, they'll very likely attempt to stump you with the iron issue. After all, iron is viewed as "the mineral from red meat," an association fostered by the meat industry and its advertising. Athletes and "real men" are conditioned to link their performance with steaks and burgers.

In this section, we examine the facts about the iron in our bodies and our food supply.

The Roles of Iron in the Body

The mineral iron is the crown jewel in the center of the hemoglobin molecule, which is comprised chiefly of protein. This molecule is found in the red blood cells that continually circulate throughout our bodies. Iron has a remarkable ability to attach itself to, and to let go of, oxygen and carbon dioxide. Thus, it is central to the breath of life.

Iron also is present in muscle tissue, where it helps to store oxygen for future use. Small amounts of iron help us regulate cell metabolism and resist infection.

We require more of this mineral during pregnancy, when blood volume increases, and during the growth spurts of childhood and adolescence. Women need more iron than men, because iron is lost each month during menstruation. Endurance athletes require extra iron because of high requirements for transport of oxygen to cells, iron losses in perspiration, and the destruction of red blood cells during high-impact exercise. For these reasons, one or two out of every ten North American women of childbearing age becomes iron deficient, and children, athletes, and the elderly (whose diets may be limited) tend to be low in this mineral.

Iron-Deficiency Anemia

In industrialized countries, many deficiency diseases have been eliminated, yet insufficient iron remains a problem for a small but significant number of people. Its effects include small, pale, red blood cells, fatigue, a weakened immune system, and a reduced ability to concentrate. Shortage of this mineral can affect children's learning abilities at school.

Recommended Intakes of Iron

Our bodies efficiently recycle iron, but we need to replace what is lost in perspiration, in cells sloughed off from our skin and our intestinal lining, and during menstruation. This amounts to less than 1.5 mg of iron per day for women who menstruate and 1 mg for men and older women. Because we absorb only a small proportion of the iron present in foods, particularly plant foods, the recommended iron intakes for adults are considerably higher than this, especially for vegetarians.

The Food and Nutrition Board recommends intakes of 18 mg for nonvegetarian women age nineteen to fifty, and 10 mg for nonvegetarian men and older women. These figures are based on the typical requirements for a day, plus an added safety factor, and should be regarded as the average daily intake over a period of time, such as a week. The iron recommendations for vegetarians are multiplied by a factor of 1.8 to account for the lower absorption from plant foods and are shown in the box at right.

Recommended Iron Intake for Vegetarians	
Women, 19–50	32.4 mg
Women over 50	18.0 mg
Men, all ages	18.0 mg
For other ages, see table 15.2, page 362.	

Are Iron Recommendations for Vegetarians Set Too High?

Not all experts agree with these greatly increased recommendations for vegetarians. Because they were based largely on one study that compared meat-based diets with vegetarian diets, this study may not reflect how most vegetarians really eat. As discussed in "Factors That Influence Iron Absorption" on page 80, the preparation and overall composition of a meal affects how iron from plant foods is absorbed. In contrast to the study, vegetarians tend to eat plenty of fruits, vegetables, and foods that are high in vitamin C, and many do not drink black tea (which contains tannins that reduce iron absorption) at meals. They often use foods prepared in ways that increase iron absorption, such as soaked, sprouted, and fermented foods. Vegetarians who adopt many of these practices usually can maintain excellent iron status with total intakes that are somewhat lower than current recommendations for vegetarians.

Furthermore, it appears that, with time, vegetarians may adapt, absorb, and retain iron with greater efficiency. (If you'd like feedback on how well you're doing, request a blood test at your next medical examination.) However, vegetarians can meet even these high recommendations, as shown in Menus 3 and 4 and table 3.6.

TABLE 3.5   IRON, ZINC, AND PROTEIN IN FOODS

Food and Category	Serving (amount)	mg per serving		
		Iron	Zinc	Protein
Legumes (cooked)				
Adzuki beans	1 cup (250 ml)	4.6	4.1	17.3
Black beans	1 cup (250 ml)	3.6–5.3	1.4–1.9	15.2
Cranberry beans	1 cup (250 ml)	3.7	2.0	16.5
Garbanzo beans/chickpeas	1 cup (250 ml)	4.7	2.5	14.5
Lentils	1 cup (250 ml)	6.6	2.5	17.9
Navy beans	1 cup (250 ml)	4.5	1.9	15.8
Kidney beans	1 cup (250 ml)	5.2	1.9	15.4
Pinto beans	1 cup (250 ml)	4.5	1.9	14.0
Soyfoods				
Soybeans, green	1 cup (250 ml)	4.5	1.6	22.2
Miso	1 tbsp. (15 ml)	0.5	0.6	2.0
Natto	1 tbsp. (15 ml)	0.9	0.33	1.6–1.9
Soybeans, cooked	1 cup (250 ml)	8.8	2.0	28.2
Tofu, firm (see label)	½ cup (125 ml)	1.8–13.2	1.3–2.0	10.1–20.0
Tofu, silken firm	½ cup (125 ml)	1.3	0.8	8.7
Tempeh	½ cup (125 ml)	2.2–3.2	1.0	15.3–24.0
Veggie "Meats"				
Yves Veggie Bologna slices (fortified)	4 (2 oz./57 g)	3.6	3.0	13
Yves Good Dog (fortified)	1 (1.8 oz./52 g)	3.6	2.2	13
Vegan GardenBurger	1 (2.5 oz./71 g)	1.0	0.5	11
Yves Good Burger (fortified)	1 (2.5 oz./71 g)	3.6	4.5	12
Yves Veggie Ground Round (fortified)	2 oz. (55 g)	2.7	3.0j35	10
Nuts, Seeds, and Their Butters				
Almonds	¼ cup (60 ml)	1.4	1.2	7.5
Cashew nuts	¼ cup (60 ml)	2.1	1.9	5.2
Flaxseeds	2 tbsp. (30 ml)	1.9	0.4	3.7
Hazelnuts	¼ cup (60 ml)	1.6	0.8	5.1
Pecans	¼ cup (60 ml)	0.7	1.2	2.5
Pine nuts	¼ cup (60 ml)	3.1	1.4	8.2
Pistachios	¼ cup (60 ml)	1.4	0.7	6.6
Pumpkin seeds	¼ cup (60 ml)	5.2	2.6	8.5
Sunflower seeds	¼ cup (60 ml)	2.7	1.8	8.1
Sesame tahini	3 tbsp. (45 ml)	1.2–2.9	2.1–4.7	7.8–8.8
Nondairy Milks				
Soymilk (see label)	½ cup (125 ml)	0.4–0.9	0.3–0.5	3.2–5.0
Rice milk	½ cup (125 ml)	0.2–0.5	0–0.4	0.5–1.6
Grains and Grain Products				
Barley, pearled, cooked	½ cup (125 ml)	1.0	0.6	1.8
Barley, whole, cooked	½ cup (125 ml)	1.0	0.8	3.7
Millet, cooked	½ cup (125 ml)	0.8	1.1	4.2
Oatmeal, cooked	½ cup (125 ml)	0.8	0.6	3.0
Quinoa, cooked	½ cup (125 ml)	2.1	0.8	3.0
Rice, brown, cooked	½ cup (125 ml)	0.5	0.6	2.3
Rice, white, enriched, cooked	½ cup (125 ml)	1.0	0.4	2.1

Food and Category	Serving (amount)	mg per serving		
		Iron	Zinc	Protein
Grains and Grain Products				
Rye flour*	¼ cup (60 ml)	0.5–2.1	0.5–1.8	2.1–4.5
Whole wheat flour	¼ cup (60 ml)	1.2	0.9	4.1
Wheat germ	2 tbsp. (30 ml)	0.9	1.8	3.3
Fortified dry cereals (see labels)	1 oz. (28.4 g)	2.1–18	4 0.7–15	4.2
Vegetables				
Mung bean sprouts, raw	1 cup (250 ml)	1.0	0.4	3.2
Broccoli, raw	1 cup (250 ml)	0.8	0.4	2.6
Carrot, raw, 7.5 inches (20 cm) long	1	0.4	0.1	0.7
Cauliflower, cooked	½ cup (125 ml)	0.2	0.1	1.1
Corn, cooked	½ cup (125 ml)	0.5	0.4	2.7
Green/yellow beans, cooked	½ cup (125 ml)	0.8	0.2	1.2
Eggplant, cooked	½ cup (125 ml)	0.2	0.1	0.4
Kale, raw	1 cup (250 ml)	1.1	0.3	2.2
Mushrooms, cooked	½ cup (125 ml)	1.4	0.7	1.7
Okra, cooked	½ cup (125 ml)	0.4	0.4	1.5
Potato, baked, medium	1 (4 oz./115 g/)	1.7	0.4	2.8
Romaine lettuce, raw	1 cup (250 ml)	0.6	0.1	0.9
Spinach, raw	1 cup (250 ml)	0.8**	0.2	0.9
Sweet potato, baked, medium	1 (4 oz./115 g)	0.5	0.3	2.0
Turnip, cooked and mashed	½ cup (125 ml)	0.2	0.2	0.8
Winter squash, cooked and mashed	½ cup (125 ml)	0.3–0.7	0.1–0.3	0.8–1.8
Fruits				
Apple, medium	1	0.2	0.1	0.3
Apricots, dried	8 (¼ cup/60 ml)	1.3	0.2	1.0
Banana, medium	1	0.4	0.2	1.2
Cantaloupe or honeydew melon	¼	0.2–0.3	0.2	1.2–1.5
Figs, dried	5 (3 oz./85 g)	2.1	0.5	2.9
Strawberries	½ cup (125 ml)	0.3	0.1	0.4
Orange, medium	1	0.1	0.1	1.2
Prunes	7 (¼ cup/60 ml)	1.5	0.3	1.5
Raisins	¼ cup (60 ml)	1.1	0.1	1.0
Other				
Blackstrap molasses	1 tbsp. (15 ml)	3.6	0.2	0
Sugar	1 tbsp. (15 ml)	0	0	0
Oil	1 tbsp. (15 ml)	0	0	0
Dairy Products and Eggs				
Cow's milk, 2%	½ cup (125 ml)	0.1	0.5	4.1
Cheese, cheddar	¾ oz. (21 g)	0.1	0.6	5.2
Yogurt, low-fat	½ cup (125 ml)	0.1	1.1	6.4
Egg, large	1 (1.75 oz. /50 g)	0.6	0.5	6.3
Animal Products (for comparison)				
Ground beef	2 oz. (60 g)	1.1	2.3	10.6
Chicken, roasted	2 oz. (60 g)	0.6	0.6	17.9
Cod, baked/broiled	2 oz. (60 g)	0.3	0.4	13.7
Salmon, baked/broiled	2 oz. (60 g)	0.3	0.3	13.4

*Amounts of iron, zinc, and protein are highest with dark rye flour.

**Don't count spinach as an iron or calcium source; it's high in oxalates that inhibit absorption of iron and calcium.

How Much Iron Do Vegetarians Get?

Many studies show that vegetarians have higher iron intakes than nonvegetarians and that vegetarian men are likely to meet their iron recommendations. But, similar to nonvegetarian women, many vegetarian women have intakes that fall short of the recommendations. Since they don't eat meat, do vegetarians get sufficient dietary iron? Let's examine another myth:

Myth: Most vegetarians end up with iron-deficiency anemia.

Iron Status of Vegetarians

We can determine whether vegetarians are getting enough iron by looking at various measures of iron status, such as levels of hemoglobin, transferrin (an indicator of the iron transportation system), and stored iron (ferritin). Studies in the United States, Australia, Canada, and other parts of the world have shown vegetarians to have similar levels of iron in their blood and transport systems compared with nonvegetarians. This means that vegetarians have as much iron in their systems as nonvegetarians and experience no higher rates of iron-deficiency anemia.

At the same time, the iron stores (ferritin) of vegetarians tend to be lower than those of nonvegetarians. The average nonvegetarian man has about 1,000 mg of stored iron, which could supply his iron needs for about three years, and the average nonvegetarian woman has about 300 mg, enough to meet her iron needs for six months. Average iron stores in vegetarians are about half these levels—480 mg for men and 160 mg for premenopausal women. What does this mean? Unless you are undergoing a period of starvation, high iron stores do not provide any particular advantage. In fact, having a lot of iron stored in your body may be a disadvantage. This is because iron is a pro-oxidant, which means it promotes the oxidative damage that is linked to many chronic diseases, including heart disease and some cancers, particularly colorectal cancer. Iron stores in vegetarians seem to be sufficient, and the fact that they are lower may be protective.

Iron in Foods

Iron is essential for both humans and animals because it helps transport oxygen in the blood and between cells. It also plays key roles in the respiration and enzyme systems of plants and aids photosynthesis and chlorophyll formation. Not surprisingly, iron is abundant in plant foods. Plants get this mineral from the earth, and animals get their iron from the plant foods they eat. It's the same mineral that we can adapt for our various uses. We do not require flesh foods as our iron sources.

TABLE 3.6	IRON IN MENUS	
	Iron (mg)	
Menu and Page	2,000 calories	2,800 calories
1 Nonvegetarian, page 70	18.9	26.3
2 Lacto-Ovo Vegetarian, page 71	14.5	22.6
3 Lacto-Ovo Vegetarian with More Legumes, page 72	34.0	44.7
4 Vegan, page 73	23.4-35.4	30.7-42.7

As illustrated in table 3.5, pages 76 to 77, the amounts of iron in plant foods compare very favorably with those in animal products. We tend to eat more servings and larger quantities of plant foods, so, by making smart choices, we can reach even the higher intake levels that are recommended. Table 3.6 above shows iron intakes from the four menus that were given earlier in this chapter.

Levels of iron in the 2,000-calorie, lacto-ovo vegetarian Menu 2 are somewhat low. When people stop eating meat, they often replace it with familiar dairy-based dishes, such as pizza, macaroni and cheese, grilled cheese sandwiches, cream soups, and cheese lasagne. To a certain extent, this pattern is reflected in Menu 2. Unfortunately, dairy foods are poor sources of iron; to make matters worse, they actually inhibit iron absorption. For these reasons, it is wise to replace meat with legumes and other meat alternatives that are good iron sources, as has been done in Menu 3, rather than with dairy products.

When the emphasis shifts to legumes, nuts, seeds, plenty of vegetables, and other iron sources, intakes increase significantly. Menu 4 includes tofu, a good source of iron and other minerals. Because amounts of added iron vary considerably from one brand to another, there is quite a range in how that can affect total intake.

Heme and nonheme iron

There are two forms of iron present in foods: heme iron and nonheme iron. Forty percent of the iron in meat, and a lesser amount in fish and poultry, is called heme iron. It is present in animal flesh in the form of muscle myoglobin and blood hemoglobin. People usually absorb 15 to 35 percent of the heme iron in foods. The remainder of the iron in meat and all of the iron in plant foods and eggs is called nonheme iron.

Factors That Influence Iron Absorption

Nonheme iron

Nonheme iron is absorbed differently from heme iron and is much more sensitive to dietary factors that decrease or increase iron absorption. Understanding this difference can help all of us make the most of our dietary iron, since more than 85 percent of the iron in nonvegetarian Western diets and all of the iron in vegetarian diets is the nonheme form. The proportion of nonheme iron that is absorbed varies from 2 to 20 percent or more of the total in a particular meal, depending in part on the foods and beverages that are eaten at the same time. Accompanying foods have relatively little effect on the absorption of heme iron.

Beverages with meals

If you're concerned about iron absorption, pay attention to the beverages you have with your meals. Beverages that inhibit iron absorption include dairy products, black tea, some herb teas (peppermint, chamomile, vervain, lime flower, pennyroyal), coffee, and cocoa. In contrast, citrus, tomato, and vitamin C—enriched juices will help you absorb iron from your cereal, sandwich, soup, or salad.

Phytates and fiber

There has long been a concern that two beneficial components of whole grains and legumes, fiber and phytate, can also inhibit iron absorption. (Phytate is a form of phosphorus in plants.) Yet it turns out that the effects of fiber and phytate on the iron status of vegetarians are somewhat less than we might expect. This gives us some insights into our bodies' natural balances. First, vitamin C and other organic acids found in fruits and vegetables can reduce the effects of phytate—and vegetarian diets tend to be high in these. Second, food preparation techniques, such as soaking and sprouting beans, grains, and seeds and leavening breads, reduce the amount of phytate that binds minerals and inhibits their absorption. These techniques, commonly used by vegetarians, can make a big difference. Third, the effects of fiber appear to be minor. Fourth, foods that are high in phytate also tend to be high in iron, and the actions of phytate may help us strike the right balance and protect us from iron overload.

Vitamin C

Foods rich in vitamin C work wonders with the iron from plants. Breakfast is a great time to boost our iron intake. For example, studies have shown that the amount of iron absorbed from cereal or toast doubles or triples when eaten with a large orange or a glass of juice, which provides 75 to 100 mg of vitamin C. In one study, papaya accompanying a grain meal increased iron absorption up to six times. Fruits and vegetables with smaller amounts of vitamin C also enhance the absorption of nonheme iron, but to a lesser extent. This contradicts popular ideas of food combining, which dictate that fruits be eaten separately from other foods. If you want to do your hemoglobin a favor, include a vegetable or fruit high in vitamin C along with iron-rich foods. Fruits and vegetables provide the maximum amount of vitamin C when they are raw, although cooked foods (for example, onions, or tomatoes in a soup or casserole) also can be effective.

Cast-iron cookware

Another sure way to increase iron intake is to use cast-iron cookware. Use of these heavy, iron-containing pots and pans have been shown to significantly increase the amount of iron in food and that we absorb from the food, especially when we cook acidic items in them, such as tomato or sweet-and-sour sauce. Steel woks also have been shown to add iron to the foods cooked in them.

Oxalates

Sorry, Popeye, but spinach isn't really the best source of iron, after all. Although his example was widely used to inspire children to eat their greens, the iron in spinach is bound with oxalates, making it largely unavailable. Oxalates are acids found in spinach, beet greens, rhubarb, Swiss chard, and chocolate. In contrast, the low-oxalate greens—broccoli, kale, collards, Chinese cabbage, okra, and bok choy—provide abundant iron that is readily absorbed.

In summary, although the iron in plant foods tends to be less well absorbed than the heme iron that makes up some of the iron in meat, this tends to be offset by the increased quantity of iron-rich foods that vegetarians eat. Additional smart dietary choices and preparation techniques also help vegetarians enhance their iron absorption.

Challenges to Iron Out: Common Errors and Solutions

The following situations illustrate potential pitfalls that could lead to low iron intakes for those shifting toward plant-based diets:

✗   A vegetarian teen eats just the nonmeat portion of family meals and snacks on fries, shakes, and granola bars.

✗   A busy parent finds cheese to be such a convenient source of protein that it becomes a mainstay for many quick meals.

✗   A business executive eats a significant number of meals at restaurants, often ordering pasta and cheese-laden entrées, with black tea as a beverage.

All of these people risk a decline in their iron status and a drop in their energy levels. As a result, they might become uncertain that a vegetarian diet is adequate to meet their nutritional needs, yet a few simple changes will easily solve their problems.

✓   The teen needs to explore the wonderful world of vegetarian convenience foods. Burgers, luncheon slices, instant bean soups, and frozen entrées all make meals more interesting and higher in iron. Youngsters can easily learn to make hummus and keep it handy at the front of the fridge for a quick after-school snack. Families with members whose dietary patterns differ—and there are more of these all the time—can still enjoy tacos together, with optional vegetarian chili (cooked in a cast-iron pot) or meat filling. The increased availability of veggie "meats," soy dogs and burgers, and delicious flavors of marinated tofu make meal planning easier all the time. Though common and inexpensive, peanut butter is a good source of protein, iron, zinc, and calories, making it a valuable part of the diet of many youngsters. Its uses go far beyond a spread for toast or a sandwich filling. For example, try it in the African Stew, page 343.

✓   The busy parent could prepare a delicious tofu or lentil dish in minutes after work. Some good examples are Hot Tofu and Cool Greens (page 338) or Easiest–Ever Curried Lentils (page 347). Calcium-set tofu is rich in three minerals—iron, zinc, and calcium—in addition to protein. This parent can buy a bean salad from a deli or stock up on the convenience foods listed above for the teen. An economical solution is to have a cooking spree once a week and stock the freezer with meal-size portions of entrées, soups, or stews based on beans, lentils, split peas, or tofu. Almond butter, or a thin layer of tahini and molasses, makes a mineral-rich spread for toast in the morning. Fortified ready-to-eat dry cereals or Cream of Wheat also add iron.

✓ The restaurant eater may frequent ethnic or vegetarian restaurants and order Asian tofu dishes, bean curries, burritos, and lentil or split pea soups; the accompanying vegetables will increase iron absorption. Before traveling out of town, he or she could check the website www.vegdining.com for vegetarian restaurants en route and at the destination. It also is wise for those who are concerned about iron status to drink juice or water in place of tannin-containing teas with meals.

Ironclad Rules

Here are tips to help vegetarians increase iron intakes.

1. Build meals around iron-rich foods. Follow the Vegetarian Food Guide on page 193, as every one of the food groups will contribute iron. Don't waste many calories on junk foods, which are high in fat and sugar and lack iron.

2. Help your body absorb the iron you do take in. Eat vitamin C–rich fruits and vegetables at meals. Avoid consuming black tea or wheat bran with your iron sources. Use foods that are yeasted (such as bread), sprouted (such as bean sprouts), roasted (such as nuts), and fermented (such as tempeh).

3. Use cast-iron cookware.

4. If in doubt, have your iron status checked to see how you are doing while you get used to this new plant-based way of eating.

TIME TO THINK ABOUT ZINC

While it is unlikely that you will be faced with questions about zinc, it is one nutrient that does present a challenge for vegetarians, as it does for nonvegetarians. Zinc is not as well studied as iron; there are unanswered questions regarding the many ways in which it supports our health, exactly how much we need, and whether people in North America get a sufficient amount of it.

Zinc in the Body

Zinc plays crucial roles in metabolism from our first moments of conception. It is required for the activity of nearly a hundred enzyme systems and affects the fundamental processes of life. It is essential for reproduction, growth, sexual maturation, wound healing, and a strong immune system. It helps to protect against the destructive action of free radicals. It also enables us to build molecules that are fundamental to our existence and to use carbohydrate as a source of energy. Zinc plays a role in our ability to taste; some seniors who have lost their sense of taste are actually zinc deficient. Infants and children whose diets are short on zinc will have slower physical growth and poor appetites. For those with anorexia nervosa, zinc deficiency could worsen the condition by promoting a true loss of appetite.

How Do We Know If We're Getting Enough Zinc?

There is not a single specific and precise way to assess zinc status. Instead, a combination of tests is used, such as determining the amounts in plasma and the activity of enzymes that depend on zinc. Testing is expensive and is not done on a routine basis. As a result, we have limited feedback about our zinc status. Our best plan is to aim for the recommended dietary intakes.

Recommended Zinc Intakes

Zinc recommendations are based on the average requirements plus a safety factor. The safety factor has been set to account for the wide range in people's requirements and variations in the availability of zinc from different diets. We absorb about 20 percent or more of the zinc we consume, and just over ⅓ cup (90 ml) of cashews provides 3 mg of zinc. Pumpkin seeds are another good choice.

One reason men need zinc is that they lose an estimated 0.6 mg of zinc with each seminal emission. (Ardent vegetarians might be well advised to keep a bowl of cashews on the bedside table!)

Recommended Zinc Intakes	
Women, 19 and older	8 mg
Men, 19 and older	11 mg

Intakes and Nutrient Status

Studies show that the average zinc intake of nonvegetarians is about 11.1 mg per day, and significant numbers fall well below the recommended amounts. The average for lacto-ovo vegetarians is even lower at about 9.1 mg per day. Intakes of vegans can be worse still. A typical example of low intake is a young woman on a low-calorie vegetarian diet who eats salads and refined pasta, but avoids nuts, seeds, and tofu in an effort to cut dietary fat. (In fact, these mineral-rich foods are the best choices one can make for fat sources.)

One popular misconception among some vegetarians is that any diet based on wholesome plant foods will automatically provide all the nutrients necessary for good health.

Myth: **Eating any combination of plant foods will provide you the recommended amounts of zinc and other trace minerals.**

Not so. With good planning, vegetarians can get plenty of zinc, but it does not happen automatically. Take a look at the zinc column in table 3.5 and you'll see some powerful sources of this mineral that can be added to your diet. Many of these foods have been integrated into Menus 3 and 4 in ways that are simple and very tasty.

In Menu 1 (nonvegetarian), almost half the zinc was provided by beef and chicken, with peas being the next most important source. Refined flour in the white roll and bread has lost most of its zinc. In Menu 2, the main sources are dairy products, whole grains, and egg. When the use of animal products is decreased, people may think their zinc intake also will be decreased. Yet in Menus 3 and 4, legumes, plentiful amounts of whole grain products, and frequent use of nuts and seeds contribute significant amounts of zinc. Other zinc-rich foods are wheat germ and asparagus.

TABLE 3.7 ZINC IN MENUS		
	Zinc (mg)	
Menu and Page	**2,000 calories**	**2,800 calories**
1 Nonvegetarian, page 70	8.4	13.9
2 Lacto-Ovo Vegetarian, page 71	7.3	12.3
3 Lacto-Ovo Vegetarian with More Legumes, page 72	13.1	18.2
4 Vegan, page 73	13.0	13.9

Factors That Increase or Decrease Zinc Absorption

The amount of zinc we absorb from our diets can vary greatly, from an average of about 20 to 30 percent to as much as 50 percent from the readily available zinc that infants receive in breast milk. Some of the zinc in our bodies is secreted into the intestine (for example, in pancreatic juices), and a variable amount of this is reabsorbed. We seem to be able to adapt to lower zinc intakes by absorbing more from our food and by reabsorbing more of the zinc that is secreted. Though more studies would help us understand the intricacies of zinc balance, research has shown that vegetarians have lower zinc intakes but also lose less, providing a similar overall balance to that of nonvegetarians.

Phytate-calcium-zinc combinations

The compound phytate, present in whole grains and legumes, and very concentrated in wheat bran, can bind zinc and lower the amount we absorb, especially when calcium is present. This phytate-calcium-zinc combination can result from a meal of whole grain cereal, plus wheat bran, plus cow's milk or fortified soymilk. Naturally, we want to consume adequate intakes of calcium. So what's the solution? While there is no need to avoid the occasional delicious bran muffin, vegetarians should not add bran to their foods; they already get plenty of fiber. (Wheat germ is quite different; it is low in phytate and is an excellent source of zinc.) Also, it's best not to take a calcium supplement at the same time you are eating zinc-rich whole grains and legumes, or with wheat bran.

Reducing phytate action with food preparation

When we soak or sprout seeds, nuts, grains, or legumes, we decrease the amount of phytate and increase the amount of zinc we absorb from these foods. Many vegetarians soak nuts overnight before using them, and legumes are generally presoaked before cooking. Sprouted brown, green, and French lentils are mineral-rich, high-protein additions to salads (see page 330).

The yeasting of bread increases the availability of zinc from whole grain flours (in contrast to unleavened breads). The moist action of fermentation in foods such as tempeh can also increase zinc availability. Scientists are just beginning to understand some advantages of food preparation methods that long-term vegetarians have used for years to ensure good nutrition.

Dietary fats

Dietary fats are important as they help us absorb zinc (plus other minerals, phytochemicals, and fat-soluble vitamins). On an extremely low-fat diet, absorption can be decreased.

Choose a Good Multivitamin-Mineral Supplement over Single Mineral Supplements

Don't rush out and buy zinc pills. Zinc, iron, copper, and calcium all interact with each other, and large intakes of zinc can interfere with your utilization of one of the other minerals. If you wish to use supplements, choose a multi-vitamin-mineral complex in the general range of recommended (rather than higher) mineral levels. For recommended intakes, see tables 15.1 and 15.2 (pages 361 and 362). Check that the supplement you use contains zinc; many do not. Supplements that are below recommended levels are fine too, because your diet should be supplying most of your needs. If you use a separate calcium supplement, take it at a different time than when eating zinc-rich foods.

Guidelines for Maximizing Zinc Intake

For optimum zinc intake, follow these guidelines.

1. Consume a variety of zinc-rich foods. Eat good sources of zinc throughout the day, including whole grains, wheat germ, tofu, tempeh, miso, legumes, nuts, and seeds. Lacto-ovo vegetarians can add eggs and dairy products. Zinc-fortified cereals and veggie "meats" can significantly increase your intake.

2. Make the most of the zinc in your diet. Use yeasted breads, sprouts, roasted or soaked nuts, and presoaked legumes.

3. Eat foods that retain the mineral wealth that nature gave them rather than refined foods. White flour and products made from white flour, white rice, and other refined grains have lost most of their zinc.

4. Wheat bran, added to a diet high in whole grains and legumes, is not only unnecessary, but can interfere with mineral absorption.

Putting Protein, Iron, and Zinc into Your Meals

Our best sources of zinc also tend to be rich in iron and protein too, so choosing these is a win-win-win situation—and more! Here are some examples of how nuts, seeds, beans, and whole grains can enrich your meals at breakfast, lunch, supper, and snack time.

Breakfast

Almond butter, sesame tahini, or peanut butter on toast

Cereal with soymilk

Wheat germ

Granola with nuts

Veggie bacon or ham

Banana Walnut Pancakes (page 309)

Cashew French Toast (page 308)

Marvelous Morning Muesli (page 311)

Whole Grain Cereal (pages 312 and 313)

Scrambled Tofu (page 314) with whole grain toast

Lunch or Supper

Marinated tofu with rice

Peanut butter on bread

Nuts or seeds on a salad

Sesame tahini in place of salad oil in dressing

Hummus and pita bread

Pea soup with French bread

Vegetarian chili with tortillas

Soy burger or dog on a bun

Lunch or Supper (continued)

Dahl with chapatis

Red beans with rice

Falafel (garbanzo bean croquettes) on pita bread

Pasta with pine nuts

Black Bean Soup (page 318)

Timesaving Tacos (page 342)

Shepherd's Pie (page 344)

Zucchini Chedda Soup (page 319)

Muenster Cheeze (page 320)

Veggie Clubhouse Sandwich (page 326)

Angelic Tofu Sandwich Filling (page 322)

African Stew (page 343)

Easiest-Ever Curried Lentils (page 347)

Hot Tofu with Cool Greens (page 338)

Chunky Red Lentil Tomato Sauce (page 340) over whole grain pasta

Desserts

Muscle Muffins (page 348)

Chocolate Mint Nut Bars (page 352)

Nutty Date Cookies (page 350)

Beverages and Snacks

Trail mix

Soy nuts

Pumpkin seeds

Hazelnut Pâté (page 323)

Quick Chocolate Shake (page 315)

Summing Up Protein, Iron, and Zinc

It is clear that meat, fish, and poultry can be replaced by a wealth of nutritious alternatives that can meet your needs for protein, iron, and zinc while reducing your intake of saturated fat and cholesterol. Generally, these nutrients are not as concentrated in plant foods as they are in animal products, but we don't *need* such concentrated sources. In fact, as we'll see in the next chapter, more moderate protein intakes can help our calcium balance.

For scientific references for this chapter, see
http://www.nutrispeak.com/bvreferences.htm

Chapter 4

BONE BOOSTERS

MILKS, GREENS, AND OTHER CALCIUM CHAMPIONS

If we go into any third grade classroom and ask the children why we need calcium, their likely answer would be, "To build strong bones, of course." Some may even tell us that if we don't eat enough calcium, we could get osteoporosis when we are old. If we ask the children where we get our calcium, most will not hesitate to tell us it comes from milk. Some might even mention cheese, yogurt, or other dairy products. There is no doubt about it, few nutrition messages are more strongly promoted than this one. Yet, despite the best efforts of the government and the dairy industry, many people fail to meet calcium recommendations. For example, 50 percent of North American women are expected to have at least one osteoporosis-related fracture in their lifetime. The answer to this problem seems so simple—drink more milk. While we know that milk is a rich source of calcium, could there be something missing in this nutrition education message?

In this chapter we will explore the many ways in which calcium, a mineral that is fifth in abundance in the earth's crust, can become part of our diets. In the process, we will challenge several myths—some widely held by the general population, others prevalent among some vegetarians.

Myth #1:	It is virtually impossible to get enough calcium in our diets without dairy products.
Myth #2:	Vegetarians need much less calcium than meat-eaters.
Myth #3:	Due to its high protein content, milk actually drains our bodies of calcium.
Myth #4:	Getting enough calcium ensures strong bones.

We also will look at how we get vitamin D, which is a key player in bone metabolism and essential for our absorption of calcium.

Myth #5:	Vitamin D is not a concern; we get plenty from sunshine.

Finally, we'll discover the various dietary sources of riboflavin, a vitamin present in milk and many plant foods.

CALCIUM

Calcium in the Body

Ninety-nine percent of our body's calcium is found in bones and teeth. Bones are living systems permeated by blood vessels and fluid. The minerals that harden bones are in a state of constant turnover throughout our lives, remodeling up to 15 percent of the bone mass annually, with about 700 mg of calcium entering and leaving bone every day. Though just 1 percent of our calcium is present in blood and soft tissues, its functions here are so vital that our bodies retrieve calcium from our bones to perform them if our dietary sources are insufficient. Calcium is a part of all cell membranes, allowing substances to enter and leave, and is involved with muscle contraction and relaxation, blood clotting, the transmission of nerve impulses, and enzyme activity.

Calcium Balance

No matter how much calcium is in our diets, our bodies maintain optimal levels of calcium in our blood and inside our cells with a complex system of checks and balances. Even as you read this, your body is adjusting the amount of calcium in your blood. To support this fine-tuning, we have some ability to control the proportion absorbed from foods, to alter the quantity of calcium lost in urine, and, if necessary, to draw on the calcium in our bones. The relationship between calcium intake and calcium losses from the body is known as calcium balance.

We achieve our maximum or peak bone mass in our early thirties. We gain 45 percent of this bone mass during our first eight years of life and another 45 percent during the next eight years. As adults, the total calcium in our bodies weighs between 2.2 and 3.3 pounds (1 and 1.5 kilograms). Through the growing years, we need to maintain a positive calcium balance by taking in much more calcium than we lose. Attaining good bone mass during our first few decades of life is extremely important for long-term bone health. Generally, at stages when we most need calcium, we absorb the highest percentage from our diets. Absorption is greatest during pregnancy, lactation, and the growing years. Thus, children may absorb up to 75 percent of dietary calcium, whereas young adults absorb 20 to 40 percent and most adults absorb just 15 to 20 percent.

When intake and output (losses) are roughly equal, we are in calcium balance. This is a good goal during our adult years. After about age forty-five, bone mass typically declines as much as 0.5 percent each year. In the decade before and after menopause, the rate of women's calcium losses accelerates to as much as 2 to 5 percent loss of total bone mass in a single year, and then it slows. Our diet and lifestyle choices through the years can help keep our bones strong by maximizing absorption, minimizing losses, and helping us retain the calcium we have. This is of prime importance after menopause and in the later years.

Factors Contributing to Calcium Balance

Though adequate intake is important, it is just one part of the rather complex equation of calcium balance. A study of hundreds of women looked at how calcium balance is determined, and showed that 11 percent was determined by calcium intake, 15 percent by absorption, and 51 percent by urinary excretion. Most people are very aware of the importance of calcium intake for bone health, as a great deal of resources are directed toward this message. On the other hand, calcium absorption and excretion are seldom recognized. Yet these are also extremely important for long-term bone health. Ignoring excretion is like trying to fill your bathtub without putting in the plug!

Calcium absorption

For adults, about 15 to 20 percent of the calcium from our food and beverages is absorbed from the intestine into the bloodstream. There can be a great deal of variation. For example, infants, whose bones are growing, absorb as much as

75 percent of the calcium from breast milk. When our needs increase, vitamin D steps into action and absorption also increases. Vitamin D plays a key role in helping us absorb and retain calcium (see page 109).

We absorb calcium more efficiently when small amounts are eaten throughout the day, rather than consuming the total amount at one sitting. For example, we might drink 2 cups (500 ml) of fortified soymilk or cow's milk all at once, or we could divide it into four smaller servings consumed at different times. Either way, we'll take in 600 mg calcium. Yet we will absorb much more calcium if we have the smaller servings over the course of the day.

Certain substances in foods, particularly oxalates (which are present in spinach, Swiss chard, rhubarb, and beet greens), can bind calcium. As a result, we absorb only about 5 percent of the calcium in these foods. In contrast, we absorb about 40 to 70 percent of the calcium in kale, collards, broccoli, and turnip greens. (For more on this, see table 4.4, page 103.) These foods have negligible amounts of oxalates, so we can rely on them as good calcium sources. To a lesser extent, phytates can reduce calcium absorption. Wheat bran, for example, is a concentrated source of phytates.

Calcium excretion

Every day, about 8,000 mg of calcium passes through our kidneys' filter, and we reabsorb about 98 percent of the mineral. Our overall diet has a large effect on the acidity and composition of our urine, which in turn determines how much calcium we lose. There are two major "calcium thieves," protein and sodium, plus several minor ones.

Protein. Research has shown that for every gram of dietary protein above 47 grams per day, we lose about 0.5 mg of calcium through the urine. This happens because a by-product of protein breakdown combines with calcium and carries it out of the body. The by-product is sulfate from the sulfur-containing amino acids. (These were discussed on page 63.) Sulfates make our blood more acidic than is optimal, so our bodies restore pH balance by drawing on calcium reserves—which are our bones—or with calcium from our diet. All dietary protein contributes to urinary calcium losses; however, meat, fish, poultry, and eggs are particularly high both in protein and in the sulfur-containing amino acids. Thus, their impact can be particularly strong, causing more calcium to be excreted. Dairy products, legumes, nuts, and grains

CALCIUM NEEDS

People with diets high in animal protein are likely to need more calcium than those with plant-based diets. (Exactly how much more is difficult to determine, as there are so many variables that interact.) Thus, excess protein can be an important factor in the epidemic of osteoporosis. Two other primary factors are high salt intakes and lack of exercise.

contain moderate amounts of protein and sulfur-containing amino acids, while fruits and vegetables contain even less. These foods do not have as great an impact on urinary calcium excretion. Protein is essential for building body tissues (including bone) and meeting recommended allowances is important. At the same time, too much protein can have a negative effect on calcium balance, *especially when calcium intakes are low.*

Sodium. The amount of sodium we require each day is very low, only about 500 mg. Intakes in some parts of the world are much higher. For instance, North Americans tend to consume about five to ten times that amount. The average intake from food alone is over 4 grams (4,000 mg) for men and almost 3 grams (3,000 mg) for women. Total intakes are even higher, because salt added at the table and whatever amounts might be present in our drinking water are not included in these values. High sodium intakes decrease our kidneys' ability to reabsorb the calcium that passes through it. For every 1,000 mg (1 gram) of sodium in our diets, we lose about 20 to 40 mg of calcium. One level teaspoon (5 ml) of salt provides 2,400 mg sodium; this also is the amount that many experts suggest as our maximum (from all sources) for the day.

TABLE 4.1	SODIUM IN FOODS	
Food	**Amount**	**Sodium (mg)**
Bread, slice	1	100–180
Canned tomatoes	1 cup (250 ml)	24–504
Corn chips	3 oz. (85 g)	182–869
Dill pickle, medium	1	900
Doughnut	1	210–380
Kraft Dinner, prepared	1 cup (250 ml)	1,460
Miso	1 tsp. (5 ml)	209
Peanut butter	2 tbsp. (30 ml)	80–150
Potato chips	3 oz. (85 g)	360–660
Pretzels	1 oz. (28.4 g)	450
Ready-to-eat cereal	1 cup (250 ml)	200–350
Salsa	½ cup (125 ml)	450–1,300
Soup, commercial	1 cup (250 ml)	700–1,100
Table salt or sea salt	¼ tsp. (1 ml)	581
Tamari or soy sauce	1 tsp. (5 ml)	335
Tomato sauce	1 cup (250 ml)	40–1,680
Veggie "meats"	3 oz. (85 g)	114–1,148
Suggested maximum intake per day		**2,400**

Generally, we can meet our basic requirements through the sodium that is naturally present in food and water, without added salt. Though few of us would shake one teaspoon (5 ml) of salt over our food at the table, we may add that much to a recipe and then eat a sizable portion of the dish. Still, only 15 percent of our salt intake comes from what we add to foods during cooking or at the table. The processed foods in our diets are a more significant source, as these have massive amounts of salt added to appeal to our taste buds. Seventy-five percent of North Americans' sodium intake comes via processed foods, such as salad dressings, soups, pickles, fast foods, and snacks. Specific examples are shown in table 4.1. Note the wide range of sodium in many products. It is smart to read labels!

There's one more bit of math that may convey further the impact salt can have on our health. Above, we said, "For every 1,000 mg (1 gram) of sodium in our diets, we lose about 20 to 40 mg of calcium." When this occurs, we're losing 20 to 40 mg of calcium that has been absorbed. If we absorb only 15 to 20 percent of our dietary calcium, this means that each extra gram of sodium in our diets should be counterbalanced by about 100 to 267 mg of dietary calcium. Considering that the average sodium intake is about 4 grams per day, we should be increasing our daily calcium intake by at least 400 to 1,068 mg to offset our sodium consumption. Scientists have calculated that for adult women, each extra gram (1,000 mg) of dietary sodium per day could produce additional bone loss of 1 percent per year if all the calcium loss comes from the skeleton. Research on postmenopausal women supports these results.

To protect our bones as we age, we should read labels to check the amount of sodium in the foods we buy and replace some of the salt in our cooking with other seasonings. Aim for about 2,400 mg of sodium or less per day.

Coffee. If we have two or three cups (500 to 750 ml) of coffee per day or less, the effect on calcium balance appears to be negligible, as long as our diets meet recommended calcium intakes. However, studies have shown that even 2 cups (500 ml) of coffee can encourage bone loss in women whose calcium intake is less than 800 mg per day.

Phosphoric acid. Some of the most popular sodas (cola beverages) contain phosphoric acid to balance their sweetness and inhibit the growth of micro-organisms. Phosphoric acid can increase calcium excretion, although the effects are considered relatively minor. However, if these beverages become a primary fluid, there could be more of a problem.

Calcium retention

Although several lifestyle factors can affect bone health, two primary considerations are hormonal balance and exercise.

Hormonal balance. Our hormonal balance plays a significant part in bone health. Estrogen appears to aid in calcium absorption and help our bones retain calcium. Vegetarians tend to have lower lifelong serum estrogen. This is thought to be due to the onset of menstruation at a later age, lower fat intakes, and increased fecal output of estrogen (due to higher-fiber diets). The reduced estrogen levels, while an advantage when it comes to cancer, may increase the risk of osteoporosis. For about five years around menopause, women may lose as much as 3 percent of their total bone mass each year. Hormone-replacement therapy has been used by postmenopausal women to prevent calcium loss; however, there can be unwanted side effects. New research is exploring the gentler effects of similar plant estrogens derived from soyfoods (isoflavones) and flaxseeds (lignans). Research shows that regular use of foods containing plant estrogens (for example, about 1½ servings of soymilk or tofu per day) may improve our bone density. With calcium-rich soyfoods, our odds are even better!

Calcium deficiency

Our bodies carefully control the calcium levels in blood and other fluids, maintaining these levels even if dietary calcium is low. Consequently, we can't determine the adequacy of our calcium intake over recent months by taking a simple blood test, as we can with iron. If blood levels of calcium drop, our bodies automatically make a withdrawal from our bone-calcium bank account. Eventually, of course, repeated withdrawals will result in fragile bones. During periods of high need, low intake, or increased excretion, output exceeds intake, so we are in negative calcium balance.

Osteoporosis has been called "a disease of childhood that manifests in old age." This description conveys how this complex condition can reflect years of diet and lifestyle choices that affect calcium balance. This includes intakes of many other nutrients that make up or affect our bones. Decades later, we learn the outcome of our choices. For more information on osteoporosis, and the many factors that lead to it, see page 107.

> ## EXERCISE
>
> The importance of exercise to bone health cannot be overemphasized. Exercise communicates a powerful message to the bones to preserve calcium and keep bones strong. Apart from diet, there is nothing we can do that is more valuable for our bones than to exercise. The best ways to help our bones retain calcium are by taking part in forty-five minutes to an hour of weight-bearing exercise (such as walking, running, cycling, or dancing) three to five times a week, plus a session of resistance exercise (such as free weights, exercise machines, or life activities that provide similar resistance exercise) two to three times a week. Bones appreciate being used!

Recommended Intakes of Calcium

Establishing recommended intakes for calcium is a tricky business. Nutrition experts have observed that defining the adult requirement, upon which a recommended intake is usually based, has proved to be one of the most difficult problems in the history of human nutrition. Because blood levels are maintained whether our diets are adequate or not; and because the feedback, in terms of bone density, comes decades later; and because there are so many variables that interact in the equation of calcium balance, it's difficult to determine exactly how much we need. However, combining the wisdom of scientists in the United States, Canada, Europe, Australia, New Zealand, and many other parts of the world, amounts have been set as Acceptable Intakes (a sort of "best guess") for various ages (shown in the box at right).

Acceptable Intakes for Calcium	
1–3 years	500 mg
4–8 years	800 mg
9–18 years	1,300 mg
19–50 years	1,000 mg
51 and over	1,200 mg

Upper limits also have been set and are called *Tolerable Upper Intake Levels* (UL). We are advised not to consume more than 2,500 mg of calcium daily on an ongoing basis. Generally, this would occur only with supplement use. Excessive calcium intakes can lead to kidney stones, which can be a particular problem when plenty of high-oxalate plant foods (such as spinach, Swiss chard, beet greens, and rhubarb) are consumed. High calcium intakes also may interfere with our absorption and use of other minerals: iron, zinc, magnesium, and phosphorus.

How Much Calcium Do Nonvegetarians, Lacto-Vegetarians, and Vegans Get?

With virtually all diets, average calcium intakes typically fall short of the recommendations for people nine years of age and older. U.S. national surveys show calcium intakes of teenage girls and women to be about 60 percent of recommended levels. Diets of men come a little closer to recommendations, providing a daily average of about 900 mg of calcium until the age of fifty, when intakes drop off to 700 mg. For both sexes, intakes of lacto-vegetarians are similar to those of nonvegetarians, or even a little higher. Vegan diets tend to be lower in calcium, providing about two-thirds of recommended levels for men and one-half the recommended levels for women. All in all, it's not enough!

Do Vegetarians (Including Vegans) Need This Much Calcium?

It is well known that many people in nonindustrialized countries, whose diets are mainly plant based, have strong bones despite calcium intakes that are far below the adult intakes recommended in the box above. We also know that excessive intakes of animal protein increase urinary calcium losses, and that requirements theoretically could be lower when these excesses are avoided. This combination of fact and theory has led some vegetarians to assume that they don't need to worry about calcium and can manage very well on intakes of 400 or 500 mg per day.

Myth: Vegetarians need *much* less calcium than meat-eaters.

It's important to recognize that people in other cultures who manage on these low calcium intakes often lead lives that are far different from urban dwellers in North America, Britain, Australia, and New Zealand. Their main mode of transportation may be walking outdoors in the sunshine. Carrying heavy loads, such as children, water, and food, is a part of their everyday life. Our lives are often very sedentary. We may be indoors much of the time, sitting at a desk during the day and watching TV at night. Even when we exercise, we drive to the gym or use a golf cart. When we are outside, we often smear on the sunscreen. Some of us also live at latitudes that limit sun exposure. These factors, including those that determine vitamin D levels, affect our calcium retention.

Vegetarians, along with vegans, should meet the calcium intakes recommended for their age group. This can be accomplished by following the Vegetarian Food Guide (page 193). Many people find it easier to meet recommended calcium levels if fortified foods or supplements are included as part of the day's intake.

Taking part in weight-bearing exercise, steering clear of excess salt, and avoiding the extremes of insufficient or far too much protein are habits that can work to our advantage. One good predictor of our bone health may be the ratio between our calcium and protein intakes. As shown in table 4.2, the ideal ratio appears to be 16 mg of calcium for every gram of protein in our diet. Lacto-ovo vegetarians fit this pattern very closely. The ratios for nonvegetarians and vegans are fairly similar and lower—between 9 and 12 mg of calcium for each gram of protein in the diet. Vegans have the advantage of less excessive protein intakes, but this is offset by lower calcium intakes.

Vegetarians may also have lower amounts of estrogen in their bodies over a lifespan. This carries certain anticancer health benefits, but it could possibly have a negative impact on bone health. Overall, while some vegetarians un-doubtedly have lower calcium needs than the general population, we do not have evidence, based on differences in lifelong bone health, that the vegetarian population as a whole needs less calcium than is generally recommended. Some studies have shown that vegetarians and nonvegetarians lose the same amount of

TABLE 4.2	RATIO OF CALCIUM TO PROTEIN; SODIUM INTAKE	
	Ratio of Calcium to Protein (mg:g)	Sodium (mg)
Ideal	16:1	Less than 2,400
Lacto-Ovo Vegetarians	15:1 to 17:1	2,000–3,800
Nonvegetarians	10:1 to 12:1	2,000–3,600
Vegans	9:1 to 12:1	1,800–2,800

calcium in their urine when their calcium intakes are similar. Until we have actual clinical studies showing that vegetarians can have healthy bones with lower calcium intakes, the goal for vegetarians, including vegans, should certainly be to meet calcium recommendations.

The availability of calcium-fortified beverages and food (such as soymilk, orange juice, and calcium-set tofu) has improved immensely in recent years. Most studies of vegan dietary patterns were done before excellent fortified products appeared in the marketplace. Though kale, calcium-set tofu, and other nondairy sources of calcium (in table 4.3, page 99) are not yet listed on national food guides, our range of choices is becoming more widely acknowledged. Vegans, and people whose intakes fall short of recommendations, would be well advised to take advantage of the many calcium sources available to them!

Myth: Due its high protein content, milk actually drains our bodies of calcium.

Rumors circulate among vegetarians that cow's milk is not a good source of calcium and even that it depletes us of calcium. This is quite simply untrue. Cow's milk has an excellent calcium-to-protein ratio, which is reflected in the diets of lacto-ovo vegetarians. The proportion of calcium that is absorbed is respectable, about 32 percent. While it's not as high as the calcium from low-oxalate greens, it is comparable to calcium-set tofu (see table 4.3). Including dairy products in our diets certainly can help people achieve recommended calcium intakes. Although many Americans drink an average of 2 cups (500 ml) of cow's milk per day, an amount that provides about 600 mg of calcium, many others do not.

There are a number of reasons why some people choose to avoid dairy products. These include health concerns (for instance, the desire to avoid saturated fat and the hormone known as IGF-1 or insulin-like growth factor, which has been shown to accelerate tumor growth); environmental issues and the impact of animal agriculture (for example, land and water pollution from manure); and compassion for animals (in particular, the abbreviated lives of veal calves and their mothers, the dairy cows). Intolerances and allergies to milk's sugar and several of its proteins are widespread. These topics are discussed in more detail in *Becoming Vegan* by B. Davis and V. Melina, *Dairy-Free and Delicious* by B. Davis, B. Clark Grogan, and J. Stepaniak, and *The Ultimate Uncheese Cookbook* by J. Stepaniak (all published by Book Publishing Company, Summertown, TN). The last two books include excellent recipes.

TABLE 4.3	CALCIUM IN FOODS

Food and Amount	Calcium (mg)
Amounts listed are those in the Guide to Daily Food Choices, page 194.	
Green Vegetables	
Bok choy, raw, 2 cups (500 ml)	147
Bok choy, cooked, 1 cup (250 ml)	178
Broccoli, raw, 2 cups (500 ml)	84
Broccoli, cooked, 1 cup (250 ml)	70–94
Chinese broccoli, cooked, 1 cup (250 ml)	88
Chinese (Pe-Tsai/napa) cabbage, raw, 2 cups (500 ml)	117
Chinese (Pe-Tsai/napa) cabbage, cooked, 1 cup (250 ml)	158
Chinese cabbage flower leaves, cooked, 1 cup (250 ml)	478
Chinese mustard greens, cooked, 1 cup (250 ml)	424
Chinese (luffa/loofah) okra, 1 cup (250 ml)	112
Collard greens, cooked, 1 cup (250 ml)	226
Kale, raw, 2 cups (500 ml)	181
Kale, cooked, 1 cup (250 ml)	94–179
Mustard greens, 1 cup (250 ml)	128
Okra, 1 cup (250 ml)	101
Romaine lettuce, raw, 2 cups (500 ml)	40
Sea vegetable, hijiki or arame, dry, ½ cup (125 ml/10 g)	100–140
Turnip greens, 2 cups (500 ml)	209

Food and Amount	Calcium (mg)
Nondairy Milks and Yogurts	
Fortified soy and grain milks, ½ cup (125 ml)	100–150
Unfortified soy and grain milks, ½ cup (125 ml)	5–10
Silk Cultured Soy, ½ cup (125 ml)	333

Food and Amount	Calcium (mg)
Fruits and Juices	
Figs, 5 (3 oz./85 g)	137–197
Orange, 1 medium	52
Fortified orange juice, ½ cup (125 ml)	150–154

Food and Amount	Calcium (mg)
Amounts listed are those in the Guide to Daily Food Choices, page 194.	
Legumes and Soyfoods	
Black turtle beans, cooked, 1 cup (250 ml)	84–102
Cranberry beans, cooked, 1 cup (250 ml)	94
Garbanzo beans/chickpeas, cooked, 1 cup (250 ml)	80
Kidney beans, cooked, 1 cup (250 ml)	50
Lentils, cooked, 1 cup (250 ml)	38
Navy beans, cooked, 1 cup (250 ml)	127
Pinto beans, cooked, 1 cup (250 ml)	82
Great Northern beans, cooked, 250 ml (1 cup)	120
White beans, cooked, 1 cup (250 ml)	226
Green soybeans, 1 cup (250 ml)	185
Soybeans, cooked, 1 cup (250 ml)	175
Soy nuts (roasted soybeans), ½ cup (125 ml)	120–162
Tofu, firm (calcium–set), ½ cup (125 ml)	152–336
Tofu, silken firm, ½ cup (125 ml)	40
Tempeh, ½ cup (125 ml)	92
Yves Veggie Ground Round, 3 oz. (85 g)	62

Food and Amount	Calcium (mg)
Nuts, Seeds, and Butters	
Almonds, ¼ cup (60 ml)	115
Almond butter, 3 tbsp. (45 ml)	130
Flaxseeds, 2 tbsp. (30 ml)	47
Hazelnuts, ¼ cup (60 ml)	38
Sesame tahini, 3 tbsp. (45 ml)	50–63

Food and Amount	Calcium (mg)
Other	
Blackstrap molasses, 1 tbsp. (15 ml)	176
Fortified breakfast cereals, 1 oz. (25 g)	55–1,000

Food and Amount	Calcium (mg)
Dairy Products	
Cow's milk, nonfat, 2%, or whole, ½ cup (125 ml)	143–153
Cheese, cheddar, ¾ oz. (21 g)	151
Yogurt, ½ cup (125 ml)	156–200

Calcium-Rich Plant Foods: Plenty of Options

Our culture teaches us that milk and its products are an essential food group, and government publications tell us that we must eat foods from each group to be healthy. Children learn that if they don't drink milk, they won't grow strong bones. Adults get the impression that the best way to prevent, or even cure, osteoporosis is to drink more milk. While milk is a key source of calcium for people consuming animal-centered diets, it is not essential to human health. As it turns out, there are a great many ways for the calcium that originates in the earth's crust to become part of our bones. Cow's milk is just one. A great many people, dairy consumers or not, will benefit by knowing some of the plant foods that provide this mineral.

Table 4.3 shows a variety of these foods, along with the amount of calcium they contain. The calcium content in plants can be expected to vary somewhat from one crop to another. There also can be great differences between brands of tofu, so check the package label. When labels state that a serving provides a certain percent of the Daily Value (DV), this is based on 1,000 mg of calcium as 100 percent; thus, 10 percent means 100 mg calcium. Table 4.4, on page 104, takes this one step further and combines the research on how well we absorb calcium (where this is known) with amounts in various foods.

Greens: broccoli, Asian greens, collards, kale, okra, mustard greens, and turnip greens

Because calcium is an important structural component in the cell walls of leaves and many other parts of plants, various veggies can easily become important calcium contributors in our diets. In some plants (see box at right), the calcium is tightly bound by plant acids called oxalates, which make little of it available to us. In contrast, many other greens are low in oxalates and are good sources of easily absorbed calcium. These include bok choy, broccoli, collards, kale, many Asian greens (apart from Chinese spinach), okra, mustard greens, and turnip greens. The proportion of calcium we absorb from these low-oxalate greens is somewhat higher than from cow's milk.

> **HIGH-OXALATE GREENS**
> **GOOD FOODS,**
> **BUT NOT FOR CALCIUM**
>
> Spinach, Swiss chard, beet greens, and rhubarb contain plenty of calcium. Unfortunately, the calcium is tightly bound by plant acids called oxalates; thus, we can absorb only a small proportion of the calcium in these foods (only about 5 to 8 percent), so they can't be counted as calcium sources (see table 4.4). We don't need to avoid these high-oxalate greens, as they are rich in other very important nutrients, such as folate and phytochemicals.

Greens are among our best bone builders for reasons beyond their unbeatable calcium absorption. They're high in vitamin K—the darker the leaf, the better. Vitamin K plays a mysterious but essential role in helping our bone-building cells perform their task. Consuming 3.5 ounces (100 grams) per day of dark leafy greens, such as kale, provides enough vitamin K to cut our risk of fracture in half. Greens also contribute plenty of potassium to the bone-building team.

Kale is a hardy crop that many gardeners can grow throughout much of the year. It's well worth learning how to prepare kale and other greens in delicious ways (see the recipes on pages 327 and 338).

Sea vegetables

Vegetables from the sea, often called seaweeds, are commonly used in Japan and are packed with minerals. Hijiki (also known as hiziki) and arame are particularly high in calcium; wakame contains calcium, too. These sea vegetables are available in dried form in most natural food stores, though they also can be found at a far less expensive price in Asian markets. They can be rehydrated and added to soups, salads, and stir-fries.

Calcium-set tofu

Tofu is made from soymilk that is allowed to set by adding a coagulant. Traditional methods in Japan involve adding a sea vegetable extract called nigari. Today, either calcium or magnesium salts are commonly added in amounts that vary considerably from one brand or variety to another (check the nutrition panel on the package). Calcium-set tofu can be one of the most significant sources of calcium in our diet.

Tempeh, a fermented, highly digestible soyfood originating from Indonesia, also contains calcium, though less than calcium-set tofu.

White beans, black turtle beans, and soybeans

Although all beans contain calcium, some have more than others. One cup (250 ml) of white beans contains as much calcium as ¾ cup (185 ml) of cow's milk. Other legumes particularly rich in calcium include green soybeans, navy beans, black turtle beans, and Great Northern beans. (See table 4.3 for the calcium content of these and other legumes.)

Figs

Although considered a fruit, the fig actually is a flower that is inverted onto itself. Break open a fig, fold it back, and you will see all the seeds. The fig tree is a member of the mulberry family; one grew in the Garden of Eden and its fruit is mentioned throughout the history of many cultures. Figs were a favorite of the prophet Mohammed. This sweet fruit was a training food for early Olympic athletes. In Rome, Pliny (52–113 A.D.) wrote, "Figs are restorative. They increase the strength of young people, preserve the elderly in better health and make them look younger with fewer wrinkles." (Wouldn't it be nice if this were true? It surely would boost the sales of figs!) Certainly dried figs are an excellent treat to carry in our backpack, glove compartment, or purse; they give us an energy boost, complete with plenty of calcium, iron, potassium, and fiber. Five dried figs, or ⅔ cup (170 ml), contain as much calcium as ½ cup (125 ml) of cow's milk.

Calcium-fortified beverages

Soymilk, rice milk, and orange juice are available in calcium-fortified versions, generally containing the same amount of calcium per cup as cow's milk. In fortified soymilk and rice milk this is accompanied by vitamin D (which helps us absorb calcium). Check labels for the words "fortified" or "enriched"; read the ingredient list for a calcium salt (such as calcium gluconate, calcium citrate malate, or tricalcium phosphate), or see if the nutrition information panel states, for example, "Calcium...30% of DV," which means 300 mg of calcium per 1 cup (250 ml) serving (as in cow's milk). The calcium tends to settle to the bottom of the container rather than staying in suspension, so if we want to end up with the calcium inside us, we need to shake the closed container well each time before using.

Almonds, sesame seeds, and their butters

Almonds are a good choice for a high-calcium trail mix. Different nuts have different nutritional profiles; almonds are particularly rich in calcium. Some fortified almond milks contain about 200 mg of calcium per cup, plus vitamin D. Unfortified almond milk made from ground almonds is tasty, but is not a suitable calcium-rich beverage for children; it has nowhere near the 300 mg of calcium per cup that we find in fortified soymilk or cow's milk. Almond butter makes an excellent spread for toast. The sesame seed butter called tahini has less calcium than almond butter, but significantly more than peanut butter or most other nut or seed butters.

Blackstrap molasses

You've likely heard that white sugar has been stripped of everything but refined carbohydrates. Where do the nutrients go when the sugarcane plant is converted to this nutritionally barren white powder? They end up in a byproduct of the sugar refining industry known as blackstrap molasses, a rich concentrate of the minerals that were in the original plants. If you make baked beans, use blackstrap (not regular) molasses for calcium (the beans have calcium, too). Molasses can contain concentrated residues from pesticides and other chemicals that were sprayed on the cane, so organic brands are our best option. (Barbados molasses and sorghum molasses are far less concentrated and have less than one-third the mineral content of blackstrap.)

Fortified cereals

Some ready-to-eat cereals contain added calcium. In the United States, amounts reach levels that are recommended for the entire day's intake. (Note that calcium is better absorbed from small servings in food throughout the day rather than from a large amount served all at once.)

Foods falsely assumed to be calcium-rich

Soy yogurt, cheese substitutes, and soy ice creams often are thought to provide the same amount of calcium as their dairy counterparts, but they generally are

TABLE 4.4 CALCIUM FROM FOODS AND ESTIMATED ABSORPTION			
Food	Calcium (mg)	Percentage absorption*	Estimated absorbable calcium (mg)
Beans and Products			
Tofu with calcium, ½ cup (125 ml)	258	31%	80
White beans, cooked, ½ cup (125 ml)	113	22%	25
Pinto beans, ½ cup (125 ml)	45	27%	12
Red beans, ½ cup (125 ml)	41	24%	10
Fortified Beverage			
Fruit punch with calcium citrate malate, 1 cup (250 ml)	300	52%	156
Low-Oxalate Greens			
Bok choy, cooked, ½ cup (125 ml)	79	53%	42
Broccoli, cooked, ½ cup (125 ml)	35	61%	21
Chinese cabbage flower leaves, cooked, ½ cup (125 ml)	239	40%	96
Chinese mustard greens, cooked, ½ cup (125 ml)	212	40%	85
Kale, cooked, ½ cup (125 ml)	61	49%	30
Mustard greens, cooked, ½ cup (125 ml)	64	58%	37
Turnip greens, cooked, ½ cup (125 ml)	99	52%	51
High-Oxalate Foods			
Chinese spinach, cooked, ½ cup (125 ml)	347	8%	28
Spinach, cooked, ½ cup (125 ml)	115	5%	6
Rhubarb, cooked, ½ cup (125 ml)	174	8.5%	15
Nuts and Seeds			
Almonds, dry roasted, 1 oz. (28.4 g)	80	21%	17
Sesame seeds, without hulls, 1 oz. (25 g)	37	21%	8
Dairy Products			
Cow's milk, 1 cup (250 ml)	300	32%	96
Cheddar cheese, 1.5 oz. (43 g)	303	32%	97
Dairy yogurt, 1 cup (250 ml)	300	32%	96

* Note that absorption varies with serving size, and amounts vary from one crop to another.

much lower in calcium. When in doubt, check labels. Calcium-fortified soy yogurt is now available, so be sure to look for it.

Estimated Absorbable Calcium

Dr. Connie Weaver of Purdue University and others have done excellent studies that give us an idea of how much calcium we can absorb from an assortment of plant foods. Research of this type has not been done on all the plant sources of calcium available to us; however, it is clear that we can readily absorb calcium from many foods, not just from dairy products.

Calcium in Our Menus

We can see from tables 4.3 and 4.4 that we have many options when it comes to calcium-rich foods. Table 4.5 shows the amounts of this mineral that are provided by the four menus in the previous chapter (pages 70 to 73). As we move from Menu 1 (nonvegetarian) to Menu 4 (vegan) there is increasing reliance on the plant sources of calcium. In Menu 1, we find that 80 percent of the calcium comes from dairy products and little use is made of nondairy sources of calcium. In Menu 2, we see that 66 percent of the calcium comes from dairy products, while Whole Grain Cereal (pages 312 and 313), green salad, and breads add a little. If ¾ cup (185 ml) of calcium-fortified orange juice was used instead of the regular variety, the calcium would increase by 208 mg, bringing the total in the 2,000 calorie menu up to 1,036 mg. Menu 3 contains 265 mg of calcium from dairy products—just over one-quarter of the day's total supply. All the calcium in Menu 4 comes from plant foods; the exact amount will depend on the type of tofu chosen. Some brands are extremely high in calcium, and the Hot Tofu recipe (page 338) provides a hefty serving of tofu. In addition, 480 mg come from other calcium sources.

TABLE 4.5 CALCIUM IN MENUS

Menu and Page	Calcium (mg) 2,000 calories	2,800 calories
1 Nonvegetarian, page 70	839	1,098
2 Lacto-Ovo Vegetarian, page 71	827	1,177
3 Lacto-Ovo Vegetarian with More Legumes, page 72	1,260	1,239
4 Vegan, page 73	768–1,707	964–1,913

Boosting Calcium from Dawn to Dusk

Here are some ways we can increase our calcium intakes at meals and snacks throughout the day.

Breakfast

✓ Cook porridge in fortified soy, rice, or cow's milk instead of water.

✓ Spread toast with almond butter or tahini and a thin layer of blackstrap molasses.

✓ Add fortified soy, rice, or cow's milk to a smoothie.

✓ Choose the calcium-fortified variety of orange juice.

✓ Scramble some calcium-set tofu.

✓ Munch on Marvelous Morning Muesli (page 311).

✓ Top fruit salad with yogurt (dairy or calcium-fortified soy yogurt) and granola.

✓ Use blackstrap molasses as the sweetener in muffins, on porridge, and on toast.

✓ Add milk powder (fortified soy or cow's) to muffins, pancakes, waffles, or porridge.

Lunch

✓ Make a sandwich of marinated tofu or Angelic Tofu Sandwich Filling (page 322) using calcium-set tofu.

✓ Pack raw broccoli florets along with the carrot sticks.

✓ Eat your vegetables with hummus or a yogurt-based dip.

✓ Bring a thermos of black or white bean soup.

✓ Add fortified soymilk or cow's milk to cream soups.

✓ Make a salad with calcium-rich greens and top it with marinated tofu and toasted almonds.

Supper

✓ Make a huge marinated salad with broccoli, many other vegetables, edamame (fresh green soybeans), and white or black beans. (This keeps well.)

✓ Use calcium-set tofu, a variety of Asian greens, and toasted almonds in a stir-fry.

✓ Dine on Hot Tofu with Cool Greens (page 338).

✓ Add white or black beans to stews and chili.

✓ Turn World's Greatest Greens into a family favorite (page 327).

✓ Enjoy the Go-for-the-Green Salad (page 328).

Snacks and Desserts

✓ Keep a bag of dried figs and almonds in your glove compartment, desk drawer, or backpack.

✓ Spread a bagel or bread with almond butter.

✓ Snack on soy nuts or edamame (green soybeans in the shell).

✓ Use calcium-rich ingredients such as tahini, blackstrap molasses, fortified soymilk or cow's milk powder, almonds, and almond butter in making treats such as cookies, squares, or muffins (see recipe for Muscle Muffins on page 348).

✓ Freeze calcium-fortified soy yogurt in Popsicle trays to make frozen yogurt treats.

✓ Serve yogurt or puddings made with fortified soy or rice milk, or cow's milk for dessert.

✓ Eat the whole German Chocolate Cake (page 356). Just kidding!

Beverages

✓ Combine 1 cup (250 ml) of calcium-fortified orange juice with 4 ounces (115 g) of calcium-set tofu and a ripe banana to make a smoothie.

✓ Drink calcium-fortified soymilk, rice milk, or cow's milk as a cold beverage or in cocoa.

What about Supplements?

The diets of many people fall short of recommended intakes for calcium, and supplements can help to assure that our needs are met. U.S. surveys show that one in five adults takes a supplement that contains calcium and one in four takes a supplement that contains vitamin D. The amount of calcium in a multivitamin-mineral supplement is often about 150 mg, which may be enough. (Adding as much as 1,000 mg of calcium to a tablet would make it very bulky. Chewable multivitamin-mineral supplements can be a little larger, and may contain as much as 250 mg of calcium.) If we're using a "single mineral" supplement, such as calcium with vitamin D, the directions may suggest that we take several tablets for the day's recommended intake, but this much is probably unnecessary, as our diet can provide most of our calcium needs. If you take more than one tablet in a day, or use a liquid form, note that several small doses of calcium are absorbed much more efficiently than the same total amount taken all at once. Thus, try to spread larger doses, such as 500 mg, over the course of the day.

What kind of calcium supplement is best?

Research on the absorption of various forms of calcium shows as many differing results as there are studies. Should we get calcium carbonate, calcium citrate, calcium citrate malate, or chelates? In truth, all of these are well absorbed; any differences are negligible as long as the pill breaks apart and doesn't just pass through our system whole. (Vegetarians should be aware that hydroxyapatite is made from the bones of cows, and oyster shell supplements really are made from oyster shells!) Our physical responses to various formulations are quite individual. Some people find that calcium carbonate causes constipation; others find it relaxing when taken before bedtime. What really matters for overall bone health (and health in general) is to have a good source of vitamin D (from the sun or a supplement, as vitamin D helps us absorb calcium) and an assortment of trace minerals: boron, vanadium, fluoride, and others. Vegetarians may not need supplementary magnesium, because plant foods are high in this mineral—it is a part of the green pigment chlorophyll.

What about mineral interactions?

High calcium intakes can interfere with iron absorption, so if you're short of iron, it's best to take a high-dosage calcium supplement separately from iron-containing supplements and from iron-rich meals. This is because minerals can compete, and calcium could hinder iron absorption. The lower amounts of calcium in a multivitamin-mineral supplement are closer to the amounts in a typical meal, and at these levels, minerals are well absorbed.

Building a Strong Defense against Osteoporosis

In the United States, Britain, Canada, Australia, and New Zealand, more than one in three women over the age of fifty has osteoporosis. By age sixty, the numbers increase to over 50 percent. Because women have slightly smaller bones than men, the risk of fractures for women is higher, yet rates among men are escalating, too. Our best protection is to develop good bone density early in life, and then maintain what we have with adequate nutrition and exercise. Studies have shown that in our later years we still are capable of increasing our bone density and can even repair some osteoporotic damage. Exactly how do we do this? Is the solution calcium, calcium, and more calcium?

Myth: Getting enough calcium ensures strong bones.

If we trust advertising, we may get the impression that the way to avoid osteo-porosis is to load up on calcium. However, relying on this single mineral to pre-vent osteoporosis is like trying to play baseball with only a pitcher on our team. In truth, we need other team members on bases, behind the plate, and in key spots out in the field. Bone health involves a similar team of players, including calcium, vitamin D, protein, magnesium, boron, copper, zinc, manganese, fluo-ride, and vitamins K, C, B_{12}, B_6, and folic acid. Physical activity, which is vital, would no doubt take the position of "team coach." Bone health is a complex interplay of many lifestyle factors. Thousands of milligrams of calcium will not do us much good if our diets generally are unbalanced or if we ignore com-monsense rules of healthy living.

Here are a few examples of roles played by the members of the "bone team." Vitamin C, found in fruits and vegetables, helps build cross-links between mol-ecules of collagen, a protein in bone. Vitamin K, from leafy greens, binds cal-cium to three types of protein that make up bone structure. Boron, a mineral in apples and other fruits, flaxseeds, nuts, vegetables, and legumes, plays a role in preventing calcium loss and seems to support the action of vitamin D.

VITAMIN D—FOR DULL DAYS

When we expose our hands or face to warm sunlight, even for just a few min-utes, our skin cells form vitamin D. Vitamin D also is added to a limited range of foods: milks (fortified soy, rice, and dairy), breakfast cereals, cereal grain bars, margarine, and infant formulas. Sunlight, fortified foods, and supplements are our sources of this essential substance.

The importance of sunlight to the sturdiness of the skeleton was referred to even in ancient times. More recently, folk wisdom recognized the importance of time spent in the sun, especially for children. In the twentieth century, we found that certain ultraviolet rays in sunlight would help our bodies create vitamin D. It also was discovered that vitamin D could be taken orally, in foods or supplements, and that both sources were equally effective treatments for a once common disease called rickets.

Natural Sources of Vitamin D

For those growing up in the mid–twentieth century, doses of cod-liver oil were a daily feature of childhood—although the practice never gained popu-larity among the children involved. The livers of oily fish, particularly cod and halibut, are among the few food items that are naturally high in vitamin D. The skins of animals (sheep, pigs, and cows) also contain vitamin D. As in humans, their skin is a production center for the vitamin. Vitamin D extracted from skins and wool is used to fortify cow's milk and margarine. Eggs provide small amounts of vitamin D if the chickens have been fed a high–vitamin D diet. The form of this vitamin that is derived from oily fish and other animal products is called vitamin D_3. Vitamin D also is present in a few plants; however, we do not rely on these as food sources. When exposed to ultraviolet light, certain sea vegetables, mushrooms, and yeasts can produce a vegetarian form of this nutrient known as vitamin D_2. Yeast, irradiated by light, is the source of the vitamin D_2 in many vitamin D–fortified vegetarian foods and supplements.

Vegetarian Sources of Vitamin D

Vegetarians typically get vitamin D from sunlight, fortified foods (look for vitamin D_2 on labels), and supplements. Vegetarian food sources include fortified soymilk, rice milk, and cow's milk, margarines, and infant formula. Manufacturers use a variety of words to describe beverages with added nutrients, such as enriched, fortified, plus, or extra. Because excess vitamin D can be toxic, legislation limits the types of foods to which manufacturers are allowed to add vitamin D.

The Role of Vitamin D in the Body

Vitamin D is essential for the proper formation of the skeleton. If we have too little vitamin D, the skeleton will be inadequately mineralized, leading to a condition called rickets in children and osteomalacia in adults. One of vitamin D's best-known roles is to maintain blood calcium at exactly the right level. It does this by regulating the movement of calcium in three places: absorption in the intestine, losses through the urine, and storage in the bones. Vitamin D also affects the process of cell division in a manner that may protect against cancer.

Rickets: the first air pollution disease

In the past, sunlight was the major provider of vitamin D for most of the world's population, and it still is for many people. For those who ventured to northern regions where there was little ultraviolet light in winter months, fish liver oils were a lifesaver centuries before their vitamin D content was identified.

With the Industrial Revolution, things changed. From the seventeenth to the early twentieth century, rickets plagued children who played in narrow, dark city streets, or who worked indoors. Very little sunlight made its way through the coal smoke from factories or between closely packed buildings. In 1900, four out of five children in some smoggy, urban areas of North America and Europe had rickets, a crippling disease that resulted in bowed legs, knock-knees, and misshapen skeletons. These children grew, but with insufficient vitamin D, their bones did not adequately mineralize or harden. Instead of being strong and straight, their legs bent in inward or outward arcs under the weight of their body.

By 1925, scientists had recognized the effectiveness of both sunlight and the vitamin from fish liver oil in preventing and treating rickets. Across North America in the 1930s, cow's milk was chosen as a vehicle to distribute vitamin D to the entire population and to children in particular. This public health measure proved to be tremendously effective. With mandatory fortification of cow's milk, along with nutrition education that promoted milk drinking, rickets became a rarity. With time, several other ways to deliver vitamin D through the food supply have been added, including fortified soymilk, rice milk, margarine, and infant formula.

Despite sunlight and fortification, occasional cases of rickets continue to be reported. Typically, these occur in toddlers under three years of age who have not received vitamin D in a supplement or fortified beverage. Often these are children with darker skin, meaning that they require somewhat more sun exposure to develop vitamin D. Occasional cases have occurred in vegan children who are not given vitamin D–fortified soymilk, and macrobiotic children if, for example, their parents are opposed to the use of supplements and fortified foods.

The Sunshine Vitamin

People who are regularly exposed to adequate amounts of sunlight do not need vitamin D from foods or supplements. When our skin is exposed to ultraviolet light, we can make vitamin D out of a cholesterol compound that is naturally present in the skin. These ultraviolet light rays don't pass through glass, so we can't get the beneficial effects of sunlight through a window. To determine whether an individual is getting enough sun for adequate vitamin D production, a number of factors must be taken into consideration.

Age

As we age, our skin's ability to produce vitamin D diminishes by 25 to 50 percent. Yet we continue to need the vitamin to help us absorb and use calcium and to ward off osteoporosis. Thus, supplements and fortified foods, in addition to some sun exposure, can become even more important in our later years.

Skin color

People with dark skin require substantially more exposure to sunlight for vitamin D production. Whereas light-skinned people need ten to fifteen minutes of sunlight a day on their face, hands, and forearms, people with increasingly darker skin need thirty minutes to three hours daily. The melanin pigment in dark skin absorbs some of the ultraviolet radiation. This appears to be a protective adaptation developed by people in sunny climates. It has been suggested that over the evolution of humankind, as people moved to northern latitudes, skin pigmentation decreased to allow for adequate production of vitamin D. Have you ever wondered why Scandinavians in the north have blond hair and light skin and people closer to the equator have dark hair and dark skin? These differences in skin pigment probably developed in large part because of our need for vitamin D!

Use of sunscreen

Sunscreen protection factors (SPF) of 8 and above will prevent vitamin D synthesis. Most people apply far less sunscreen than manufacturers recommend, so the blocking effect may be only partial. Our need for vitamin D must be balanced with the obvious need for protection from overexposure to the sun, especially during the hot hours of the day. For vitamin D synthesis, mid-morning sun is fine.

Amount of clothing worn

Vitamin D production varies with the amount of clothing worn and the total surface area of skin that is exposed. For example, the attire of some Middle Eastern women covers the head and face completely, preventing vitamin D production. The elderly tend to cover more of their skin with clothing. The people on *Baywatch* likely get their vitamin D supply in a minute or so!

Sunlamps

Sunlamps can be used to produce vitamin D in the skin. As with overexposure to sunlight, they can cause skin damage, so use caution or controlled ultraviolet light chambers.

Time of year and geographical location

Vitamin D production in skin differs seasonally and according to the latitude at which we live, as these factors affect the amount of ultraviolet radiation. On a cloudy summer day, even the "skyshine" will stimulate some vitamin D production. It has been estimated that the amount of ultraviolet radiation received even on sunny days in winter is sixteen times less than in summer. At latitudes above 40 degrees north (and in the southern hemisphere at latitudes below 40 degrees south), we experience "vitamin D winter." In other words, for three or four months, little or no vitamin D production occurs in skin. "Vitamin D winter" is longer the closer we get to the poles. In Los Angeles (34 degrees north) there is no vitamin D winter, while in Boston (42 degrees north) people do not produce vitamin D between November and February. Vitamin D winter lasts longer still, from about October to March, in Edmonton (52 degrees north).

We have the ability to store vitamin D, so to a certain extent we can get by with more sun in the summer and less in the winter. Yet, for populations living along the forty-ninth parallel, adults can expect their serum levels of the vitamin to drop to the lower end of the normal range, or even below, during winter months. Many will fare better with taking a supplement to augment whatever sun exposure they can get while taking out the trash or walking a few blocks. Infants and children have limited vitamin D reserves, so they need a supplement or fortified food source in regions farther from the equator.

Young men living in a submarine with no vitamin D–fortified foods or supplements found that their serum vitamin D dropped to less than two-thirds of normal levels after just one and one-half months. Their levels shot back up again when they returned to the surface and were able to get regular sun exposure. This situation has relevance for older and younger people who are institutionalized, bedridden, or unable to get outdoors for extended periods.

Researchers found that a total of three hours of sun exposure per week improved calcium balance in a group of elderly people (whose average age was eighty-three) in Stockholm, which is at 59 degrees latitude.

As you might have guessed, making a recommendation for the minimum sunlight exposure necessary for vitamin D production can be complicated by all of the above factors. However, the guidelines in the box at right will help you meet your vitamin D needs.

There are many circumstances in which our exposure to ultraviolet light

GETTING ENOUGH VITAMIN D FROM SUN EXPOSURE

A general guideline for light-skinned people is a daily average of ten to fifteen minutes of mid-morning to late afternoon sun on the face and hands. Darker-skinned people need more (thirty minutes to three hours daily, depending on skin color). At the same time, we need to take care to avoid overexposure, which can increase our risk of skin cancer; moderate sun exposure is the wisest course.

At latitudes far from the equator, infants and children cannot depend on adequate skin exposure to sunlight for vitamin D synthesis, especially during winter months.

is insufficient for the optimal production of vitamin D. We cover ourselves with clothing, stay indoors, live in smoggy cities amid tall buildings that shield us from sunlight, use sunscreens that block ultraviolet rays, and live in geographical regions that do not receive adequate sunlight. Thus, dietary sources of the vitamin become crucial, particularly during winter months. When sunlight is in short supply, we can choose fortified foods, supplements, or a combination of all three.

Recommended Intakes from Foods or Supplements

Current guidelines advise that if we do not have adequate exposure to sunlight, our intake should be 5 micrograms (mcg) of vitamin D per day up to the age of fifty-one, then double that amount until the age of seventy-one, when it should increase yet again. Requirements rise as we get older because our skin production drops. Vitamin D supplementation has proven to be effective in preventing bone loss and is deemed especially necessary after seventy years of age.

Amounts of vitamin D in foods and supplements are listed in mcg or international units (IU). One mcg is equivalent to 40 IU.

Recommended Vitamin D Intakes	
Birth–50	5 mcg (200 IU)
51–70	10 mcg (400 IU)
71 and over	15 mcg (600 IU)

Forms of vitamin D

There are two forms of vitamin D: vitamin D_2 (ergocalciferol, generally made from yeast) and vitamin D_3 (cholecalciferol, from the skins of sheep, cows, and pigs, and from sheep's wool). Our bodies can use either form.

Researchers have found vitamin D_2 to be about 60 percent as effective as vitamin D_3 in raising serum vitamin D levels. It makes sense for vegetarians, who prefer to use the form that is not of animal origin (vitamin D_2), to increase their intakes accordingly (multiply by 1.7). This means our daily intake up to fifty years of age should be 8.5 mcg of vitamin D_2; from fifty-one to seventy years it should be 17 mcg, and after the age of 70 it should be 25.5 mcg.

Beware of excess vitamin D

Whereas a little vitamin D is a good thing, too much is toxic. Three to five times the recommended intake of vitamin D over an extended period can cause hypercalcemia (too much calcium in the blood). This is a serious condition in which calcium is deposited in soft tissues, resulting in possible heart and kidney damage. An upper limit has been set, and that is 25 mcg of vitamin D per day for infants up to one year of age and 50 mcg after that. Care must be taken not to leave supplements within the reach of infants and children. Getting too much sunlight will not lead to vitamin D toxicity, though it can result in a sunburn.

TABLE 4.6	VITAMIN D IN FOODS	
Food and Amount		**Vitamin D (mcg)**
Enriched Soy Dream or Rice Dream, 1 cup (250 ml)		2.5
Fortified So Nice, Silk, or Westsoy Plus, 1 cup (250 ml)		2.5
Vitasoy Enriched, 1 cup (250 ml)		2.0
Edensoy Extra, 1 cup (250 ml)		1.0
Fortified cow's milk, 1 cup (250 ml)		2.5
Fortified breakfast cereals, 1 oz. (28.4 g)		0.5–1.0
Fortified margarine, 1 tsp. (5 ml)		0.5–0.75
Cod-liver oil, 1 tsp. (5 ml)*		11.0

*(for comparison)

RIBOFLAVIN

There has been occasional concern that plant-based diets could be low in riboflavin, a vitamin also known as vitamin B_2. This is because, for many people, dairy products, meat, poultry, fish, and eggs are the primary contributors of this vitamin. Yet there are good riboflavin sources in the plant world, too. Grains, both whole and enriched, typically provide about 30 percent of our riboflavin intakes. Leafy greens also contain riboflavin; other food sources are listed in table 4.7.

BULLETIN FOR BABIES

All breast-fed babies and toddlers should receive vitamin D drops. These are available at pharmacies; sometimes they are behind the counter, so you may need to ask for them. The recommended dose is 200 IU per day. If you have questions about how to measure the dose, ask a community health nurse or pharmacist. It should be given just before or after a feeding. Keep giving the vitamin D drops until your toddler is drinking 2 cups (500 ml) of infant formula or fortified soymilk or whole cow's milk every day. Two cups (500 ml) of any of these contain a suitable amount of vitamin D. (Breast milk generally cannot be relied on as a source.)

Your breast-fed infant should be given vitamin D drops if, during your pregnancy, you did not get vitamin D (from fortified soy or cow's milk or from a prenatal supplement) and did not have regular exposure to the sun's rays. Vitamin D supplementation is especially important for babies born in spring and early summer (when mom had little sun) and for those born prematurely or with a birth weight under 53 ounces (1,500 g). Youngsters don't get a chance to make vitamin D from sunlight during the wintertime, or when faces and hands are covered with scarves, gloves, or baby carriage covers.

A baby's skin production of vitamin D will be good when hands and face (without sunscreen) are exposed to ten minutes of sunlight a day for those with light skin, with more time allowed for those who have darker skin. For protection from sunburn in hotter months and latitudes, avoid the sun between 11 A.M. and 3 P.M.

As with other B vitamins, riboflavin is involved with energy metabolism and is active in every cell in the body. It also helps to maintain body tissues, including skin and mucous membranes, such as those in the mouth and eyes. Riboflavin deficiencies, although rare, show up as cracks at the corner of the mouth and changes in the tongue and mucous membranes of the mouth. Riboflavin is a fluorescent yellow vitamin that often shows up in the urine after we take a multivitamin supplement. That's the extra that we didn't need! Apart from the bright yellow urine, extra riboflavin doesn't seem to cause any problems.

Recommended Intakes of Riboflavin

Recommended intakes are 1.1 mg for women and 1.3 mg for men. American vegetarians and nonvegetarians generally get about one and one-half times the recommended daily intakes. Although some research suggests that vegans consume slightly less, they meet recommended intake levels.

Riboflavin in Foods

A few studies have shown vegetarian and vegan intakes of riboflavin to be low or borderline. This is both surprising and unnecessary, because riboflavin is plentiful in many plant foods. Table 4.7 shows several foods that provide 15 percent or more of the recommended daily intake.

Amounts in Menus

Menus 1 and 2 in chapter 3 (pages 70 and 71) each provide about one and one-half times the recommended intake of riboflavin. Menus 3 and 4 (pages 72 and 73) provide more than twice the recommended intake, with a big boost from nutritional yeast in the Liquid Gold Dressing (page 329) and the Hot Tofu with Cool Greens (page 338). Another recipe that will raise your riboflavin intake is the Scrambled Tofu (page 314).

TABLE 4.7 RIBOFLAVIN IN FOODS	
Food	**Riboflavin (mg)**
Almonds, 1/4 cup (60 ml)	0.3
Avocado, 1 medium	0.2
Beans, assorted, 1 cup (250 ml)	0.1–0.2
Cereal, ready-to-eat, fortified, 1 oz. (28.4 g)	0.2–1.7
Cow's milk, whole, 2%, or skim, 1/2 cup (125 ml)	0.2
Egg, large, 1 (1 3/4 oz./50 g)	0.6
Fortified instant oatmeal, 1 packet	0.3
Lotus root, 10 slices, 3 oz. (85 g)	0.2
Marmite or Vegemite yeast spread, 1 tsp. (5 ml)	0.7
Mushrooms, raw or cooked, 1/2 cup (125 ml)	0.2
Nutritional yeast mini-flakes, 1 tbsp. (15 ml)	1.9
Soymilk, fortified, 1/2 cup (125 ml)	0.2
Spinach, cooked 1/2 cup (125 ml)	0.2
Sweet potato, 1/2 cup (125 ml)	0.2
Yogurt, 1/2 cup (125 ml)	0.2–0.3

Note: Foods providing smaller amounts of riboflavin (0.1 mg of riboflavin per serving) include alfalfa sprouts, asparagus, bananas, broccoli, figs, kale, lentils and their sprouts, mung bean sprouts, peas, raspberries, seeds, sesame tahini, tofu, tempeh, wheat germ, whole grain bread, and enriched bread and pasta.

In a vegan diet, one-third of the riboflavin may come from vegetables and fruits, one-quarter from legumes, nuts, and seeds, and the remainder from grains. Vegans often include good sources that are not commonly used by non-vegetarians, such as nutritional yeast, yeast extracts (including spreads such as Marmite and Vegemite), wheat germ, and sprouts. A desire to meet riboflavin intakes may inspire us to try a few new foods! We can easily meet recommended intakes by including a variety of riboflavin-rich foods and by following the Vegetarian Food Guide (page 193).

STEPS FOR STRONG BONES

This chapter has focused on the many ways to meet our requirements for the nutrients necessary to build and maintain strong bones. There is little evidence that bone mineral density differs between Western nonvegetarians and lacto-ovo vegetarians, though the latter may have some advantages. Because at this time there are few lifelong vegans (and because the advent of calcium-fortified beverages and soyfoods is still fairly new), it's hard to give reliable data on the bone health of North American vegans. Studies suggest that bone health is poorer among vegan women with marginal protein and calorie intakes (perhaps due to continual dieting). Since we require vitamin D for calcium absorption, adequate intakes of this nutrient are essential. Certain features of vegetarian diets may help to maximize bone health, such as higher intakes of magnesium, potassium, and vitamin K. We have evidence that soy protein, rich in isoflavones, can help postmenopausal women retain bone in their spinal column.

Here are ten tips for strong bones:

1. **Follow the Vegetarian Food Guide**. Learn which foods are in the "Milks and Alternates" group.

2. **Eat dark green vegetables daily.** Include broccoli, kale, collards, bok choy, and Chinese cabbage on your regular shopping list. Find an Asian grocery store, grow greens in your garden or on your balcony, or arrange for these to be delivered weekly to your door. Learn delicious ways to prepare greens. Some minerals (and vitamins) are lost in the cooking water, so steam vegetables or use the mineral-rich cooking water in soups or in grain preparation.

3. **Use calcium-set tofu**. People who haven't tried tofu (or have tried it but haven't enjoyed how it was prepared) may not realize that it is just an ingredient, like flour. We wouldn't want to eat a bowl of flour, even though we may love many baked goods. Tofu is unusually versatile and takes on delicious flavors; it can be made into everything from soups to desserts, so it can be used often without your menus becoming repetitive.

4. **Take advantage of calcium-fortified beverages**. Fortified nondairy milks and juices can help raise your total calcium intake to recommended levels.

5. **Make almonds, almond butter, sesame tahini, and blackstrap molasses a part of your meals and snacks**. Every time you replace 2 tablespoons (30 ml) of peanut butter with an equal amount of almond butter, you increase your calcium intake by 73 mg. By replacing 1 tablespoon (15 ml) of jam with the equivalent of blackstrap molasses, you gain a surprising 168 mg of calcium. These wonderfully flavorful options add iron and zinc as well!

6. **Don't keep company with the calcium thieves**. Avoid high intakes of salt, alcohol, and caffeine, excessive amounts of animal protein, and a sedentary lifestyle.

7. **When you go out for dinner, frequent Japanese, Chinese, Middle Eastern, and vegetarian restaurants**. These cuisines do a masterful job of teaching us about the many wonderful sources of calcium that are seldom recognized in the Western world. You may learn delicious ways to use sea vegetables, such as hijiki, in stir-fries and soups. You'll discover flavorful dishes made with tofu, greens, beans, and tahini.

8. **Build strong bones during the growing years**. Emphasize a broad spectrum of calcium-rich foods, along with a balanced, varied diet for children. Infants need breast milk or commercial infant formula. As children get older, they can switch to fortified soymilk or cow's milk (see chapter 10).

9. **Add some sunshine to your day**. Take the opportunity to stretch your legs and walk around the block on your lunch break. You'll not only feel good, but with ten minutes (for Caucasians) to thirty minutes (for dark-skinned people) of sunlight you can achieve your vitamin D quota for the day.

10. **Exercise!** Walking, jogging, dancing, ballgames, hiking, step exercises, or other forms of weight-bearing exercise are essential for lifelong bone health. Even in the elderly, these activities strengthen bones. With bones, it's a case of use 'em or lose 'em.

For scientific references for this chapter, go to
http://www.nutrispeak.com/bvreferences.htm

Chapter 5

ENERGY PLUS

GOODNESS FROM GRAINS

When you hear the word "grains," what comes to mind? Perhaps you imagine fields of golden wheat, freshly baked bread, steamed rice, or piping hot oatmeal. Most people regard grains as healthful food, the kind that sticks to your ribs. Governments and health authorities encourage the use of grains as dietary staples. Grains have been awarded a prime position in food guides around the world. For example, in the United States and the Philippines, grains form the foundation of the food pyramid; in Canada, they occupy the largest arc of the rainbow; in Germany, they claim the largest wedge of a dinner plate; in Australia, they are featured as the biggest section of a circle; and in China and Korea, they serve as the base of the pagoda. Yet, despite all the positive press grains have received from health authorities, many of the most popular diet books on the market urge consumers to avoid grains and other carbohydrate-rich foods, claiming they are the root of almost every disease that plagues the Western world. All of this leaves consumers wondering whether grains are truly friend or foe. This chapter explores the myths and realities regarding grains as food staples and provides practical tools to help us select the kinds of grains that best support our health.

WHAT ARE GRAINS?

Grains or "cereal grains" are the seeds of a specific group of grasses. Worldwide, the grains people most commonly use are varieties selected for cultivation because of their high yields. These include wheat, spelt, kamut, oats, corn, rye, rice, millet, triticale, Job's tears, barley, sorghum, and teff. While sweet corn is eaten fresh as a vegetable, all varieties of corn are technically grains. Two common, highly nutritious seeds, quinoa and amaranth, often are mistakenly classified as cereal grains. However, they actually come from nongrass species, so they sometimes are referred to as pseudocereal. Quinoa is a member of the goosefoot family, along with common lamb's quarters, beets, chard, and spinach. Amaranth is in the amaranth family, along with pigweed. Buckwheat, also incorrectly thought of as a cereal grain, is a member of the buckwheat family, as is rhubarb. While quinoa, amaranth, and buckwheat are not grains in the true sense, we will include them as such for practical purposes, as that is how they are used.

There are three parts to any grain: the bran (the outer layer containing most of the fiber), the germ (the core containing much of the protein, vitamins, minerals, and fat), and the endosperm (the large middle mass, which is mainly pure starch). Intact grains are also known as whole grains. The whole grain can be rolled (e.g., rolled oats), cut (e.g., cracked wheat), or ground into flour (e.g., whole wheat or whole rye flour) for use in whole grain breads, cereals, pasta, and other prepared products.

ARE WHOLE GRAINS NUTRITIOUS FOODS?

Absolutely—whole grains are nutrition powerhouses. They are excellent sources of carbohydrates and a number of valuable vitamins and minerals, including many B vitamins, vitamin E, selenium, zinc, copper, magnesium, manganese, iron, potassium, and chromium. They also are great sources of fiber, plant sterols, and numerous phytochemicals, such as phenolic compounds and, in some cases, phytoestrogens.

Nutritional Composition of Whole Grains

The nutritional composition of whole grains is noteworthy. They provide a healthful balance of protein, carbohydrates, and fat, as well as a wide range of vitamins and minerals, and a host of other protective components such as fiber and phytochemicals. In the following text, we examine the principal nutrients found in grains and the value of these nutrients for human health. We consider the contribution grains can make to our daily intakes of these nutrients, by calculating nutrients provided in six servings of grains a day: three servings of whole wheat products, and one serving each of oats, barley, and brown rice. The products selected for our analysis are not fortified with additional nutrients. While quinoa and amaranth were not included in this particular analysis, their nutrient profiles are even more impressive than those of true grains.

Energy-giving nutrients

Protein. The contribution made by grains to the world's protein intake is far higher than most people imagine. Close to 50 percent of our protein comes from grains. Typically, 10 to 15 percent of the calories in grains are provided by protein, although for some grains it is even higher. While grains are relatively low in the important amino acid lysine, the typical combinations of plant foods that vegetarians eat offset this imbalance. Quinoa and amaranth provide about twice as much lysine as true cereal grains.

Fat. Grains are low in fat—only about 5 to 15 percent of their total calories come from fat. Most of this is polyunsaturated, from the omega-6 family. Saturated and monounsaturated fats each generally comprise less than 20 percent of the total fat content in grains.

Carbohydrates. Approximately 70 to 85 percent of the calories in grains come from carbohydrates, making grains the world's most important source of food energy. For many years, carbohydrates were divided into two categories: simple carbohydrates (single sugars or two sugars bound together) and complex carbohydrates (starches and fiber made of chains of many sugars). Simple carbohydrates were considered to be damaging to our health; complex carbohydrates were thought to be beneficial. Most people associated simple sugars with white sugar, brown sugar, and other concentrated sweeteners, while complex carbohydrates were associated with bread, pasta, and rice.

Today, these terms are becoming obsolete, because we now know that many foods rich in simple carbohydrates can be very good for us, and others rich in complex carbohydrates can be detrimental. For example, supernutritious vegetables and fruits, such as red peppers and blueberries, are generally low in starches and contain mostly simple sugars. Other far less nourishing foods, such as potato chips and doughnuts, are high in complex carbohydrates. Rather than focusing on simple carbohydrates as "bad guys" and complex carbohydrates as "good guys," experts now are encouraging us to look at foods in terms of their overall nutritional value. Whole grains stand out as excellent carbohydrate sources, providing a wonderful balance of starches and fiber, in addition to many other nutrients and protective components.

Vitamins

Grains are valuable sources of several vitamins, including the B vitamins and vitamin E.

B vitamins. Grains are a treasure trove of B vitamins, including thiamin, riboflavin, niacin, vitamin B_6, pantothenic acid, biotin, and folate. The only B vitamin not present is vitamin B_{12}. Although each has unique and varied functions, the B vitamins work as a team to convert carbohydrates, protein, and fat to energy. They also are important for maintaining healthy skin, and for nervous system and digestive functions. In addition, folate is needed for building new cells, pantothenic acid for synthesizing hemoglobin, and riboflavin for maintaining healthy vision. Taking into account our daily B vitamin requirements, six servings of whole grains every day would provide about 50 percent of our thiamin, niacin, B_6, and biotin; 25 percent of our riboflavin and pantothenic acid; and 15 percent of our folate.

Vitamin E. Although grains are not our most concentrated sources of vitamin E (nuts, seeds, and oils are higher), they do make a significant contribution. Vitamin E helps stabilize cell membranes and is a powerful antioxidant. Six servings of whole grains provide approximately 10 percent of our daily requirements. This figure would be considerably higher if we added wheat germ, which is where vitamin E is stored in wheat.

Minerals

Grains contribute to our intake of many minerals, including some of the trace minerals that tend to be lacking in our diets.

Chromium. A valuable trace mineral often low in diets high in processed foods, chromium is essential for the metabolism of sugar (glucose). It also is a component of glucose tolerance factor (GTF), a compound that works with insulin to move glucose into cells where it can be used to produce energy. Eating six servings of whole grains provides roughly 50 to 100 percent of our daily chromium needs.

Copper. As a critical part of a number of body enzymes, copper plays a role in energy production, connective tissue formation, and iron metabolism, as well as brain and nervous system function. Six servings of whole grains each day provide about half of our total copper needs. Quinoa and amaranth have about five to eight times more copper than true grains.

Iron. As an essential component of hundreds of proteins and enzymes, iron is necessary for oxygen transport and storage, electron transport, energy metabolism, and DNA synthesis. Whole grains provide a significant contribution to overall iron intake. Six servings a day provide about 6 mg of iron or about 20 to 40 percent of recommended intakes for most vegetarian adults. Quinoa and amaranth contain about four to six times more iron than true grains.

Magnesium. Magnesium is necessary in more than three hundred essential metabolic reactions, including energy production; synthesis of DNA, RNA, and glutathione (a potent antioxidant); and transport of ions such as potassium and calcium across cell membranes. It also is an integral part of the structure of bones, cell membranes, and chromosomes. Whole grains are an important source of magnesium, and six servings provide approximately one-half of our daily requirements.

Manganese. Manganese is a constituent of some enzymes and an activator of others. It serves as an antioxidant, protecting the mitochondria of cells, which are highly susceptible to oxidative damage. Manganese also is important in the formation of healthy bones, cartilage, and collagen. Six servings of whole grains give us all the manganese we need for the day.

Potassium. Both an essential mineral and an electrolyte, potassium is indispensable to every cell in our body. It is the most prevalent positively charged ion in the fluid of our cells and is critical for nerve impulse transmission, muscle contractions, and every beat of our heart. Potassium also is required for the activity of certain enzymes that are important to carbohydrate metabolism. When we think of potassium, bananas and perhaps potatoes or other vegetables and fruits generally spring to mind. Few people would imagine that whole grains are significant contributors to our potassium intake, with six servings providing about 30 percent of our daily needs.

Selenium. Selenium is required for the function of at least eleven enzymes, also known as selenoproteins. Most of these function as powerful antioxidants, reducing potentially damaging free radicals. One selenoprotein activates our thyroid hormones, making selenium essential for normal growth and development. Another selenoprotein plays a role in muscle metabolism. The selenium content of foods varies considerably, depending on the selenium content of the soil. The richest known plant source of selenium is Brazil nuts; a single nut contains approximately 110 micrograms, approximately double our daily requirement. Other rich sources include nuts, seeds, and grains. Six servings of whole grains provide about 90 percent of our daily selenium needs. Vegetables and fruits generally contribute little selenium.

Zinc. The functions of zinc in the human body are numerous and varied. Zinc plays central roles in growth and development, our immune response, neurological function, and reproduction. Nearly one hundred different enzymes are dependent on zinc for their function. Whole grains can contribute significantly to our overall zinc intake, as six servings provide 30 to 45 percent of the recommended daily amount. (See figure 5.1, page 125.) Quinoa and amaranth provide about three to six times more zinc than true grains.

Other protective components

In addition to providing energy-giving nutrients, vitamins, and minerals, whole grains also contain appreciable amounts of fiber, phytochemicals, and plant sterols. While not currently considered nutrients, these valuable components are found exclusively in plants.

Fiber. Required for the healthy functioning of the digestive system, fiber also helps to keep blood lipids and blood sugar under control. (For more on fiber, see pages 129 to 133.) Whole grains are an important source of fiber—six servings provide about 12 to 20 grams, or about one-third to one-half of the 30 to 50 grams recommended.

Phytochemicals. As with all plant foods, whole grains provide a unique mix of phytochemicals, which perform a remarkable array of protective activities. The phytochemicals most plentiful in grains include phenolic acids such as ferulic acid, p-coumaric acid, and caffeic acids (which have antioxidant and anticancer activity); lignans (phytoestrogens that may reduce the risk of estrogen-related cancers); and tocotrienols (forms of vitamin E with antioxidant activity).

Plant sterols. Another important group of health protectors in grains are plant sterols or phytosterols. These compounds are similar to cholesterol in structure, but they have remarkably different effects on the body. Plant sterols appear to compete with dietary cholesterol, reducing its absorption from the gut. Studies suggest that plant sterols can reduce our blood cholesterol levels; improve blood sugar control; inhibit breast, prostate, and colon cancer cell growth; and reduce inflammation.

The Great Grain Robbery

If grains are such marvels of rich and diverse nutrients, why have they been so viciously maligned? The sad truth is that food manufacturers do something that defies logic: they generally refine grains, which removes the two most nutrition-packed parts—the bran and germ. What is left is the endosperm, otherwise known as starch. To make matters worse, the value of grains often is undermined further by the addition of hydrogenated fats, sugar, and salt. Thus transformed, grains shift from being health promoters to potentially damaging foods. Figure 5.1 helps to quantify the magnitude of this nutritional loss.

As you can see, the losses (gray area) are staggering. Gone are approximately 95 percent of the phytochemicals, 80 percent of the fiber, and 70 percent of the vitamins and minerals. Sometimes several nutrients are added back to refined flour and the breads, cereals, and other foods made from it in an effort to prevent nutritional deficiency diseases. This process is called *enrichment*, and the laws regarding this practice vary tremendously from country to country. In the United States, all refined grains must be enriched with thiamin, riboflavin, niacin, and iron. In addition, as of January 1, 1998, all manufacturers are required to add from 0.43 mg to 1.4 mg of folic acid per pound of refined white flour, bread, rolls and buns, farina, corn grits, cornmeal, rice, and noodle products. It is estimated that this contributes about 100 micrograms (mcg) of folic acid to the average daily diet. While these regulations help compensate for a small portion of the nutrient losses shown in figure 5.1, they are a drop in the bucket when compared to the wide array of vitamins, minerals, fiber, and phytochemicals originally present in the whole grain.

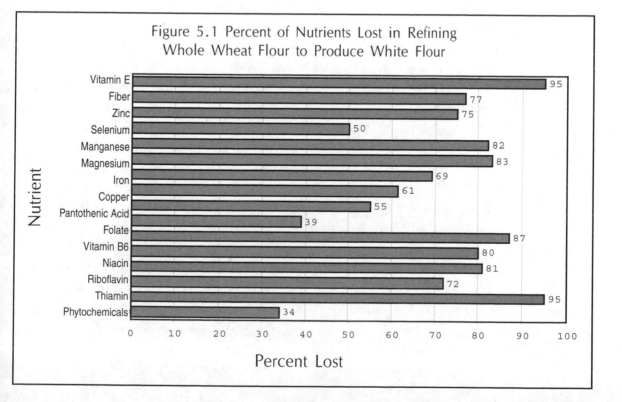

Figure 5.1 Percent of Nutrients Lost in Refining Whole Wheat Flour to Produce White Flour

Unfortunately, close to 95 percent of all grains in the American diet are refined, which means that a scant 5 percent of the grains eaten are whole. These refined grains (usually in the form of white flour) are used to produce many favorite foods: bread, pasta, cereals, crackers, pretzels, cookies, and other baked goods. There is substantial evidence to suggest that this reliance on refined grains as a dietary staple has significant negative repercussions on our health.

DO WHOLE GRAINS PROVIDE PROTECTION AGAINST DISEASE?

The evidence that whole grains provide protection against ailments such as heart disease, type 2 diabetes, and certain cancers is hard to ignore. In fact, it is so strong that recommendations to increase whole grain consumption have become a standard part of health recommendations from governments and health organizations around the world. The Iowa Women's Health Study showed that women who increased their consumption of whole grains reduced their risk of death from all health-related causes. Let's consider the evidence as it currently stands in relation to heart disease, cancer, and type 2 diabetes.

Heart Disease

The evidence linking our intake of whole grains with reduced rates of heart disease is very strong. Eating higher amounts reduces our blood cholesterol and blood pressure levels. While experts are not certain how whole grains work their magic, the presence of phytochemicals, fiber, plant sterols, and vitamin E are thought to be key. Some of the most convincing data are provided in the following studies:

➤ The Nurses' Health Study, which observed the diets of close to 70,000 women, found that those who ate the most whole grains reduced their risk of disease by 23 percent compared with those who ate the least. The fiber in grains was found to be even more protective than the fiber from other foods. For every 5 gram increase in cereal fiber (the amount in a bowl of multigrain cereal), the risk of heart disease dropped by 37 percent.

➤ The Iowa Women's Health Study, which examined the diets of nearly 35,000 women, also showed that eating whole grains reduced the risk of heart disease. This study suggested that components of grains other than fiber may be responsible for these protective benefits.

➤ The Health Professionals Study, which involved almost 44,000 men, found that those eating the highest amounts of fiber (an average of 29 grams per day) had a 41 percent lower risk of heart attacks compared with men eating the lowest amounts (an average of 12 grams per day). The fiber from grains appeared to be even more protective than the fiber from vegetables and fruits.

➤ In a Finnish study, which assessed the diets of 22,000 men, those eating approximately 35 grams of fiber a day (mostly from whole grain rye bread) enjoyed a 31 percent lower risk of heart disease compared with those eating only 16 grams of fiber a day.

➤ A Korean study of seventy-six men with heart disease examined the effects of switching from white rice to whole grains and powdered legumes for a period of sixteen weeks. Significant beneficial effects on blood sugar, insulin secretion, and homocysteine levels were noted, along with less free-radical damage to body fats.

Cancer

There is solid evidence that eating a high proportion of whole grains can protect us from cancer. Experts speculate that these protective effects may be due to the phytochemicals and antioxidants they contain, both of which reduce free-radical damage to body tissues and DNA. Fiber also protects against colorectal cancer. Two large reviews have confirmed this beneficial effect.

➤ One large report reviewed forty different studies that looked at intakes of whole grains and cancer risk. On average there was a 34 percent risk reduction for those eating the highest amount of whole grains compared with those eating the smallest amount. These benefits were confirmed in over 95 percent of the studies examined.

➤ A second large review showed that a high intake of whole grains reduced the risk of cancer in almost every part of the body. Those eating the most whole grains cut their risk of cancer of the upper digestive tract by 70 to 80 percent, and of the stomach, colon, and gallbladder by 50 percent, compared to those eating the fewest whole grains.

How dangerous is acrylamide in grains?

Acrylamide is a chemical used in the manufacture of plastics. It is a known carcinogen (cancer-causing substance) that produces nerve damage in animals. It was first discovered in certain foods in a Swedish study in April 2002. Researchers discovered that acrylamide is formed when starch-containing foods such as rice, potatoes, and bread are heated. Higher temperatures seem to further increase their formation. Following the release of this study, the World

Health Organization (WHO) and the United Nations Food and Agriculture Organization (FAO) assembled a panel of experts to consult on the implications of acrylamide in food. The experts agreed that most people's intake of acrylamide is likely to be even higher than the carcinogenic aromatic hydrocarbons that form in meat when it is cooked at high temperatures. Clearly this is cause for concern.

At this point, we have more questions than answers about acrylamide. We don't know how much acrylamide it takes to cause cancer in humans. We don't even know what fraction of acrylamide in the body actually comes from starch-based foods. Other foods and environmental contaminants such as cigarette smoke may also increase exposure. We have known for some time that high-temperature cooking can create damaging by-products, for example, in grilled meats and deep-fried foods. We now are seeing that the effects of high-temperature cooking may extend to other products that were thought to be safe. While we don't really know enough to make specific recommendations, it makes sense to practice moderation when consuming starchy foods that have been cooked at high temperatures. In practical terms, this means eating fewer highly processed foods, such as French fries, potato chips, and doughnuts.

Type 2 Diabetes

Whole grains have more favorable effects on blood sugar and insulin response than refined grains. There are important components in whole grains that ward off diabetes, including fiber, phytochemicals, and trace minerals such as chromium, magnesium, and zinc. Some of the most compelling studies are described below.

➤ In a study of close to 3,000 middle-aged adults, whole grains were associated with improved insulin sensitivity. Insulin, the body's key blood sugar-regulating hormone, tends to be present in the bloodstream in greater amounts in those who are at risk for type 2 diabetes. People who were overweight or obese had the highest insulin levels and consumed the least whole grain foods.

➤ The Health Professionals Follow-Up Study, which looked at 43,000 men, found that the risk of developing type 2 diabetes was 42 percent lower in those consuming the highest amounts of whole grains compared with those consuming the least. This benefit appears to be linked with the cereal fiber and magnesium in whole grains.

➤ In a six-year U.S. study of over 65,000 healthy people, 915 cases of type 2 diabetes were reported. The researchers found that diets with a high glycemic index and glycemic load increased the risk of diabetes, while those high in cereal fiber reduced the risk. (Glycemic index is a measure of how much a food affects blood sugar. The higher the glycemic index, the greater the effect. Glycemic load takes into account not only the glycemic index but the amount of carbohydrates eaten as well.) The combination of high glycemic load and low cereal fiber intake made things even worse, increasing the risk of diabetes by two and one-half times. The researchers concluded that grains should be eaten in a "minimally refined form" to reduce the risk of diabetes.

➤ In a small, controlled experiment with eleven participants, researchers compared insulin sensitivity using similar diets (55 percent carbohydrate and 30 percent fat, with six to ten servings per day of breakfast cereal, bread, rice, pasta, muffins, cookies, and snacks). Half of the participants received whole grain products and the other half received refined products. After six weeks the diets were reversed, so each person received both diets at different periods of time. While the participants were on the whole grain diet, their fasting insulin levels were 10 percent lower and their insulin sensitivity improved.

FIBER FUNDAMENTALS

Whole grains contribute more dietary fiber than any other group of foods. Fiber is the part of plants that we cannot digest. All plant foods contain fiber, as it gives plants their structure. In contrast, animals get their structure from bones and are fiber free. Fiber is often divided into two categories based on whether or not it dissolves in water.

Structural fibers—such as celluloses, some hemicelluloses, and lignins—are *insoluble*. Wheat bran is an example of a food rich in insoluble fiber. When mixed with water, wheat bran absorbs the water but does not dissolve or become gluey. Almost all whole plant foods are good sources of insoluble fiber.

Gel-forming fibers—such as pectins, gums, and mucilages—are *soluble*. Oat bran is a rich source of soluble fiber. When mixed with water, it becomes sticky. Other good sources of soluble fiber are beans, peas, several fruits (such as canned plums), barley, some vegetables (such as okra), flaxseeds, and psyllium (used in some cereals and bulk fiber laxatives). Most plant foods contain a mixture of insoluble and soluble fiber; though generally two-thirds to three-quarters of the total fiber is insoluble.

Fiber Functions

Fiber provides a host of benefits to health. The most notable are listed below.

➤ *It keeps our gastrointestinal system clean and healthy.* Fiber, especially insoluble fiber, adds bulk to stool, ensuring that foods pass quickly and easily through our intestinal tract. This helps to protect us against diverticular disease, constipation, hemorrhoids, and anal fissures. It may also provide protection from colorectal cancers, duodenal ulcers, gallstones, and irritable bowel diseases.

➤ *It helps to control blood cholesterol, triglyceride, and blood sugar levels.* Soluble fiber is mainly responsible for these benefits. The most effective types of soluble fiber are those that are stickiest, as they help to remove bile acids that digest fat. Soluble fiber coats the gut's lining, causing the stomach to empty more gradually. As a result, it can slow the rate that sugar is absorbed into the bloodstream and may reduce the need for insulin. Soluble fiber is thought to improve blood sugar control in people with diabetes and reduce the risk of heart disease.

➤ *It increases satiety or feelings of fullness after eating.* Fiber is bulky and makes us feel full, which can help us control our total food intake. As a result, high-fiber diets are linked to more healthful body weights.

Recommended and Actual Fiber Intakes

Unfortunately, the majority of Americans eat far too little fiber to enjoy these tremendous health benefits; most average about 15 grams per day. The World Health Organization recommends that we include 15 to 22 grams of fiber per day per 1,000 calories. For those who eat between 2,000 and 2,500 calories a day, this works out to about 30 to 50 grams of fiber. An upper limit of 54 grams per day is recommended for adults. It is interesting to note that lacto-ovo vegetarians, on average, consume approximately 30 to 40 grams of fiber a day, and vegans about 40 to 50 grams a day. Of course, the amount of fiber in any diet depends on the way the diet is constructed. Eating patterns rich in legumes, whole grains, and high-fiber vegetables and fruits will be far higher in fiber than those built more on refined foods.

This is well illustrated by the menus on pages 70 to 73. (See table 5.1 for fiber content of each menu.) In the nonvegetarian menu, the fiber content is slightly higher than the average intake of 15 grams. Almost two-thirds of the fiber in this

TABLE 5.1	FIBER IN 2,000-CALORIE MENUS
1 Nonvegetarian, page 70	19 g
2 Lacto-Ovo Vegetarian, page 71	24 g
3 Lacto-Ovo Vegetarian with More Legumes, page 72	55 g
4 Vegan, page 73	42 g

menu comes from vegetables and fruit (peas, potatoes, carrots, and apple), while an additional 10 percent comes from the slice of whole wheat bread. The first lacto-ovo vegetarian menu (Menu 2) is lower in fiber than typical lacto-ovo vegetarian diets because more processed foods are eaten. In this menu, 40 percent of the fiber comes from whole grains, while about one-third comes from fruits and vegetables. The second lacto-ovo menu (Menu 3) contains more than double the fiber of the previous menu. This menu contains more whole foods, including legumes, which are especially high in fiber. In this menu, about one-third of the fiber comes from legumes, one-third from whole grains, and the final one-third from vegetables and fruits. In the vegan menu (Menu 4), the total fiber is slightly lower than the legume-rich lacto-ovo menu, because a greater proportion of the legumes used are in the form of tofu and soymilk, and the processing of these foods removes much of the fiber. About 40 percent of the fiber comes from whole grains, one-third from vegetables and fruits, and only about 10 percent from legumes.

What Are Our Best Sources of Fiber?

The richest sources of fiber in the plant kingdom are legumes, the coarse part of grains, dried fruits, berries, and other fruits and vegetables. Table 5.2 provides a list of the fiber content of various foods.

Can Too Much Fiber Be Harmful?

Yes, it is possible to get too much of a good thing! Too much fiber can reduce the absorption of certain minerals, such as calcium, iron, and zinc. Yet when compared to refined foods, high-fiber whole foods provide enough extra minerals to more than compensate for any losses incurred. The upper limit of 54 grams a day suggested by the World Health Organization is based on the maintenance of mineral balance. When fiber does bind minerals, a significant proportion is freed by the action of bacteria in the large bowel. Short-chain fatty acids (also products of fermentation) help to facilitate their absorption from the large bowel. As a general rule, eating a wide variety of whole plant foods will not result in excessive intakes of fiber. It is important to note, however, that problems with mineral absorption can occur if concentrated fiber foods, such as wheat bran or fiber supplements, are added to a plant-based diet already rich in fiber. While these fiber boosters can be helpful to people eating low-fiber, animal-centered diets, they are both unnecessary and potentially damaging to those eating high-fiber, plant-based diets.

TABLE 5.2	FIBER IN SELECTED FOODS

Ultra High-Fiber foods (2 to 20 g)

Most legumes, green peas
High-fiber bran cereals (e.g., All Bran, Bran Buds with Psyllium), ½ cup (125 ml)

Very High-Fiber foods (8 to 11 g)

Lima beans, soybeans, black-eyed peas	Pea soup
Grains (bulgur, buckwheat groats)	Cereals (Raisin Bran and other bran-enriched cereals)
Dried fruits (4 figs or pears, 7 peaches, 20 apricots)	Berries (raspberries, blackberries)

High-Fiber Foods (5 to 7 g)

Grains (barley, cornmeal, whole wheat pasta, oat bran)	Potatoes, regular or sweet, 1 medium, baked
Cereal (whole grain, e.g., Shredded Wheat)	Artichoke, 1 medium
Cereal (Grape Nuts, granola), ½ cup (125 ml)	Berries (strawberries, blueberries), fresh
Bread, high-fiber whole grain, 2 slices	Fruit (papayas, Asian pears, avocado), 1 medium
Vegetables, (broccoli, Brussels sprouts, squash, eggplant, okra, dark greens, parsnips, carrots)	Flaxseeds, ground, 2 tbsp. (30 ml)

Moderate-Fiber Foods (2 to 4 g)

Grains (oats, millet, brown rice)	Bread, whole grain, 2 slices (read label)
Pasta, white	Fruit, most, 1 medium, 2 small, or 1 cup (250 ml)
Vegetables (cabbage, cauliflower, green beans, asparagus, turnips, mushrooms, peppers, leeks, celery), 1 cup (250 ml) cooked; 1 to 2 cups (250 to 500 ml) raw	Nuts and seeds, most, $1/4$ cup (60 ml)
	Popcorn, 3 cups (750 ml)

Low-Fiber Foods (1 g or less)

Refined grains (white rice, Cream of Wheat cereal)	Fruits (melon)
White bread, two slices	Fruit juice, all varieties
Baked white flour products (crackers, cookies, cakes, pastries, etc.), 1 serving.	Vegetables (lettuce, iceberg or Bibb, cabbage), raw
Cereals (Cornflakes, Rice Krispies, and other refined grain cereals—read labels)	Potato chips, 1 oz (28.4 g)

Fiber-Free Foods (zero fiber)

Meat, poultry, fish	Milk, cheese, ice cream, and other dairy products
Eggs	Fats and oils

The amount of fiber is rounded to the nearest gram.
All grains and legumes are cooked; all serving sizes are 1 cup (250 ml) unless otherwise noted.

Won't Eating This Much Fiber Cause a Lot of Gas?

Gas production is a normal, healthy function of our intestines. It is the result of bacteria in the large intestine utilizing undigested carbohydrates (fiber) and releasing their by-products (hydrogen, carbon dioxide, methane, water, and short–chain fatty acids). It may come as a surprise that this process can protect the colon against damage. However, excessive gas production can create bloating and painful cramping unless, of course, we choose to pass the gas and risk the social consequences.

Fortunately, there are a number of steps you can take to live happily with a high-fiber diet. There are two distinct causes of gas production: fermentation of carbohydrates that reach the large intestine and swallowing of air. You can reduce the amount of air you swallow by eating more slowly, avoiding carbonated beverages and beer, and not chewing gum or sucking on candy. If you wear dentures, make sure they fit properly so you chew more thoroughly. As for reducing the fermentation of carbohydrates, here are a few simple tips:

✓ Increase your intake of high-fiber foods gradually so your gastrointestinal system has time to adapt.

✓ Eat beans and other fibrous foods regularly. This will encourage the growth of bacteria that are more efficient at completely digesting bean sugars, thereby reducing gas production.

✓ Moderate your intake of foods that are particularly problematic, especially at first. Among the worst offenders are the oligosaccharides (raffinose and stachyose), which are found in beans, and vegetables in the cabbage family.

✓ Watch for combinations that make gas worse. For instance, some people avoid eating sugar or fruits along with foods that are digested more slowly.

✓ Try lentils, split peas, or other small legumes rather than larger beans, which seem to cause more problems.

✓ Don't overeat. Overeating increases the amount of food that ends up undigested in the colon.

✓ Take enzymes designed to break down the undigestible carbohydrates before they reach the colon.

RECOMMENDED AND ACTUAL INTAKES OF GRAINS

Recommended Intakes

The U.S. Food Guide Pyramid recommends that six to eleven servings of grains be eaten each day. The *Dietary Guidelines for Americans* advocates that several of these servings should be whole grains. It also suggests that a variety of grains be selected, such as whole wheat, brown rice, oats, whole corn, and barley. Consumers are advised to select grain products with little or no added fats and sugars.

Actual Intakes

Food consumption surveys suggest that North Americans eat five to seven servings of grains a day, with slightly lower intakes in Canada than in the United States. A mere 5 percent of the grains eaten are whole grains, primarily in the form of breakfast cereals. Only 13 percent of North Americans consume one or more servings of whole grains each day. There is some evidence that vegetarians consume a greater proportion of whole grains or grains that have been minimally processed.

GREAT GAINS IN GRAINS: PRACTICAL GUIDELINES

Increasing your intake of whole grains is a valuable step toward a healthier diet. The following practical suggestions will help make great grains a natural part of your day.

Replace refined grains with whole grains. Begin by taking an inventory of your grain habits. What grains and grain products do you eat at breakfast, lunch, dinner, and between meals? How many of these foods are refined grains and how many are whole grains? Decide which of the refined grains you would be willing to replace with whole grains. To start, at least half of all the grain products you choose should be whole grains. For example, if you eat an average of eight grain servings a day (see the Guide to Daily Food Choices, page 194, for serving sizes), *at least* four of these should be whole grains. Some people are willing to eat whole grain breakfast cereals and whole grain breads but prefer refined pasta and white rice. Others are happy to eat brown rice and kamut pasta but couldn't bear to give up their crispy rice cereal and poppy seed bagels. The choice is entirely yours. In time, you can work your way up to the point where all, or almost all, of your grain intake is whole grains.

Increase consumption of intact or minimally processed whole grains. Not all whole grains are created equal. The following list places whole grain foods into one of five categories from the very best (least processed) to the least desirable (most processed) choices. The top category is awarded a five-star rating, while the lowest category receives a single star. Attempt to gradually shift your selections to the most nutritious foods.

★★★★★   **Best choices**. The best possible way to eat your grains is intact—that is, without removing a thing. Whole grains such as brown rice, barley, millet, kamut, wheat or spelt berries, oat groats, and quinoa can be cooked as a breakfast cereal (see the recipes for Basic Whole Grain Cereal and Your

Very Own Whole Grain Cereal on pages 312 and 313); used in casseroles, soups, and stews (see the recipe for African Stew on page 343); or as pilafs (see page 334). Instructions for cooking grains start on page 332. Many grains can be sprouted or soaked. (Raw food cookbooks provide excellent recipes and ideas for using uncooked grains.)

★★★★   **Great choices.** Other great choices are grains that have been "minimally processed," such as those that are cut, rolled, or stone-ground, with little or nothing added or removed. These methods of processing do little damage to the grain. Examples include rolled oats (see the recipe for Marvelous Morning Muesli on page 311), cracked wheat, mixed-grain hot cereals, muesli, sprouted wheat breads, manna bread, and heavy German rye breads with whole seeds.

★★★   **Good choices.** Whole grains that are more highly processed still can be good choices. The damage caused by grinding (as in making stone-ground whole wheat flour) is only slightly higher than for rolling or cutting. A little more damage occurs with flaking (as in making flaked cereals), although much of the original value can be retained. To identify foods made with whole wheat, look for "whole wheat flour" as the first ingredient, rather than "wheat flour" or "unbleached wheat flour," both of which are refined flours. Whole grain products (for example, pancakes, muffins, and other prepared items made with whole grain flours), may have healthful additions, such as nuts, seeds, nut butters, dried fruits, and small amounts of nonhydrogenated oils or sweeteners. (See the recipes for Muscle Muffins on page 348, Banana-Walnut Pancakes on page 309, Lemon Teasecake on page 354, and Nutty Date Cookies on page 350.) Examples of good choices are whole wheat or whole grain breads, whole rye crispbreads, flaked whole grain cereals, shredded wheat and whole wheat, spelt, kamut, brown rice, or quinoa pasta.

★★   **Fair choices.** These include whole grain products that have undergone considerable processing, products with higher amounts of fat and sugar added, and those with small amounts of hydrogenated fats. Products that contain a portion of whole grain flour would also qualify as fair choices. Examples of fair choices include most whole grain cookies, cakes, and baked treats, whole grain breads containing hydrogenated fats, 50/50 breads and pastas (half white flour, half whole wheat flour), and puffed cereals. (See the recipes for German Chocolate Cake and Chocolate Mint Nut Bars on pages 356 and 352.)

✳   **Less desirable choices**. Among the whole grain products, the poorest choices are those with large amounts of potentially harmful additions, such as hydrogenated fats and sugar. Examples are whole grain crackers made with hydrogenated vegetable oil, whole grain pie crust made with shortening, whole wheat cinnamon buns loaded with butter and sugar, and deep-fried grain or corn chips.

For scientific references for this chapter, go to
http://www.nutrispeak.com/bvreferences.htm

Chapter 6

PERFECT PROTECTORS

VEGETABLES AND FRUITS

Getting kids to eat their vegetables and fruits is a part of every parent's job description. Moms and dads don't need to go to school to learn how to do this; the ability comes from a sort of divine intervention with the birth of their first child. The words "Eat your vegetables" naturally flow off parents' lips at dinner tables everywhere. It is quite beautiful and perhaps one way the universe is trying to preserve our species.

Even though vegetables and fruits have been recognized for centuries as extraordinarily healthful, their status has been growing progressively stronger. Scientists are learning more about the specific components these foods contain, how they function in our bodies, and the potential of their protective effects.

WHAT SEPARATES VEGETABLES FROM FRUITS?

Have you ever heard that tomatoes are actually a fruit, not a vegetable? While this is true botanically, legally in the United States it is not. In 1893 there was a conflict about the true nature of tomatoes, and a U.S. Supreme Court judge ruled that the tomato is legally a vegetable. The justification for this decision was that fruits tend to be relatively sweet and are typically served as a dessert, while vegetables tend to be savory and are typically eaten with the main course. Most of us continue to use the "savory versus sweet" or "main course versus dessert" method to distinguish vegetables from fruits. Webster's *New World Dictionary* (second edition) concurs. It defines a vegetable as a plant that is eaten whole or in part, raw or cooked, generally with an entrée or in a salad but not as a dessert. Botanists look at this a little differently. They define a fruit as the matured ovary of a flower containing the seed. What we eat is the fleshy part surrounding the seed or seeds. Almost any vegetable that contains seeds is botanically a fruit, including tomatoes, okra, squash, cucumbers, beans, pea pods, peppers, and eggplant. A "botanical" vegetable includes the edible "non-fruit" part of a plant. True vegetables include roots, tubers, leaves and leafy heads, immature flower clusters, stems, and bulbs. In the grand scheme of things, whether we call these foods vegetables or fruits matters far less than whether or not we eat them. For practical purposes, in this book we will stick with the gastronomical definitions of vegetables and fruits rather than the botanical ones.

THE NUTRITIONAL VALUE OF VEGETABLES AND FRUITS

Vegetables and fruits provide people with a unique and marvellous complement of nutrients. In their natural state, it is hard to find fault with any of them. With the exception of a few, such as avocados and olives, vegetables and fruits are very low in fat. All are cholesterol free. Vegetables and fruits are outstanding sources of several vitamins and minerals, and they provide most of the vitamin C and the plant form of vitamin A in our diets. They also are our primary sources of folate and potassium. If that wasn't enough, vegetables and fruits come packaged with fiber and are the most concentrated sources of protective phytochemicals. With a few exceptions (such as potatoes), most vegetables are lower in calories and higher in protein and trace minerals than fruits. Compared to other foods, vegetables (and fruits to a lesser extent) have very high nutrient densities.

What Is Nutrient Density?

Nutrient density is the measure of nutrients in a food in relation to its calories. A food with high nutrient density is one that provides a lot of nutrients for a minimum number of calories. For simplicity, we often compare the nutrients per 100 calories of food. Vegetables (except tubers) are well known to be the most nutrient-dense foods in the diet. In other words, vegetables provide more nutrients per 100 calories than most other foods. When a food is particularly nutrient dense, it means that we can eat large portions of the food without getting a lot of calories. If we eat tiny portions, the nutrient contribution from the food will be relatively small. When it comes to vegetables, we'd be well advised to take a lesson from our raw-food friends and supersize our servings! For example, per 100 calories, romaine lettuce provides 257 mg of calcium, while 2 percent milk provides 243 mg of calcium. Thus, where calcium is concerned, romaine lettuce is more nutrient dense than 2 percent milk. However, 100 calories' worth of romaine lettuce amounts to 12.5 cups (3.125 L). By comparison, we would get 100 calories in only ⅖ cup (200 ml) of 2 percent milk.

In addition to comparing different types of foods, we can compare the nutrient density of a food that has been prepared in various ways. For example, a baked potato is more nutrient dense than French fries, and an apple is more nutrient dense than apple pie. Table 6.1 provides the nutrient densities of several vegetables and fruits, along with a range of other foods, including prepared

| TABLE 6.1 | NUTRIENT DENSITY OF SELECTED FOODS |

Food	Nutrient Density Nutrients per 100 Calories							Amount of Food Equivalent to 100 Calories
	Protein (g)	Iron (mg)	Calcium (mg)	Potassium (mg)	Vitamin A (RAE*)	Vitamin C (mg)	Folate (mcg)	
Vegetables								
Broccoli, raw	10.4	3	169	1,144	271	328	250	4 cups (1 L), chopped
Kale, raw	6.6	3.4	270	900	894	241	58.2	3 cups (750 ml), chopped
Romaine lettuce	12	7.8	270	2,030	910	168	952	12.5 cups (3.125 L), chopped
Mushrooms, cooked	8.1	6.5	22	1,330	0	15	66	2.4 cups (600 ml), sliced
Sweet potato, baked	0.9	0.2	14	177	556	126	12	1 small (3.5 oz./100 g)
White potato, baked	2.2	0.7	11	578	1	13.3	40	1 small (3.5 oz./100 g)
French fries	1.2	0.2	4	199	0	3	11	1 oz. (28.4 g) (⅓ small order)
Fruits								
Apple	0.3	0.3	12	196	5	9.6	5	1 large (6 oz./170 g)
Apple pie	0.8	0.2	5	28	12	1	2	1/24 of pie
Orange	2	0.2	85	382	21	112	63	2 small
Watermelon	2	0.5	25	364	57	31	6	2 cups (500 ml), diced
Blueberries	1.2	0.3	11	159	9	23	10	1¼ cups (310 ml)
Other Foods								
Oatmeal	4.2	1.1	13	92	0	0	7	¾ cup (185 ml)
Navy beans	6.1	1.7	48	254	0	1	97	⅓ cup (85 ml)
Pumpkin seeds	6.4	2.9	9	156	4	0	11	4 tsp. (20 ml)
Eggs	8	0.8	33	82	127	0	31	2 small or 1 jumbo
Milk, 2%	6.6	0.1	243	308	112	0	10	¾ cup (185 ml)
Fish, cod, baked	21	0.5	13	232	13	1	8	3.5 oz. (100 g)
Hamburger, lean	10.5	1.1	8.5	148	0	0	3	1.5 oz. (43 g)

RAE = retinol activity equivalency

foods and animal products. As you can see, unprocessed vegetables and fruits have remarkable nutrient densities. Dark green vegetables are the most nutrient dense of all.

Key Vitamins in Vegetables and Fruits

Vegetables and fruits contain almost every vitamin we need, with two exceptions: vitamins B_{12} and D. While it is possible to get a tiny amount of vitamin B_{12} (from dirt clinging to vegetables) and some vitamin D (from certain seaweeds and mushrooms), vegetables and fruits are not reliable sources of these nutrients. The vitamins that vegetables and fruits are most noted for are vitamin A (present as provitamin A carotenoids), vitamin C, vitamin K, and folate (a B vitamin). Let's consider each of these nutrients and the important role vegetables and fruits play in supplying them.

Vitamin A

Vitamin A is widely recognized as the "vision vitamin." A deficiency of this vitamin is the leading cause of blindness in children throughout the world. Few people are aware that vitamin A is important for much more than good eyesight. It helps us fight off infection and supports reproduction, growth, and the production of red blood cells and many proteins.

Vitamin A is an umbrella term for two main categories of compounds. The first is preformed vitamin A. This is the active form of vitamin A. It is present in animal products, such as liver, fish, eggs, and dairy products, but is not found in plant foods. Preformed vitamin A has no antioxidant activity. The second category of vitamin A compounds is called provitamin A carotenoids. These are carotenoids that can be converted by the body into the active form of vitamin A. While plants make over six hundred different carotenoids, only about 10 percent of these can be converted to vitamin A. Brightly colored orange, yellow, and green fruits and vegetables, such as carrots, sweet potatoes, and dark greens, are the richest sources of provitamin A carotenoids. These components serve as important antioxidants for the body.

Measuring vitamin A activity from carotenoids. The way we measure the vitamin A activity from various carotenoids is by looking at their retinol activity equivalency (RAE). One microgram (mcg) of preformed vitamin A equals one mcg RAE. Provitamin A carotenoids are less easily absorbed than preformed vitamin A and must be converted to the active form of vitamin A by the body. Thus, we need greater amounts of beta-carotene and other carotenoids to provide the same vitamin A activity as preformed vitamin A. It takes 12 mcg of beta-carotene and about 24 mcg of other provitamin A carotenoids to make one microgram RAE. An older standard for measuring vitamin A is the international unit (IU). One IU equals 0.3 mcg of preformed vitamin A or RAE.

Recommended intakes. The recommended dietary allowance (RDA) for vitamin A is 700 mcg RAE a day for women and 900 mcg RAE a day for men. The upper limit (UL) that is advised for vitamin A is 3,000 mcg of preformed vitamin A per day. The upper limit has been set based on three primary adverse effects of excess vitamin A: liver damage, reduced bone mineral density, and birth defects in infants. While large amounts of provitamin A carotenoids (for example, from drinking quarts of carrot juice) can make your skin orange, it is not toxic and does not contribute to the damaging effects of excess preformed vitamin A.

Current intakes. The average intake of vitamin A ranges from 750 to 810 mcg RAE in men and 530 to 720 mcg RAE in women. In the general population, approximately 25 to 35 percent of this intake is from provitamin A carotenoids, while in vegetarians the proportion would be higher. In vegans, provitamin A carotenoids contribute all of the vitamin A unless vitamin A–fortified foods are used.

Meeting recommended intakes. By eating five to ten servings of vegetables and fruits each day, vegetarians and vegans can easily meet the RDA for vitamin A. Just one carrot provides enough provitamin A carotenoids to meet our daily needs. (For other good sources, see table 6.2.) It is wise to eat deep green, yellow, or orange vegetables or fruits for at least three of our servings of vegetables and fruits. While many people assume that our best sources of vitamin A are raw foods, it turns out that cooking can improve our absorption. We can further enhance our absorption of provitamin A carotenoids in vegetables and fruits by eating some fat with them or by pureeing or finely chopping them.

Vitamin A supplements. Vitamin supplements containing more than 3,000 mcg of preformed vitamin A are not recommended, as they exceed the upper limit for safety. Taken over several months or years, these high doses can cause a condition called hypervitaminosis A. (This is due only to excesses of preformed vitamin A; it cannot be caused by carotenoids.) Multivitamin-mineral supplements generally contain a mix of preformed vitamin A and provitamin A carotenoids; however, the amounts are almost always within a safe range.

Vitamin C

Vitamin C is most well-known as the vitamin that prevents scurvy, the scourge of the navy that sent countless sailors to the bottom of the ocean centuries ago when they were deprived of fresh produce for months on end. The name of one of the active forms of vitamin C, ascorbic acid, literally means "no scurvy." We need vitamin C in order to produce collagen, an important structural component of our blood vessels, tendons, ligaments, and bone. Vitamin C also helps us to fight infection. An effective antioxidant, vitamin C can protect proteins, fats, carbohydrates, DNA, and RNA from damage by free radicals. While most mammals can make their own vitamin C, humans cannot, so we must get it through our diet.

Current intakes. Average daily intakes of vitamin C from food are about 105 mg for men and 90 mg for women. Vegetarians consume about 150 mg of vitamin C per day; vegan intakes are higher still.

Recommended intakes. The RDA for vitamin C is 75 mg a day for women and 90 mg a day for men. This is considerably higher than the previous recommendation, which was 30 mg per day for women and 40 mg for men. A new, separate RDA for smokers also has been set at 35 mg per day above nonsmoker requirements (125 mg for men; 110 mg for women). The upper limit (UL) for vitamin C is 2 grams a day, based on adverse effects including diarrhea and other gastrointestinal disturbances.

Vitamin C sources. About 90 percent of our vitamin C comes from vegetables and fruits. Our richest sources include citrus fruits and other tropical fruits, some berries and melons, and several vegetables, including peppers, leafy greens, cruciferous vegetables (e.g., broccoli, cabbage, cauliflower), and potatoes. See table 6.2 for the vitamin C content of selected vegetables and fruits.

Vitamin K

Vitamin K gets its name from the word for coagulation as it is spelled in Denmark and Germany (*koagulation*). Once recognized only for its role in building proteins that help us coagulate and clot blood, vitamin K is now in the spotlight. Recent evidence suggests that it plays a key role in bone health by making the proteins needed for bone metabolism. Because recommended intakes are set mainly on the basis of healthy blood clotting, some experts believe that higher levels may be needed for optimal bone health.

Current intakes. Research suggests that average vitamin K intakes range from 80 to 120 mcg a day, although some studies have shown lower intakes of 70 to 80 mcg per day. While there is very little research on vitamin K intakes in vegetarians, there is some evidence that intakes are higher than in nonvegetarians.

Recommended intakes. The RDA for vitamin K is 90 mcg a day for women and 120 mcg for men. However, for bone health, we may need as much as 150 to 200 mcg a day.

Vitamin K sources. The most concentrated sources of vitamin K are green leafy vegetables. Some vegetable oils (soybean, cottonseed, and canola) and other vegetables and fruits also provide significant amounts, with lesser amounts distributed throughout the food supply. Early analyses overestimated the vitamin K content of foods, particularly of animal foods, such as liver, cheese, and eggs. (See table 6.2 for the vitamin K content of selected fruits and vegetales.) Now we know that these animal foods are poor sources of this nutrient.

Folate

The terms folic acid and folate refer to two different forms of the same vitamin, and the two words often are used interchangeably. Folate is the form of the vitamin that occurs naturally in foods. Folic acid, the more stable form of the vitamin, is used in vitamin supplements and fortified foods. Folate supports the metabolism of amino acids and the enzymes that are necessary for building cells and genetic material. It is most commonly recognized as the nutrient that helps prevent neural tube defects in unborn children (spina bifida and anencephaly). Insufficient folate can significantly increase our risk for heart disease, as deficiencies are linked to elevated levels of homocysteine (see page 26 for more information).

Measuring folate activity. When the current dietary recommended intakes (DRI) for folate were established, a new unit of measure was introduced called the dietary folate equivalent (DFE). With this measure, the differences in the availability of folate and folic acid from various sources are taken into consideration (see box at right).

Current intakes. The average intakes of folate were reported to be approximately 250 mcg a day for adults

---

CALCULATING FOLATE

One mcg of folate from food is equal to 1 mcg DFE. However, in fortified foods or supplements, the folic acid has a greater potency. For example:

➤ One mcg of folic acid in fortified foods or in a supplement taken with meals provides 1.7 mcg of DFE.

➤ One mcg of folic acid from a supplement taken on an empty stomach is equal to 2 mcg of DFE.

Thus, if you eat a food providing 100 mcg of folate, it would equal 100 mcg of DFE. On the other had, if you eat a fortified food providing 100 mcg of folic acid, it would equal 100 x 1.7 or 170 mcg of DFE.

prior the mandatory addition of folic acid to enriched grains in the U.S. However, it is estimated that intakes would be at least 80 to 100 mcg higher today for those consuming foods fortified with folic acid. Vegetarians consume about 25 to 50 percent more folate (from whole foods) than nonvegetarians, although total intakes may be comparable to that of nonvegetarians who use greater amounts of fortified foods.

Recommended intakes. The new RDA for folate is 400 mcg of DFE. This is approximately twice the earlier recommendation. During pregnancy, the RDA is 600 mcg of DFE. The upper limit (UL) for folate is 1,000 mcg of DFE

TABLE 6.2	VITAMINS AND MINERALS IN SELECTED VEGETABLES AND FRUITS					
Food/ Serving Size	Vitamin A (RAE)	Vitamin C (mg)	Vitamin K (mcg)	Folate (mcg)	Potassium (mg)	Magnesium (mg)
Vegetables						
Asparagus, cooked, 1/2 cup (125 ml)	24	10	80	131	144	9
Beets, cooked, 1/2 cup (125 ml)	1.7	3	1.2	68	259	20
Broccoli, cooked, 1/2 cup (125 ml)	54	58	113	39	228	19
Carrots, cooked, 1/2 cup (125 ml)	958	2	10	11	177	10
Cauliflower, cooked, 1/2 cup (125 ml)	1	27	20	27	88	6
Green beans, cooked, 1/2 cup (125 ml)	21	6	11	21	187	16
Kale, raw, 1 cup (250 ml)	298	80	547	19	300	23
Mushrooms, raw, 1 cup (250 ml)	0	2	0	8	259	7
Peas, cooked, 1/2 cup (125 ml)	24	12	4	50	217	31
Sweet potato, cooked, 1/2 cup (125 ml)	1,091	25	1	23	348	20
Potato (white), cooked, 1/2 cup (125 ml)	0	10	1	8	296	17
Romaine lettuce, raw, 1 cup (250 ml)	72	14	58	76	162	4
Spinach, raw, 1 cup (250 ml)	369	9	360	131	419	78
Winter squash, cooked, 1/2 cup (125 ml)	132	10	1	28	448	8
Fruits						
Apple, 1 medium	4	8	2	4	159	7
Avocado, 1 medium	62	16	125	7	1,204	78
Banana, 1 medium	5	11	0	22	467	34
Blueberries, 1/2 cup (125 ml)	3	9	6	4	65	4
Cantaloupe, 1/2 cup (125 ml)	126	33	0	13	241	9
Grapes, 1/2 cup (125 ml)	3	9	4	3	148	5
Kiwi, 1 medium	8	89	23	35	302	27
Orange, 1 medium	269	70	0	39	237	13
Peach, 1 medium	26	6	2	3	193	7
Pear, 1 medium	2	7	6	12	208	10
Strawberries, sliced, 1/2 cup (125 ml)	23	47	1	15	138	9
Watermelon, 1 wedge	51	27	0	6	332	31

Source: USDA nutrient database: <http://www.nal.usda.gov/fnic/foodcomp/index.html>

for adults. The reason for this relatively low UL is that excess folate intake may mask a vitamin B_{12} deficiency. (For more information, see page 179.)

Folate sources. The name folate comes from the word foliage, so it is not surprising that green leafy vegetables are among the richest sources. Other important sources of folate include citrus fruit juices, legumes, and vegetables other than leafy greens. Since 1998, all enriched cereal grains (e.g., enriched bread, pasta, flour, breakfast cereal, and rice) are required to be fortified with folate in the United States, thus these products are also important contributors to overall intake. (Table 6.2 provides the folate content of various vegetables and fruits.)

Key Minerals in Vegetables and Fruits

Vegetables and fruits are key sources of potassium and magnesium and can be important contributors to the intakes of most other minerals essential to human health, including calcium, iron, zinc, chromium, and copper. (For the potassium and magnesium content of various vegetables and fruits, see Table 6.2.)

Potassium

Potassium is an electrolyte—a charged particle capable of conducting electricity. It acts with sodium to keep the right amount of fluid inside and outside of cells and to pass nerve impulses to the brain. It also is necessary for muscle contraction, including every beat of the heart.

There is no specific RDA for potassium, although the estimated minimum requirement for adults is approximately 2,000 mg a day. Increasing intakes to 3,500 mg has been found to have beneficial effects on blood pressure.

When we think of potassium-rich foods, often the first one that comes to mind is bananas. While bananas do contain a lot of potassium, it's surprising that their fame is not shared with other fruits and vegetables, as there are many other notable sources, such as avocados. Although animal products do contribute some potassium to the diet, they are not big contributors for most people. Vegetarians seldom have problems meeting potassium needs.

Magnesium

Magnesium plays key roles in both the structure and function of the human body. It is necessary for strong bones and teeth (50 to 60 percent of the magnesium in our bodies is in our bones) and helps to convert food to usable energy. Magnesium is essential for building numerous enzymes and our genetic material, DNA and RNA. It also is needed to transport potassium and calcium across cell membranes. This is one busy mineral, so we need to ensure a plentiful supply.

The RDA for magnesium is 310 mg for women nineteen to thirty years of age, 320 mg a day for women over thirty, 400 milligrams for men nineteen to thirty years of age, and 420 milligrams for men over thirty. Green vegetables are a primary source, because the center of the chlorophyll molecule contains magnesium. Other vegetables, fruits, legumes, whole grains, nuts, and seeds also are good sources. Most of the magnesium in our diets comes from plant foods, although animal products do contribute lesser amounts. The best way to ensure magnesium needs are met is to eat plenty of whole plant foods, including at least five servings of vegetables and fruits each day. Vegetarians tend to have excellent magnesium intakes unless they rely too heavily on refined grains.

Other Beneficial Components: Phytochemicals

For many years, experts presumed that vegetables and fruits were healthful because of all the vitamins, minerals, and fiber they contained. Of course they were right, but only partly so. During the past few decades, scientists have discovered a new category of protective compounds loaded into each and every vegetable and fruit. Collectively, these compounds are called phytochemicals ("phyto" means "plant"). Phytochemicals regulate the growth of plants, defend against attacks by insects or fungi, and provide the plant's flavor, color, texture, and odor. While vegetables and fruits are the best sources for phytochemicals, other plant foods, such as grains and legumes, also contribute significantly to our total intakes. When we eat plants, these powerful little protectors go to work on our behalf.

The beneficial effects of phytochemicals are quite remarkable. Many phytochemicals are strong antioxidants, helping to quench destructive free radicals. Others have potent anticancer activity, blocking cell division and helping to rid our bodies of carcinogens. Phytochemicals work to protect us against heart disease and reduce cholesterol production, blood pressure, blood clot formation, and damage to blood vessel walls. Phytoestrogens or "plant estrogens" block the destructive action of the potent form of human estrogen. They do this either by competing with estrogen for locations to attach to the cells or by reducing the production of the potent form of estrogen while increasing the production of the less potent form. In this way, phytoestrogens possibly reduce the risk of osteoporosis and certain types of hormone-dependent cancers. Some phytochemicals have powerful anti-inflammatory activity; others are immune enhancing or prevent motion sickness; while still more work against viruses, bacteria, fungi, and yeasts.

Choosing a glorious, rainbow-hued assortment of whole plant foods is the secret to a phytochemical-rich diet. Among the most outstanding choices are dark leafy greens (kale, collards, and spinach), cruciferous vegetables (especially broccoli and broccoli sprouts), garlic, tomatoes, blueberries, and citrus fruits. Let's take a closer look at what makes these foods so protective.

Phytochemical superstars of the vegetable and plant kingdom

Blueberries. In a study by the U. S. Department of Agriculture's Center for Aging at Tufts University, the ability of over forty vegetables and fruits to quench free radicals (oxygen radical absorbance capacity or ORAC) was measured. Of all the foods, blueberries came out number one, ahead of the most revered dark green, leafy vegetables. Indeed, blueberries had five times the ORAC of most other fruits and vegetables. The primary active component in blueberries is a powerful antioxidant called anthocyanin, which is responsible for their deep blue color. (Other anthocyanin-rich foods are plums, deep purple grapes, and other berries.) Blueberries contain several other phenolic compounds, including flavonols and phenolic acids. In addition to their antioxidant activity, blueberries protect against urinary tract infections, improve "tired eyes," and may help reduce the effects of aging.

Citrus fruits. Oranges, grapefruits, lemons, and limes contain vitamin C, folic acid, and a wonderful array of phytochemicals. A single orange contains over 170 different types of phytochemicals (with thousands of copies of each), including 60 flavonoids, 40 limonoids, and 20 carotenoids. Flavonoids and carotenoids are strong antioxidants with significant anticancer and anti–cardiovascular disease activity, while limonoids help reduce our production of cholesterol and detoxify our systems.

Garlic. A king of the allium family, garlic is loaded with sulfur-containing compounds that give it its characteristic aroma. These unique compounds help to lower blood pressure, reduce the stickiness of blood cells, dilate blood vessels, and destroy cancer cells. They also stimulate the immune system and act against bacterial, fungal, and yeast infections. It is little wonder that 2,400 years ago Hippocrates used garlic to treat infections and pneumonia.

Kale. Competing against nineteen other veggies, kale was tops in phytochemical activity. Kale is rich in carotenoids such as lutein and zeaxanthin (antioxidants that protect the eyes), indoles, sulforaphane (anticarcinogens that help rid the body of carcinogens), and quercetins (anti-inflammatory agents).

Other dark greens such as spinach, collards, broccoli, and chard were also strong contenders.

Tomatoes. The superstar status of tomatoes is largely based on their exceptional content of lycopene, the carotenoid responsible for their red color. Some, but not all, red vegetables and fruits contain lycopene. (Red and pink grapefruit, watermelon, and guava are colored, in part, by lycopene, while red peppers and strawberries are not.) Lycopene has strong antioxidant properties, and several studies have suggested that it may protect against prostate cancer and slow the growth of prostate tumors. In addition, there is some compelling evidence that lycopene is a powerful protector against the development of heart disease. Cooking improves the absorption of lycopene, so eating tomatoes that are cooked (as in stewed tomatoes, tomato sauce, and tomato paste) provides us with considerably more lycopene than raw tomatoes.

Phytochemicals from pills

Some people think they can get all the phytochemicals they need by popping a pill containing a variety of concentrated phytochemicals. However, several studies have suggested that this practice could backfire. In some (but not all) cases, isolating individual phytochemicals has actually increased the risk of disease. It seems as though phytochemicals work synergistically with one another, and the collaborative action of two or more chemicals may be needed to produce beneficial effects. At this time, we just do not know enough about the complicated interactions of these dietary components to be confident about turning them into pills. Besides, whole vegetables and fruits come packaged with fiber, vitamins, minerals, plant sterols, and other protective components, and they are infinitely more pleasurable to consume!

VEGETABLES AND FRUITS FIGHT DISEASE

The evidence that vegetables and fruits protect us against disease is highly impressive and continually gaining ground. Those who eat the highest amounts of these foods seem to enjoy the greatest protection against cancer, heart disease, stroke, type 2 diabetes, obesity, osteoporosis, and gallbladder disease. Here are some of the more impressive findings.

Cancer. According to the World Cancer Research Fund and the American Institute for Cancer Research, if we eat five servings or more of a variety of vegetables and fruits, we will reduce our risk of cancer by at least 20 percent.

Heart disease. Data from the Nurses' Health Study and the Health Professionals Follow-Up Study (over 120,000 people in total) found that those who ate the most vegetables and fruit reduced their risk of coronary artery disease by 20 percent compared to those with the lowest intakes. For every serving of vegetables or fruits included in the daily diet, the risk of coronary artery disease was reduced by approximately 4 percent. Green leafy vegetables and vitamin C–rich fruits and vegetables appear to offer the greatest protection.

Stroke. Data from the Nurses' Health Study and the Health Professionals Follow-Up Study suggests that people who eat the most vegetables and fruits reduce their risk of stroke by 31 percent compared to those eating the least.

Type 2 diabetes. A large 1999 study showed that those eating the greatest amounts of vegetables were least likely to develop type 2 diabetes. Eating fruit also reduced risk, but to a lesser extent.

RECOMMENDED AND ACTUAL CONSUMPTION

The USDA's Food Guide Pyramid suggests that we eat five to nine servings of vegetables and fruits each day. The Vegetarian Food Guide (chapter 9, page 193) recommends five or more servings of vegetables and fruits each day. This advice is consistent with the recommendations of numerous other health organizations and governments. In the United States, Canada, and Australia, plus some countries in Europe, Asia, and Africa, a campaign called "Five A Day for Better Health" encourages consumers to eat at least five servings a day of fruits and vegetables. Many experts believe that increasing the minimum to seven or eight servings could bring further benefits. Most suggest at least three servings of vegetables and two servings of fruits.

Only one in four Americans meet these recommended intakes (27 percent of women and 19 percent of men). A U.S. study found the most frequently consumed vegetables and fruits to be iceberg lettuce, tomatoes, French fries, bananas, and orange juice. Intakes of dark green and cruciferous vegetables were quite dismal at 0.2 servings per day. Not surprisingly, vegetarians eat more vegetables and fruits than nonvegetarians. This is demonstrated in the menus on pages 70 to 73. Both the nonvegetarian menu (Menu 1) and the lacto-ovo vegetarian menu (Menu 2) provide five and one-half servings of vegetables and fruits. The lacto-ovo vegetarian menu with more legumes (Menu 3) contains eight servings of vegetables, while the vegan menu has ten servings. Consuming seven to ten servings of vegetables and fruits a day is typical for many vegetarians and vegans.

GETTING THE GOODS: GUIDELINES FOR EATING MORE VEGETABLES AND FRUITS

Think about how many vegetables and fruits you eat each day. Do you eat the minimum five servings? How about seven or more servings? Do you choose dark leafy greens, citrus fruits, berries, and other deeply colored produce daily? If you know you should be eating more vegetables and fruits, why aren't you? One common reason people give for failing to eat their veggies is that they take too much time to prepare. Some people are unfamiliar with many of the choices in the produce department, and the thought of preparing them may be overwhelming. Many complain that vegetables and fruits aren't as satisfying as a bowl of cereal, a sandwich, or a bag of chips, especially at snack time. Others say that fruits and vegetables are boring, tasteless, or expensive. Whatever challenges are limiting your intake, the following tips will help you sail past them, giving vegetables and fruits the celebrated position they deserve on your plate.

Make It Easy

✓ Prepare vegetables ahead of time. Wash, cut up, and store them in airtight plastic containers or bags for handy snacking. There are terrific produce storage bags on the market that help prolong the life of vegetables in your refrigerator.

✓ Prepare a huge salad, enough to last for up to five days, and store it in an airtight Tupperware-type container. This half hour of washing and chopping can be a pleasant event once or twice a week, especially if shared with family members or while listening to your favorite radio program.

✓ Keep a large marinated vegetable salad and a fruit salad in the refrigerator. This will make it very easy for everyone in the family to have instant access to fresh vegetables and fruits.

✓ Take advantage of the salad bars and deli counters at natural food stores and grocery stores. They offer ready-to-eat raw vegetables and fruit, as well as prepared salads made with fruits and vegetables.

✓ Look for precut and cleaned fruits and vegetables. Many grocery stores now carry prewashed, bagged salad greens and vegetable pieces, such as baby carrots, celery sticks, and broccoli and cauliflower florets. Some also offer packaged precut fruits, such as melons and pineapple.

✓ Keep canned and frozen fruits and vegetables on hand, and stock up on frozen, canned, and bottled juices, and dried fruits and vegetables.

Know Your Vegetables and Fruits

✓ Buy an unfamiliar vegetable or fruit at least once a month. Search out information about the new produce, such as where it originated, its historical uses, and its nutritional value. Check for suggested methods of preparation and good accompaniments. Share this new information with your family.

✓ Ask your local produce manager or the owner of your favorite ethnic store how to prepare or use a specific item that interests you.

✓ Take a cooking class that focuses on vegetables and fruits. Ethnic classes are a great option.

✓ Buy a few good vegetarian cookbooks. Purchase (or borrow from the library) a book that has pictures of the various plant foods available and a description of how to use them. An Internet search will also prove fruitful!

✓ Subscribe to an organic produce delivery service. You can arrange for a set list or a wide variety of vegetables and fruits. Many services will provide suggestions for how to use them.

✓ Order a menu item that includes a vegetable or fruit you have never tried.

Give Them Substance

✓ Serve cut-up vegetables with a hearty dip, such as hummus.

✓ Make a big batch of vegetable soup with beans and barley. Keep it handy for a quick lunch or satisfying snack. Freeze it in individual portions.

✓ Top salad with nuts, seeds, beans, and/or marinated tofu for a filling meal.

✓ Fill pita bread with a mix of lettuce, sprouts, grated carrots, and peanut sauce.

✓ Make vegetable and bean stews using a variety of different vegetables such as winter squash, greens, sweet potatoes, and corn.

✓ Be creative with stir-fries. Add cashews, tofu, or seitan (wheat gluten).

✓ Add grated carrots or zucchini to muffins, cookies, and other baked goods.

✓ Use fruits in smoothies with tofu or soymilk. You can easily get three or four fruit servings in a single smoothie.

✓ Make a big fruit salad and top it with granola and yogurt (soy or dairy).

✓ Use fruits as the key ingredient in desserts, such as fruit crumble, cakes, and muffins.

Think Economy

✓ While vegetables and fruits may seem expensive, they are a nutritional bargain. Compare the cost of 100 percent fruit juice with soda pop. While there is little difference in cost, there is a huge difference in nutrition.

✓ Buy straight from the farmer whenever you can. Frequent farmers' markets. Co-ops, organic delivery services, and produce stands offer excellent options. If you live near farming country, take advantage of it. Many farmers sell directly to the consumer, and some even allow you to pick produce, which can be great fun for family members of all ages.

✓ Keep an eye out for bargains. Every week there are great sales on produce. Stock up when you can.

✓ Buy in season. The prices are always more reasonable.

✓ Can or freeze produce when you get it in volume.

✓ Clip money-saving coupons for your favorite canned and frozen fruits, vegetables, and juices.

✓ Buy store brands over name brands, which can cost much more.

Make Them Tasty

✓ Always buy the freshest produce available. Quality makes a tremendous difference where taste is concerned.

✓ Do not overcook. When vegetables are overcooked, they get mushy and lose flavor, texture, and color. Instead, cook vegetables just until they are tender crisp (except for tubers and some root vegetables, which need longer cooking).

✓ Try eating more of your vegetables raw. Grate or dice them into salads or slice and serve them as finger foods with meals.

✓ Make nutritious dips and sauces for vegetables. Vegetarian cookbooks will give you some wonderful, novel ideas on how to do this. *The Saucy Vegetarian* by J. Stepaniak (Book Publishing Company; Summertown, TN) is a complete book of delicious and easy sauces and dressings. *Cooking Vegetarian* by V. Melina and J. Forest (Wiley and Sons; New York, NY) also offers some great options.

✓ If you aren't so fond of eating vegetables and fruits, try juicing them. Invest in a juicer and a few good juicing books to help you get started.

Keeping Your Produce Safe

Although not commonly associated with food poisoning, raw fruits and vegetables can harbor some not-so-friendly bacteria. About 5 percent of food poisoning is caused by contamination in these foods. The source is generally animal manure or contamination during food preparation. To avoid food poisoning from vegetables and fruits:

✓ Rinse all produce well with clean drinking water before eating (even if you don't eat the rind or skin). Use a small, clean vegetable brush to remove dirt from cracks in the food. Do not use detergent or bleach when washing fruits and vegetables. Most produce washes are safe and effective, but costly.

✓ Refrigerate whole and cut-up raw fruits, vegetables, and salads to keep bacteria from multiplying.

✓ Keep a separate cutting board for produce. Boards used for cheese, eggs, and, of course, any other animal products should not be used for produce.

✓ Wash your hands with warm water and soap for at least twenty seconds before and after handling food.

For scientific references for this chapter, go to
http://www.nutrispeak.com/bvreferences.htm

SHOULD I BUY ORGANIC PRODUCE?

The debate about conventional-versus-organic produce rages on. Proponents of conventional growing, including the controlled use of pesticides, argue that pesticides help protect crops from insects, diseases, weeds, and mold, increasing crop yield. This, they say, makes vegetables and fruits more affordable for the average consumer. Government authorities tell us that the amounts of pesticides on our vegetables and fruits are well within safe limits and pose little threat to human health. They remind us that all major studies examining diet and pesticide residues have concluded that the benefits of eating produce far outweigh any risk.

On the other side of the fence stand the proponents of organic farming. They contend that organic produce tastes better, is lower in toxic pesticides, and is more nutritious. Organic food supporters stress that organic farming can help return our land and water to a healthy, natural state, which, in turn, protects our health and the health of all other living things. They add that most organic farms are small, family-owned businesses, and by buying organic, we help save family farms. In addition, we protect farm workers who would otherwise be exposed to high levels of pesticides. Among the strongest arguments put forward by organic enthusiasts is that organic foods are not genetically engineered. Genetic engineering isolates and transfers genes from one species into a foreign species. Once this technology is released into the environment, it cannot be recalled. Proponents of organic farming methods declare that while genetic engineering holds great promise from a nutrition standpoint, thus far it has failed to deliver. Instead, it has harmed nontarget (beneficial) insects and soil microorganisms, led to resistance in weeds and insect pests, and spread into wild environments, breeding with wild relatives.

In May 2002, the first detailed scientific analysis comparing the pesticide residues of conventionally and organically grown vegetables and fruits was published in the *Food Additives and Contaminants Journal*. This study showed that organic foods contain about one-third as many pesticide residues as conventionally grown foods.

So what's the verdict? While eating conventionally grown vegetables and fruits is a positive first step for health, there are solid reasons to opt for organic beyond and including health benefits.

Chapter 7

FAT FEUDS

WHO'S WINNING?

Few health concepts have been as strongly promoted or zealously embraced as the notion that fat is bad. Some health authorities urge consumers to eat only very low-fat foods and avoid whole foods that are naturally high in fat, such as nuts and seeds. Not surprisingly, a backlash has occurred. Naysayers have brought forth two distinct arguments. The first is that fat is not the villain, carbohydrates are. This theory is wildly popular among consumers of diet books who relish the thought of dining on steak, bacon, eggs, and cheese. The second argument is that it is not high intakes of fat that contribute to our health problems, but bad fats in particular. Proponents of this theory contend that high-fat diets (for example, the Mediterranean-style plan that is rich in nutritious plant fats, such as olive oil and avocados) are among the most health-promoting of all the approaches. To make matters even more complicated for vegetarians, heart health organizations urge people to eat a couple servings of fatty fish each week to increase intakes of omega-3 fatty acids. It is enough to make your head spin.

Fat nutrition is tricky because there are so many different types of fat, all with distinct effects on our health. Many people assume the switch to a vegetarian diet guarantees a more healthful fat intake. While it is true that most vegetarians eat less total fat, less of the potentially damaging saturated fats and cholesterol, and more unsaturated fats, becoming vegetarian is no guarantee that fat in the diet will be decreased. After all, there are plenty of junk food snacks that do not contain a single speck of meat. In addition, when we switch to a vegetarian diet, our concerns tend to shift from getting too much of the "bad fats" to getting enough of very specific types of "good fats."

This chapter sheds light on the volumes of literature about fat, helping to clarify what we know and what is mere speculation. It lays outs the significant issues for vegetarians and provides solid, practical guidelines for making choices that support optimal health. Our examination of the issues will focus on four key questions:

1. What is more important, the amount or type of fat?
2. Can vegetarian diets provide sufficient essential fats?
3. How much fat is optimal?
4. What are the healthiest fat sources?

WHAT IS MORE IMPORTANT, THE AMOUNT OR TYPE OF FAT?

There is no question that both the quantity and quality of fat we eat can have a significant effect on our health. However, it is becoming increasingly clear that the *type* of fat consumed has a greater influence on our risk of disease than the *amount* of fat we eat. This does not mean that our total fat intake is not important—it is. It means that eating a relatively high-fat diet can have minimal health consequences if the fat comes from the right kinds of foods and we are not overeating. On the other hand, our risk of disease increases considerably when the fat comes from the wrong kinds of foods, even when our total fat intake is moderate.

What Are Fats?

In scientific jargon, fats are known as lipids. Lipids are a family of compounds that do not dissolve in water. They include fats and oils (made up of fatty acids), sterols (such as cholesterol), and phospholipids (such as lecithin). As you can see, while fats are only one type of lipid, the words *fat* and *lipid* are commonly used interchangeably. Fatty acids do not generally roam free in the body; most of them travel in threesomes as part of larger molecules called *triglycerides*. Most of the fatty acids we need for survival can be produced in the body, but there are two we cannot make and must obtain from food. These are called *essential fatty acids*.

The main feature that distinguishes fats from oils is that fats are hard at room temperature and oils are liquid. Fats generally are found in animal products (such as meat, poultry, and dairy), and oils are commonly derived from plant seeds (such as olives, canola, corn, and sunflowers).

Fatty acids are saturated, monounsaturated, or polyunsaturated, depending on the amount of hydrogen they contain. All fats and oils contain varying amounts of fatty acids from each of these three categories. For example, corn oil contains about 58 percent polyunsaturated fat, 29 percent monounsaturated fat, and 13 percent saturated fat. It is referred to as polyunsaturated oil because most of the fat it contains is polyunsaturated. The breakdown of fatty acids in a variety of fats and oils is shown in table 7.4 (page 178).

What Are the Most Damaging Types of Fat?

Fats that have been shown to have negative effects on health, when eaten in excess, are saturated fats, trans-fatty acids, and cholesterol. Here's what you need to know about each of these types of fat.

Saturated fat

Saturated fats have been pegged as "bad fats" for good reason. Excessive consumption of saturated fats increases our risk for several diseases, including heart disease, several cancers, gallstones, kidney disease, and possibly type 2 diabetes.

Saturated fat is hard at room temperature. The harder the fat, the more highly saturated it is. The primary sources of saturated fat are:

Animal fat: Beef and pork fat are about 40 to 45 percent saturated, chicken and turkey fat about 30 to 33 percent, and fish fat 20 to 30 percent.

Dairy fat: Dairy fat is about 65 percent saturated.

Tropical "oils": Coconut fat is about 91 percent saturated, palm kernel oil about 87 percent, and palm oil about 51 percent.

By contrast plant fats (excluding tropical oils) are about 6 to 25 percent saturated, with most in the 10 to 20 percent range.

How much saturated fat do we eat? Most North Americans eat too much saturated fat. The average person eats about 20 to 30 grams of saturated fat a day, which comes out to 11 to 12 percent of the total calories consumed by most American men and women. Vegetarian diets are naturally lower in saturated fat than nonvegetarian diets. Lacto-ovo vegetarians average 8 to 10 percent of calories from saturated fat. Vegans eat even less, averaging 4 to 7 percent of calories from saturated fat. In the menus provided in chapter 3 (pages 70 to 73), saturated fat contributes the following proportions of total calories:

Saturated fat in menus	Percent of calories
Menu 1: Nonvegetarian	14.9
Menu 2: Lacto–Ovo Vegetarian	11.6
Menu 3: Lacto–Ovo Vegetarian with More Legumes	2.1
Menu 4: Vegan	3.7

Are there specific recommendations for saturated fat intake? Most governments and health authorities recommend that saturated fat should not exceed 10 percent of calories. Official nutrient recommendations in the U.S. and Canada (DRI Macronutrients 2002)* do not suggest an upper limit (UL) for saturated fat because "any incremental increase in saturated fatty acid intake increases CHD [coronary heart disease] risk." The Joint WHO/FAO Expert Consultation on Diet, Nutrition, and the Prevention of Chronic Diseases (WHO/FAO Diet and Diseases, 2002) suggests intakes of less than 10 percent of calories, and 7 percent for high-risk groups.

What does this mean in grams? It depends on your energy needs. For those consuming 2,000 calories a day, 10 percent of calories means a maximum saturated fat intake of 22 grams, and 7 percent of calories amounts to a maximum saturated fat intake of 16 grams. A fast-food meal that includes one double cheeseburger, a milkshake, and a large order of fries provides about 31 grams of saturated fat. Vegetarians who eat a lot of full-fat dairy products could find themselves over the top almost as quickly. Two ounces (57 grams) of cheddar cheese contain 12 grams of saturated fat, and 1 cup (250 ml) of whole milk has over 5 grams. On the other hand, a person could eat ten servings of fruits and vegetables, eight servings of whole grains, two serving of beans, one serving of tofu, 2 ounces (57 grams) of nuts, and 2 ounces (57 grams) of seeds, and still come in under 10 grams of saturated fat.

Should vegetarians avoid tropical oils? Is coconut an unhealthy food? What about foods with coconut, palm kernel, or palm oil added? While tropical oils are unquestionably high in saturated fat, moderate amounts can have a place in nutritious vegetarian diets. Some experts believe that saturated fats from tropical oils are less damaging than saturated fats from animal sources because they are not packaged with cholesterol. In whole foods, such as fresh coconut, the oil comes with protective fiber and phytochemicals. Studies suggest that when moderate amounts of coconut or tropical oils are consumed as part of a high-fiber, low- or no-cholesterol, plant-based diet, their use does not increase our risk of heart attack. In contrast, adding tropical fats to a standard

---

The Dietary Reference Intakes for Energy, Carbohydrates, Fiber, Fat, Protein, and Amino Acids (Macronutrients) (2002) issued by the Food and Nutrition Board, Institute of Medicine

North American diet already containing excessive saturated fat and cholesterol may simply be adding fuel to the fire. Here is the bottom line for healthy individuals eating a high-fiber, plant-based diet: small amounts of tropical oils, coconut milk, or, better still, fresh coconut can be enjoyed in moderation.

Trans-fatty acids

Do you recall when the newly discovered connection between saturated fat and heart disease was splashed across the front pages of newspapers and magazines? Consumers responded by demanding that lard and tropical oils be removed from their favorite products. Manufacturers provided the perfect solution to allay their fears—vegetable fat. Liquid vegetable oil was processed to look and taste like animal fat. Margarine was designed to replace butter and vegetable shortening was intended to replace lard.

Manufacturers were delighted, because the replacements were economical and stable—they could sit on a shelf for a long time without going rancid. Consumers were pleased, because they believed that these products were more healthful choices.

The process that turns vegetable oils into solid fats is called hydrogenation. This process changes the configuration of some of the healthful unsaturated fats to trans-fatty acids. Technically, trans-fatty acids are still unsaturated fats, but unlike the more common form of unsaturated fats, which are flexible and curved in shape, trans-fatty acids are straighter, more rigid molecules. These molecules behave much like saturated fat—only worse.

For many years trans-fatty acids were considered a relatively minor player in health and disease. There are two reasons for this. First, we eat far less trans-fatty acids than saturated fat (2 to 4 percent of calories come from trans-fatty acids compared to 11 to 12 percent of calories from saturated fat). Second, studies have shown that trans-fatty acids increase total cholesterol levels only 80 percent as much as saturated fat. This figure is deceiving to say the least. While trans-fatty acids do not affect total cholesterol as much as saturated fat, their overall damage to heart health is greater. Trans-fatty acids not only raise total cholesterol, they lower HDL (good cholesterol). They also raise damaging lipoprotein(a), a particularly harmful form of LDL (bad cholesterol), and potentially increase triglycerides. Gram for gram, the adverse effect of trans-fatty acids is estimated to be at least double that of saturated fatty acids.

What foods are highest in trans-fatty acids? Close to 90 percent of the trans-fatty acids in foods come from hydrogenated or partially hydrogenated oils. These fats are used extensively in processed foods such as crackers, granola bars, chips and other snack foods, pies, cakes, pastries, cookies, and other baked goods, margarine, and shortening. Hydrogenated oils also are widely used in the fast-food industry and in restaurants for deep-frying foods. (See table 7.1 for a list of the amounts of trans-fatty acids in some common foods.)

The remaining 10 percent of trans-fatty acids come from animal foods, including meat and dairy products, and are also formed naturally from bacterial fermentation within the intestinal tracts of ruminant animals.

TABLE 7.1	TRANS-FATTY ACID CONTENT OF SELECTED FOODS		
Food		**Total Fat (g)**	**Trans-Fatty Acids (g)**
Microwave popcorn, 3.5 oz. (100 g)		25.0	7.5
French fries, large		23.7	5.0
Cookies, chocolate chip, 4		12.0	5.0
Doughnut, honey-glazed, 1		15.0	3.8
Shortening, 1 tbsp. (15 ml)		14.0	3.7
Cake, yellow commercial with frosting, 1 piece		12.8	3.2
Margarine, hard, 1 tbsp. (15 ml)		12.0	3.1
Crackers, 8		7.0	2.6
Margarine, soft, 1 tbsp. (15 ml)		12.0	1.4
Potato chips, 2 oz. (57 g)		19.6	1.1

Source: The USDA Nutrient Database.

How much trans-fatty acids do people eat? It is estimated that 2 to 4 percent of the average North American's calories come from trans-fatty acids. Vegetarians generally consume fewer trans-fatty acids than nonvegetarians, although any differences are negated when vegetarians regularly eat large amounts of processed food. Vegans generally consume the least trans–fatty acids, with estimates averaging 0 to 2 percent of calories. In the menus provided in Chapter 3 (pages 70 to 73), trans–fatty acids contribute the following proportion of calories:

Trans-fatty acids in menus		Percent of calories
Menu 1:	Nonvegetarian	1.4
Menu 2:	Lacto-Ovo Vegetarian	1.9
Menu 3:	Lacto-Ovo Vegetarian with More Legumes	0.7
Menu 4:	Vegan	0.2

It is important to note that the use of processed and deep-fried foods is low in the first two menus and negligible in the second two menus.

How much should we limit trans-fatty acids? The DRI Macronutrients (2002) does not suggest an upper limit for trans-fatty acids because "any incremental increase in trans-fatty acid intake increases CHD risk." However, the WHO/FAO Diet and Diseases (2002) suggests that intakes of trans-fatty acids should be less than 1 percent of calories.

For someone eating 2,000 calories a day, that amounts to no more than 2.2 grams of trans-fatty acids. In practical terms, this means limiting or completely avoiding foods containing hydrogenated or partially hydrogenated fats, especially when they are major ingredients in a product. Fried foods should also be minimized.

Cholesterol

Have you ever wondered how much cholesterol is in a bowl of nuts or a whole avocado? The answer is zero—not a single gram. Animals, not plants, make cholesterol. Thus, all animal products contain cholesterol and all plant foods are cholesterol free.

Cholesterol is an essential part of every human cell. The body makes about 800 to 1,000 milligrams of cholesterol each day, so we don't need any additional cholesterol from food. Too much cholesterol can cause blood cholesterol levels to rise, increasing the risk of blood clots, heart attack, and stroke. It may also increase the risk for certain types of cancer. For this reason, most governments and health authorities, including the WHO, recommend that we limit total dietary cholesterol to less than 300 mg a day. The DRI Macronutrients (2002) does not suggest an upper limit for cholesterol because "any incremental increase in cholesterol intake increases CHD risk."

How much cholesterol do people eat? The general population eats about 200 to 400 mg of cholesterol a day. In the menus provided in chapter 3 (pages 70 to 73), cholesterol intakes are as follows:

Cholesterol in menus		mg cholesterol
Menu 1:	Nonvegetarian	315
Menu 2:	Lacto-Ovo Vegetarian	86
Menu 3:	Lacto-Ovo Vegetarian with More Legumes	11
Menu 4:	Vegan	0

None of these menus contains eggs, which would increase the cholesterol content significantly. (A single egg contains over 200 mg of cholesterol.)

The most concentrated sources of cholesterol are organ meats and eggs. Contrary to what many people believe, there is little difference in the cholesterol content of meat, poultry, or fish. Dairy products are moderate sources of cholesterol.

What Are the "Healthy Fats"?

Fats that have been found to cause little or no adverse health effects, or to be protective to human health, are plant sterols, monounsaturated fats, and polyunsaturated fats.

Plant sterols and stanols

While animals make cholesterol, plants make their own family of similar compounds called sterols and stanols. These naturally occurring plant compounds are similar in structure to cholesterol, but they do not behave the same way as cholesterol in the body. We absorb far less plant sterols and stanols, which also help to block cholesterol absorption from the gut. All whole plant foods contain small amounts of these compounds. New margarines on the market that have added sterols and stanols contain higher amounts. Vegetarian diets are naturally higher in plant sterols and stanols than nonvegetarian diets.

Monounsaturated fat

Monounsaturated fat has been shown to have a neutral or slightly beneficial effect on health, with minimal effect on blood cholesterol levels. There is some evidence that monounsaturated fat may slightly reduce blood pressure and enhance blood flow.

Oils rich in monounsaturated fat generally are liquid at room temperature but become cloudy and thick when refrigerated, as with olive oil. The richest dietary sources of monounsaturated fat are olives, olive oil, canola oil, avocados, most nuts (except for walnuts and butternuts), high-oleic sunflower oil, and high-oleic safflower oil. ("Oleic" is the main type of monounsaturated fat. Sunflower and safflower oils normally contain mainly polyunsaturated fats, but the high-oleic varieties are bred to have a high monounsaturated fat content.) See table 7.4 for the amount of monounsaturated fat in various fats and oils.

Polyunsaturated fat

Polyunsaturated fats have been shown to have numerous benefits to health and are the most complex of all fatty acid families. It is within this group that we find the *essential fatty acids*—fatty acids that cannot be made by our bodies and must be obtained through our diets. These fats are needed for the formation of healthy cell membranes. They also help cells keep their shape and flexibility and allow substances to flow in and out. They are critical to the development and functioning of the brain and nervous system, and are involved in the production of hormone-like substances called *eicosanoids*, which regulate many organ systems.

There are two distinct families of polyunsaturated fats, each with unique properties. They are known as the omega-6 family and the omega-3 family, and both are vital to health. Within each family there is one *essential fatty acid*.

In the omega-6 family this is *linoleic acid* (LA). In the omega-3 family it is *alpha-linolenic acid* (ALA). There are several other very important fats in each family called *highly unsaturated fatty acids* (HUFA). These fatty acids are critical to health; however, because they can be made in the body from the essential fatty acids, they are not "essential" in our diets.

Highly unsaturated fatty acids (HUFAs)

Highly unsaturated fatty acids (HUFAs) are even more active in the body than essential fatty acids and have a powerful effect on our health. In the omega-6 family, the most important HUFAs are *arachidonic acid* (AA) and *gamma-linolenic acid* (GLA). In the omega-3 family, the most important HUFAs are *eicosapentaenoic acid* (EPA) and *docosahexaenoic acid* (DHA). All of these HUFAs, except DHA, serve as raw materials for making eicosanoids. The eicosanoids formed from AA are

Fatty Acid Abbreviations	
Omega-6 Fatty Acids	
Linoleic acid	LA
Arachidonic acid	AA
Gamma-linolenic acid	GLA
Omega-3 Fatty Acids	
Alpha-linolenic acid	ALA
Eicosapentaenoic acid	EPA
Docosahexaenoic acid	DHA

very potent, increasing blood pressure, inflammation, cell proliferation, and many markers of heart disease. The eicosanoids formed from EPA and GLA protect against these responses. While we need the eicosanoids formed from AA, when we produce too much, our risk of chronic disease increases.

DHA cannot form eicosanoids, but it is an important part of the gray matter of our brains, the retina of our eyes, and specific cell membranes. Low levels of DHA have been associated with several neurological and behavioral disorders, such as depression, schizophrenia, Alzheimer's disease, and attention deficit hyperactivity disorder (ADHD). In addition, low levels of DHA can negatively affect brain and eye development in infants. Thus, while these long-chain fatty acids are not "essential" in our diets, we must get enough, either by making them from essential fatty acids or by getting them directly from foods.

Sources of Essential Fatty Acids

The primary sources of the two essential fatty acids—LA and ALA—are plants grown in soil and in the sea. The most common sources of the long-chain fatty acids—AA, EPA, and DHA—are animal foods (although DHA and EPA also are available from sea plants). Table 7.4 lists specific amounts of these fatty acids in a variety of foods.

Sources of omega-6 fatty acids

LA: seeds and seed oils (sunflower, safflower, hemp, grape, pumpkin, sesame, cottonseed); nuts and nut oils (walnuts, butternuts); grains and grain oils (corn, wheat germ); and soybeans and soybean oil.

GLA: primrose oil, borage oil, black currant oil, hempseed oil, spirulina.

AA: meat, poultry, and dairy products.

Sources of omega-3 fatty acids

ALA: seeds and seed oils (flax, chia, hemp, canola); nuts and nut oils (walnuts, butternuts); green leaves of plants (dark green leafy vegetables, broccoli); sea vegetables; soybeans and soybean oil.

EPA and DHA: fish (especially cold-water fish); eggs (especially those from chickens fed flax or microalgae); sea vegetables; and DHA-rich microalgae (not blue-green algae, which contains little or no DHA and EPA).

How much omega

6 and omega-3 fatty acids do we need?

Most healthy vegetarian adults eating about 2,000 calories a day should strive for about 12 to 18 grams of omega-6 fatty acids and 3 to 6 grams of omega-3 fatty acids in their daily diet. A tablespoon of omega-6-rich oil (such as sunflower, safflower, or grapeseed oil) contains about 10 grams of omega-6 fatty acids; a teaspoon of flaxseed oil contains about 2.7 grams of omega-3 fatty acids.

How did we arrive at these figures? While there are no official recommendations for essential fatty acid intakes for vegetarians, we do have official recommendations for nonvegetarians and can adjust these figures for vegetarians based on our knowledge of their essential fatty acid status. The Joint WHO/FAO Expert Consultation on Diet, Nutrition, and the Prevention of Chronic Diseases (2003) recommends 5 to 8 percent of calories from omega-6 fatty acids and 1 to 2 percent of calories from omega-3 fatty acids for the general population. For vegetarians and vegans who consume little, if any, direct sources of the highly unsaturated omega-3 fatty acids EPA and DHA, a ratio of omega-6 to omega-3 fatty acids from 2:1 to 4:1 (with an upper limit of 6:1) has been suggested by experts in essential fatty acid nutrition. Most vegetarian diets have higher ratios of omega-6 to omega-3, in the range of 10:1 to 20:1. This means that we do not eat enough omega-3 fatty acids and possibly that we eat too much omega-6 fatty acids. To achieve the recommended 2:1 to 6:1 ratio, vegetarians would need to follow the 5 to 8 percent omega-6 fatty acid recommendation and increase the omega-3 fatty acid recommendation to

1.5 to 2.5 percent of calories. Thus we arrive at our recommendation of 12 to 18 grams of omega-6 fatty acids, and 3 to 6 grams of omega-3 fatty acids (based on a 2,000-calorie diet).

How much omega-6 and omega-3 fatty acids do we eat?

Vegetarians eat more omega-6 fatty acids than nonvegetarians. Vegans consume an average 9 to 12 percent of their fats (20 to 27 grams per 2,000 calories) as omega-6 fatty acids, and lacto-ovo vegetarians about 6 to 10 percent (13 to 22 grams per 2,000 calories). Omega-3 fatty acid intakes are similar for vegans, vegetarians, and nonvegetarians, averaging 0.5 to 1 percent of total calories (1 to 2 grams per 2,000 calories). As you can see, we get slightly higher amounts of omega-6 fatty acids than we should and only about one-third of the omega-3 fatty acids recommended.

Intakes of very long-chain omega-3 fatty acids (EPA and DHA) are remarkably different in vegetarians and nonvegetarians. Vegans consume little, if any, EPA and DHA, and vegetarians consume minimal EPA (less than 5 mcg a day) and varying amounts of DHA depending on their egg consumption. (The average DHA from eggs in lacto-ovo vegetarian diets is approximately 33 mg a day.) Nonvegetarian EPA and DHA intakes vary with the use of fish and eggs, with averages ranging 100 to 150 mg a day.

In the menus provided in chapter 3 (pages 70 to 73), intakes of omega-6 fatty acids fall within the usual ranges listed above. However, Menus 3 and 4 are much higher in omega-3 fatty acids than the average intake because of the inclusion of flaxseed oil, which in Menu 3 provides 87 percent of omega-3 fatty acids and in Menu 4 provides 74 percent. For the amount of essential fatty acids in all four menus, see table 7.2.

TABLE 7.2 **ESSENTIAL FATTY ACID INTAKES IN MENUS**				
	Omega-6		Omega-3	
Menus	Total (g)	Percent of Calories	Total (g)	Percent of Calories
1 Nonvegetarian, page 70	10.2	5%	1.2	0.5%
2 Lacto-Ovo Vegetarian, page 71	21.5	10%	2.0	0.9%
3 Lacto-Ovo Vegetarian with More Legumes, page 72	14.6	6%	4.9	2%
4 Vegan, page 73	19.4	9%	7.0	3%

CAN VEGETARIAN DIETS PROVIDE SUFFICIENT ESSENTIAL FATTY ACIDS?

Yes, we can be confident that vegetarian diets can provide plenty of both essential fatty acids: the omega-6 fatty acid (LA) and the omega-3 fatty acid (ALA). Vegetarian diets are rich in LA; however, as with nonvegetarian diets, they tend to be low in ALA. The primary sources of ALA are plants, so if vegetarians select ample amounts of omega-3-rich plant foods, they can easily obtain sufficient amounts of ALA. The challenge for vegetarians is to convert these fats to the active, long-chain omega-3 fatty acids, EPA and DHA. Several studies have shown that vegetarians generally have lower EPA and DHA in their body tissues compared to nonvegetarians. Vegans are reported to have the lowest EPA and DHA status, with levels only about half those of nonvegetarians. Breast milk DHA levels in vegan and lacto-ovo vegetarian women are also lower than in nonvegetarians. While this is somewhat of a concern, there is good evidence to show that vegetarians and vegans can achieve excellent essential fatty acid status at every stage of life with the right food choices.

Vegetarian Guide to Getting Enough Omega-3 Fatty Acids

TABLE 7.3	**OMEGA-3 FATTY ACIDS (ALA) IN FOODS**
Food	**Omega-3 Fatty Acids**
Flaxseed oil, 1 tbsp. (15 ml)	8.0 g
Hempseed oil, 1 tbsp. (15 ml)	2.7 g
Canola oil, 1 tbsp. (15 ml)	1.6 g
Soybean oil, 1 tbsp. (15 ml)	1.0 g
Walnuts, 1 oz. (28.4 g)	2.7 g
Flaxseeds, 1 tbsp. (15 ml)	2.6 g
Soybeans, cooked, 1 cup (250 ml)	1.1 g
Leafy greens, raw, 1 cup (250 ml)	0.1 g
Wheat germ, 2 tbsp. (30 ml)	0.1 g

The keys to improving omega-3 fatty acid status for most vegetarians are getting enough omega-3 fatty acids, producing optimal amounts of EPA and DHA, improving our intake of ALA, and achieving the right balance between omega-6 and omega-3 fatty acids. There are three simple steps that will help us ensure our intakes of omega-3 fatty acids are adequate.

1. **Include good sources of alpha-linolenic acid (the plant omega-3 fatty acid) in the diet**. The very best sources are flaxseeds, flaxseed oil, hempseeds, hempseed oil, canola oil, walnuts, and green leafy vegetables. Aim for 3 to 6 grams per day for most adults. Flaxseeds are by far the richest source of ALA (57 percent of the fat is ALA). One teaspoon (5 ml) of flaxseed oil or 1½ tablespoons (23 ml) of ground flaxseeds, plus your usual intake of vegetables, walnuts, and other foods, provides plenty of omega-3 fatty acids for most people. (See table 7.3 for the amounts of ALA in various plant foods.) One delicious way to use flaxseed oil is in salad dressing. (See the recipe for Liquid Gold Dressing on page 329.)

2. **Consider including a direct source of EPA and/or DHA in the diet**. There has been some concern that vegetarians and others who do not include fish in their diets may not be able to make enough EPA and DHA from the ALA they consume. (Fish are the primary sources of EPA and DHA for the general population.) There is considerable evidence to suggest that most healthy people can effectively convert ALA to EPA and DHA if appropriate amounts of essential fatty acids are consumed. People with increased requirements (for

instance, pregnant and lactating women and those with diseases associated with poor EFA status) or those at risk for poor conversion (such as people with diabetes and the elderly) may enjoy more benefits from consuming direct sources of EPA and DHA. Although fish is the most concentrated direct source of EPA and DHA, fish do not produce these fatty acids: the plants and microalgae that fish consume make them. EPA is found in sea vegetables; in some varieties, up to 30 percent of the fat is EPA. (Sea vegetables have little DHA.) However, sea vegetables are so low in fat that we'd need to eat a lot of them to make a significant contribution to our intake. One hefty serving of 3½ ounces (100 grams) of sea vegetables provides about 100 mg of EPA. DHA also is found in specific types of microalgae (not blue-green algae); some contain as much as 40 percent DHA by dry weight. This type of microalgae currently is being cultivated, extracted, and sold as a DHA supplement with 100 to 300 mg of DHA per capsule. (Some are available in gelatin-free capsules.) Eggs from chickens fed flaxseeds or DHA-rich microalgae also are reasonable DHA sources for lacto–ovo vegetarians; each egg provides about 60 to 150 mg of DHA. For those who want to supplement their diets with DHA, 100 to 300 mg of DHA from microalgae is recommended (the higher end of the range is appropriate for pregnant and lactating women).

3. Moderate the use of oils rich in omega-6 fatty acids and high-fat processed foods rich in these oils. Eating too much omega-6 fatty acids relative to omega-3 fatty acids can reduce omega-3 conversion by up to 40 to 50 percent. While increasing omega-3 fatty acids is an important first step in correcting the imbalance, vegetarians with especially high omega-6 intakes would be well advised to moderate their

WHY NOT JUST EAT FISH?

Fish is loaded with omega-3 fatty acids. High-fat, cold-water fish contains up to 1,600 mg of DHA and 1,000 mg of EPA for each 3½-ounce (100-gram) serving. So why not just eat fish?

There are plenty of sound reasons to forgo fish. For starters, fish is our most concentrated source of two types of contaminants: heavy metals (such as lead, mercury, and cadmium) and industrial pollutants (such as PCBs, DDT, and dioxins). Needless to say, these are compounds that need to be minimized in the diet. Fish also is a primary source of foodborne illness, poisoning hundreds, perhaps thousands, of people in North America each day.

There also are compelling ecological and ethical arguments for avoiding fish. Large commercial fishing operations are leaving the vast majority of our fish stocks in jeopardy. The Natural Resources Defense Council estimates that about 70 percent of the world's fish populations are now fully fished, overexploited, depleted, or slowly recovering. From an ethical perspective, eating fish requires taking a life, or several lives. Indeed, commercial fishing operations generally have huge "bycatches" (fish and other sea life that are unintentionally caught). These creatures generally do not survive and simply are tossed back into the water.

omega-6 intake. The best way of doing this without compromising our overall nutrient intake is to reduce our use of processed foods containing large amounts of omega-6-rich oils and our use of oils rich in omega-6 and poor in omega-3. Sunflower, safflower, corn, grapeseed, soybean, and cottonseed oils contain the greatest amounts of omega-6 fatty acids relative to omega-3 fatty acids. While hempseed and walnut oils are rich in omega-6 fatty acids, they are beautifully balanced with omega-3 fatty acids, so they are good options (although they cannot be used for cooking, as the omega-3s are destroyed by high heat). The best choices for cooking oils are those rich in monounsaturated fats, such as olive, canola, and high-oleic sunflower or safflower oils. Omega-6-rich whole foods, such as sunflower seeds, pumpkin seeds, sesame tahini, tofu, and wheat germ, are wonderful nutrition powerhouses, so there is no need for us to reduce our consumption of them.

HOW MUCH FAT IS OPTIMAL?

How do we decide how much fat to eat? This favorite fat feud of health authorities and diet-book gurus continues despite the growing body of evidence that provides us with reasonable answers.

The DRI Macronutrients (2002) does not set a recommended dietary allowance (RDA), adequate intake (AI), or upper limit (UL) for total fat (except for the first year of life), but they do suggest something called the acceptable macronutrient distribution range (AMDR). The AMDR for fat is 20 to 35 percent of calories for everyone four years of age and older, and 30 to 40 percent of calories for children age one through three. The Joint WHO/FAO Expert Consultation on Diet, Nutrition, and the Prevention of Chronic Diseases (2003) recommends a range for total fat of 15 to 30 percent of calories. This is consistent with many governments and health organizations.

The optimal amount of fat for each person depends on his or her unique constitution. People who have very efficient metabolisms (those who require fewer calories) generally need less fat than people with less efficient metabolisms (those who require a lot of calories). In addition, activity level, climate, and gastrointestinal function can affect caloric and fat needs. For example, a person who is very lean, constantly hungry, and lives in a cold, northern climate will likely find that a diet in the upper range of fat intake would be most supportive to health (around 30 to 35 percent of calories). In contrast, a person who is overweight, sedentary, and lives in a hot climate would very likely do better with a diet containing fewer calories from fat (in the range of 15 to 20 percent). For the average healthy adult, a diet providing 20 to 25 percent of calories from fat would prove most beneficial for long-term health (providing the fat is from good sources).

It is important to recognize that there can be disadvantages to diets that are either very low in fat (under 15 percent of calories) or very high in fat (over 35 percent of calories). Very low-fat diets may provide insufficient calories (especially for children) and very low intakes of omega-3 fatty acids. They also reduce the absorption of fat-soluble vitamins and protective phytochemicals. In some cases, people who become very "fat phobic" may choose nutritional washouts, such as fat-free cookies or fat-free pretzels, over nutritious, whole plant foods, such as nuts, seeds, and soy products. The end result may be a diet deficient in vitamin E and several trace minerals.

Very high-fat diets also can spell trouble. Large amounts of fat can contribute to overeating and add unwanted pounds. This is because fat is two and one-half times more concentrated in calories than carbohydrates or protein. In addition, if the fat comes mainly from concentrated fats and oils, it can be a challenge to get all the nutrients and protective components we need from our food. Fats and oils contain almost no vitamins and minerals and lack fiber and phytochemicals. There also is some evidence that very high fat intakes contribute to certain types of cancer.

WHAT ARE THE HEALTHIEST FAT SOURCES?

People often look at nuts much the way they do potato chips: as high-fat snack foods that clog our arteries. Conventional wisdom tells us that nuts and other high-fat plant foods—such as seeds, avocados, and olives—are unhealthful. That wisdom is based upon the myth that all high-fat foods are bad for us. There is absolutely no evidence that eating moderate amounts of higher-fat, whole plant foods is in any way detrimental to our health. In fact, the evidence is quite the opposite.

High-Fat and Healthful

The highest quality fat is naturally present in fresh nuts, seeds, soybeans, avocados, olives, and other plant foods. There simply is no contest between the fats found in these foods and the chemically altered fats found in margarine, shortening, and other hydrogenated vegetables oils or the highly saturated fats found in animal products. Even vegetable oils that are regarded as very healthful pale in comparison to the whole foods from which they were extracted. Why? Plant foods carry with them valuable vitamins, minerals, phytochemicals, plant protein, plant sterols, essential fatty acids, and fiber. Consider what we know about the health benefits of nuts and seeds.

Nuts. The studies that have examined the healthful effects of eating nuts debunk the myth that "all fat is bad fat." During the last decade, studies have consistently confirmed the health benefits of these foods. In three large studies, people who ate nuts most frequently had a 39 to 60 percent reduction in their risk of dying from heart disease compared with those who ate nuts the most infrequently. Numerous smaller studies investigating the effects of individual nuts, including peanuts (not technically a tree nut, but a legume), have provided further evidence that nuts are extremely protective to our health. Another large study found that consuming a 1-ounce (28.4 gram) serving of nuts five or more times a week resulted in a 27 percent lower risk of developing type 2 diabetes compared to those who rarely or never ate nuts.

What is it that makes nuts so nutritious? Nuts are loaded with good fats, low in saturated fat, and free of trans-fatty acids and cholesterol. They contain primarily monounsaturated fat, except for walnuts, which are high in polyunsaturated fats and are excellent sources of essential fatty acids. Nuts are great sources of antioxidant vitamins (including selenium and vitamin E), as well as plant protein and fiber. Nuts are rich sources of several trace minerals, such as copper, magnesium, selenium, chromium, zinc, and potassium. Of course, as with all whole plant foods, nuts provide a unique complement of phytochemicals. So, next time you get the urge to throw a few cashews in your stir-fry, sprinkle almonds on your salad, or crack open some walnuts after dinner, just do it!

Seeds. Seeds are complete nutrition packages, designed to nourish new plants and allow them to carry on their species. The value of seeds in human nutrition is sorely underestimated. These concentrated foods are our most plentiful sources of essential fatty acids. Pumpkin seeds, sunflower seeds, poppy seeds, hemp seeds, and sesame seeds are all rich in the omega-6 fatty acid, linoleic acid (LA). Flaxseeds, chia seeds (grown in the deserts of Mexico), canola seeds, and hemp seeds (hemp contains plentiful amounts of both essential fatty acids) are all rich in the omega-3 fatty acid, alpha-linolenic acid (ALA). Seeds vary in their protein content, ranging from about 12 percent of calories to over 30 percent of calories. They are among our richest sources of vitamin E and provide an impressive array of other vitamins, minerals, phytochemicals, and fiber.

Flaxseeds offer a significant advantage for vegetarians, as they have the highest omega-3 content of any plant food, averaging about 57 percent ALA. Thus, flax can go a long way toward correcting any imbalances in essential fatty acids.

Flax is very high in soluble fiber (the type of fiber that lowers cholesterol) and is one of the richest known sources of boron, a mineral important to bone health. Studies show that flaxseeds can help reduce blood cholesterol levels, triglycerides, and blood pressure. They also improve blood sugar response in people with diabetes and may improve immune and inflammatory disorders. Flaxseeds are the best food source of lignans, which may provide protection against cancer.

Do flaxseeds and flaxseed oil increase the risk of prostate cancer?

At least seven studies since 1993 have found a positive connection between blood levels of ALA (the type of omega-3 fatty acids found in plants and animals, excluding fish) and prostate cancer. As a result, prostate cancer experts often warn men to limit their use of ALA-rich foods. Flaxseed and flaxseed oil, with their exceptionally high ALA content, have been singled out as foods to be cautiously avoided, especially by those with prostate cancer or by those who are at high risk for the disease. Many experts suggest that men should stick to fish as their primary source of omega-3 fatty acids. While it certainly makes sense to assume that flaxseeds would be a problem if high ALA increases the risk of prostate cancer, there are a few important details about these studies that are often overlooked and seldom mentioned. To begin, flaxseeds and flaxseed oil were not the source of the ALA in any of these studies. Indeed, several of the authors made it clear that the ALA was animal derived. In addition, the actual differences in the ALA intakes of the study participants (from the highest to lowest intakes) were small. At least four other large studies have found that high ALA does not increase prostate cancer risk. In one study, there was no association, and in three studies, higher ALA was associated with a reduced risk of prostate cancer.

In 1991, a research team decided to look specifically at the effects of flaxseed use in men with prostate cancer. While this was a small, short-term, pilot study with only twenty-five participants, the results were most encouraging. The participants were given a low-fat diet (20 percent of calories from fat or less) and about 3 heaping tablespoons (45 ml) of finely ground flaxseeds per day for an average of thirty-four days. The findings showed a trend toward a decrease in prostate-specific antigen (PSA) levels in men with early-stage prostate cancer. Also, there was a reduction in tumor cell division and a greater rate of tumor cell death in the entire group. Larger studies will be needed before conclusions can be made about flaxseeds, flaxseed oil, and prostate cancer. However, for practical purposes, it is probably wise for vegetarians with prostate cancer to stick with ground flaxseeds rather than flaxseed oil as a primary source of omega-3 fatty acids until more research is completed.

Could we get sufficient fat without using any concentrated fats and oils?

Absolutely! Just as we can get all the carbohydrates our bodies need from whole foods, without any added refined starches or sugars, so we can get all the fat our bodies need without using any concentrated fats and oils. However, we do need to include a wise selection of fresh, whole plant foods that are naturally high in fat. Nuts and seeds and their butters, avocados, olives, soybeans, and soy products all are excellent sources of good-quality fats.

Is it okay to use some concentrated fats and oils?

While there is no question that the best-quality fat comes from whole plant foods, moderate amounts of concentrated fats and oils can fit into a nutritious vegetarian diet. High-quality oils can make meals more enjoyable, add extra calories (without adding bulk), and help to improve the absorption of certain vitamins and protective phytochemicals.

Although refined oils offer important advantages over hydrogenated oils, they provide little nutritional value other than fat calories. It is best to select unrefined, mechanically pressed, organic oils when they are available, as these oils contain higher amounts of phytochemicals and antioxidant nutrients. Extra-virgin olive oil is generally the only unrefined oil available on supermarket shelves. The high monounsaturated fat content makes it an excellent choice.

Other high-quality, fresh-pressed oils are available in natural food stores. (Those with high omega-3 content will be kept refrigerated.) Among the best choices are flaxseed, hempseed, canola, walnut, almond, and hazelnut oil. Your primary cooking oil should be mainly monounsaturated—olive, canola, or high-oleic sunflower or safflower oil. Nonorganic canola oil often is produced from genetically engineered crops, so if you want to be sure to avoid these products, buy organic.

The most highly unsaturated oils (flaxseed, hempseed, and walnut oil) should not be used in cooking at all. They are best reserved for salad dressings or on foods at the table. Only stable oils, higher in saturated or monounsaturated fats, are appropriate for higher-temperature heating (e.g., olive, high-oleic sunflower or safflower, or peanut oil). Lower-temperature cooking, such as baking, is less destructive to oils.

TABLE 7.4 FATTY ACID COMPOSITION OF SELECTED FOODS

Food/Serving Size	Total Fat % of total calories	Sat. Fat % of fatty acids	Mono. Fat % of fatty acids	Omega-6 % of fatty acids	Omega-3 % of fatty acids	ALA (g)	EPA (mg)	DHA (mg)
Oils, 1 tbsp. (15 ml)								
Canola oil	100	7	61	21	11	1.3	0	0
Coconut oil	100	91	7	2	0	0	0	0
Corn oil	100	13	29	58	0	0	0	0
Cottonseed oil	100	26	22	52	0	0	0	0
Flaxseed oil	100	9	18	16	57	8.0	0	0
Grapeseed oil	100	6	17	77	0	0	0	0
Hempseed oil	100	8	16	57	19	2.7	0	0
Olive oil	100	15	75	9	1	0.8	0	0
Palm oil	100	51	39	10	0	0	0	0
Palm kernel oil	100	87	11	2	0	0	0	0
Peanut oil	100	19	48	33	0	0	0	0
Safflower oil	100	6	14	75	0	0	0	0
Safflower oil, high-oleic	100	6	75	14	0	0	0	0
Sesame oil	100	14	42	44	0	0	0	0
Soybean oil	100	15	24	54	7	0.9	0	0
Sunflower oil	100	11	20	69	0	0	0	0
Sunflower oil, high-oleic	100	10	86	4	0	0	0	0
Walnut oil	100	9	23	53	13	1.7	0	0
Nuts, Seeds, Soy, and Wheat Germ, 1 oz. (28.4 g) (about 3.2 tbsp/48 ml)								
Almonds	80	10	66	24	0	0	0	0
Butternuts	84	2	19	63	16	2.5	0	0
Cashews	72	21	61	18	0	0	0	0
Flaxseed, whole, 2 tbsp. (30 ml)	41	9	18	16	57	5.2	0	0
Flaxseed, ground, 2 tbsp. (30 ml)	41	9	18	16	57	3.8	0	0
Hazelnuts	87	7	78	15	0	0	0	0
Macadamia nuts	95	17	81	2	0	0	0	0
Peanuts	76	15	52	33	0	0	0	0
Pecans	94	8	63	28	1	0.3	0	0
Pistachios	72	12	56	32	0	0	0	0
Pumpkin seeds	76	19	31	45–50	0–5	0–0.7	0	0
Soybeans, cooked, 1 cup (250 ml)	47	15	24	54	7	1.0	0	0
Sunflower seeds	77	10	19	66	0	0	0	0
Tofu, firm 1/2 cup (125 ml)	54	15	24	54	7	0.7	0	0
Walnuts	90	7	15	63	15	2.6	0	0
Wheat germ, 2 tbsp. (30 ml)	24	19	15	58	8	0.1	0	0
Sea Vegetables, 3.5 oz. (100 g) raw								
Irish moss	<1	33	14	7	46	.001	46	0
Kelp	12	58	23	17	2	.004	4	0
Spirulina	13.5	50	12	23	15	0.2	0	0
Wakame	13	32	14	8	46	0.001	186	0
Fruits and Land Vegetables								
Avocado, 1 medium	86	17	69	13	1	0.25	0	0
Greens, 1 cup (250 ml)	12–14	28	5	11	56	0.1	0	0
Olives, 10 large	84	14	77	8	0.1	0.02	0	0
Animal Products (for comparison)								
Egg, 1 large	61	37	48	14	0.4	.02	5	51
Wild Atlantic salmon, 3 oz. (85 g)	40	18	40	3	39	0.1	517	948
Cod, 3 oz. (85 g)	7	31	22	1	46	0	54	111

FINE-TUNING THE FAT: SIX SIMPLE STEPS

1. Aim for 15 to 35 percent of calories from fat for everyone four years of age and older and 30 to 40 percent for children one to three years of age. Those who are inactive, overweight, or have chronic diseases should aim for the lower end of this range, while children, athletes, and those who are lean and active should aim for the higher end of this range. How much fat is 15 to 35 percent of calories? For a person eating 2,000 calories, it would allow for 2.5 to 5 tablespoons (38 to 75 ml) of fat, including fat naturally present in whole foods and concentrated fats and oils. The following foods provide approximately 1 tablespoon (15 ml) of fat each:

✓ ¼ cup (60 ml) nuts or seeds
✓ 1 cup (250 ml) medium-firm tofu or ½ cup (125 ml) firm tofu or tempeh
✓ 2 cups (500 ml) full-fat soymilk
✓ ¾ cup (185 ml) boiled soybeans
✓ ½ of a medium avocado
✓ 20 olives
✓ ½ cup (125 ml) shredded coconut

2. Minimize intake of trans-fatty acids. Trans-fatty acids should make up less than 1 percent of total calories. To accomplish this, all foods containing hydrogenated or partially hydrogenated fats should be restricted. This includes processed foods (e.g., cookies, crackers, pastries, pies, and snack foods), hydrogenated margarine, shortening, and most fried foods. Don't be fooled by a declaration of "all-vegetable oil" on the label. Be sure to read the list of ingredients!

3. Limit foods rich in saturated fats. Aim to keep saturated fat under 7 percent of total calories. To reduce saturated fat in a vegetarian diet, limit your use of butter, cheese, and other high-fat dairy foods; eggs; and tropical oils. If you use dairy products, replace high-fat items such as whole milk and sour cream with nonfat or low-fat items, such as skim milk and nonfat yogurt, and replace butter with oil or nonhydrogenated margarine. Try scrambled tofu instead of scrambled eggs for breakfast, and substitute ground flaxseeds or commercial egg replacer for eggs in baking.

4. Moderate intake of omega-6 fatty acids. Most vegetarians consume plenty of omega-6 fatty acids, and some consume excessive amounts. Aim for 5 to 8 percent of calories from omega-6 fatty acids. The best way to do this is to avoid using omega-6-rich oils as your primary oils (e.g., corn, safflower, sunflower, grapeseed, soy, and cottonseed oils). Instead, replace these oils with oils rich in monounsaturated fats (such as extra-virgin olive oil) and/or omega-3 fatty acids (such as flaxseed oil and organic canola oil). Do not restrict your consumption of highly nutritious, omega-6-rich whole foods such as sunflower seeds, pumpkin seeds, and sesame seeds.

5. Select reliable sources of omega-3 fatty acids each day. Aim for 1.5 to 2.5 percent of total calories as omega-3 fatty acids (3 to 6 grams per day for most people). The best omega-3 sources for vegetarians are flaxseeds and flaxseed oil, hempseeds and hempseed oil, canola oil, walnuts, soybeans (and products made from soybeans), dark green leafy vegetables, and wheat germ. The following foods provide roughly 1 gram of alpha-linolenic acid:

- ✓ ⅓ teaspoon (1.7 ml) flaxseed oil
- ✓ 2 teaspoons (10 ml) ground flaxseeds
- ✓ 10 cups (2.5 L) raw dark greens
- ✓ 1⅓ teaspoons (7 ml) canola oil
- ✓ 1 teaspoon (5 ml) hempseed oil
- ✓ 1 cup (250 ml) soybeans
- ✓ 6 ounces (170 g) firm tofu
- ✓ 1½ tablespoons (23 ml) walnuts

Consider getting a direct source of long-chain omega-3 fatty acids in your diet. The best source for vegetarians is DHA from a special type of microalgae that is cultured and sold in gelatin-free capsules. When using these supplements, 100 to 300 mg of DHA per day is generally recommended. (The higher end of the range is for pregnant and lactating women.) For lacto-ovo vegetarians, omega-3-rich eggs also are an option.

6. Rely on whole foods for the bulk of your fat. The highest quality fat comes from fresh, whole foods, such as nuts, seeds, olives, avocados, and soybeans. Wherever possible, rely on these foods instead of concentrated fats and oils for most of your fat. Whole foods come carefully packaged by nature to protect them from damaging light, heat, and air. Whole plant foods provide phytochemicals, including antioxidants, plant sterols, vitamins, and minerals, and are the very best sources of essential fatty acids. Remember that fats and oils are essential for good health, so make the effort to choose the highest quality.

How are high-fat plant foods and oils best stored?

High-fat plant foods can easily become rancid if not properly stored. This could well be nature's way of letting us know that a food has lost its freshness and is no longer wholesome. Foods and oils rich in essential fats, especially omega–3 fatty acids, are best stored in the refrigerator or freezer. Nuts and seeds that are naturally preserved by a hard shell will keep for about a year in a cool, dry place. Once this protective covering has been removed or broken, they will keep for three to four months in the refrigerator and up to a year in the freezer. Walnuts, ground flaxseeds, hempseeds, and wheat germ are best stored in the freezer, as they are higher in the more unstable omega–3 fatty acids.

For scientific references for this chapter, go to
http://www.nutrispeak.com/bvreferences.htm

Chapter 8

FINE-TUNING THE VEGETARIAN DIET

VITAMIN B$_{12}$

Have you ever heard someone say that if we can't get all the nutrients we need from plants, it proves we are designed to eat meat? During such arguments, vitamin B$_{12}$ is often used as the case in point. People may then go on about the Paleolithic diet and the evolutionary process. Obviously, they say, if B$_{12}$ is found only in animal products, nature is telling us something.

The truth is that our requirement for B$_{12}$ has nothing to do with a need for meat, nor does it indicate that vegan diets are inferior. Animals do not make vitamin B$_{12}$; bacteria do. Whatever is contaminated with B$_{12}$-producing bacteria can provide us with B$_{12}$—plants or animals. In the past, people got vitamin B$_{12}$ from dirt clinging to plants, from water, and from bacterial contamination in animals. In our modern, sanitary food environment, we wash any bits of dirt from vegetables before eating them and chlorinate our water before drinking it. In meat, the B$_{12}$ produced by bacteria is contained within the product itself. This does not make meat a superior food. So where can people who prefer not to eat animal products get their B$_{12}$? They can get it from carefully grown B$_{12}$-producing bacteria. These bacteria provide a convenient, reliable, and well-absorbed supply of vitamin B$_{12}$ that is added to fortified foods and used to make supplements. Today, we are fortunate to have the option of choosing a diet that not only supports human health, but promotes a healthy environment and a more compassionate world. The amount of vitamin B$_{12}$ that we need each day is tiny—smaller even than the period at the end of this sentence. A number of false B_{12} beliefs exist; in some cases, these myths have led to major health problems.

Myth #1: **Some people manage perfectly well without a source of vitamin B_{12}.**

Myth #2: **Vitamins from supplements are never as good as those from foods.**

Myth #3: **Vegetables grown in B_{12}-rich soil can meet our vitamin B_{12} needs.**

Myth #4: **Reliable sources of vitamin B_{12} include spirulina, algae, sea vegetables, fermented foods (such as miso, tempeh, tamari, sauerkraut, and umeboshi plums), or raw foods.**

To begin, let's consider the nature of vitamins.

Vitamin B_{12} was first isolated in 1948 and was the very last vitamin to be discovered. It is the largest and most complex of all vitamins, a beautifully symmetrical molecule, similar in many respects to hemoglobin. Whereas hemoglobin has an atom of iron in a central position, the mineral cobalt is at the center of vitamin B_{12}. As you'll see, vitamin B_{12} is complicated in many ways, not only in its molecular structure. This chapter aims to make the role of B_{12} understandable.

Vitamin B_{12} in the Body

Vitamin B_{12} helps our red blood cells mature normally. This vitamin is essential to the function of our brain, spinal cord, and nerves; it helps maintain the protective myelin sheaths that surround nerve fibers. During our body's processing of protein, a molecule called *homocysteine* is created. The buildup of this molecule can be toxic, resulting in heart disease and other damage. As part of its role, vitamin B_{12} helps clear away homocysteine.

Symptoms of Deficiency

If we don't get sufficient B_{12}, either in our food or from supplements, we will eventually develop a vitamin B_{12} deficiency. In some people, the deficiency can take years to manifest; while for others, symptoms can show up in a matter of months. Early signs of deficiency often are nonspecific, such as fatigue, weakness, or loss of menstruation. However, symptoms can escalate and may involve many body systems. If left for too long, the damage can be irreversible. The following list provides a range of possible symptoms, though not all appear in every case of vitamin B_{12} deficiency.

Effects related to blood. Among the very first symptoms of B_{12} deficiency are fatigue and a lack of energy. (Of course, there can be plenty of reasons for fatigue apart from a lack of this vitamin.) Shortness of breath and palpitations (abnormal, rapid beating of the heart and shaking) also can occur. These symptoms arise because the lack of vitamin B_{12} prevents red blood cells from maturing and dividing properly, which affects the blood's ability to deliver oxygen. This condition is called *macrocytic* (large cell) anemia. With a microscope, lab technicians can view unusually large, oddly shaped red blood cells. Tests that detect this condition are listed on lab reports as MCV (which stands for "mean cell volume," a measure of the size of individual red blood cells) and hematocrit (a count of the red cells in a certain volume of blood). As soon as our bodies get enough vitamin B_{12}, this problem can be repaired and normal blood cells can be created.

Yet even when vitamin B_{12} is in short supply, another B vitamin, known as folate or folic acid, can step in and help red blood cells form normally. Vegetarian diets typically are high in folic acid. (Folate is related to the word foliage; it is found in leafy greens, legumes, oranges, whole grains, and fortified flours.) However, folate can't help with the neurological symptoms of B_{12} deficiency described in the next section.

WHAT IS A VITAMIN?

Vitamin is one of those words people toss around without being entirely sure what it means. Put down this book for a moment and ask someone near you to define the word *vitamin*. Odds are you'll hear something vague, such as "one of those tiny little things that keeps us healthy." We asked our neighbors and received these interesting responses: "A vitamin is something you take so you don't feel guilty about having a diet consisting primarily of luncheon meats, potato chips, and beer," and, "What we give our kids because their diets are so desperately limited," and, "A vitamin is what you take to avoid eating all that green stuff. You need vitamins on a boat; otherwise you will get scurvy. I'm not sure what scurvy is, but it's bad."

So what is the correct definition of a vitamin? Vitamins are organic molecules that are vital to life. (In this case, *organic* doesn't mean "grown without pesticides"; it means "carbon-containing.") These compounds are essential in tiny amounts and cannot be made by our bodies. Vitamins are not fuels, as are carbohydrate, fat, and protein; yet they act as necessary catalysts in many reactions, including processes that support growth or allow us to convert food to usable energy.

Effects related to the nervous system. Because of vitamin B_{12}'s importance in creating a fatty myelin sheath that protects our nerves, spine, and brain, a deficiency of this vitamin can be very serious. Numbness and tingling occur, especially in the hands and feet. This is the first nervous system sign of a B_{12} deficiency. Eventually, balance and the ability to walk are affected. Memory and the ability to concentrate decrease; dizziness, disorientation, and mood changes occur, including delusions and paranoia. Bladder and bowel control may be lost. Vision may blur and optic nerves could be damaged. These changes happen gradually. If nerve damage is severe, it can be irreversible.

Effects related to artery walls. In the section "Vitamin B_{12} in the Body," we mentioned the vitamin's role in helping us clear away potentially damaging homocysteine, which can cause plaque to form along the inner wall of arteries and increase our risk of heart attack. (For more information about this, see table 2.3, page 26.)

Effects related to the gastrointestinal tract. The tongue can become sore and its color and surface texture may change. Appetite may be lost.

Effects in infants and children. Because babies have not built up stores of this vitamin, B_{12} deficiency will develop much more rapidly than in adults. Symptoms include loss of energy, appetite, and alertness, and can progress to coma and death. Because vitamin B_{12} plays a role in cell division, it is especially necessary during times of growth. Thus, an adequate intake of vitamin B_{12} is particularly important for pregnant and lactating women, and for infants and children. Breast-fed infants can become severely deficient if the mother has low B_{12} intake, even if the mother has no deficiency symptoms. Therefore, a regular source of the vitamin is crucial for pregnant and breast-feeding mothers, and for breast-fed infants if the mother's diet is not supplemented.

All symptoms are reversible if caught early enough; otherwise damage can be permanent, particularly in children. Nerve damage from prolonged vitamin B_{12} deficiency can be severe and irreversible, yet it rarely occurs because deficiencies generally are diagnosed before this point. Such tragedies can easily be prevented by supplementation.

Causes of Vitamin B_{12} Deficiency

Vitamin B_{12} deficiency is most often the result of one of two factors:

1. Reduced absorption of B_{12}
2. A lack of B_{12} in the diet

In the general population, reduced absorption is the usual cause of B_{12} deficiency. In vegetarians, and especially in vegans, low or negligible dietary B_{12} may be implicated.

Reduced absorption

Absorption of vitamin B_{12} is a complex process. As the vitamin moves through the gastrointestinal tract to spots along the small intestine where it can be absorbed, it must be shielded from bacteria and enzymes that would consume or destroy it. Substances in our saliva, pancreatic juices, and stomach secretions help accomplish this task. Three substances produced by the cells that line our stomachs are of particular interest. These are a digestive enzyme called *pepsin*, hydrochloric acid, and a protein substance called *intrinsic factor*.

Decreased production of pepsin and hydrochloric acid. In order for us to absorb the protein-bound form of vitamin B_{12} in animal products, the joint action of hydrochloric acid (HCl) and pepsin are required to split the vitamin apart from the protein that binds it. If cells lining the stomach decrease their production of pepsin and hydrochloric acid, we lose our ability to absorb the protein-bound form of vitamin B_{12}. However, in this situation we are capable of absorbing the simpler form of the vitamin—a form that is not bound to protein—in fortified foods and supplements.

As we age, our stomach lining gradually becomes less adept at producing HCl and pepsin, and this is the cause of most of the B_{12} deficiency in North America. One out of every three people over the age of fifty has lost the ability to absorb the protein-bound B_{12} present in animal products.

Decreased production of intrinsic factor. The stomach lining also releases intrinsic factor, which acts as a B_{12} bodyguard, shepherding it along, protecting it from bacteria and enzymes that would otherwise consume or destroy it, until it reaches particular spots along the small intestine where the vitamin can be absorbed into the bloodstream. Without intrinsic factor, our body absorbs very little vitamin B_{12}, resulting in a condition known as *pernicious anemia*, which must be treated with vitamin B_{12} injections. A physician may order a Schilling test to check for pernicious anemia.

Senior needs. Sometimes, senior citizens who are admitted to nursing homes with a diagnosis of confusion are suffering from a loss of ability to absorb vitamin B_{12}. When this is the case, the condition frequently can be reversed quickly by injections of the vitamin.

Those who lack pepsin and HCl can manage well thereafter with fortified foods and supplements, whereas those who lack intrinsic factor will continue to require monthly B_{12} injections.

Absorption, Recycling, Storage, and Interpersonal Differences

We secrete vitamin B_{12} into our intestines (through bile from the liver), and then reabsorb as much as 75 percent of it. Some people's recycling systems are more efficient than others. Excess vitamin B_{12} can be stored in the liver and other tissues. Most people have a supply that will last three years or more; however, stores vary considerably. (Infants have very little.)

Myth: Some people manage perfectly well without a source of vitamin B_{12}.

From one person to another, there are great differences in how efficiently we absorb vitamin B_{12} and how well we reabsorb what is secreted (in bile) into the intestine. These variations explain why deficiency symptoms may arise in less than a year in a person who has no dietary source of B_{12}, especially someone whose initial vitamin B_{12} stores are low. Yet another individual with no B_{12} intake might recycle internal stores of the vitamin efficiently and problems may not become obvious for a decade or more. Genetic variations between individuals influence how early damage to the nervous system begins, how quickly homocysteine accumulates, and what degree of damage results. This much is certain: no one manages indefinitely without a sufficient intake of this essential nutrient. The effects of a deficiency on the nervous system and artery walls are not something we want to risk when potential problems are so easily prevented with fortified foods or a supplement! It may come as a surprise that the form of vitamin B_{12} used in supplements and fortified foods is one that is well suited to our needs. In fact, as we age, this becomes the preferred form. This brings us to another myth listed at the beginning of this chapter.

Myth: Vitamins from supplements are never as good as those from foods.

The form of B_{12} in supplements and fortified foods is not bound to protein the way it is in animal products, and this actually makes it easier for people to absorb, especially those whose gastric acidity and pepsin production is beginning to decline.

Laboratory Testing for Vitamin B_{12} Status

Vitamin B_{12} deficiency can be detected by blood tests, even at the early stages. Certainly this should be done before serious problems develop, and it is strongly recommended for the following people:

➤ anyone with early symptoms of B_{12} deficiency, such as numbness and tingling in the fingers and toes;

➤ anyone who eats little or no animal products and has not had a regular, reliable source of this vitamin for many months (or several weeks, in the case of children);

➤ a woman in an early stage of pregnancy who is concerned about past intake;

➤ a person over fifty years of age with doubts about his or her vitamin B_{12} status.

Since adults have reserves of this vitamin that can last months or years, a simple and effective course of action for a symptom-free adult who simply has gone for a few months without any B_{12} intake is just to start using fortified foods or supplements regularly! This will get B_{12} to a healthy level and keep it there.

Normal levels

Several lab tests are used to detect vitamin B_{12} deficiency. The following are the two most commonly used.

Serum B_{12}. Blood serum levels above 300 picomoles per liter (pmol/L) of vitamin B_{12}, or 400 picograms per milliliter, indicate that we have sufficient B_{12}. With levels below 300 picomoles per liter, the amount of homocysteine in the blood increases to a point at which it could have a detrimental effect on health. (Note that the serum B_{12} test is not valid for people who regularly eat spirulina or sea vegetables, as these contain analogs that fool the blood test.)

Methylmalonic acid. In the section "Vitamin B_{12} in the Body," we mentioned that as part of its role, vitamin B_{12} helps clear away homocysteine. In B_{12} deficiency, a related compound, called *methylmalonic acid* (MMA), builds up. One sensitive test for vitamin B_{12} status is a measure of MMA in blood or urine. Levels should be less than 370 nanomoles per liter in blood or less than 4 micrograms (mcg) per mg creatinine in urine.

Recommended intakes: simple solutions

Because vitamin B_{12} is effectively conserved, our required intake of it is miniscule. The actual amount to take depends on how frequently we consume a source, as we absorb a much higher percentage from a small amount than from a large dose. For example, when we consume 1 mcg of vitamin B_{12} in ½ cup (125 ml) of fortified soymilk, we are likely to absorb about 50 percent of the B_{12} present. Yet, from a 2,000-mcg vitamin B_{12} supplement, we may absorb only about 1 percent. The recommendations that follow allow for a range of personal choices.

Recommended intake based on several small amounts over the course of a day. The recommended dietary allowance (RDA) for those above the age of thirteen years is 2.4 mcg per day. The RDA is based on the assumption that our intake is spread over the course of a day; for example, by using fortified foods, eggs, or dairy products at various meals. When we take in about 1 mcg or less at a time, we absorb 50 to 60 percent of the B_{12} present.

Recommended intake from a single daily supplement. If we have our total in a single supplement instead of spread over several meals, we should take 10 mcg per day. Most multivitamins provide at least 10 mcg, so this is certainly an option for most people.

Recommended intake from a single weekly supplement. Some people prefer to take a larger-dose supplement once a week. In this case, we must take 2,000 mcg per week. High intakes do not seem to present problems; we absorb only a small percentage of the total.

Needs during stages of growth. Because vitamin B_{12} is used for the creation of red blood cells and for building the fatty sheath that protects nerves, it is very important throughout times of growth. During pregnancy, a fetus depends on the mother's intake of vitamin B_{12}, rather than on the mother's stores. Thus, intake every day is advised during pregnancy, either spread over several meals or in a daily supplement. For B_{12} amounts recommended for children and pregnant and lactating women, see page 361.

Needs for those above fifty years of age. The Institute of Medicine of the National Academy of Sciences recommends that most or all of our B_{12} should be supplied by fortified foods or a daily supplement, rather than by animal products, for those above fifty years of age. (B_{12} from animal products is bound to protein and can be more difficult to absorb.) The form in most supplements and fortified foods is called cyanocobalamin and is not bound to protein.

Intakes and B_{12} Status in Nonvegetarians and Vegetarians

Nonvegetarians tend to have vitamin B_{12} intakes that meet or exceed recommended amounts, and deficiency generally is due to absorption problems, not a shortage in the diet. Past studies have shown the intakes and vitamin B_{12} status of some vegans and other vegetarians to be relatively low compared to nonvegetarians. Often lacto-ovo vegetarian intakes were within the normal range, as were the intakes of vegans who used B_{12}-fortified foods or supplements. Studies have demonstrated that the longer people remain on a diet without a source of vitamin B_{12}, the lower their serum B_{12} drops, and eventually problems can develop.

A 1999 study by Dr. Ella Haddad and her colleagues at Loma Linda University observed serum B_{12} and MMA in two groups: nonvegetarians and vegans. The latter had followed a vegetarian diet for twelve years and had been vegan for four years. Serum B_{12} and MMA were found to be similar in the two groups. This is because B_{12} intakes were similar in the vegans and nonvegetarians. Nonvegetarian women averaged 5.7 mcg of vitamin B_{12} from foods and supplements, while vegan women averaged 6.0 mcg. Nonvegetarian men averaged 5.3 mcg of vitamin B_{12} from foods and supplements, while vegan men averaged 5.0 mcg. This demonstrates that when a reliable source of B_{12} is provided in vegan diets, vitamin B_{12} status is similar to nonvegetarians. Indeed, vegans using adequate amounts of fortified foods or B_{12} supplements are much less likely to suffer from B_{12} deficiency than the typical meat-eater. This is because the type of B_{12} that vegans consume is exclusively cyanocobalamin; they do not rely on protein-bound B_{12} that is poorly absorbed by many people past fifty years of age.

Our Sources of Vitamin B_{12}

The actual sources of vitamin B_{12} are some very helpful microorganisms that are capable of building the intricate vitamin B_{12} molecule. We humans cannot make the vitamin in our bodies, nor can animals. We rely on bacteria and several other microorganisms for our entire supply. Some of these bacteria live in the lower intestines of animals and humans. Unfortunately, we can't absorb the vitamin B_{12} made by these bacteria because absorption takes place higher up in the intestine than where they live (and they don't swim upstream).

B_{12} in animal products

For most North Americans, dietary vitamin B_{12} comes primarily from animal products, yet animal products are not the original source of this B_{12}. The B_{12} in animal flesh, seafood, eggs, and dairy products comes from bacteria and other one-celled organisms.

B_{12} in the cycle of nature

We may think fondly of times when we humans were "closer to nature." In the natural cycle, intestinal waste from humans, grazing animals, and wild animals, and waste from beetles, worms, and little burrowing creatures puts vitamin B_{12} back into the soil. Bugs and little bits of dirt, along with B_{12}, ended up on plant foods eaten by our ancestors. This was beneficial in terms of B_{12} intake, but frankly, there are downsides to being that "close to nature."

B_{12}, **earth, and modern hygiene.** Today we choose to be more hygienic and avoid the pathogens (disease-causing organisms) that can also be present in soil. When plant foods are washed, bacterial contamination and vitamin B_{12} are scrubbed off along with the dirt. Humanity's progress in hygiene certainly has cut down on many microorganisms that we don't want, along with infectious disease and related deaths—but it has reduced the B_{12}, too.

Myth: Vegetables grown in B_{12}-rich soil can meet our vitamin B_{12} needs.

B_{12} **and agriculture.** Certainly there is more vitamin B_{12} in cobalt-rich soils that contain organic waste and have plenty of little "critters" burrowing through the earth. But we scrub this dirt off the veggies that go into our salads. Even in those that are not rinsed, the amount of B_{12} would be quite variable, although generally negligible. Unfortified plant foods simply cannot be relied on as B_{12} sources.

Myth: Reliable sources of vitamin B_{12} include spirulina, algae, sea vegetables, fermented foods (such as miso, tempeh, tamari, sauerkraut, and umeboshi plums), or raw foods.

B_{12} **and food production methods.** Fermented foods such as tempeh and miso are reputed to contain vitamin B_{12}. This assumption arose during a time when less hygienic, less tightly controlled production methods were used to produce these foods. In traditional methods, all sorts of bacteria could get into the fermenting food, including some that produce vitamin B_{12}. Modern sanitation controls eliminate the B_{12}-producing bacteria. These foods cannot be relied on as sources of the vitamin, nor can spirulina or algae. If there is any B_{12} on sea vegetables, the amount is unpredictable and depends on the type of sea vegetable and on the waste and bacteria present in the water in which it grew. Don't count on seaweed for your vitamin B_{12}.

B_{12} **analogs.** Sea vegetables, spirulina, and other types of algae may contain vitamin B_{12} analogs (also known as *noncobalamin corrinoids*). These analogs are similar to true vitamin B_{12}, but are not exactly the same. They are near-identical twins, with something missing. Analogs can occupy the same locations on cell surfaces that are used by true vitamin B_{12} and crowd out B_{12} molecules from their rightful receptor sites. In the process, the analogs can prevent the true vitamin from performing its necessary functions. A substance that contains substantial amounts of analogs won't help you meet your need for vitamin B_{12}. In fact, it could make the situation worse.

Scientific reports have shown that sea vegetables, spirulina, and other types of algae are ineffective in reversing cases of vitamin B_{12} deficiency. To add to the confusion, some lab tests that detect vitamin B_{12} in foods have been unable to distinguish true B_{12} from analogs.

Foods that are not reliable sources of vitamin B_{12}. None of the following should be relied on as B_{12} sources: fermented foods (such as miso, tempeh, tamari, sauerkraut, and umeboshi plums), sea vegetables, spirulina, algae, raw plant foods, and unfortified plant foods.

Lost in label lingo?

Unless fortified, no plant food contains significant amounts of true vitamin B_{12} (cobalamin). Labels of fortified foods

Recommended B_{12} Intakes and Dietary Value Standard for Food Labels	
Adult recommended dietary allowance (RDA)	2.4 mcg
Daily value (DV)	6.0 mcg

show them to contain B_{12}; however, it can be very confusing to figure out how much of your day's ideal supply is in a serving. This is because the amount set as 100 percent some years ago (and used ever since as the basis for food labels) is not the same as 100 percent of the day's recommended dietary allowance (RDA) for an adult today. (It would be immensely expensive for manufacturers to redesign their food labels every time nutritional scientists decided to adjust the recommended intake for any one of dozens of nutrients.)

Whereas the RDA for adults is now 2.4 mcg of vitamin B_{12}, the DV or Daily Value, a standard used for U.S. labels and based on an earlier recommended intake, is 6 mcg. Thus, a serving that contains 1.2 mcg, or half of our recommended intake (RDA) for the day, is labeled as providing 20 percent of the DV for vitamin B_{12}. For RDAs at other ages, see page 361.

TABLE 8.1 VITAMIN B_{12} IN FOODS		
Fortified Foods	**Vitamin B_{12} (mcg)**	**% DV**
Cereals, ready-to-eat, fortified, 1 oz. (28.4 g)	0.6–6.0	10–100%
Nutritional yeast (Red Star Vegetarian Support Formula), mini-flakes, 1 tbsp. (15 ml)	1.5	25%
Soymilk or other nondairy milks, fortified, ½ cup (125 ml)	0.4–1.25	7–21%
Veggie "meats," fortified, 1½ oz. (43 g)	0.6–1.2	10–20%
Infant formula	See label	–
Animal Products	**Vitamin B_{12} (mcg)**	**% DV**
Cow's milk, ½ cup (125 ml)	0.4	7%
Cheddar cheese, ¾ oz. (21 g)	0.1–0.2	2–3%
Yogurt, ½ cup (125 ml)	0.3–0.7	5–12%
Egg, 1 large, (50 g)	0.5	8%

Reliable food sources of B_{12} that are used by vegetarians are listed in table 8.1. Yeasts other than the brand listed here generally are not fortified.

To determine the amount of true B_{12} in a particular food, you can write a letter to the technical department of the company that produces the food and request a laboratory report to verify the presence of cobalamin (vitamin B_{12}) and the absence of noncobalamin corrinoids (vitamin B_{12} analogs).

Vitamin B_{12} in Menus

Menu 1 meets recommendations. In the 2,000-calorie Menu 2, egg and dairy products contribute some B_{12}, though less than recommended intakes. Adding one or more fortified foods could easily bring the total up to recommended levels.

For a vegan, a suitable intake that meets the RDA of 2.4 mcg of vitamin B_{12} might include a serving of fortified breakfast cereal and, at another time during the day, ½ cup (125 ml) of fortified soymilk or a serving of a fortified veggie "meat," each providing 1.5 mcg of vitamin B_{12} (with the food label showing 25 percent of the DV). On another day, the intake might come from a multivitamin-mineral supplement.

TABLE 8.2	VITAMIN B_{12} IN MENUS	
	Vitamin B_{12} (mcg)	
Menu and Page	2,000 Calories	2,800 Calories
1 Nonvegetarian, page 70	3.1	4.3
2 Lacto-Ovo Vegetarian, page 71	1.9	2.6
3 Lacto-Ovo Vegetarian with More Legumes, page 72	3.5	3.6
4 Vegan, page 73	4.9	5.0

What about B_{12} Supplements?

When it comes to vitamins and minerals, generally our best plan is to try to meet our recommended intakes from foods, especially plant foods, because they contain a wide assortment of phytochemicals, fiber, and other nutrients.

Yet in the case of vitamin B_{12}, the situation is a little different. Some vegetarians use plenty of eggs and dairy products, while others use very little or none of these. Vitamin B_{12} from supplements and fortified foods is essential for those who consume little or no animal products, and it is the preferred form for older people.

In fact, most vitamins are absorbed well from vitamin pills. Though pills are no substitute for the many healthful components of plant foods, using supplements or fortified foods to reach recommended intakes can work very well.

B*₁₂* Basics: What You Really Need to Know

➤ Low B_{12} intakes can cause serious health consequences, especially in babies.

➤ Aim for enough B_{12} to prevent deficiency and to reduce homocysteine.

➤ Do not fool around with insufficient vitamin B_{12}!

Reliable Vegan B*₁₂* Sources

1. Foods fortified with vitamin B_{12} (for example, nondairy beverages, some veggie "meats," some ready-to-eat cereals, and some nutritional yeasts)

2. Vitamin supplements

How Much Vitamin B*₁₂* Do We Need?

1. **From fortified foods:** At least 2.4 mcg daily when spread among two or more doses throughout the day

2. **From supplements:** At least 10 mcg a day when taken daily; at least 2,000 mcg when taken once a week

For scientific references for this chapter, go to
http://www.nutrispeak.com/bvreferences.htm

Chapter 9

DESIGNING THE DIET

THE VEGETARIAN FOOD GUIDE

In chapters 3 through 8 we discussed the key areas of vegetarian nutrition. We challenged myths about protein, iron, and zinc and specified the best plant-based food sources of these valuable nutrients. We explored the amazing world of calcium and vitamin D and revealed the many little-known calcium powerhouses of the plant kingdom. A fresh perspective on grains was presented, as we uncovered the important contribution these little gems can make to our overall nutrient intakes. We talked about the most highly protective, nutrient-dense foods in our diet—vegetables and fruits. The world of fat was explored, and a strong case was built for including higher-fat, whole foods in our daily diets in place of processed fats and animal fats. Finally, we investigated vitamin B_{12}, the one nutrient that vegetarians sometimes fall short on, even with a varied vegetarian diet. Now we will summarize this information in a simple, practical illustration called the Vegetarian Food Guide. This guide will assist us in designing a vegetarian diet that is virtually foolproof!

As you might imagine, it's no simple task to develop a tool that is suitable for people of many ages, activity levels, and food preferences. A single guide must support the nutritional health of a teenage marathon cyclist, his preschool sister, and his grandmother. A vegetarian guide applies to those who use eggs and dairy products and those who don't. It must assist beginners to "get it right" and help long-term vegetarians fine-tune their way of eating.

In fact, there are enough variations on a vegetarian theme to keep all of us in excellent health. Some like a simple, basic menu, repeated day after day with just a few changes. Others prefer gourmet meals and an elegant presentation. Many people don't want (or don't have the time) to cook, and rely on restaurant meals and take-out delis. Others eat much of their food raw. For some, preparation must be quick and easy, while for others the top priority is economy.

The Vegetarian Food Guide covers all these possibilities. It emphasizes whole foods, yet it also allows for the use of some processed foods. It supports us in meeting recommended intakes for the full spectrum of essential nutrients. At the same time, it helps us avoid the diseases of excess.

These practical pointers will help you plan an excellent diet using the Vegetarian Food Guide:

✓ **Eat a wide variety of foods from each group.** Variety helps to ensure sufficient nutrients, phytochemicals, and fiber. It also makes our meals much more interesting!

✓ **Be moderate in your intake of concentrated fats, oils, and added sugars, if used.** These generally are high in calories, but poor sources of nutrients. Fats and sugar can crowd out foods that offer valuable nutrients.

✓ **Aim for an hour of physical activity each day.** Exercise is central to energy balance and overall health.

✓ **Drink six to eight glasses of water and other fluids each day.** Water is essential to good health. Drinking pure water is a great way to provide needed fluids. However, using vegetable or fruit juices and herbal teas to provide fluids is an excellent option, too.

Additional notes about the different groups in the guide are provided below.

Grains

The whole grains, breads, cereals, and pasta in this group are key contributors of energy (each serving typically provides about 80 calories), protein, B vitamins, and minerals, such as iron. Whole grains are preferred, as they provide a wide assortment of vitamins and minerals plus fiber. The number of servings suggested ranges from six to eleven per day. The minimum of five servings is suitable for those who have low energy needs, such as people who are inactive or small in stature, and those who are limiting their caloric intake. Does a total of six servings sound like a lot? It is less than you might imagine. For example, one cup of cooked cereal at breakfast (two servings), a sandwich with two slices of bread at lunch, and one-half cup of rice or pasta at supper add up to five servings. Athletes and teenage boys, who have high energy requirements, can easily eat eleven servings from this group (or more)!

The Vegetarian Food Guide

A GUIDE TO DAILY FOOD CHOICES

The ranges in servings allow for differences in body size, activity level,
and age. For example, smaller and less-active people need fewer servings;
larger and more-active people need more.

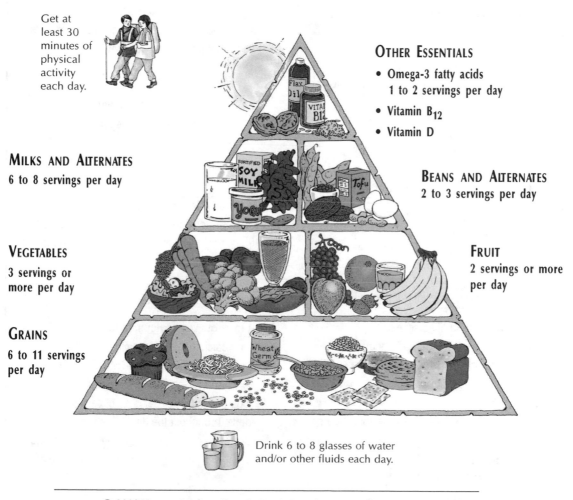

Get at least 30 minutes of physical activity each day.

OTHER ESSENTIALS
- **Omega-3 fatty acids 1 to 2 servings per day**
- **Vitamin B$_{12}$**
- **Vitamin D**

MILKS AND ALTERNATES
6 to 8 servings per day

BEANS AND ALTERNATES
2 to 3 servings per day

VEGETABLES
3 servings or more per day

FRUIT
2 servings or more per day

GRAINS
6 to 11 servings per day

Drink 6 to 8 glasses of water and/or other fluids each day.

A Guide to Daily Food Choices

The left column gives amounts for one serving of each food group in the Vegetarian Food Guide on the previous page. The ranges in servings allow for differences in body size, activity level, and age. For example, smaller and less-active people need fewer servings; larger and more-active people need more. Comments about each food group are given in the right column.

Grains: 6 to 11 servings per day

1 slice of bread
1 oz. (28.4 g) ready-to-eat cereal
2 tbsp. (30 ml) wheat germ
1/2 cup (125 ml) cooked grains, cereal, or pasta
1 oz. (28.4 g) other grain products

Choose mainly whole grains.
Include intact whole grains, such as brown rice,
   quinoa, millet, barley, and kamut.
Enjoy whole grain breads and cereals.
Limit refined grains, such as white flour products
   and white rice.

Vegetables: 3 servings or more per day

1/2 cup (125 ml) vegetables
1 cup (250 ml) salad
1/2 cup (125 ml) vegetable or fruit juice

Eat a wide variety of colorful vegetables.
   Include deep green, leafy vegetables.

Fruits: 2 servings or more per day

1/2 cup (125 ml) fruit or fruit juice
1 medium apple, banana, orange, pear
1/4 cup (60 ml) dried fruit

Include a wide range of fruits.
Vitamin C–rich choices, such as citrus and tropical
   fruits, help us to absorb iron from foods eaten at
   the same meal.

Milks and Alternates: 6 to 8 servings per day

1/2 cup (125 ml) fortified soymilk
1/2 cup (125 ml) cow's milk or yogurt
1/2 cup (125 ml) calcium-fortified orange juice
1/4 cup (60 ml) calcium-set tofu
1 cup (250 ml) cooked or 2 cups (500 ml) raw
   high-calcium greens (kale, collards, Chinese
   greens, broccoli, okra)
1 cup (250 ml) high-calcium beans (soy, white,
   navy, great Northern, black turtle beans)
1/4 cup (60 ml) almonds
3 tbsp. (45 ml) almond butter
3/4 oz. (21 g) cheese
1 tbsp. (15 ml) blackstrap molasses
1/4 cup (60 ml) dry hijiki seaweed
5 figs

Get to know your calcium sources!
Include calcium-rich foods with every meal.
Foods should provide about 15% of the DV per
   serving to be included in this group.
Include several small servings of calcium-rich
   foods throughout the day.
For lower-calorie choices, pick greens more often.

A Guide to Daily Food Choices

Beans and Alternates: 2 to 3 servings per day

1 cup (250 ml) cooked legumes (beans, lentils, split peas)

$^1/_2$ cup (125 ml) tofu or tempeh

1 serving veggie "meat" (burger, wiener, slices)

3 tbsp. (45 ml) nut or seed butter

$^1/_4$ cup (60 ml) nuts or seeds

2 cups (500 ml) soymilk

2 eggs

For maximum benefit, eat a wide range of these protein-rich foods.

Select beans and lentils often for extra fiber.

Include nuts and seeds for a boost of vitamin E and minerals.

Try veggie "meats" for more concentrated protein.

Omega-3 Fatty Acids: 1 to 2 servings per day

1 tsp. (5 ml) flaxseed oil

$^1/_4$ cup (60 ml) shelled hempseeds

$1^1/_2$ tbsp. (22 ml) ground flaxseeds

4 tsp. (20 ml) canola oil

1 tbsp. (15 ml) hempseed oil

3 tbsp. (45 ml) walnuts

Add excellent sources of omega-3 fatty acids to your daily diet.

For supplementary veggie DHA, see page 166.

Vitamin B$_{12}$ (cobalamin) for recommended intakes

Fortified foods, supplements, eggs, dairy products supplying 2.4 mcg (adults);

2.6 to 2.8 mcg (pregnancy/lactation);

0.9 to 1.8 mcg (youth)

Be sure to include a reliable source of vitamin B$_{12}$ in your diet.

Select either vitamin B$_{12}$–fortified foods or a supplement.

Vitamin D for recommended intakes

Sunshine; fortified foods or supplements supplying

5 mcg /day (through age 50);

10 mcg /day (51–70 years);

15 mcg (70+ years:)

If you don't get enough sunshine, use vitamin D–fortified beverages or supplements.

Vegetables

Vegetables provide a wealth of vitamins, minerals, fiber, and phytochemicals, yet a serving of vegetables averages about 25 calories, so we can eat plenty without worrying about our waistlines. Calcium-fortified juices and many leafy greens do double duty as calcium sources. Greens are rich in folate, vitamin K, and other vitamins. Vegetables that are particularly high in vitamin C (such as red and orange bell peppers, broccoli, kale, and Brussels sprouts) improve iron absorption when eaten along with foods that provide this mineral.

Variety is important in our choice of vegetables (and fruits, too) because each delivers its own special package of nutritional benefits, including some of the rainbow range of phytochemicals.

Fruits

Fruits make a wonderful alternative to sweet, high-calorie desserts, delivering, on average, just 60 calories per serving. Calcium-fortified juices and figs give extra benefit by acting as calcium sources. Oranges and orange juice are excellent sources of folate.

The following fruits are particularly high in vitamin C: guava, citrus fruits and juices, kiwi, papaya, cantaloupe, strawberries, and mangos. One-half cup of any of these will provide more than one-third of our day's vitamin C. Many other fruits provide lesser amounts of the vitamin and larger servings can provide enough vitamin C to boost iron absorption.

Milks (Cow's Milk, Fortified Soymilk) and Alternates

Increasingly, food guides are recognizing the importance of calcium sources that go beyond cow's milk. *The Manual of Clinical Dietetics*, developed by the American Dietetic Association and Dietitians of Canada, lists all of the options shown here in its vegetarian section. China's Food Guide Pagoda (similar to the pyramid) recognizes beans and calcium-set tofu as good calcium sources. The American Food Guide Pyramid includes fortified soymilk as an option, listed as a footnote.

Each serving in this group contains approximately 150 mg of calcium. (We also get small amounts of calcium from foods other than those in this group.) An excellent way to meet goals of 1,000 mg of calcium for adults up to age fifty, or 1,200 mg for those over fifty, is by consuming at least six to eight of these calcium-rich foods at meals and snacks throughout the day. The percentage we absorb is highest when our calcium is delivered in small doses.

On national food guides, the size of a serving of cow's milk is doubled (1 cup/250 ml) and there are half as many servings in this group (two to four), so total amounts work out to be the same or slightly less than in this guide. In the Vegetarian Food Guide, a serving of fortified soymilk or cow's milk is ½ cup

(125 ml). Label readers, note that foods and beverages containing about 150 mg of calcium are listed as providing about 15 percent of the Daily Value (DV).

Nutrient-wise choices

This calcium-rich group includes such a wide variety of foods that you can emphasize those that best suit your personal needs. For example, if you are trying to lose weight, opt for those that are low in fat and calories, such as greens (1 cup of cooked greens provides only about 20 to 40 calories), skim milk, nonfat yogurt, fortified orange juice, or mineral-rich blackstrap molasses. While beans and figs are very low in fat, we need larger servings of these foods to get our calcium, so total calories are higher with these foods. However, beans are important mainstays in any vegetarian diet, and figs can take the place of less-nutritious desserts.

Those who need extra calories can select those items that are more concentrated in fat and calories, such as tofu, fortified soymilk, almond butter, and higher-fat dairy products. These high-calorie foods are particularly valuable during the growing years, for athletes, and for people who tend to be underweight.

As we have mentioned, many foods in this group qualify as servings from other food groups too. For example, ½ cup (125 ml) of calcium-fortified orange juice counts as a fruit serving as well; ½ cup (125 ml) of calcium-set tofu counts in the beans group; and 1 cup (250 ml) of cooked kale counts as two servings of vegetables. Note that unfortified soymilk, rice milk, and orange juice are not options in this group.

It's wise to choose a crosssection of these various ways to get our calcium. For ideas about how to include them over the course of a day, see "Boosting Calcium from Dawn to Dusk," pages 104-06.

Beans and Alternates

Beans, peas, lentils, and soyfoods stand out as protein powerhouses for vegetarians. At first we might think, "I could never eat two servings of beans in a day." In fact, this group is rich with possibilities that take us far beyond beans, satisfying every taste. Choices run the gamut from fat-free, protein-packed veggie "meats" (about 80 calories per 2 oz./57 g serving) to hearty foods that deliver about 200 calories per serving (beans, soymilk, tofu, nuts) or as high as 270 calories per serving (3 tbsp./45 ml of nut or seed butter).

Legumes provide iron, zinc, a range of B vitamins, and both insoluble and soluble fiber. Some beans are good calcium sources, and calcium-set tofu and fortified soymilk are great ways to get this mineral. Soyfoods deliver isoflavones. When it comes to nuts, each has its own special features. For example, walnuts are high in omega-3 fatty acids; almonds and almond butter are sources of calcium; cashews contain zinc. Peanuts, which are actually legumes, are economical, higher in protein than tree nuts, and contain health-protective phytochemicals.

Remember that iron absorption is increased substantially when we eat a vitamin C–rich fruit or vegetable at the same time. This occurs, for example, when beans or lentils are served in the same meal with red pepper or other vitamin C–rich vegetables, or when tofu is combined with orange juice or strawberries in a shake.

Omega-3 Fatty Acids

We require two essential fats, the omega-6 and omega-3 fatty acids. Generally we have no difficulty at all in getting enough of the omega-6 fatty acids from vegetable oils and an assortment of plant foods in the various food groups. However, we must take particular care to include the omega-3 fatty acids, as these are less widely distributed in the food supply. Our most efficient way to get omega-3s is from flaxseeds or flaxseed oil. Other good options are hempseeds or hempseed oil, canola oil, walnuts, or a hearty serving of tofu.

We can get DHA, one of the long-chain omega-3 fatty acids present in fish, from the same source that fish get theirs—microalgae. DHA from microalgae is cultured and sold in veggie caps containing 100 to 300 mg of DHA per capsule. (See chapter 7.)

Vitamin B_{12}

People who eat little or no animal products need fortified foods that supply at least 2.4 mcg of vitamin B_{12} (cobalamin) over the course of the day or a supplement that provides 10 mcg per day. (Note that the DV on food labels is 6 mcg.)

Dairy products or eggs supply some B_{12} (see table 8.1, Vitamin B_{12} in Foods, on page 187, for amounts). However, for everyone over the age of fifty (including nonvegetarians, lacto-ovo vegetarians, and vegans), fortified foods or a supplement are advised. A weekly B_{12} supplement of 2,000 mcg is another option.

Vitamin D

Be sure to get adequate vitamin D from daily sun exposure or through fortified foods or supplements. Fortified soymilk, cow's milk, breakfast cereals, and margarines are fortified with vitamin D. Label readers, note that milk (soy or cow's) that is fortified with 2.5 mcg of vitamin D per cup is shown on the label as providing 25 percent of the DV. Also, the vegetarian form is vitamin D_2 (ergocalciferol).

> For recommended intakes of vitamins and minerals for children and during pregnancy and lactation, see pages 361 and 362.

ASSESSING YOUR DIET

How do you figure out whether you're meeting your nutritional needs? You can check your day's food intake by photocopying the Score Sheet on page 200 and using it to assess your diet for a few days. This will give you an idea of the strengths and weaknesses of your current way of eating. If you find that you're short in a certain group, choose foods that you like from that group and put them on your shopping list. You can extend your cooking repertoire with the recipes in chapter 14; these emphasize highly nutritious ingredients. After scor-

---

TABLE 9.1 VEGETARIAN FOOD GUIDE SCORE SHEET

Columns list the number of servings from each group.

Food	Grains	Vegetables	Fruits	Beans and Alternates	Milks and Alternates	Omega-3 Fatty Acids	Vitamin B_{12}	Vitamin D
Breakfast								
Cereal, cooked, 1 cup (250 ml)	2							
Fortified soymilk or cow's milk, 1 cup (250 ml)					2		3 mcg	2.5 mcg
Fruit or juice, ½ cup (125 ml)			1					
Lunch								
Whole wheat pita bread, 2	2							
Hummus, 1 cup (250 ml)				1	1			
Raw veggies, ½ cup (125 ml)		1						
Supper								
Rice, 1 cup (250 ml)	2							
Calcium-set tofu, ½ cup (125 ml)				1	1			
Steamed broccoli, 1 cup (250 ml)		2			1			
Salad, 1 cup (250 ml)		1						
Dressing, 2 tsp. (10 ml) flaxseed oil						2		
Snack								
Shake with fortified soymilk or cow's milk and fruit			1		1			2.5 mcg
TOTAL	**6**	**4**	**2**	**2**	**6**	**2**	**3 mcg**	**5 mcg**

200

TABLE 9.2	VEGETARIAN FOOD GUIDE SCORE SHEET							

Under "Food," list your day's intake. Then, in the appropriate column, write the number of servings from each group.

Food	Grains	Vegetables	Fruits	Beans and Alternates	Milks and Alternates	Omega-3 Fatty Acids	Vitamin B$_{12}$	Vitamin D
TOTAL								
GOAL	6–11	3 (+)	2 (+)	2–3	6–8	1–2	2.4 mcg	5–15 mcg

ing your diet for a while and making a few adjustments, you can relax and feel confident that you're on the right track.

The Simple Life

Table 9.1 gives a sample meal plan with cereal, a milk, and fruit for breakfast; hummus, pita, and veggies for lunch; tofu with rice, salad, and broccoli for supper; and a fruit smoothie as a snack. This simple menu is packed with 75 grams of protein and plenty of vitamins, minerals, essential fats, and fiber. The whole day's eating pattern comes to just 1,680 calories, so most active people will be able to add foods, such as larger portions or favorite treats. It's no harder to plan a nutritionally adequate vegetarian (or vegan) diet than a nonvegetarian diet. If you are aiming for a balanced diet, with plenty of fiber and protective antioxidants, you actually are at an advantage with your vegetarian eating pattern.

Common Questions (and Answers)

Q. If I follow the guide, should I take a supplement?

A. If you score your diet according to the Score Sheet and meet the minimum servings in the Vegetarian Food Guide each day, then you can likely maintain excellent health without a supplement. However, there is good evidence to suggest that those who take a multivitamin-mineral supplement (occasionally or regularly) enjoy better health. This may be because taking this type of supplement can help us boost some of the nutrients that may be marginal on certain days, depending on our food intake. In addition, there are several micronutrients that tend to be marginal for many people. There also are specific situations in which supplements are well advised. Here are five examples.

1. If your vitamin B_{12} requirement is not met by fortified foods, eggs, or dairy products, a vitamin B_{12} supplement or a multivitamin-mineral supplement that contains vitamin B_{12} is essential.

2. If the need for vitamin D is not met by sunlight, fortified soymilk, cow's milk, breakfast cereals, or margarine, then a vitamin D supplement or a multivitamin-mineral supplement that containins vitamin D is necessary.

3. When life is extra busy, meals can become irregular and nutrient intakes may suffer. In such cases, supplements taken occasionally or routinely can be helpful.

4.   When calories are limited or portions are very small (for example, with a finicky child or someone with a poor appetite), giving a supplement can help meet vitamin and mineral needs.

5.   At times of growth (such as during pregnancy), it can be a challenge to meet the recommended intakes shown on page 217 or to consume the suggested amounts of food. Supplements give us reassurance during these times.

Q. Do I need to drink water or are other fluids okay?

A. Water is ideal, and it's a good goal to drink six to eight glasses during the day. We can count herbal teas, juices, various milks, and the water in soups, too. Caffeinated beverages (tea and coffee) don't fully count in the way water does, as these beverages have a diuretic effect; that is, they encourage water losses through our kidneys.

Q. Do fruit "drinks" count as a fruit serving?

A. No! They'd count as servings of sugar, if we had a sugar group—but we don't! Whereas real fruit juice gives us an assortment of vitamins, minerals, and phytochemicals, beverages that are called "drinks" do not. Even if a fruit "drink" has added vitamin C and a small percentage of real juice, it is still primarily sugar and water plus a vitamin.

Q. Where do oils and sugar fit in? Do I need to count them?

A. Oils rich in omega-3s, such as flaxseed, hempseed, canola, or walnut oils, are in a special category and make an important contribution. Other oils provide vitamin E and healthful fats but are not necessary, as these dietary components can be obtained in whole foods. Sugars provide carbohydrates with few additional nutrients. The best way to regard these other oils and sugar is to allow them some space in our diet after the recommended servings for the food groups have been met. If we still have room in our day's menu (without taking in excess calories), these can be included. This is more likely to be the case for active people who have higher caloric requirements. Generally, it's best to make fresh and dried fruits our favorite sweets, and whole foods, such as avocados, olives, nuts, and seeds, our first choice in fats.

Q. How do I get iodine?

A. The mineral iodine is present in plant foods in amounts that vary from one geographic area to another, depending on how much iodine is present in the soil. In the past, people in low-iodine regions throughout the world developed iodine deficiency. Symptoms included the overgrowth of the thyroid gland to form a goiter in the area of the throat, and the tragic outcome of deficiency during pregnancy in which the child would be born with cretinism. This problem still occurs in some parts of the world. In some countries, iodine is added to table salt. This addition is mandatory in Canada and optional in the United States, Britain, Australia, and New Zealand. About 10 percent of Australian households, 50 percent of Americans, and 70 percent of New Zealanders use iodized salt. The adult recommended intake for iodine (150 mcg) is easily met by ½ teaspoon (2 ml) of iodized salt. Sea salt generally is not iodized (although it may be—check the package label) and contains negligible amounts of natural iodine, as this mineral is lost in the drying process. Salty seasonings—such as tamari, soy sauce, Bragg Liquid Aminos, and miso—do not provide iodine.

In addition to variable amounts in plant foods, bread can be a source of iodine, because the mineral is present in some dough stabilizers. Iodine is present in some dairy products in Britain, for example, due to animal feed or cleaning agents used in the dairy industry. Sea vegetables and supplements, such as kelp powder or kelp tablets, can be very high in iodine, leading to intakes by some vegetarians in excess of the recommended upper limit, which is 1,100 mcg.

For scientific references for this chapter, go to
http://www.nutrispeak.com/bvreferences.htm

Chapter 10

VEGETARIAN FOR LIFE

There are several stages of life that deserve special attention. These include the years of peak growth (pregnancy and lactation, infancy, childhood, and adolescence) and the senior years. Each stage of growth is characterized by physical changes that result in unique nutritional requirements. During pregnancy and lactation, infancy, childhood, and adolescence, our needs for many nutrients are greater (per pound or kilogram of body weight) than at any other time in our lives. As we approach our senior years, our caloric requirements decline, while our needs for some nutrients actually increase. This means we must be especially diligent about our food choices to ensure that our nutrient needs are met.

Although the dietary goals of optimal health and well-being are the same throughout the various stages of life, the food patterns that best support these goals naturally differ. During the adult years, a primary focus is the avoidance and sometimes treatment of chronic diseases, such as heart disease, cancer, and type 2 diabetes. Diets relatively low in fat and high in fiber are generally the most suitable choices. In contrast, diets for infants and children require greater emphasis on adequate growth and development, so sufficient concentrated sources of calories and nutrients are necessary. However, these years establish the basis for prevention of chronic disease in later life, so laying the foundation for lifelong healthy eating patterns also is essential. By recognizing the fundamental differences in our nutritional needs, the positive health consequences of a vegetarian diet can be fully realized at every stage of life.

Regardless of whether we are near-vegetarian, lacto-ovo vegetarian, or vegan, a plant-centered diet can support excellent health. The guidelines offered in this chapter will help to ensure that the special needs of those in the growing years and prime of life are met in a simple and enjoyable manner. This chapter will take us through each of these five important life stages:

1. Pregnancy and Lactation
2. Infancy (Birth to Two Years)
3. Childhood (Two to Twelve)
4. Focus on Teens (Thirteen to Eighteen)
5. The Prime of Life (Fifty Years Plus)

PART 1: PREGNANCY AND LACTATION

The months of pregnancy are filled with excitement and anticipation. At no other time in our lives are we are more focused on taking good care of ourselves. This is because we have the awesome responsibility of a precious little soul depending on us for her or his growth and development. It is not uncommon during this time to question whether or not our plant-centered diets are adequate to support this little person who shares our food. Sometimes concerned friends, relatives, and even health professionals start drilling us with questions that further shake our resolve. Thankfully, with a little planning and good sense, we can get all the nutrients we need for both our babies and ourselves.

Both lacto-ovo vegetarian and vegan diets can meet all the nutrient and energy needs of pregnant women. Babies of vegetarian mothers have birth weights that are, on average, similar to those of infants born to nonvegetarian mothers, and well within a healthy range. Vegetarians enjoy some advantages when it comes to pregnancy and lactation, including a lower risk for obesity, hypertension, and pre-eclampsia. The recommended nutrient intakes during pregnancy and lactation are provided in table 10.3, page 217.

Nutrition Guidelines for Pregnancy and Lactation

1. Increase food intake by approximately 100 calories a day during the first trimester of pregnancy, 300 calories a day during the last two trimesters, and 500 calories a day during lactation. One of the key factors for a healthy pregnancy is the mother's weight gain. Insufficient weight gain can cause the baby to be very small. Low birth-weight babies (under 5½ pounds /2.5 kilograms) are at higher risk for illness and death than are babies of normal weight. How much weight gain is best? For most adult women beginning pregnancy with a healthy body weight, a gain of 25 to 35 pounds (11.5 to 16 kilograms) is recommended. Table 10.1 lists recommended weight gain during pregnancy for a variety of circumstances.

In order to produce the desired weight gain during pregnancy, about 100 extra calories a day are needed during the first trimester and about 300 extra calories a day in the last two trimesters, in addition to normal food intake. A total caloric intake of 2,500 to 2,700 calories a day is appropriate for most women. A glass of soymilk or a slice of whole grain bread provides about 100 calories; a bowl of cereal (with milk) or a muffin with a piece of fruit provides about 300 calories.

TABLE 10.1	RECOMMENDED WEIGHT GAIN DURING PREGNANCY AND LACTATION	
Weight Category		**Weight Gain Recommended****
Normal Weight (BMI* 19–24.9)		25–35 lbs. (11.5–16 kg)
Underweight (BMI < 19)		28–40 lbs. (12.5–18 kg)
Adolescent (< 2 years after 1st menstruation)		28–40 lbs. (12.5–18 kg)
Overweight (BMI ≥ 25)		15–25 lbs. (7–11.5 kg)
Normal weight with twins (BMI 19–24.9)		35–45 lbs. (16–20 kg)
Normal weight with triplets (BMI 19–24.9)		50 lbs. (23 kg)

*   BMI means body mass index. For a definition, see page 259. BMIs listed are prior to pregnancy.

** African-Americans and young adolescents should strive for weight gain at the upper end of the range, while short women should aim for gains at the lower end of the range.

During lactation, we need an additional 200 calories above pregnancy needs, or about 500 additional calories each day. This is because it takes a lot of energy to produce enough milk for a baby. Total calorie requirements are approximately 2,700 to 2,900 for most lactating women. Five hundred calories can be found in a sandwich and a glass of fortified soymilk or cow's milk. The 500-calorie recommendation is based on the assumption that we will be using about 300 calories a day from the body fat stores that we have accumulated during pregnancy. For moms who do not have extra fat stores, the increase in calories needs to be in the 800- to 1,000-calorie range. It is important not to let caloric intake slip below 1,800 calories a day, as this can reduce milk production.

WHAT IF I HAVE MORNING SICKNESS?

If you experience morning sickness (varying degrees of nausea), you are not alone. It affects 50 to 75 percent of all pregnant women, especially during the first trimester. Morning sickness can reduce appetite, slow weight gain, and even cause weight loss. To help reduce the nausea associated with morning sickness, it is best to eat several small meals a day and avoid having an empty stomach. Bland, starchy, low-fat foods—such as pasta, bread, cereal, rice, potatoes, and crackers—are good choices. Ginger, a natural antinausea herb, also can be helpful. Sweets and fatty foods can make matters worse, while sour and salty foods are said to be helpful. Drink plenty of water. Be sure to take prenatal supplements.

2. Eat a wide variety of nutritious foods, as outlined in the Vegetarian Food Guide. During pregnancy, nutrient needs shoot up, but calorie requirements increase only slightly. What this means is that there is less room for "junk food" that provides little nutritional value. Instead, we must load up on the many wholesome foods described in the Vegetarian Food Guide (page 193). Include a wide variety of foods from each food group to achieve the best balance of nutrients possible. Avoid skipping meals, as a good supply of vitamins and minerals are needed throughout the day. To make the food guide work during pregnancy and lactation, strive for the higher end of the recommended number of servings within each food group.

A suggested meal plan based on the Vegetarian Food Guide, with the additions recommended during pregnancy and lactation, is provided in table 10.2, Sample Menu Plan for Pregnancy and Lactation. This menu supplies the recommended dietary allowances (RDA) for all nutrients during lactation, and all nutrietns except for vitamin D and iron during pregnancy (although intakes are very high). About half the vitamin D is supplied by fortified soymilk. The other half can be obtained through sunshine or supplements. The iron in the menus provided is very close to the recommended intakes during pregnancy and far exceeds the recommended intakes for lactation (45 mg in the menu for pregnancy and 50 mg in the menu for lactation).

3. Include three to four servings of beans and alternates each day. During pregnancy, needs for protein, iron, and zinc increase, while during lactation, protein and zinc requirements increase. These nutrients are important for the growth of the uterus and expanding blood volume, as well as the infant's growth and development. (See chapter 3 for more information on these nutrients.) The increases in the RDA for each of these nutrients are as follows:

Recommended Number of Servings during Pregnancy and Lactation	
Beans and alternates	3 to 4 servings
Milks and alternates	6 to 8 servings
Vegetables and fruits	7 to 10 servings
Grains	7 to 11 servings
Other Essentials	
Omega-3 fatty acids	2 servings
Vitamin B$_{12}$	2.6 mcg (pregnancy)
	2.8 mcg (lactation)
Vitamin D	5 mcg

• **Protein**: The RDA for protein goes up by 25 grams a day throughout pregnancy and lactation. On average, this means an increase from 46 grams of protein to 71 grams a day. More precisely, protein needs climb from 0.4 to 0.6 grams per pound (0.8 grams to 1.1 grams per kilogram) of body weight. For vegetarians who eat a primarily whole foods diet and very little tofu, soymilk, and veggie "meats," an additional 10 percent is suggested to compensate for the reduced protein digestibility in whole plant foods. This would bring protein requirements up to 0.6 grams per pound (1.2 grams per kilogram) of body weight, or about 78 grams of protein a day.

• **Iron:** The RDA for iron rises from 32.4 mg a day for nonpregnant vegetarians to 48.6 mg for pregnant vegetarians. (This is 1.8 times greater than the nonvegetarian RDA of 18 mg a day for nonpregnant women and 27 mg a day for pregnant women.) Getting 48.6 mg of iron from any diet is very difficult, so iron supplements are recommended for pregnant vegetarians, as they are for all pregnant women. There currently is little evidence to suggest that the risk for iron deficiency in pregnancy is any greater for vegetarians than it is for nonvegetarians. However, vegetarian iron stores are lower, so, theoretically, risk may be increased. To help ensure sufficient iron intake, an iron supplement of 30 mg per day is recommended for all pregnant women, and 60 to 120 mg is recommended per day for those with a low hemoglobin or hematocrit.

Iron needs are not increased during lactation; actually the RDA drops below nonpregnant levels to 16.2 mg a day for lactating vegetarians (9 mg a day for nonvegetarians). This is because women do not generally menstruate during lactation.

• **Zinc:** The RDA for zinc increases from 8 mg a day for nonpregnant women to 11 mg a day during pregnancy and 12 mg a day during lactation. Vegetarians may need as much as 50 percent more zinc if intakes of zinc inhibitors, such as phytate and calcium, are high. Although zinc supplementation is not routinely recommended during pregnancy, it may be wise for pregnant vegans to select a prenatal supplement that includes approximately 15 mg of zinc. This supplement should also contain 2 mg of copper, as zinc can reduce copper absorption.

• **Meeting the RDAs for protein, iron, and zinc:** Increasing our intakes of beans and alternates to three to four servings a day will help ensure sufficient protein, iron, and zinc. While this may seem like a lot of beans, when you include a variety of alternates, it is quite manageable. The following food combinations are examples of just what three to four servings of beans and alternates can look like:

A. ½ cup (125 ml) tofu
1 cup (250 ml) soymilk
1 cup (250 ml) kidney beans

C. ¼ cup (60 ml) cashews
1 cup (250 ml) black beans
½ cup (125 ml) tempeh

B. 3 tablespoons (45 ml)
almond butter
2 veggie burgers
1 cup (250 ml) pea soup

D. 2 eggs
3 slices veggie bacon
1 cup (250 ml) soymilk
¼ cup (60 ml) pumpkin seeds

4. Include six to eight servings of milks and alternates each day, and a reliable source of vitamin D. The RDA for calcium remains at 1,000 mg a day during pregnancy and lactation. There is no increase in calcium requirements because calcium is more efficiently absorbed during this time. Getting sufficient calcium during pregnancy is important for proper formation of a baby's bones and teeth, as well as proper nerve, muscle, and blood functioning. It also is important for a woman's own bone health.

The following examples provide six or more servings from the milks and alternates group:

A. 3 tablespoons (45 ml) almond
butter
1 tablespoon (15 ml)
blackstrap molasses
½ cup (125 ml) tofu
made with calcium
2 cups (500 ml) fortified nondairy or cow's milk
(8 servings)

C. 1 cup (250 ml) broccoli
1 cup (250 ml) black turtle
beans
¼ cup (60 ml) hijiki sea
vegetable
¾ ounce (21 grams) cheese
1 cup (250 ml) calcium-
fortified orange juice
(6 servings)

B. 1 cup (250 ml) fortified
nondairy or cow's milk
1 cup (250 ml) yogurt
1 cup (250 ml) Chinese greens
¼ cup (60 ml) almonds
(6 servings)

D. 1 cup (250 ml) steamed kale
1 cup (250 ml) baked beans
5 figs
1 cup (250 ml) fortified nondairy soymilk or cow's milk
1 cup (250 ml) calcium-
fortified orange juice
(7 servings)

For those who consume less than the recommended number of servings from the calcium-rich group, a calcium supplement may be warranted. While there are modest amounts of calcium in most prenatal supplements (about 100 to 250 mg), this may not be sufficient to make up for a diet containing few calcium-rich foods. If a calcium supplement is needed, select one that provides about 500 mg of calcium daily. Absorption is improved when this amount is taken in two doses at different times. It is best to take calcium supplements between meals, separately from iron supplements, as calcium can interfere with the absorption of iron and zinc.

Vitamin D partners with calcium to assist in its absorption. While vitamin D needs do not increase during pregnancy and lactation, a reliable source is necessary for the bone health of both mother and infant. Most prenatal supplements contain sufficient vitamin D. We also can get our vitamin D from sunshine or from fortified foods. (See chapter 4 for more information on the amounts of sunshine required and fortified foods available.)

5. Eat seven to ten servings a day of colorful vegetables and fruits, including leafy greens. During pregnancy and lactation, our need for several vitamins and minerals increases, including many that are concentrated in vegetables and fruits, such as vitamins A and C, and folate. (See table 10.3, Nutrient Recommendations for Pregnancy and Lactation, on page 217 for more information about each nutrient.)

• **Vitamin A:** Our need for vitamin A increases by just under 10 percent during pregnancy, but by almost 100 percent during lactation. The greater requirements during lactation are because an average of about 400 mcg RAE (see page 140) of vitamin A goes into breast milk each day. Thus, vegetarians must take special care to include vitamin A–rich foods in the diet during this time. (See chapter 6 for more information about vitamin A.) Most of our vitamin A comes from brightly colored orange and deep yellow vegetables and fruits, and green leafy vegetables. It is best to strive for at least three to four servings of vitamin A–rich vegetables and fruits each day.

• **Vitamin C:** The RDA for vitamin C increases by 12 percent during pregnancy and 60 percent during breast-feeding. The higher amounts needed during lactation reflect the 40 mg of vitamin C that appear in breast milk each day. Additional vitamin C can be obtained easily by eating the recommended number of servings of vegetables and fruits. Especially rich vitamin C sources are citrus fruits, strawberries, tropical fruits, broccoli, Brussels sprouts, spinach, and peppers.

• **Folate:** The RDA for folate increases to 600 mcg of Dietary Folate Equivalent (DFE) a day during pregnancy and 500 mcg of DFE a day during lactation. Folate is of tremendous importance because it is estimated that the occurrence of neural tube defects in newborns, including spina bifida and anencephaly, can be reduced by at least 50 percent if the mother increases her folate intake before conception and during early pregnancy. In fact, all women who are capable of becoming pregnant are advised to consume at least 400 mcg of folic acid a day, either from fortified foods or a supplement. (Folic acid is the form of the vitamin in supplements and fortified foods, while folate is the form of the vitamin in foods. The two terms are often used interchangeably—see chapter 6 for more information.) Note that very high folate intakes can mask a vitamin B_{12} deficiency. Therefore, while getting sufficient folate is necessary, intake from supplements and fortified foods should be limited to not more than 1,000 mcg a day (excluding folate from foods).

6. Include at least seven to eleven servings of grains each day. Our requirements for a number of B vitamins rise about 20 to 30 percent during pregnancy and lactation. Eating more whole grains will ensure that these additional needs are easily met. The most nutritionally dense grains are intact whole grains such as quinoa, amaranth, oat groats and rolled oats, kamut, spelt and wheat berries, rye, and brown rice. Use these more often. See pages 332 to 334, 312, and 343 for cooking instructions and recipe ideas. Muffins, breads, and cereals made with whole grains also are good options. If you are experiencing severe morning sickness, you may prefer refined grains at least part of the time. If you opt for refined pasta, bread, cereal, and other processed grains, select those that are enriched with B-vitamins.

7. Increase your intake of omega-3 fatty acids to 2 percent of your total calories. During pregnancy and lactation, our needs for long-chain omega-3 fatty acids, particularly DHA, increase. DHA is critical to the development and function of many different organ systems and for the structure of the brain and retina of the eye. The primary source of DHA for nonvegetarians is fish. Vegetarians can get their DHA from the same place fish do—microalgae. Today, we culture microalgae so it is free of environmental contaminants and sell it in gelatin-free capsules. However, this DHA source has only recently become available, so DHA in vegetarian (and particularly vegan) diets has been very low in the past. Lacto-ovo vegetarians can get some DHA from eggs, especially the omega-3-rich varieties. Vegetarians generally have reduced DHA status compared with nonvegetarians. Past studies show vegans to have approximately one-half the DHA of nonvegetarians in their body tissues and breast milk, while vegetarians have slightly higher levels. While we do not know what the optimal levels of DHA are, there is some indication that higher levels provide some benefit to infants. Vegetarians have two ways of improving their DHA status. First, we can maximize our conversion of alpha-linolenic acid (ALA, the form of omega-3 fatty acids in plants) into DHA by ensuring sufficient ALA in our diets. (See chapter 7, pages 166 to 167, for more information about DHA conversion from ALA.) Second, we can take a supplement of vegetarian, microalgae-based DHA providing 200 to 300 mg of DHA a day. Many experts advise a direct DHA source during pregnancy and lactation, as conversion of ALA to DHA is very limited (about 2 to 5 percent).

How much ALA do we need? Increasing our intake to at least 2 percent of calories is recommended. For someone eating 2,400 calories a day, about 5 grams of ALA should be sufficient. We can get 5 grams of ALA in two servings from the omega-3 fatty acid group. Each of the following examples provides 2 servings from the omega-3 rich group:

✓ 2 teaspoons (10 ml) flaxseed oil

✓ 1 tablespoon (15 ml) hempseed oil and
3 tablespoons (45 ml) walnuts

✓ 1½ tablespoons (22 ml) ground flaxseeds and
4 teaspoons (20 ml) canola oil

8. Include a reliable source of vitamin B$_{12}$ in the diet every day. The importance of getting sufficient vitamin B$_{12}$ throughout pregnancy and lactation cannot be overemphasized. A lack of this nutrient during pregnancy can result in an extremely low amount of stored B$_{12}$ in newborn infants. If the mother's intake of vitamin B$_{12}$ continues to be insufficient during lactation, the baby may end up with severe vitamin B$_{12}$ deficiency, potentially resulting in weakness, loss of reflexes, failure to thrive, delayed development, muscle wasting, and irreversible brain damage. The key determinant of a baby's vitamin B$_{12}$ status appears to be the mother's current intake, rather than her B$_{12}$ stores, so it is especially important to include a reliable source of vitamin B$_{12}$ each day. To add to the concern, recent research has demonstrated that high homocysteine levels caused by insufficient vitamin B$_{12}$ during pregnancy may increase the risk for neural tube defects in infants.

All pregnant and lactating women should aim for 5 to 10 mcg of vitamin B$_{12}$ every day from fortified foods or supplements. (Most prenatal vitamins contain this much.) While the RDA is 2.6 mcg a day during pregnancy and 2.8 mcg a day during lactation, the higher intakes will help to keep homocysteine from rising. The best dietary sources of vitamin B$_{12}$ for vegetarians are Red Star Vegetarian Support Formula nutritional yeast and vitamin B$_{12}$–fortified nondairy beverages, cereals, and meat substitutes. For lacto-ovo vegetarians, dairy products and eggs are another source of this vitamin, though the amounts of

B_{12} in them are small. (See chapter 8 for more information on B_{12} sources.) Sea vegetables, fermented soyfoods (such as tempeh and miso), and organic vegetables are not reliable vitamin B_{12} sources.

9. **Take a prenatal multivitamin-mineral supplement.** Prenatal vitamin and mineral supplements provide protection against nutrient shortages during pregnancy, so they are advised for all pregnant women. All women capable of becoming pregnant should consume 400 mcg of folic acid each day from supplements, fortified foods, or both, in addition to consuming folate from other foods. Also, an iron supplement of 30 mg per day is recommended for all pregnant women. Those who do not eat sufficient calcium-rich foods would be wise to use a daily supplement of 500 mg of elemental calcium.

Remember that vitamin and mineral supplements do not provide protein, carbohydrates, fats, fiber, or phytochemicals, so they cannot compensate for a poor diet. Make a healthful, balanced food plan your top priority. Higher-dose supplements are not advised unless medically indicated, as they provide no added benefit and can interfere with the absorption of other nutrients. Single-nutrient supplements can be toxic to the developing baby and generally are best avoided unless medically indicated. There are three notable exceptions to the caution on single-nutrient supplements: calcium, vitamin B_{12}, and essential fatty acids (specifically DHA).

10. **Avoid alcohol during pregnancy.** Pregnant women who drink alcohol increase the chance of their babies being born with fetal alcohol syndrome (FAS), the world's leading cause of mental retardation. This devastating condition also can result in central nervous system disorders, growth deficiencies, and abnormal facial features. Although the risk to the infant increases with the amount of alcohol consumed, safe lower limits are not known. For this reason, alcohol should be completely avoided during pregnancy.

11. **Keep caffeine consumption under 300 mg per day.** There is limited evidence that excess caffeine may contribute to premature birth, low birth weight, and reduced head circumference in infants. Caffeine passes easily across the placental barrier and is very poorly metabolized by the unborn baby. Caffeine is found primarily in coffee, tea (black and Asian green teas), cola beverages, chocolate, and some medications. While a limit of 300 mg a day generally is accepted, some studies suggest that intakes as low as 150 mg a day could contribute to low birth weight and increase the risk of a spontaneous abortion. A 5-ounce (156 ml) cup of coffee contains about 85 mg; 1 ounce (30 ml) of

TABLE 10.2	SAMPLE MENU PLAN FOR PREGNANCY AND LACTATION	
Food	**Pregnancy (2,400 calories)**	**Lactation (2,600 calories)**
Breakfast		
Whole grain breakfast cereal (p. 312)	1 cup (250 ml)	1 cup (250 ml)
Fortified soymilk	1 cup (250 ml)	1 cup (250 ml)
Blueberries	½ cup (125 ml)	½ cup (125 ml)
Whole grain toast	1 slice	1 slice
Almond butter	1½ tbsp. (22 ml)	1½ tbsp. (22 ml)
Blackstrap molasses	1 tbsp. (15 ml)	1 tbsp. (15 ml)
Calcium-fortified orange juice	1 cup (250 ml)	1 cup (250 ml)
Lunch		
Black Bean Soup (p. 318)	1½ cups (375 ml)	1½ cups (375 ml)
Rye crackers	6	6
Muenster Cheeze (p. 320)	¼ cup (60 ml)	¼ cup (60 ml)
Raw veggies (carrots, peppers, cucumbers)	1 cup (250 ml)	1 cup (250 ml)
Nutty Date Cookies (p. 350)	1	2
Snacks		
Fruit smoothie	1 cup (250 ml)	1 cup (250 ml)
Muscle Muffin (p. 248)	0	1
Dinner		
Hot Tofu with Cool Greens (p. 338)	6 oz. (170 g) tofu	6 oz. (170 g)
Go-for-the-Green Salad (p. 328)	3 cups (750 ml)	3 cups (750 ml)
Liquid Gold Salad Dressing (p. 329)	2 tbsp. (30 ml)	2 tbsp. (30 ml)
Pumpkin seeds	2 tbsp. (30 ml)	2 tbsp. (30 ml)
Lemon Teasecake (p. 354)	1/16 of cake	1/16 of cake
Servings from Each Food Group		
Grains	8	11
Vegetables and fruits	10	10
Beans and alternates	4	4
Milks and alternates	8	8
Omega-3 fatty acids	2	2
Vitamin B$_{12}$	Yes	Yes
Vitamin D	In part*	In part*

*From soymilk; additional needed from sunshine or supplement

espresso has about 40 mg; a 5-ounce (156 ml) cup of tea about 30 mg, and a 12-ounce (375 ml) cola about 36 mg.

Caffeine-free, grain-based beverages made from ingredients such as roasted malt, barley, chicory, and carob may be useful substitutes. Decaffeinated coffee also is an option, but its effects are not known. Herbal teas, such as rosehip, mint, lemon, and fruit teas, also are good alternatives, although not all herbal teas are safe. Examples of herbal teas that are not recommended for pregnant or lactating women include comfrey, pennyroyal, lobelia, sassafras, barberry, devil's claw root, chamomile, dong quai, gol-den seal, lily of the valley, rue, uva ursi, yarrow, coltsfoot, hawthorne berries, juniper berries, mandrake root, mistletoe, wormwood, and Scotch broom.

12. **Minimize your intake of environmental pollutants.** Environmental contaminants such as DDT and PCBs are highly toxic compounds that are extremely difficult to excrete from our bodies. Sadly, one way women get rid of some of these contaminants is through breast milk, so it's necessary to minimize our exposure to them as much as possible. Vegetarians are at a considerable advantage in this regard, as the most concentrated sources of environmental contaminants are fish and animal fat. Not surprisingly, vegetarians, and especially vegans, have lower levels of pesticide residue (from pesticides

such as DDT and PCBs) in their blood and breast milk. In one large study, vegans had only 1 to 2 percent of the amounts found in nonvegetarians. These findings have been supported by at least three other studies, with not a single study suggesting otherwise.

To further increase protection, limit pesticide-laden plant foods. Some of the worst offenders are nonorganic peanuts, raisins, and cottonseed oil, and foreign produce. A simple solution is to purchase organically grown foods whenever possible. All produce should be thoroughly washed before eating, even if it is organic!

Additional Considerations for Breast-Feeding

There is no better food for the mind and body of the human infant than the warm milk of his or her mother. It is exquisitely designed to provide the perfect balance of nutrients and protective substances for optimal growth and development. Plus, there are numerous health benefits for mom: breast-feeding helps us relax and return to our prepregnancy weight and shape more quickly; it prevents menstruation (during full-time breast-feeding), helping to maintain iron stores and energy; it saves money; and it reduces the long-term risk of breast, uterine, and ovarian cancers.

Breast-feeding a baby for a minimum of one year—and preferably for two years or more—is best. Fortunately, more and more mothers are returning to this practice. In 1970, just one infant in five was breast-fed; now two in three babies receive this excellent start, and half of these continue for six months or more.

Moms need extra fluids while breast-feeding, so it's a good idea to keep a big glass of water handy while nursing. Drink 8 to 12 cups (2 to 3 L) of liquids a day. While water is among the very best choices, pure fruit juices, fortified milks, grain beverages, and soups can make excellent contributions to overall fluid intake. Caffeine should be limited. Alcohol does not need to be as strictly avoided as during pregnancy, although consumption should be very moderate, if it is used at all.

The nutrient needs of breast-feeding mothers are similar to what they were during pregnancy. Lactating mothers often are advised to continue prenatal vitamin/mineral supplements for a couple months after the baby is born, then switch to a regular adult multivitamin-mineral supplement that contains vitamin B_{12} and vitamin D.

For more detailed information about nutrition and breast-feeding, we highly recommend *Raising Vegetarian Children* by J. Stepaniak and V. Melina (McGraw-Hill; New York, NY).

TABLE 10.3	NUTRIENT RECOMMENDATIONS FOR PREGNANCY AND LACTATION				
Nutrient	**RDA or AI * (AI in italics)**			**Percent Increase over Nonpregnant Needs**	
	Nonpregnant*	**Pregnant**	**Lactating**	**Pregnant**	**Lactating**
Protein	46 g	71 g	71 g	54%	54%
+10%**	51 g	78 g	78 g		
Minerals					
Iron***	32 mg	49 mg	16 mg	50%	0
Zinc	8 mg	11 mg	12 mg	37%	50%
Calcium	1,000 mg	1,000 mg	1,000 mg	0	0
Magnesium	310–320 mcg	350–360 mcg	310–320 mcg	13%	0
Selenium	55 mcg	60 mcg	70 mcg	9%	27%
Vitamins					
Vitamin A	700 mcg	770 mcg	1,300 mcg	10%	86%
Thiamin	1.1 mg	1.4 mg	1.4 mg	27%	27%
Riboflavin	1.1 mg	1.4 mg	1.6 mg	27%	45%
Niacin	14 mg	18 mg	17 mg	29%	21%
Vitamin B_6	1.3 mg	1.9 mg	2.0 mg	46%	54%
Vitamin B_{12}	2.4 mcg	2.6 mcg	2.8 mcg	8%	17%
Folic Acid	400 mcg	600 mcg	500 mcg	50%	25%
Vitamin C	75 mg	85 mg	120 mg	13%	60%
Vitamin D	5 mcg	5 mcg	5 mcg	0	0
Vitamin E	15 mg	15 mg	19 mg	0	27%

* RDA (recommended dietary allowance): Average daily intake levels sufficient to meet requirements of 97 to 98 percent of healthy people. AI (adequate intake): A recommended daily intake used when the RDA cannot be determined with confidence. Based on observations and research on a group (or groups) of healthy people. Nutrients stated as AIs are in italics. All values are for ages 19–50 years.

** Protein: The additional 10 percent is to be used for vegetarians who get most of their protein from unprocessed whole foods such as beans, vegetables, whole grains, nuts, and seeds (as opposed to those who use tofu, soymilk, and meat analogs on a regular basis).

***Iron: RDAs given in this table are for vegetarians and are 1.8 times higher than they are for nonvegetarians.

Most foods can be eaten during breast-feeding without problem, although some babies are sensitive to garlic, onion, hot spices, soda pop, MSG, licorice, and artificial sweeteners. While allergy to breast milk is virtually nonexistent, a baby can have allergic responses to foods eaten by the mother, because intact proteins can make their way into breast milk. Colic, eczema, chronic congestion, or gastrointestinal distress all can be signs of allergy, especially if there is a family history of food allergies. The foods most commonly associated with these kinds of reactions are cow's milk (causing an estimated 75 to 80 percent of the cases), eggs, wheat, soy, citrus fruits, nuts, and chocolate.

PART 2: INFANCY (BIRTH TO TWO YEARS)

The first two years of life are filled with discovery. Adventurous infants delight in the colors, textures, and flavors that surround them. As parents or caregivers, we must seize the opportunity to build a foundation for health that includes a wide variety of wonderfully nourishing foods.

During the first year of life, our babies grow at an unprecedented rate, tripling their birth weight. Their requirements for most nutrients per pound of body weight are two to three times those of adults. When we consider the small stomach capacity of a baby and this tremendous rate of growth, we can understand their need for a steady supply of energy and nutrients.

Infants can be very well nourished on lacto-ovo vegetarian or vegan diets. Parents or caregivers need to become well acquainted with food patterns that work and those that don't. We must pay particular attention to the energy, protein, and vitamin B_{12} in the baby's diet. Iron, zinc, calcium, and vitamin D must also be considered. Foods that are more concentrated in energy and nutrients, such as tofu and nut and seed butters, are especially valuable for vegan infants. As vegetarian diets grow in popularity, new products appear on the market, making it easier to include a variety of nutritious foods that infants enjoy.

Poorly planned or overly restrictive diets can have serious consequences for the growth, development, and overall health of an infant. The following guidelines will help to ensure that your baby grows up to be a happy, thriving toddler.

NUTRITION GUIDELINES FOR VEGETARIAN AND VEGAN INFANTS

1. **Breast-feed for a minimum of six months, and preferably for a full two years.** The World Health Organization and the American Academy of Pediatrics recommend breast-feeding as the sole source of nutrition for the first six months of life. After solids are introduced, breast milk should remain a primary source of nutrition and fluids for at least the first year. Ideally, breast-feeding will continue until babies wean themselves, generally from two to four years of age.

Breast milk is perfectly designed to meet the needs of human infants, just as the milks of other mammals are designed to meet the needs of their young. It provides just the right amount of protein, essential fatty acids, vitamins, and minerals, and supplies special substances that protect babies from infection. The breast milk of lacto-ovo vegetarian and vegan women is similar in composition to that of nonvegetarians. Mother's milk adjusts naturally to meet an infant's changing needs. The more scientists learn about the unique composition of human milk, the more they realize that an equivalent can never be formulated in a lab.

2. If breast-feeding is not chosen or is not possible, or if an infant is weaned before one year of age, iron-fortified commercial infant formula is recommended. Commercial infant formula is the only acceptable alternative to breast milk during the first year of life. The American Academy of Pediatrics advises using the iron-fortified variety from birth for all formula-fed babies until twelve months of age. If breast-feeding stops prior to one year, or if a baby nurses fewer than three times a day, an iron-fortified commercial infant formula should be used as the replacement. Apart from breast

> ## ARE THERE ANY FORMULAS SUITABLE FOR VEGAN BABIES?
>
> Most commonly used commercial infant formulas are not vegan, as they are based on cow's milk. Soy-based commercial infant formulas are safe and adequate, and they are the only alternatives for vegan babies who are not breast-fed. However, it is important to read the label, as at least one soy-based formula contains beef fat. All soy-based formulas in North America currently use vitamin D_3 in their products (the animal-derived form of vitamin D). In addition, soybeans used in many infant formulas are not organic, so they may be genetically modified.
>
> Questions have been raised about the use of soy-based formulas for infants due to their high isoflavone content. Babies fed soy formula do have higher blood levels of isoflavones, and it is not known whether this would have a positive or negative effect on long-term health. Thus far, studies have not shown any adverse effects. Furthermore, these formulas have been in use for several decades with no apparent harm to infants.

milk and commercial infant formula, no other substitute can safely serve as the primary milk source before a baby's first birthday.

Cow's milk is not recommended during the first twelve months of life and there are several important reasons why. In the first six months of life, an infant's gastrointestinal system often is sensitive to cow's milk protein, resulting in blood loss in the stool. In addition, cow's milk contains higher amounts of protein, sodium, potassium, and chloride than the immature kidneys of an infant can handle. The early introduction of cow's milk also can increase the risk of nutritional deficiencies, especially for iron. Finally, cow's milk contains insufficient essential fatty acids, zinc, and vitamins C and E.

Never use homemade infant formulas as they provide grossly inadequate nutrition. Reports of malnutrition in vegetarian infants frequently are traced to such beverages.

3. Provide 20 to 24 ounces (625 to 750 ml) of breast milk, formula, or cow's milk, or a combination of breast milk, formula, and full-fat, fortified soymilk per day for infants between the ages of twelve and twenty-four months. Providing the appropriate milk during the second year of life helps ensure sufficient energy and high-quality protein, vitamins, and minerals to support normal growth and development. While breast milk continues to be the best option, if a baby has been weaned or is nursing only part-time (less than three times a day), a substitute can be used.

During the second year of life some milks can be safely used as substitutes. After twelve months of age, **lacto-ovo vegetarian babies** can use whole cow's milk in addition to, or in place of, breast milk or commercial infant formula. Two percent cow's milk generally is not recommended, although it is thought to be acceptable in cases where the infant is growing well and eating a wide variety of solid foods. Lower-fat cow's milk (1 percent and skim milk) is not suitable for babies up to two years of age.

HEALTHY BABIES ALERT!

Unfortified soymilk, tofu milk, rice milk, nut milk, and grain milks should not be used as the primary milk source during the first two years of a baby's life. These milks will not provide the nutrients necessary for optimal growth and development of infants.

Vegan infants and those with dairy allergies (or where there is a preference for soy) can be given full-fat fortified soymilk after one year of age. (Check with your physician regularly to ensure your baby is the appropriate height and weight for her or his age.) Because soymilk is a little lower in fat than whole milk, it is important to ensure that the baby's diet includes ample amounts of healthful fat from foods such as tofu, nut butters, and avocado. Breast milk and/or commercial infant formula should continue to be offered as a supplementary beverage until the baby is two years old, or even longer. The baby also should be eating a good variety of solid foods, as outlined in table 10.4 on page 224.

4. **Provide a vitamin D supplement of 400 international units (10 mcg) per day from birth for all breast-fed babies until sufficient vitamin D is obtained from fortified foods.** While somewhat controversial, a vitamin D supplement of 400 international units (10 mcg) for all breast-fed infants usually is recommended. Theoretically, infants can make enough vitamin D from warm sunlight; however, this is not considered a reliable source of vitamin D during infancy and certainly is not possible during winters in northern latitudes. Infants usually are protected from ultraviolet rays with clothing or sunscreen. Babies with dark skin require two to six times as much sunlight to produce sufficient vitamin D.

Breast milk typically is a poor source of vitamin D. Nursing mothers who do not receive sufficient vitamin D from food sources or sunlight will have very low levels of this nutrient in their milk. Mothers who receive sunlight and/or vitamin D–fortified foods have higher amounts of vitamin D in their milk, but amounts can be quite variable and may not be sufficient to meet the needs of their infant. Insufficient vitamin D during infancy causes rickets, a bone disease in infants and children that results in the softening and weakening of their bone structure and may cause permanent bone deformities. Bowlegs, knock-knees, and misshapen ribs and skull are common symptoms of advanced rickets. For more information on vitamin D, see page 114.

Formula-fed infants don't need a vitamin D supplement, as infant formula is fortified with this nutrient.

5. Ensure a sufficient source of iron throughout infancy. Breast-fed infants require a source of iron apart from breast milk by six months of age. In healthy, full-term infants, iron stores are plentiful at birth. Stores begin to decline at about four months of age and can become depleted by six months or shortly thereafter. Preterm and low birth-weight babies are born with low iron stores, which can very quickly become depleted. Iron deficiency is the most common nutritional deficiency among children six months to three years of age. Symptoms of iron deficiency in infants include pallor (pale skin color), fatigue, irritability, decreased appetite, slow development, and reduced cognitive function (a diminished ability to learn).

Breast milk contains small amounts of highly absorbable iron; however, by about six months of age, additional iron is needed (sooner in preterm and low birth-weight babies). Solid foods can reduce the absorption of iron in human milk, so it is very important that a baby's first foods provide iron. The first food commonly recommended is iron-fortified infant cereal. To improve the iron absorption from infant cereals, a good source of vitamin C can be served with the cereal. (See guideline 7 on page 222 to learn how to safely introduce new foods to your baby.) Iron-fortified cereals can continue to provide iron up to two years of age and beyond. If iron-fortified infant cereals are not used, an iron supplement containing 0.5 mg per pound of body weight (1 mg per kilogram) can be given when solid foods are introduced. (For additional information on iron and iron sources, see pages 74 to 83 in chapter 3.)

The use of iron-fortified formula is recommended from birth for infants who are not breast-fed. Parents are sometimes concerned that iron-fortified formula may cause constipation and stomach upset in their infant. However, studies have found no differences in gastrointestinal symptoms or stool consistency when regular and iron-fortified formulas are compared.

6. Make sure that sufficient vitamin B_{12} is provided through either breast milk, formula, or a supplement. Breast-fed infants of lacto-ovo vegetarian and vegan women can get sufficient vitamin B_{12} if the mother's vitamin B_{12} intake is adequate. It is possible for vegetarian mothers to obtain sufficient vitamin B_{12} from fortified foods and/or from dairy products and eggs.

However, when we take a prenatal or multivitamin-mineral supplement containing at least 10 mcg of vitamin B_{12} each day, we have the extra insurance that B_{12} levels will be sufficient to meet our infant's needs. Vegan mothers who do not take care to include reliable sources of this nutrient can have very low levels of vitamin B_{12} in their milk. It is essential for both mother and child to have reliable B_{12} sources. (You can read more about B_{12} requirements in chapter 8.) If mothers have any doubt about their past intake of vitamin B_{12}, it is important to have their vitamin B_{12} status assessed by their physician and through laboratory testing. If the mother's B_{12} intake is inadequate, the child should receive a supplement of at least 0.5 mcg a day (for infants from birth to twelve months) or 1.0 mcg a day (for children twelve to twenty-four months), until the child's diet provides sufficient vitamin B_{12} from fortified foods.

Commercial infant formula is fortified with vitamin B_{12}, so no additional vitamin B_{12} is needed for vegetarian babies on formula.

7. Delay the introduction of solid foods until about six months of age. Not so long ago, a baby's first bite of solid food was considered a developmental milestone. Parents and caregivers had babies eating solids as quickly as possible, often by one or two months of age. Babies usually ended up with more food dribbling down their faces than into their bellies; and the bits they did manage to swallow were more apt to trigger allergies. Today we understand that most infants are not developmentally ready for solid foods before about six months of age, although some infants may be ready as early as four or five months, particularly if they are growing very quickly. Babies let us know when they are ready in several ways. They seem constantly hungry, even after nursing eight to ten times a day or drinking 40 ounces (1.25 L) of formula; they can sit up and give signs they are full, such as turning their head away; and they can move solids to the back of their mouth and swallow without spitting out most of the food. Solids should not be delayed too much after six months of age, as the additional foods are needed to meet nutrient and calorie requirements. Six months of age also seems to be a good stage in a baby's development to start the adventure of new foods; waiting until later can result in a reluctance to try different tastes and textures.

Guidelines for introducing solid foods are provided in table 10.4, and a sample menu is provide in table 10.6. There also is the Vegetarian Food Guide for Babies Twelve to Twenty-Four Months of Age on page 226. The tips below will help to make this experience a pleasant one for both you and your baby.

❋ Embark on this exciting food adventure when your baby is rested, alert, and happy.

✳   There are no hard and fast rules regarding the order of introduction for solid foods after six months of age, although the sequence often recommended is infant cereals, vegetables, and fruits, then protein-rich foods. This sequence takes into consideration both the nutritional value of these first foods and the maturity of your infant's gastrointestinal system.

✳   Introduce new foods one at a time, with at least three to seven days between each new food. This allows us to observe for possible allergies. If there is a family history of allergy, it is best to avoid introducing the foods that are most problematic for family members until your baby is at least twelve months old. Egg whites, due to their very high potential for causing allergy, should be delayed until one year in all infants. About 95 percent of all allergies in infants are to cow's milk, eggs, peanuts, tree nuts, soy, fish, and wheat.

✳   Introduce single-ingredient foods (for example, rice or barley cereal) before offering combination foods (such as mixed cereal).

✳   Various textured foods can be introduced gradually as the infant becomes ready to chew. This usually happens around seven to nine months of age. Textured foods should not be delayed beyond nine or ten months (unless the baby's development is delayed), as your infant may continue to reject textures for some time. Progress from pureed to mashed, then soft, minced, diced, and finger foods.

✳   Begin with small serving sizes: 1 to 3 teaspoons (5 to 15 ml) at a time. Gradually increase serving sizes. Babies will let us know when they are full. Never force-feed.

✳   Some infants are ready for mashed vegetables and fruits by six months, while others are not ready for these types of foods until they are eight months old.

✳   Babies should be encouraged to feed themselves, using their hands and easy-to-handle baby utensils. Babies are naturally messy eaters. Do not worry about it; they'll learn table manners soon enough.

✳   Teething foods are unnecessary. Instead, give your baby a clean, cold, damp washcloth that has been refrigerated.

   8. Ensure sufficient high-quality protein. Vegetarian infants can get plenty of high-quality protein; however, some care must be taken to ensure that sufficient sources are provided, especially for vegan infants. From six to twelve months, vegetarian babies need about 0.8 gram of protein per pound of body weight (1.8 grams per kilogram). This is about 10 to 20 percent more than what nonvegetarian babies require. The additional protein allows for the reduced

TABLE 10.4 GENERAL GUIDE TO THE INTRODUCTION OF SOLID FOODS

5 to 6 months

Introduce:	Iron-fortified infant cereals
Amount/Comments:	1 to 4 tablespoons (15 to 60 ml) twice daily
	Begin with single grain cereals (e.g., rice, barley, or oats), then mixed cereals. Mix with breast milk, formula, or water (cereal should be thinned).

6 months

Introduce:	Vegetables and fruits
Amount/Comments:	2 to 3 tablespoons (30 to 45 ml) vegetables twice daily; puréed or mashed
	2 to 3 tablespoons (30 to 45 ml) fruits two to three times daily; puréed or mashed
	Hard fruits cooked and puréed or mashed (skin removed); soft fruit peeled and well mashed. Avoid fruit desserts with added sugar and starch.

7 to 8 months

Introduce:	Protein-rich foods
Amount/Comments:	1 to 3 tablespoons (15 to 45 ml) twice daily
	Good choices are mashed tofu, beans, and peas (and egg yolk for lacto-ovo vegetarian babies). Press beans through a sieve to remove skins.
Introduce:	Unsweetened fruit juice
Amount/Comments:	1 to 4 ounces (30 to 125 ml) daily
	Offer in a cup rather than a bottle. Juice is not a necessary addition to the diet. May be diluted, but is not necessary.

8 to 10 months

Introduce:	Finger foods
Amount/Comments:	2 to 5 tablespoons (30 to 75 ml) fruit and vegetable pieces (cooked if hard)
	½ slice toast, ¼ bagel, crackers, unsweetened cereal pieces
Introduce:	Grains and grain products
Amount/Comments:	2 to 3 tablespoons (30 to 45 ml) once or twice a day
	Offer well-cooked whole grains: rice, quinoa, millet, barley, or others, and pasta.
Introduce:	Dairy products (for lacto-ovo vegetarian babies)
Amount/Comments:	2 to 3 tablespoons (30 to 45 ml) cottage cheese, 0.5 oz. (14 g) of cheese
	¼ cup (60 ml) yogurt

10 to 12 months

Introduce:	Mixed dishes
Amount/Comments:	½ to 1 cup (125 to 250 ml)
	Mixed dishes such as stews, pasta dishes, casseroles, and loaves are good choices.
Introduce:	Meat substitutes
Amount/Comments:	¼ to ½ cup (60 to 125 ml) one or more times daily
	Example of meat analogs or veggie "meats" are soy- or gluten-based slices, veggie patties, tofu wieners, veggie nuggets, etc.
Introduce:	Whole eggs at 12 months (for ovo-vegetarian babies)
Amount/Comments:	1 egg (best prepared by boiling or poaching rather than frying)

Solids should be given 5 to 6 times per day (3 meals and 2 or 3 snacks) and total amounts should be about ¾ to 1 cup (175 to 250 ml) per meal.

digestibility of plant foods. Infants twelve to twenty-four months of age need about 0.5 gram of protein per pound of body weight (1.1 grams per kilogram). Excellent protein-rich choices for all babies include tofu, very well-cooked legumes, quinoa, and amaranth, as well as eggs, yogurt, and cottage cheese for lacto-ovo vegetarian babies. By following the guidelines provided in table 10.4 for infants five to twelve months of age and the Vegetarian Food Guide for Babies Twelve to Twenty-Four Months of Age, protein needs are easily met.

9. Fat and energy should not be restricted during the first two years of life, unless medically indicated. Breast milk, the ideal food for infants, derives approximately 54 percent of its calories from fat. One cup (250 ml) of breast milk contains about 175 calories. This could well be nature's way of telling us that babies need food that is concentrated in both fat and calories. Plant foods can be low in fat and calories and high in fiber. Thus, it is important when planning vegetarian diets for infants to ensure that diets provide sufficient calories and fat and that fiber is not excessive. As we introduce solid foods, the following suggestions will help us keep our baby's fat and calorie intakes at safe and adequate levels

* Include plenty of low-fiber, high-fat foods in the diet. Tofu, smooth nut and seed butters and creams, mashed avocados, soy yogurt, puddings, and soups made with an appropriate milk (in addition to dairy products and eggs for lacto-ovo vegetarian babies) are excellent choices.

* Avoid fat-reduced food products. While many healthful foods are naturally low in fat, special fat-reduced products are not appropriate for babies. Low-fat or skim milk, low-fat cheese, and other fat-reduced foods are best avoided, as are foods containing fat substitutes.

* Avoid excessive fiber. Concentrated fiber products—such as raw wheat bran, bran cereals, and bran muffins—should not be used for vegetarian babies. Use mainly whole grain breads and cereals (for example, brown rice, millet, quinoa, and oatmeal bread), as they contribute important minerals to the diet. Lesser quantities of refined grain products—such as bread, pasta, and cereal—can help to keep total fiber intake in check.

* Serve regular meals and snacks. Infants have very small stomachs, so they need to eat five to six times a day. Choose snacks carefully, making sure that they contribute to your infant's overall nutrient needs. (Younger infants still are receiving enough breast milk or formula between meals so that regular snacks are not as important.) A few energy-packed favorites include spreads (hummus, tofu spreads, or nut butters) on crackers; bread with cheese (soy or dairy); homemade, wholesome cookies, muffins, or squares; rice, cornmeal, quinoa, or other whole grain puddings with fruit; and yogurt (soy or dairy).

VEGETARIAN FOOD GUIDE FOR BABIES
TWELVE TO TWENTY-FOUR MONTHS OF AGE

Include a wide variety of foods

Breast milk, commercial infant formula, cow's milk, full-fat fortified soymilk

Total 20 to 24 oz. (625 to 750 ml)

About three 6- to 8-oz. (175 to 250 ml) servings of breast milk, commercial infant formula, cow's milk, or full-fat fortified soymilk (breast milk or formula should supplement fortified soymilk)

Grains and Cereals: 4 to 6 toddler-size servings

½ slice bread
¼ cup (60 ml) cooked grain or pasta
½ cup (125 ml) ready-to-eat cereal
¼ cup (60 ml) cooked cereal

Vegetables: 2 to 3 toddler-size servings

½ cup (125 ml) salad or other raw vegetable pieces
¼ cup (60 ml) cooked vegetables
⅓ cup (80 ml) vegetable juice

Fruits: 2 to 3 toddler-size servings

½ to 1 fresh fruit
¼ cup (60 ml) cooked fruit
¼ cup (60 ml) fruit juice (limit to about 1 cup/250 ml a day)

Beans and Alternates: 2 to 3 toddler-size servings

½ cup (125 ml) cooked beans, peas, or lentils
2 ounces (57 g) tofu
½ to 1 ounce (14 to 28.4 g) veggie "meat"
1 egg

Other Essentials

Vitamin B$_{12}$	1.0 mcg in fortified foods or supplement
Vitamin D	200 IU (5 mcg) vitamin D from fortified foods or supplements
Omega-3 Fatty Acids	½ tsp. (2 ml) flaxseed oil or other source to provide 1.5 g omega-3 fatty acids

10. Include a good source of omega-3 fatty acids in the diet. The very best source of omega-3 fatty acids for infants is breast milk. To maximize the long-chain omega-3 fatty acid DHA (the fat critical for infant brain development), the mother must consume reliable sources of omega-3 fatty acids. (See part 1 of this chapter.) One of the most important reasons for extending the breast-feeding of vege-

TABLE 10.5	SUPPLEMENTS FOR BREAST-FED VEGETARIAN INFANTS
Vitamin K	A single dose at birth is given routinely in the hospital.
Vitamin D	400 IU (10 mcg) daily from birth until sufficient amounts are provided by fortified foods.
Vitamin B_{12}	0.5 mcg daily beginning at birth, unless the mother's diet contains adequate, reliable sources (fortified foods, supplements, dairy products, or eggs).
Iron	0.5 mg per lb. (1 mg per kg) daily beginning when solid foods are introduced (can be provided in fortified foods).
Zinc	3 mg per day, if insufficient sources are provided in the diet.
Fluoride	0.25 mg per day beginning at 6 months if water supply contains less than 0.3 ppm fluoride.

tarian infants into the second year of life and beyond is that they continue to receive this valuable fat. After twelve months of age, vegetarian infants should begin to receive good sources of omega-3 fatty acids, such as flaxseed oil. Aim for about ½ teaspoon (2 ml) of flaxseed oil a day. Blend it into infant cereal, smoothies, puddings, cereal, soup, or mashed potatoes. Flaxseed oil should not be heated or cooked with food; instead, mix the oil into cooked food after it has been removed from direct heat.

11. Include dietary supplements, if needed. Vegetarian and vegan infants' needs for nutritional supplements are similar to nonvegetarian infants, with the possible exceptions of vitamin B_{12} and zinc. A complete list of supplements recommended for breast-fed babies can be found in table 10.5 at right. (Formula-fed infants require only vitamin K at birth.) Multivitamin and mineral supplements are not absolutely necessary, although they can provide an excellent way to ensure that infants get adequate vitamin D, vitamin B_{12}, iron, and zinc. Take care to store all supplements away from children.

12. Avoid giving infants foods that may cause choking or food poisoning or could otherwise be harmful. There are several foods that pose a risk of choking, food poisoning, or toxicity in infants and therefore should never be given to them.

✗ Foods that may cause choking: Unsafe foods are those that do not easily dissolve in the mouth and are of a size and shape that can block the airway. These include very hard foods, small and round items, and smooth or very sticky foods. Examples are veggie dogs (cut veggie dogs in half or quarters lengthwise to reduce risk); nuts and seeds; raw peas; raw carrots and other hard, raw vegetable or fruit pieces; popcorn; whole grapes (grapes can be cut in half or quartered); and hard candies. Peanut butter and other nut or seed butters should not be served on a spoon or a finger, nor should they be served on bread or crackers until children are one year of age. However, nut and seed butters may be mixed into prepared foods or thinned (for instance, with breast milk, formula, or water) and used as a "cream." Infants should be seated and supervised while eating.

✗ Foods associated with foodborne illness: Babies have less resistance to harmful bacteria than older children or adults. For this reason, high-risk foods such as unpasteurized milk, unpasteurized apple cider, raw eggs, or foods containing raw eggs should not be fed to infants. Honey (and possibly other liquid sugars, such as corn syrup) may contain Clostridium botulinum spores, causing a rare but very dangerous form of food poisoning in infants under twelve months of age, so these sweeteners should also be avoided during the first year. Care must be taken when handling foods for infants. All fruits and vegetables should be thoroughly washed, and all prepared foods should be stored in the refrigerator. If using commercial infant foods in jars, the safety seal in the middle of the lid should pop up when the jar is opened. If it does not, the food should be discarded. Do not feed your baby directly from the jar and then return an uneaten portion of food to the fridge, as bacteria from the baby's saliva can cause the remaining food to spoil quickly. Instead, transfer a small portion of food to a bowl first. The unused food left in the jar can be stored in the refrigerator for up to three days.

✗ Excessive amounts of fruit juice: Too much fruit juice can cause diarrhea in infants and toddlers. It also can displace the primary milk (breast milk or formula in the first year), reducing nutrient intake. When given, juice should be limited to no more than 4 ounces (125 ml) a day for babies under twelve months and 8 ounces (250 ml) a day for babies twelve to twenty-four months. Juice should be offered in a cup, not a bottle. Putting juice in a bottle encourages excessive intakes and may lead to nursing bottle syndrome, a pattern of tooth decay in infants caused by prolonged exposure of the teeth to sweet beverages from a nursing bottle.

✗ Inappropriate beverages: Fruit "drinks," fruit punches, soft drinks, sports drinks, coffee, tea, herbal tea, and hot chocolate should not be given to infants. These beverages contain too much sugar, caffeine, or other potentially damaging components to be given to babies.

✗ Added sugar: The addition of sugar and salt to infant foods is both unnecessary and potentially harmful. Adding sugar to infant foods dilutes the nutritional value of the food and may contribute to dental decay.

✗ Fried foods and hydrogenated fat: Fats used in fried foods are generally hydrogenated and heated to very high temperatures. These fats are not appropriate for infants. Shortening and hydrogenated margarines also should not be given to infants.

TABLE 10.6 SAMPLE MEAL PLANS FOR INFANTS SIX TO TWELVE MONTHS OF AGE

6 to 9 months	9 to 12 months
Breast milk or iron-fortified formula	
Nursing 3 to 5 times a day or 24 to 32 oz. (750 ml to 1 L) formula daily	Nursing 2 to 4 times a day or 24 to 32 oz. (750 ml to 1 L) formula daily
Morning (on waking)	
Breast milk or formula	Breast milk or formula
Breakfast	
Breast milk or formula 2 to 4 tbsp. (30 to 60 ml) iron-fortified infant cereal 2 to 3 tbsp. (30 to 45 ml) fruit	Breast milk or formula 4 to 6 tbsp. (60 to 90 ml) iron-fortified infant cereal 2 to 3 tbsp. (30 to 45 ml) fruit
Mid-morning	
Breast milk or formula	Toast, crackers, dry (unsweetened) cereal, tofu cubes, cheese cubes, soy or dairy yogurt
Lunch	

Breast milk or formula
2 to 3 tbsp. (30 to 45 ml) vegetables
2 to 3 tbsp. (30 to 45 ml) fruit
1 to 4 tbsp. (15 to 60 ml) beans, peas, lentils,
  tofu, or tempeh
	Breast milk, or formula
	3 to 5 tbsp. (45 to 75 ml) vegetables
	3 to 4 tbsp. (45 to 60 ml) fruit
	3 to 4 tbsp. (45 to 60 ml) beans, peas, lentils,
	  tofu, or tempeh

Afternoon	
Breast milk or formula	Breast milk or formula Soft vegetables or fruit in small pieces Crackers or dry (unsweetened) cereal
Supper	
Breast milk or formula 2 to 4 tbsp. (30 to 60 ml) iron-fortified infant cereal 2 to 3 tbsp. (30 to 45 ml) vegetables 2 to 3 tbsp. (30 to 45 ml) fruit	Breast milk or formula 3 to 5 tbsp. (45 to 75 ml) vegetables 3 to 4 tbsp. (45 to 60 ml) fruit 2 to 4 tbsp. (30 to 60 ml) beans, peas, or lentils, tofu, or tempeh 2 to 4 tbsp. (30 to 60 ml) grains or pasta (optional)
Evening	
Breast milk or formula	Breast milk or formula Finger foods
Food texture	
Cereal, thick Pureed, mashed, or soft foods	Cereal, thick Soft, mashed, minced, or diced table foods Finger foods, appropriate size and shape

✗   Heavily pesticide-laden foods: To reduce exposure to pesticides, select organic foods for your baby whenever possible.

PART 3: CHILDHOOD (TWO TO TWELVE)

The years of childhood provide an opportunity to introduce a world of interesting and enjoyable foods to impressionable little ones. In receiving a wide variety of wholesome vegetarian foods, children reap the benefits twofold. First, as youngsters they'll be less likely than their nonvegetarian peers to become obese. Second, as adults they'll be at reduced risk for several chronic degenerative diseases (including heart disease, type 2 diabetes, and cancer) compared with the general population. Scientists are discovering that diets during childhood and adolescence can set the stage for later health problems—or help prevent these conditions. There's a third advantage, which is a bonus for adults. As we make efforts to ensure our children's diets are balanced and packed with nutritious foods, our diets as caregivers and role models inevitably improve!

In past decades, a common criticism of vegetarian and vegan diets was that they might place children at risk for nutritional deficiencies. The reality is that such insufficiencies are related to poorly designed diets in general, not to whether the meals are vegetarian or nonvegetarian. Studies have clearly established that well-planned vegetarian and vegan diets can support normal growth and development in children.

In planning a child's diet, it helps to consider how his or her needs differ from those of an adult. Small children have limited stomach capacities along with high nutrient requirements. A diet consisting mostly of fruits and vegetables, big bowls of salad, and whole grains can be too low in calories and certain minerals and too high in fiber to meet a child's needs. Their menus must emphasize more-concentrated sources of calories and minerals, such as soyfoods, nut butters, and plenty of the meal and snack ideas mentioned in this chapter.

Children who are raised from birth as vegetarians usually accept a wide variety of healthful foods without any problem, especially when the adults around them model these attitudes. If a family becomes vegetarian or shifts from a heavily meat-centered, highly processed diet to a vegetarian, whole foods diet a number of years after a child is born, there may be a little resistance, as would be expected with other major changes. Do not despair. There are ways we can ease the transition and make life easier for everyone.

✓   Include children in food preparation. They love to help stir, knead, roll, decorate, and do just about anything else in the kitchen that they can safely handle.

✓ For those with small appetites, try Sneaky Dad's Power Smoothie, page 316, or create your own version.

✓ Involve little ones in selecting food. Of course this process may prove more successful at a farmers' market, in the garden, or after you've purchased the groceries and brought them home, rather than in the middle of the sugar-laden cereal aisle!

✓ Consider children's preferences when planning menus and include something that they enjoy at each meal.

✓ Serve vegetarian versions of traditional favorites: pizza, spaghetti, lasagne, tacos, chili, burgers, hot dogs, stews, and stir-fries.

✓ Stock the cupboards and refrigerator with a variety of foods that are both wholesome and appealing for children.

✓ Include "fun foods." It can be tough to be vegetarian among friends who love cheeseburgers and shakes, so allow healthful versions of these treats. When our veggie burger or dog celebration includes plenty of colorful fixin's—ketchup, barbecue sauce, mustard, mayo, pickle relish, chili sauce, lettuce, sprouts, sliced tomato, dill pickles, onion, and avocado slices—everyone has a great time assembling his or her own creation, and no one misses the meat. Also try the shakes and smoothies on pages 315 to 317.

✓ Keep offering new foods, even if they are rejected. A child who turns up his or her nose at something one day could adopt it as a favorite meal a month later—it really does happen!

✓ Respect a child's right to dislike a few foods. Children can't be expected to love everything, nor is it necessary for good nutrition.

✓ Let a child decide when he or she has had enough to eat.

✓ Make mealtime a pleasant time. Set a pretty table, light a candle, and encourage positive family interaction.

As parents, we are responsible for providing our children with safe and adequate food. Our children are responsible for how much they eat from the items we provide. The process can seem a little overwhelming at times, especially when children go through periods of food refusal or strange eating behaviors. Be assured that if we provide a variety of nourishing foods in a pleasant atmosphere, food intake balances out over time and children will manage to get enough to eat.

Nutrition Guidelines for Vegetarian Children

1. Include a variety of foods from all food groups in the Vegetarian Food Guide. The foods children grow up with are the ones they learn to enjoy. If they are served whole grains, a wide variety of vegetables and fruits, legumes, tofu, and other healthful foods as described in the Vegetarian Food Guide for Preschool Children (Two to Four Years) on page 234, and after that, the Vegetarian Food Guide (page 193), they are likely to accept and enjoy these foods throughout their lives. When we offer a variety of foods from each food group, a child becomes familiar with different tastes and textures. When children are very young, they need the number of servings at the lower end of the range and portions may be somewhat smaller than those listed on the guide. Toward adolescence, portion size and the number of servings increase dramatically. Every child has his or her unique pattern of growth, appetite, and preferences.

2. Include sufficient servings of Milks and Alternates each day. at least four servings for preschoolers (two to four years), six servings for young, school-age children (five to eight years), and eight servings for children nine years or older and adolescents. Sufficient calcium can be obtained from appropriate milks or alternates. Using milks as the primary calcium source, particularly for preschoolers and young children, is the easiest and most efficient way of meeting calcium needs. Appropriate milks for preschoolers include breast milk, formula, fortified soymilk, and cow's or goat's milk. These are valuable sources of calcium, vitamin D, riboflavin, protein, and other nutrients. Although it is uncommon in our culture to continue breastfeeding beyond two years of age, human milk can continue to provide immune protection and a valuable complement of nutrients for preschoolers. From a nutritional perspective, the longer we continue to provide our preschoolers with human milk and its unique balance of high-quality protein, vitamins, minerals, and long-chain omega-3 fatty acids, the better. Although the idea might not occur to us, commercial iron-fortified infant formula could also save the day for a child who isn't eating well. Formula, or expressed breast milk, can be mixed into cereals, puddings, and other dishes. Every little bit helps! Two to four years of age is a time of nutritional vulnerability when children's diets are in transition and nutritional needs are high because of growth and activity.

By five years of age, children can progress to using the Vegetarian Food Guide (page 193). From ages five to eight, children require at least six servings from the Milks and Alternates group. While needs can be met by using a variety of calcium-rich foods, providing four servings as milks (2 cups/500 ml of fortified soymilk or cow's milk) helps tremendously with meeting the recommended number of servings from this group. At age nine, recommended intakes for calcium increase dramatically from 800 mg to 1,300 mg. The density of our bones and our defense against osteoporosis in later life depends, at least in part, on getting enough calcium and vitamin D during childhood and the teen years when calcium needs are greatest. To meet these high needs, preteens and teens need about eight servings of Milks and Alternates each day.

Fortified soymilk is an acceptable choice, but unfortified soymilk does not contain the necessary calcium and vitamin D and is not included as a choice in this group. Soymilk contains 6 to 8 grams of protein per cup (250 ml), whereas the same amount of rice milk has only 0.5 grams of protein. Rice milks, other grain milks, potato milks, nut milks, and unfortified milks are not recommended for use as primary milks for children because they do not provide sufficient nutrients.

For lacto-ovo vegetarian children, 2 percent or 1 percent cow's milk may be used, depending on the needs of the individual child. If a child is overweight, lower-fat milk may be appropriate.

Milks tend to be our mainstay when it comes to meeting children's calcium needs. Yet there are plenty of other ways to get calcium into kids, too. Be sure to buy the type of tofu that is made with calcium. Tofu can be used for a breakfast scramble, Angelic Tofu Sandwich Filling, or a quick tofu stir-fry (see the recipe section). Add tofu, mashed or in cubes, to soups, stews, spaghetti sauces, and casseroles. Introduce broccoli, kale, collards, and Chinese greens early on and make them a part of the normal fare. Use the calcium-fortified variety of orange juice. If dairy products are used, include cottage cheese, other cheeses, yogurt, and puddings. Almond butter is a delicious spread; though expensive, it's a fine treat. Blackstrap molasses as a sweetener for baking adds calcium and other minerals.

Cheese, yogurt, and the alternatives listed above supply the necessary calcium, but they do not contain vitamin D, so it is important that a reliable source be provided (sunshine, fortified foods, or a supplement).

3. Provide at least two servings of Beans and Alternates to ensure sufficient protein, iron, and zinc.

   • **Protein sources and needs**: Though we also get protein from grains and vegetables, beans and the alternates in this group tend to be the most concentrated sources. When a child is getting enough calories from a variety of nutritious foods, as outlined in the Vegetarian Food Guide (page 193) and the Vegetarian Food Guide for Preschool Children (page 234), protein needs are assured.

VEGETARIAN FOOD GUIDE FOR PRESCHOOL CHILDREN (TWO TO FOUR YEARS)

Include a wide variety of foods

Milks and Alternates: 4 to 6 servings

½ cup (125 ml) breast milk, cow's milk, or full-fat fortified soymilk
¼ cup (60 ml) calcium-set tofu
½ cup (125 ml) calcium-fortified juice
3 tablespoons (45 ml) almond butter
1 cup (250 ml) cooked, calcium-rich greens (kale, collards, Chinese greens, broccoli)
1 tablespoon (15 ml) blackstrap molasses
5 figs

Grains: 4 to 6 toddler-size servings

½ slice bread
¼ cup (60 ml) cooked grain or pasta
½ cup (125 ml) ready-to-eat cereal
¼ cup (60 ml) cooked cereal

Vegetables: 2 to 3 toddler-size servings

½ cup (125 ml) salad or other raw vegetable pieces
⅓ cup (80 ml) vegetable juice

Fruits: 2 to 3 toddler-size servings

½ to 1 fresh fruit
¼ cup (60 ml) cooked fruit
¼ cup (60 ml) fruit juice (limit to 1 cup/250 ml per day)

Beans and Alternates: 2 to 3 toddler-size servings

½ cup (125 ml) cooked beans, peas, or lentils
2 ounces (57 g) tofu
½ to 1 ounce (14 to 28.4 g) veggie "meat"
1½ tablespoons (22 ml) nut or seed butter
1 egg

Other Essentials

Vitamin B$_{12}$:   1.0 mcg in fortified foods or supplement
Vitamin D: 200 IU (5 mcg) vitamin D from fortified foods or supplements
Omega-3 Fatty Acids: ½ tsp. (2 ml) flaxseed oil or other source to provide 1.5 g omega-3 fatty acids

Table 10.7 shows the amounts of protein recommended for children and teens of different ages. Due to slight differences in digestibility of plant foods and animal products, slightly more protein is advised for vegans than for nonvegans. For vegan children, the higher end of the range given applies if the diet is mostly based on whole foods, rather than some processed foods

TABLE 10.7	RECOMMENDED PROTEIN INTAKE FOR NONVEGAN/VEGAN CHILDREN/TEENS		
Age (years)	Weight	Protein per day for Nonvegans	Protein per day for Vegans
2–3	29 lbs./13 kg	16 g	18–21 g
4–6	44 lbs./20 kg	24 g	26–28 g
7–10	62 lbs./28 kg	28 g	31–34 g
11–14, male	99 lbs./45 kg	45 g	50–54 g
11–14, female	101 lbs./46 kg	46 g	51–55 g
15–18, male	146 lbs./66 kg	59 g	66–73 g
15–18, female	121 lbs./55 kg	44 g	50–55 g

and soyfoods. Still, typical intakes tend to be well above the recommended levels for children on either dietary pattern. If a child's weight is a little higher or lower, we can adjust the recommended protein intake proportionally.

• **Legumes and soyfoods**: Legumes are so nutritious that they are valuable for everyone; this is particularly true for children who do not consume animal products. Become familiar with different legumes: black beans, red lentils, pinto beans, adzuki beans, mung beans, and lima beans. Experiment with every kind of tofu you can lay your hands on, and add it to everything from appetizers to dessert. Try other soyfoods, such as tempeh, miso, soy burgers, veggie "meats," and textured soy protein. Soymilk contains 6 to 8 grams of protein per cup (250 ml).

• **Eggs and dairy**: Cow's milk provides 8 grams of protein per cup (250 ml) and a large egg has 6 grams of protein. Lacto-ovo vegetarians should note that one large egg contains 213 mg of cholesterol, and 1 cup (250 ml) of whole milk or yogurt or 1 ounce (28.4 g) of cheddar cheese each provide 30 mg of cholesterol. The American Academy of Pediatrics suggests that cholesterol be limited to not more than 300 mg per day. Plant foods contain no cholesterol.

• **Seeds, nuts, and peanuts**: Seeds have only 3 to 5 grams of protein per ¼ cup (60 ml), and nuts are lower still, yet they do provide a little. Peanuts, which actually are legumes, contain much more—there are 9 grams of protein in ¼ cup (60 ml) of peanuts, and 8 grams of protein in 2 tablespoons (30 ml) of peanut butter. You'll find nut butters in many of the recipes in this book, especially the children's favorite, African Stew, on page 343.

• **Iron**: Iron deficiency is the most widely recognized nutritional deficiency in North American children. Here are the three main reasons for iron deficiency in vegetarian children:

1. *Insufficient dietary iron.* For solutions, beans, split peas, lentils, soyfoods, and peanut butter are highly important iron sources. See table 3.5, Iron, Zinc, and Protein in Foods, for the amount of iron in specific foods. There are iron sources in other food groups, such as prunes and dark green veggies. A good source of vitamin C, eaten at the same time we eat an iron-rich food, can greatly increase our iron absorption (see the vitamin C–rich fruits listed on the next page). Iron-fortified infant cereal works, too, and not just for infants; it can be added to other hot cereals, pancakes, and baked goods. Use cast-iron cookware when possible. It will add iron to the foods that are cooked in it, especially acidic foods, such as tomato sauce.

2. *Too much of the inhibitors of iron absorption: phytates and oxalates.* One of the most concentrated sources of phytates is wheat bran, while oxalates are highest in spinach, Swiss chard, and beet greens. (Though these greens are rich sources of iron, we absorb little of it.)

3. *Too much dairy.* Lacto-vegetarian children may not get enough iron if dairy products are used as their main sources of protein. Dairy foods not only are poor sources of iron, they inhibit its absorption. It is not uncommon for a child to consume cheese, yogurt, ice cream, or other dairy foods with almost every meal and snack, in addition to drinking three or four glasses of milk during the day. When dairy products are the central focus of the diet, it can be difficult to make room for iron-rich legumes, tofu, and greens.

• **Zinc.** Although we seldom hear of problems relating to zinc deficiency, many children (and adults) have difficulty meeting the recommended intakes. Shortages can cause a lack of appetite, delays in growth and development, and slow wound healing. For sufficient zinc, serve legumes, tofu, and seed and nut butters on a regular basis. Among veggie "meats," many of the Yves products are fortified with zinc; these can be handy for lunchboxes. Nuts and seeds are concentrated sources of calories and minerals such as zinc; some families keep a little bowl of them on a kitchen counter for passers-by to nibble on.

Take a look at the amounts of protein in the various foods listed in table 3.5, Iron, Zinc, and Protein in Foods, and in the menus on pages 70 to 73. You'll find that protein intake over the course of a day can mount up fairly quickly. For children's recommended intakes of iron, zinc, and other nutrients, see pages 361 and 362.

Apart from the Beans and Alternates food group, whole grains are good zinc sources; they provide two or three times as much zinc as refined breads and cereals. Wheat germ contains zinc, too. And some ready-to-eat breakfast cereals are fortified with plenty of zinc, along with iron and other minerals, so check the labels.

4. Include six or more servings of Grains in the diet each day, at least half of which should be whole grains. Carbohydrates, meaning the complex carbohydrates in whole grains, are ideal sources of calories. Experiment with millet, quinoa, spelt, barley, amaranth, kamut, and brown, red, or wild rice, on their own or in combinations. Whole Grain Pudding can be both a breakfast cereal and a soothing dessert or snack, sweetened with dried fruit (see recipes pages 312 and 313). Instead of the same type of sliced bread day after day, provide a variety: rye, pumpernickel, pita bread, chapatis, bagels, multigrain rolls, and oatmeal scones. Of course, making our own bread can be a tremendous adventure for children, especially punching down the dough! Whole grain flours and wheat germ can be used in cookies, muffins, squares, or other home-made goodies for a more nutritious treat.

Pasta comes in assorted shapes (from letters to big tubes) and can be made from various grains, including whole grains. It's all right to use some refined grains, especially for little ones whose small stomachs can fill up quickly if their diet is very high in fiber. Aim to keep refined grains to no more than half of the total grains served.

5. Include at least three servings of Vegetables and two servings of Fruits each day. This goes for young and old alike. Even if we did not learn to enjoy vegetables when we were children, here's a chance to start. We can visit an ethnic store and discover entirely new Asian vegetables or other foods. If we ask for tips on how to prepare unfamiliar vegetables, we'll get great ideas. With children, it's so easy to make these experiences into fascinating explorations! We can sample avocados; eggplant; zucchini; different types of tomatoes, peppers, and squashes; or broccoflower (a cross between broccoli and cauliflower). Discuss from which part of the plant the vegetable comes, or make it into a guessing game. Children often love to sample unusual fruits, such as mangos, Chinese pears, and pomegranates. Vegetables and fruits provide an abundance of vitamins, minerals, and phytochemicals.

For the love of vegetables, we can try these approaches.

- ✔ Encourage an interest in vegetables by growing some in a garden or even in containers on your balcony. If that isn't possible, bring children on an excursion to a farm and let them see how these foods grow.
- ✔ Older children and teens can prepare salads, stir-fries, and all sorts of other dishes with what they harvest.
- ✔ Grow sprouts. Youngsters enjoy rinsing them and watching them change day by day (see basic sprouting instructions, page 330).

✔ Get children accustomed to dark greens early on. Broccoli often is a favorite. Use a variety of dark greens in salads, stir-fries, casseroles, and spaghetti sauces.

✔ Preserve the nutritional value and bright color of vegetables by cooking them in a minimum of water, steaming, or stir-frying them. Children often prefer their vegetables raw or tender-crisp rather than mushy, so don't overcook!

✔ Serve two or more different vegetables with dinner. Include one that your child or teen already likes.

✔ Show enthusiasm when bringing home an unusual plant food.

✔ Make these healthy foods fun to eat. Children love vegetables and dip. Cut veggies make a great snack, even before dinner. Fancy shapes and patterns are most inviting for little ones. Vegetable pieces can be arranged into entertaining pictures on a plate (faces are a favorite).

For the love of fruit, we can try these approaches.

✔ Go for variety! There are so many flavorful fruits from which to choose that it's not hard to find a dozen or two that appeal to even the fussiest eater.

✔ Serve vitamin C–rich fruit often. Whole fruits such as oranges, grapefruits, kiwi, cantaloupe, and strawberries are our best choices. Fruit juices can be used, but only in moderation; that is, not more than about 1 cup (250 ml) per day. Juice can cause chronic diarrhea in small children and displace other foods in their diet when used in excess. Do not use fruit "drinks" in place of juice, even if they do have vitamin C added and a dribble of real juice. They don't contribute much more than vitamin C; the rest is sugar, flavor, and color.

✔ Make fruit fun to eat. Kids love fruit kabobs, fruit salads, and fruit platters (arrange the fruit in a flower shape).

✔ Offer dried fruits for a change. Dried fruits are convenient, portable, and nutritious. Try something different, such as dried peaches, pears, or apples, or your own homemade fruit leather. Unfortunately, dried fruits aren't so great for the teeth; remember to brush after eating.

✔ For a real treat, occasionally squeeze your own fruit juice.

✔ If you have dessert (which certainly is not a necessity), make fruits your main theme. Fresh fruit salads or platters, blueberry crêpes, or fruit crisp make wonderful endings to special meals.

6. Include a source of omega-3 fatty acids in the diet. Omega-3 fatty acids are very important to normal growth and development and sources should be included in a child's diet each day; aim for about 2 to 3 grams of omega-3 fatty acids daily. The most concentrated sources are flaxseeds and flaxseed oil. One teaspoon (5 ml) of flaxseed oil provides about 2.7 grams of omega-3 fatty acids. Other sources include hempseeds and hempseed oil, canola oil, and walnuts. Soy products and wheat germ also provide some omega-3 fatty acids; however, they also are very high in omega-6 fatty acids. For lacto-ovo children, omega-3-rich eggs provide a good source of DHA, one of the important long-chain omega-3 fatty acids. Of course, for young children, breast milk is an excellent source of the long-chain omega-3 fatty acids, EPA and DHA. For more information about omega-3 fatty acids, see chapter 7.

7. Include a reliable source of vitamin B12 in the diet every day. Unfortified plant foods cannot meet our needs for vitamin B_{12}. It is essential that vegetarian, including vegan, children receive reliable sources of this nutrient. The RDA for vitamin B_{12} is 0.9 mcg for children ages one to three years, 1.2 mcg for four- to eight-year-olds, 1.8 mcg for nine- to thirteen-year-olds, and 2.4 mcg for everyone fourteen years of age and older. Lacto-ovo vegetarian children can obtain vitamin B_{12} from dairy products and eggs, fortified foods, or supplements. Vegan children can obtain vitamin B_{12} from supplements or from fortified foods including soymilk, meat analogs, Red Star Vegetarian Support Formula nutritional yeast, and cereals (see table 8.1, Vitamin B_{12} in Foods, on page 187). Be sure to read the labels.

8. Provide concentrated sources of calories as part of the daily fare. Vegetarian and vegan diets can be very high in bulk, making it difficult for small children to meet their needs for energy. In the few cases where this is an ongoing problem, protein will be used for energy rather than for building body tissues, and growth can be compromised. This situation is most often seen when foods rich in fat and protein are restricted.

The solution is simple. Small children need nutritious, energy-packed foods throughout the day. By following some or all of these suggestions, we will help to ensure that a child gets enough fat and calories:

✔ Provide three meals a day, plus regular snacks in between. For many children it is difficult to pack in enough food at a meal to tide them over for five or six hours until the next meal.

✔ Don't restrict fat excessively. Allow liberal use of tofu and other soy products, avocados, and nuts, seeds, and their butters. Whole nuts and seeds can be included after four years of age, but not before that due to the danger of choking. Include some fats and oils in baking and cooking. Milk, yogurt, cheese, and eggs provide concentrated fat and energy for lacto-ovo vegetarian children.

✔ Don't overdo raw foods as they can be rather bulky for small stomachs. Use some cooked vegetables and fruits and their juices.

✔ Well-cooked whole grains are fine, but avoid the use of high-fiber foods, such as wheat bran and fiber supplements. Choose whole grain breads and cereals, but do not add extra fiber to foods. It's all right to include some refined grains (such as pasta, crackers, and couscous), but don't overdo it, because their mineral content is inferior.

✔ Offer an assortment of protein-rich foods that are also low in fiber. Great choices include tofu, nut butters and creams (which are nut or seed butters thinned with milks), soy cheese and yogurt, plus dairy products and eggs for lacto-ovo vegetarians.

Meal Memo

Rather than massive meals, most children need small, frequent servings, such as three meals with snacks in between. Appetite can fluctuate considerably in this age group, and there are going to be times when your child will eat more or less than what is suggested in the guide. Having a quiet time before meals can help to improve appetite.

We might impress our neighbors by being gourmet cooks, but our children, those sometimes masters of simplicity, tend to like a carrot that still resembles a carrot, a cracker, and a simple chunk of cheese or tofu (marinated or plain).

Children should be seated while eating, rather than running around. Supervise small children in case they choke on something. (See the list of potential problem foods for infants on page 227.)

If we don't make foods into bribes or rewards, we may avoid plenty of problems, including possible obesity, because we won't be placing an unrealistic value on certain foods.

Breakfast

Children do better at school when they've eaten breakfast. But there are a lot of ways to deliver that breakfast, such as a glass of fortified soymilk or orange juice and a couple of muffins grabbed on the way out the door; a quick chocolate shake or fruit smoothie; scrambled tofu with toast; muesli prepared the night before; or leftovers from last night's supper. (See recipe list, page 307.)

Lunch

Although some youngsters have been known to get by on seven years worth of peanut butter sandwiches, they'd likely appreciate some of the selections provided in the Ten Tempting Ways to Fill a Sandwich, page 324. Be creative with children's lunchboxes. Be sure to include something from each food group.

- **Beans and Alternates**: Marinated tofu, bean or pea soup, hummus, veggie "meat" slices, and veggie burgers.

- **Milks and Alternates**: Fortified soymilk or cow's milk, fortified soy or dairy yogurt, raw broccoli florets, figs, and almonds.

- **Vegetables and Fruits**: Raw vegetables and dip, salad, whole or cut-up fruits, and dried fruits.

- **Grains**: Soups and salads using whoe grains; breads, rolls, bagels, and crackers using whole grain flours; muffins; and other nutritious baked items.

An entire book on the topic is Judy Brown's *The Natural Lunchbox: Vegetarian Meals for School, Work, and Home* (Book Publishing Company; Summertown, TN).

Supper

See the recipes for Seven Super Simple Suppers on pages 338 to 347. These were developed with families in mind. Also, *Raising Vegetarian Children* by J. Stepaniak and V. Melina (McGraw-Hill; New York, NY) contains a wealth of child- and teen-friendly recipes.

Snacks

"Snack" does not automatically mean junk food. Snacks often contribute one-third of our children's calories; they should also contribute one-third of other nutrients. Provide youngsters with appealing and wholesome snacks. Offer nutritious squares, muffins, loaves, cookies, crackers and cheese (soy or dairy), nut butters, yogurt (soy or dairy), plus trail mixes for older children. Set out a plate of sliced raw veggies or wedges of cut-up fruit for TV time and for potential nibblers who wander by the kitchen.

Let's Have a Little Action

Childhood is an important time to establish habits of exercise. Our joy in play is natural. Often the trick is how to retain it while living in an apartment or trailer, or when parents don't want all that joyful noise around. Make a commitment to get active—join a ski club, swimming club, or sports facility.

Encourage children to pick at least one sport, and sign them up. Often we adults need more of this too. All of our lives can be improved by cycling together, taking Sunday hikes, and participating in activities at the local community center.

The Question of Supplements

Children can be well nourished without supplements, as long as a balance of foods, as described in the Vegetarian Food Guide, is provided. For vegan children, vitamin B_{12}–fortified foods must be included; otherwise, a supplement of vitamin B_{12} is necessary. A regular children's multivitamin-mineral supplement generally contains enough vitamin B_{12}—but read the label to be certain. Two cups (500 ml) of fortified milk (soy or cow's) provide enough vitamin D. Otherwise, a supplement is needed, except during the warmest half of the year if there is regular, brief exposure to sunlight. If insufficient servings from the milk and milk alternates group are consumed, a supplement of approximately 200 to 500 mg of calcium per day can help augment the diet; choose a formulation that includes vitamin D.

If a supplement is used, it is best to select one that contains a variety of vitamins and minerals including vitamin B_{12}, vitamin D, zinc, and iron in amounts that approximate the recommended intakes (see the appendix). Many children's supplements contain no minerals except iron. Read the label. Avoid single-nutrient supplements other than calcium, unless medically indicated.

PART 4: FOCUS ON TEENS (THIRTEEN TO EIGHTEEN)

Many teens today are independently making the decision to eliminate meat from their menu. Their motivation often comes from concerns about the environment or animal rights rather than from a desire to improve the nutritional quality of their diet. This doesn't mean that food is not of prime importance. It just means that the criteria for food selection may be a little different than it is for the average health-conscious vegetarian adult. The two main criteria for food selection by teens generally are:

1. How fast can it be ready?

2. Does it taste good?

The most acceptable answers to these questions are "It is ready," and "It tastes great." In other words, we're talking instant, delicious food. Our society is fairly well set up for instant and delicious, but not so well for vegetarian (although this is beginning to change).

Many teens who grow up on standard North American fare simply stop eating meat when they become vegetarian. Instead of a hamburger and fries for lunch, they opt for a double order of fries. When chicken, potatoes, and corn arrive on the dinner table, they eat just the potatoes and corn. There are a few problems with this kind of approach. First, parents tend to be less than supportive, because they see their teenager eating very poorly. Second, the poor nutrition can take its toll on the teen, eventually causing him or her to feel rundown and develop nutritional deficiencies.

An immediate solution that will often satisfy parents and teens alike is to venture into the world of veggie "meats." The possibilities are endless: slices, burgers, wieners, vegetarian "ground round," and even little nuggets. Some teens learn to make hummus and even enjoy the process. Seasoned tofu is a great food for teens; it's convenient and loaded with nutrients. Parents generally become a little less resistant to the whole vegetarian idea if they know their teen is getting some concentrated sources of protein, iron, and zinc. In many cases, the parents begin to broaden their own food choices, and some even become vegetarians themselves. The result could well be a healthier family.

There also are teens who have been raised on a vegetarian diet. This group generally does very well. Some studies show that these vegetarian teens are well nourished, have less tendency to be obese, and eat less junk, less fat, and more fiber, fruit, and vegetables than their meat-eating peers. A large study by John Sabate involving Seventh-day Adventist teens showed that these vegetarians actually outgrew their omnivorous peers by an average of one inch (2.5 cm).

The nutritional needs of vegetarian teens are similar to those of any other teens. Many physical changes are taking place during the teen years, and the demands for nutrients are high. There are several approaches parents can take to help vegetarian teens be well nourished.

✔ Keep a variety of superfast and wholesome foods handy. Stock up on fresh fruits, trail mixes, nutritious baked goods, and soy or dairy yogurt and cheese, as well as whole grain breads and cereals.

✔ Encourage teens to contribute to meals by helping with meal planning and preparation. Teens can be expected to prepare whole meals; heat and serve a partially prepared meal; make a salad; or create a nutritious dessert. This will give them a head start for managing on their own. The recipes in this book are a great place to start.

✔ Offer vegetarian versions of popular dinner favorites: baked beans, bean tortillas, pizza with vegetarian sausage or pepperoni, burgers and dogs, burritos, lasagne, chili, spaghetti, sloppy Joes, cabbage rolls, and tamale pie.

Red lentils, beans, or vegetarian "ground round" all work well as meat replacements.

✔ Remember that teens are responsible for their own food choices. Your job is to stock the pantry with a wide variety of healthy foods.

✔ Encourage involvement in groups and activities that will increase their knowledge of vegetarianism and the vegetarian way of eating.

The Vegetarian Resource Group provides many resources and sponsors an annual essay contest for students nineteen and under with fifty-dollar savings bonds awarded in three categories. Details can be found at www.vrg.org. You'll also find recipes and interesting articles.

Keep up-to-date by visiting the Web site www.vegetarianteen.com. An organization founded and run by teens and young adults is YES! (Youth for Environmental Sanity). Visit their website at www.yesworld.org. This group promotes vegetarianism and informs, inspires, and empowers young people to take positive action for social justice and environmental sanity. Contact YES! at 877-293-7226 or send them an e-mail at camps@yesworld.org.

The Nutrition Guidelines for Vegetarian Children (page 232) provides practical tips. Yet many teens seem to manage even under conditions that are less than ideal. Don't get too concerned if things don't go precisely according to plan. Here are a few additional pointers (written by two moms who have been there).

The Instant Eater

> A good sense of humor will get us through most problems in life (unfortunately, mostly in retrospect).

Teenagers are notorious for skipping meals, especially breakfast and lunch. This can lead to bouts of hunger that are too often filled with potato chips and chocolate bars. We also can be fairly certain that teens will vanish for hours and then, in the company of friends, they will descend on the kitchen like a horde of locusts (or a single very hungry one).

One way to deal with this is to have nourishing "fast foods" on hand that can be ready at a moment's notice. Instant meals, especially breakfast and lunch, are great if they can be ready to grab and go. Quick snacks that also are nutritious can salvage an otherwise marginal diet.

The high quality and tremendous variety of convenient "natural" foods on the market today may surprise you—some are truly healthful! If you haven't explored your local natural food stores, you are in for a real treat. For economy, you can buy in bulk or make your own baked items and veggie burgers.

Any food that fits into the food guide is a good choice. Here are some suggestions for making the most of the choices in each food group.

Beans and Alternates

- ✔ Serve hummus as a dip with raw veggies.
- ✔ Have spaghetti sauces on hand, in jars and cans. Add vegetarian "ground round" or make Chunky Red Lentil Tomato Sauce (page 340) and store some in the freezer.
- ✔ Legumes are indispensable! Simply open a can, drain well, and add them to a home "salad bar." Marinated bean salads can be always at the ready.
- ✔ Mash pinto or kidney beans to make taco fillings.
- ✔ Tofu absorbs the flavor of any seasonings or sauces that are used, so try it with family favorites like barbecue or sweet-and-sour sauce. Tofu is one of the most versatile foods imaginable and it's great on kabobs, in sandwiches, and nibbled as snacks.
- ✔ Stir-fry meals can be made with almonds, cashews, tofu, tempeh, or firm beans such as garbanzos in place of the meat. (See recipe, pages 346-47.)
- ✔ Vegetarian patties, sausages, loaves, and deli slices are available in supermarkets, natural food stores, ethnic stores, and food co-ops. Try different products in order to find your favorite; all are fast and easy to use. Some brands, such as many of the Yves products, are fortified with vitamin B_{12} and zinc.

Milks and Alternates

- ✔ Keep a covered jug of calcium-fortified fruit juice ready-mixed and in the refrigerator at all times.
- ✔ Use fortified soymilk or cow's milk as a beverage and in cooking.
- ✔ Stock several containers of dairy or fortified soy yogurt.
- ✔ Include dried figs in trail mixes.
- ✔ Buy almonds in bulk and keep them in the freezer.
- ✔ Use almond butter instead of peanut butter on sandwiches.
- ✔ Add broccoli florets to plates of veggie sticks.
- ✔ Enjoy tofu (made with calcium) in a variety of ways: scrambled, baked, barbecued, and stir-fried.

Vegetables and Fruits

- ✔ Put out a tray of raw vegetables and a dip for everyone to munch on. Even teens who turn their noses up at cooked vegetables seem to be quite happy to polish off a platter of raw veggies and dip.

✔ Grow a garden. Teens love to plant, watch things grow, and enjoy the fruits (and vegetables) of their labor.

✔ Arrange a big bowl of colorful fresh fruits and set it on the table, ripe for the picking.

✔ Keep plenty of dried fruit or fruit leather or a bag of apple chips on hand as instant snacks (remember to brush teeth after eating).

✔ Grate vegetables into patties, loaves, and salads.

✔ Cut up a variety of fruits and offer them at snack time.

Grains

✔ Keep assorted whole grain products on hand for instant snacking. Whole grain breads, bagels, cereals, muffins, and rice cakes all work well.

✔ Stock the freezer with scrumptious homemade or healthful baked goods.

✔ Cook a variety of whole grains—quinoa, millet, amaranth, kamut, barley, and oat groats—and use them in soups, salads, pilafs, and desserts.

✔ From time to time, have whole grain pudding available as a creamy dessert.

The supplement question

A teenager's need for nutritional supplements depends entirely on her or his eating habits and individual needs. Supplements are not necessary if the Vegetarian Food Guide is being followed and your teen's diet includes foods that are fortified with vitamin B_{12} and vitamin D. However, supplements can be useful in a number of situations. A good choice is a regular (rather than high-potency or stress-type) adult multivitamin-mineral supplement that provides the recommended levels of a wide range of nutrients, including iron, zinc, and magnesium (see appendix).

Iron can be a problem for both vegetarian and nonvegetarian teens, especially girls. Those who are watching calories, are very active in sports, or have replaced the meat in their diets mainly with cheese and eggs may also have a tough time getting enough iron. A multivitamin-mineral supplement with iron and zinc may be appropriate in these cases.

A calcium supplement will be necessary if an average of eight servings from the Milks and Alternates group is not consumed: remember, we're aiming for 1,300 mg of calcium per day, and this is a challenge on any diet! If exposure to sunlight or consumption of vitamin D–fortified foods is low, a vitamin D supplement of 10 mcg also is recommended.

PART 5: THE PRIME OF LIFE (FIFTY YEARS PLUS)

When we reach the age of fifty, and again when we reach seventy and older, our requirements for certain nutrients change. Oddly, our needs veer in opposite directions simultaneously. In order to maintain the same body weight, we require fewer calories. At the same time, we need more of two vitamins (D and B_6) and one mineral (calcium), while our recommended intakes for twelve vitamins, ten minerals, and protein remain unchanged.

What does this indicate in terms of our food choices? It means that we need to get "more bang for our buck." Let's return to the idea of nutrient density that was covered in chapter 6. If we're going to get the necessary amounts of vitamins D and B_6, calcium, protein, and other vitamins and minerals while eating fewer calories, every 100 calories in our diets must deliver a little more protein, vitamins, and minerals.

Changes with Age

Calories, muscle mass, and activity

There are two main reasons that most of us need fewer calories as we get older. First, with age we lose muscle mass. Our caloric requirement depends in part on our metabolic rate, which in turn depends on our total amount of lean body mass or muscle tissue. Muscle mass tends to shrink as we age. When a person's muscle mass at age twenty-five and age sixty-five are compared, men typically have lost 26 pounds (11.8 kg) of muscle tissue and women may have lost 11 pounds (5 kg) of muscle tissue over four decades. Thereafter, 2 or 3 pounds (1 or 1.5 kg) of muscle tissue is lost each decade. This gradually reduces our caloric requirement.

Second, with age, activity levels decrease. Unfortunately, most of us exercise less as we become older. We have found so many ways to make life easy for ourselves that in wealthy nations it is customary to think of sedentary behavior as the norm. Health problems, such as adult-onset diabetes, are viewed as almost inevitable aspects of becoming older. Yet these actually are linked to inactivity and increased fat in the abdominal region rather than to age.

The amount of muscle we carry on our frame affects our rate of metabolism, insulin sensitivity, need for calories, appetite, breathing, and ability to move; ultimately it affects our independence. Losing pound after pound of muscle is not an advantage!

As we become older, perhaps some stresses from earlier stages of life—raising children, getting ahead in the world—have lessened. It is probable that we'd like to enjoy years of vibrant good health and have fun with our loved ones. According to the *Manual of Clinical Dietetics*, "The older adult who maintains a high activity level can preserve muscle mass and requires a higher energy intake to maintain body weight." In other words, by exercising we can keep our muscle mass, plus we get to eat more without getting fat!

Physical activity has an immense impact on our health and quality of life as we age. It helps us preserve our muscles and remain strong. It is crucial to our retention of bone mass. The function of our heart, oxygen delivery system, and lungs are improved. Our bodies remain more flexible. Exercise also is an important factor in mental health and general well-being. It results in our feeling better about ourselves and improves the quality of our social interactions. Our sleep and our sex life improve. We are better able to maintain a healthy body weight. In ways that can be measured, exercise improves the effective function of our immune system. It cuts our risk of chronic diseases: colon cancer, heart disease, diabetes, arthritis, and hypertension.

Would it be best if we take up marathon running? No, that's neither necessary nor ideal. There is general agreement among experts that our target for the day should be at least an hour of exercise. Which activities are best? It matters far less what activities we choose than that we do something. To keep motivated, we need to seek out forms of exercise that we really enjoy and look forward to. Gardening, cycling, swimming, or doing yoga are all great options. Join a fitness program on land or in a pool. Dance, hike, or cross-country ski. Put on music and whirl around the living room; the family dog may be pleased to join in and perhaps the person next door would, too. Stroll through inspiring places: a park, a beach, or along a quiet road. Share a brisk power walk with a friend. Play table tennis, fly a kite, or toss a Frisbee with grandchildren or neighbors. A combination of activities from this list is likely best, because the more varied our exercise, the more we can work out every part of our bodies.

> "If the effects of exercise could be bottled, it would be the most widely prescribed medication."
> — *Linn Goldberg, MD*

Protein

Whether we're twenty, fifty, or seventy years of age, our recommended protein intake is the same as that described for adults on page 53—about 1 gram of protein per kilogram (2.2 pounds) of body weight.

We need more protein if we're dealing with illness, infection, or recovery from surgery; in these situations our requirement may be around 1.25 grams of protein per kilogram (2.2 pounds) of body weight. Either level—1 gram or

1.25 grams of protein per kilogram of body weight—easily can be met on a vegetarian diet if protein-rich plant foods, such as legumes and soyfoods, are eaten daily. Table 3.5 and the menus on pages 70 to 73 give an idea of the amounts of protein in various foods.

Though our protein needs stay the same per kilogram of body weight, we actually need more protein relative to the amount of calories we eat. That means our diets need to be more protein-dense (that is, more protein per 100 calories of food). This is because, with shrinking muscle mass, our caloric requirements decrease, but our protein needs stay the same. We must make sure that good sources of protein are included in our daily diet, and take care not to squander too many calories on junk foods. Physical changes that occur with age often attract people toward plant protein and away from meats. Dental problems and swallowing difficulties, combined with cost factors, often mean that meat is less appealing. The softer textures of tofu and split pea or lentil soups can be ideal. Concern about chronic disease (both prevention and treatment) also draws people toward plant foods.

Sometimes questions are raised about beans causing stomach upset and gas. The solution is to introduce these foods gradually. Start with the smaller beans (such as lentils and split peas) and tofu, and take the time to chew foods well. If you are soaking and cooking beans at home, discard the soaking water, as it contains oligosaccharides (indigestible sugars) that result in intestinal gas. Then make sure your beans are well cooked. There is a tremendous upside to switching from meat to beans. Meat is a fiber-free food. When we eat mainly meat and processed foods, especially if we are inactive, constipation can become a real concern. The problem seems to escalate with age. The switch to a vegetarian diet rich in beans, peas, and lentils can help resolve this problem permanently.

For a quick protein boost, a shake (recipe, page 315) is a pleasant way to get 7 grams of protein. A serving of Scrambled Tofu (page 314) can provide one-half of our protein for the day. We should not discount the contribution of cooked cereal: 1 cup (250 ml) of oatmeal with ¾ cup (175 ml) of soymilk provides 11 grams of protein, which may be one-quarter of the day's requirement. We'll get the same amount from an English muffin with 2 tablespoons (30 ml) of almond butter (and more if we use peanut butter). Browse through the recipes in this book, including the nutritional analyses, to learn many ways to reach our recommended intakes of protein.

Vitamin B_6

When we reach the age of fifty-one, our recommended intake for vitamin B_6 increases dramatically by 30 percent—from 1.3 mg per day for both sexes before age fifty-one to 1.7 mg for men and 1.5 mg for women. These recommended intakes include a large safety margin, and deficiency symptoms are not common. However, typical intakes are 1.8 mg for men and 1.3 mg for women. Since these are averages, it seems that many men and more than half the women in the general population might do well to improve their intakes.

Vitamin B_6, also known as pyridoxine, plays a role in the metabolism of more than one hundred amino acids. Along with two other B vitamins (B_{12} and folate), it helps us get rid of potentially toxic homocysteine (described in more detail on page 26). Vitamin B_6 helps us build the blood protein, heme. Symptoms of deficiency are depression, anemia, and increased homocysteine levels accompanied by increased risk of heart disease.

Vitamin B_6 is present in many vegetarian foods and throughout the different food groups. A few examples are shown in table 10.8 on the next page. We can reach the level of 1.7 mg with a banana, a baked potato, a cup of lentils, plus a handful of nuts or seeds.

Calcium

As we grow older, we become less efficient at absorbing calcium. For example, from age forty to sixty, this efficiency may drop as much as 25 percent. At age fifty, our recommended intake of calcium increases to 1,200 mg per day (from 1,000 mg for adults below age fifty). To reach these levels, we need eight servings from the Milks and Alternates group, each providing about 15 percent of the DV for calcium. For more on the Milks and Alternates group, see page 197, and for more on calcium, see chapter 4. For many people, these intakes are most easily achieved at

TABLE 10.8 VITAMIN B_6 IN FOODS	
Food and Serving Size	Vitamin B6 (mg)
Fruits	
Apple, medium, 1	0.1
Banana, medium, 1	0.7
Cantaloupe or honeydew melon, ¼	0.2
Figs, dried, 5	0.2
Prunes, 7	0.2
Vegetables	
Broccoli, collards, raw, 1 cup (250 ml)	0.1
Carrot, medium, 1	0.1
Kale, raw, 1 cup (250 ml)	0.2
Potato, baked, 1 medium with skin	0.4
Squash, cooked, ½ cup (125 ml)	0.1
Sweet potato, baked and peeled, 1	0.3
Beans and Alternates	
Adzuki, garbanzo, or kidney beans, cooked, 1 cup (250 ml)	0.2
Lentils, soybeans, cooked, 1 cup (250 ml)	0.4
Navy, pinto beans, cooked, 1 cup (250 ml)	0.3
Tempeh, ½ cup (125 ml)	0.2
Tofu, ½ cup (125 ml)	0.1
Yves Veggie Ground Round, 2 oz. (57 g)	0.3
Nuts and Seeds	
Flaxseeds, 2 tbsp. (30 ml)	0.2
Hazelnuts, ¼ cup (60 ml)	0.2
Peanut butter, 3 tbsp. (45 ml)	0.2
Sunflower seeds, ¼ cup (60 ml)	0.3
Grains	
Barley, cooked, ½ cup (125 ml)	0.1
Ready-to-eat-cereal, unfortified, 1 serving	0.2
Ready-to-eat-cereal, fortified, 1 serving (see label)	0.5
Wheat germ, 2 tbsp. (30 ml)	0.2
Dairy Products and Eggs	
Cow's milk, 2%, ¼ cup (125 ml)	0.05
Egg, 1	0.05

least on some days by adding a few hundred mg in supplement form to the amount derived from food to reach the total.

Vitamin D

This vitamin, which can be derived from the effects of sunlight on our skin or from fortified foods, is essential for our absorption of calcium. In regions far from the equator, we get little sunlight during winter months, and the average serum vitamin D levels of adults hover around the low end of the normal range. This means, of course, that some people's levels are below the ideal range. To make matters worse, as we age our skin becomes much less efficient at doing its part in building vitamin D, even when sunlight does manage to reach our hands and face. Thus, at age fifty, recommended intakes for vitamin D double to 10 mcg per day, and there is a further increase to 15 mcg for those over seventy years of age.

Fortified soymilk, rice milk, and cow's milk each provide 2.5 mcg of vitamin D per cup (check labels), so people age fifty to seventy can get their quota from 4 cups (1 liter) of any of these fortified beverages. However, that's a lot of milk! For more information on vitamin D sources, see pages 109 and 114. Over the age of seventy, it is difficult to achieve recommended intakes from fortified foods alone, so supplementation with 15 mcg per day is advised.

Certain medications—such as laxatives, catabolic steroids (used to reduce the inflammation from arthritis and other ailments), and anticonvulsants—can interfere with vitamin D and increase requirements.

To get sufficient vitamin D from sunlight in spring, summer, and fall, we can expose our face, hands, and forearms to twenty minutes of sun (mid-morning to mid-afternoon); people with darker skin may require more. Of course, avoid excess sun exposure.

Vitamin B_{12}

Changes in our gastrointestinal tract as we age affect our absorption of vitamin B_{12}. (See chapter 8, page 181.) As many as one in three adults over the age of fifty may have difficulty absorbing vitamin B_{12} from animal products, so vitamin B_{12}–fortified foods or supplements are advised for all people in this age group (not just vegetarians). The amount we need in our diets is not increased over that of younger people, it's just that we need to make sure we take our B_{12} in a form we can absorb. (For a small number of older people, monthly injections are necessary.) For examples of B_{12}–fortified foods, see table 8.1 on page 187.

Omega-3 fatty acids

As we grow older, our ability to convert the plant form of omega-3 fatty acids (ALA) to long-chain omega-3 fatty acids (EPA and DHA) diminishes. Thus, we must be especially diligent to insure adequate intake of ALA. For most people, an intake of 3 to 6 grams a day is sufficient. Some people (for instance, those with chronic diseases, such as diabetes, arthritis, or neurological disorders) may wish to consider taking direct sources of the long-chain omega-3 fatty acids and GLA. (See chapter 7 for more information on omega-3 fatty acid sources.)

Other important aspects of diet for seniors

Antioxidants. Vitamins A and C (from fruits and vegetables) and vitamin E and the mineral selenium (both found in nuts, seeds, and whole grains) are powerful protectors against free-radical damage. Antioxidants are linked to a reduced risk of cataracts, macular degeneration, heart disease, various forms of cancer, and even wrinkles. Antioxidants seem to protect our brain function from deterioration, too. Vegetarian diets tend to be high in these antioxidants. We do the cells throughout our bodies a favor by following the Vegetarian Food Guide on page 193.

If we develop dental problems, there can be a tendency to cut back on our intake of fresh produce; however, soft fruits, cooked vegetables, and fresh-squeezed vegetable or fruit juices can take the place of foods that are more difficult to chew while the problems are being resolved. The shakes and smoothies on pages 315 to 317, or your own variations, also will help at times like this. Consider buying a good juicer—it will be well worth the investment.

Water and other fluids. Though we don't need more fluids as we get older, we do need the usual 6 to 8 cups (1.5 to 2 liters) each day. With age, one's sen-

---

TIPS AND TRIVIA ON HEALTH AND FITNESS

Gratitude: There is always a lot to be thankful for if we take time to look for it. For example, we can thank the mercy of nature that wrinkles don't hurt!

Bowel Health: We know we've hit middle age when we choose our cereal on the basis of fiber rather than the free toy. We know we're over the hill when our wild oats have turned to prunes and all bran.

Exercise: Use caution when you start a walking program. My grandmother began walking five miles a day when she was sixty. Now she's ninety-seven years old and we have no idea where on earth she is!

sitivity to thirst may decrease, yet it's important to drink water even when one is not particularly thirsty. Fear of incontinence also can lead to decreased fluid intake. Dehydration can result in constipation and other health problems, so it's important to drink water, juice, soymilk, grain beverages, broth soups, and herbal teas. All of these count toward our day's quota.

Community Support

All this nutritional advice may be very fine, but often it's not the lack of knowledge about vitamins or protein that is a problem—usually it's a matter of lifestyle and social support. For instance, it's not so much fun creating nourishing meals when we sit alone at the table day after day. Although ads might show a happy pair of seniors cycling off into the sunset or enjoying a candlelit dinner on the balcony, for many of us, our partner is gone and other family members live far away.

Since there are so many of us in the same situation, it's worthwhile doing some exploring. Soon problems of this sort will be a distant memory.

Solutions to isolation

Reach out. You have no idea how happy you will make someone if you do the unexpected and invite him or her over to share a meal and perhaps prepare it together. Your guest might even help pick a recipe from those at the end of this book and join you in shopping for ingredients.

Join a vegetarian association. More and more communities have a lively vegetarian association, and membership spans the spectrum from newborns to those arriving by wheelchair or in their nineties. If you don't find such a group, ask around for one or more people with whom you can start a monthly potluck (even for two). This is how the existing groups got started!

Explore cohousing or similar living solutions. One of the authors of this book lives in a cohousing community, which is the modern form of a type of village that originated in Denmark several decades ago. Hundreds of these wonderful groups have formed across North America and in the U.K., Australia, New Zealand, and many other parts of the world, and they offer the joint advantages of privacy and community. See www.cohousing.org or in the U.S. call 510-844-0790.

Assistance in obtaining food and more

Grocery delivery. Arrange to have fresh organic produce delivered to your door each week (see page 293). Many supermarkets and some natural foods stores offer delivery services.

Meal delivery. If you are housebound or have difficulty getting around or preparing meals, programs such as Meals on Wheels may be just the answer. Though not all programs cater to vegetarians, supply depends on the local demand, so do inquire. Your local provider may not be aware that a four-week set of vegetarian menus has been developed for use by the National Meals on Wheels Foundation (www.vrg.org/fsupdate/fsu974/fsu974menu.htm).

Care facilities and vegetarian food. If you or a loved one are in search of a suitable care home with expertise in vegetarian food preparation, look into those run by the Seventh-day Adventists. These often are better equipped to provide nutritious, delicious, and varied vegetarian meals than many other care homes. See your local telephone listings; a nearby Seventh-day Adventist church can help you. In other facilities, you may be pleasantly surprised to find that the kitchen staff are willing and able to accommodate a vegetarian senior, especially if you discuss with them suitable and acceptable entrées (for example, marinated tofu; soy burgers; or thick bean, pea, or lentil soups).

Seniors online. For helpful information on everything from heartburn to quick, inexpensive meals, visit the Vegetarian Resource Group's Web site at www.vrg.org and do a search for "seniors."

POTENTIAL ADVANTAGES OF VEGETARIAN DIETS IN THE SENIOR YEARS

Populations of vegetarians living in affluent countries appear to enjoy unusually good health, characterized by low rates of cancer, cardiovascular disease, and total mortality. These important observations have fueled much research and have raised three general questions about vegetarians in relation to nonvegetarians:

➤ Are these observations the result of better nondietary lifestyle factors, such as a lower prevalence of smoking and higher levels of physical activity?

➤ Are they the result of lower intakes of harmful dietary components, in particular, meat?

➤ Are they the result of higher intakes of beneficial dietary components that tend to replace meat in the diet?

Current evidence suggests that the answer to all three questions is "Yes."

— *Walter C. Willett, Department of Nutrition*
Harvard School of Public Health, Boston

Chapter 11

VEGETARIAN VICTORY OVER WEIGHT

Americans are obsessed with food. We have more food products and more fast-food outlets than anywhere on the planet. We are equally preoccupied with matters of weight and shape; women strive to be model thin, and men strive to be muscular. Yet somehow, amid all the diet foods, weight-loss centers, protein powders, and gyms, we keep getting fatter. Overconsumption leading to overweight and obesity is epidemic and the fastest-growing form of malnutrition in the world. Over 55 percent of Americans are overweight, and the proportion of American adults over twenty-five who are overweight soared from 25 percent in 1950 to 61 percent in 2002. Since 1980, obesity rates have doubled for adults and tripled for children. Not surprisingly, this increase in body weights generally signals a predictable decline in health.

Vegetarians are at a distinct advantage where body weight is concerned. We are leaner and have remarkably lower rates of obesity than the general population. While a vegetarian diet cannot guarantee a lower body weight, it can make the struggle a little less ominous. This chapter will explore issues of body weight and shape and provide practical tips for achieving a healthy weight for life.

SOCIETY'S DOUBLE-EDGED SWORD

At twenty years old, 5 feet, 4 inches (162 cm) and 156 pounds (71 kg), Jennifer felt fat. She had struggled with her weight since she was a little girl. Efforts to lose weight had been successful only in the short term. It seemed that for every pound that she lost, she would gain two. One night, a college friend asked her to a screening of a documentary film called The Witness,★ *which moved her so deeply, she decided to become a vegetarian. While she was worried about what she would eat and how her family would respond, she felt an underlying excitement. Perhaps it was more than a coincidence that she had been invited to this movie. Maybe the payoff for being kinder to animals would be a thinner body. After all, every vegetarian she could think of was a beanpole.*

Jennifer's family always centered their activities around food: big family dinners; homemade pies, cakes, and cookies; and wonderful celebratory meals. When Jennifer announced that she was giving up meat forever, her family was appalled, feeling that she was turning her back on family traditions.

For Jennifer the biggest challenge was replacing the meat. She had never eaten beans, apart from the odd can of baked beans while camping, and she had not even tasted tofu. It seemed to her that eggs and cheese were the quickest, easiest, and tastiest substitutes. Her parents tried to compensate for what they perceived as deprivation by providing Jennifer with more of her favorite dishes, such as pizza, scalloped potatoes, and hot fudge sundaes. Jennifer had a hard time resisting, as they were so much more than just food; they were tokens of love and family unity. To top it off, her younger brother constantly hassled her about her new food choices, which triggered her to eat more. To Jennifer's dismay, her vegetarianism was not producing any weight loss.

The Vegetarian Advantage

There is no doubt about it, vegetarians are thinner than nonvegetarians. These differences cannot be explained by some miraculous side effect from eating sprouts. Experts suspect that the vegetarian advantage can be attributed largely to differences in fat and fiber.

Vegetarians eat less fat, and particularly less saturated fat. Some studies suggest that relative to saturated fat, polyunsaturated fat increases metabolic rates.

★The Witness *is an award-winning documentary by Tribe of Heart about a construction worker who opens his heart to animals and spreads his message of compassion through the streets of New York City. For more information see: www.tribeofheart.org/index.htm*

Vegetarians also eat two to three times more fiber than nonvegetarians. Fiber adds bulk to the diet without adding calories. It also helps speed food through the digestive system, slightly decreasing our absorption of calories. In addition, fiber reduces hunger and gives us a feeling of fullness. Vegetarians, as a group, also tend to lead healthier lifestyles and be more active.

However, becoming vegetarian does not guarantee freedom from being overweight, as Jennifer can attest. Although eliminating cheeseburgers, fried chicken, and barbecued ribs certainly can help, we must remember that French fries, potato chips, and coconut cream pie all are classified as vegetarian foods.

Despite the fact that being vegetarian offers clear benefits for weight control, there are a significant number of overweight vegetarians who struggle every bit as much as nonvegetarians to lose weight. The reasons for their weight struggles are not much different from anyone else's.

Causes of Overweight

Popular opinion would suggest that the primary cause of obesity is a lack of willpower: overweight people are "couch potatoes" who eat too much. If only it were that simple. While it is true that too much food and too little exercise are often technically the cause of being overweight, this is rarely the whole story. For many people, being overweight has as much to do with self-preservation and social pressures as it does with overeating and underactivity. Our current popular opinion serves only to pour salt on our wounds. The main causes of being overweight fall into one of three groups: physical, cultural, or emotional.

Physical factors

Jennifer is overweight, just like her mom, her aunt, and her grandmother. She inherited her father's eyes and her mother's and grandmother's metabolism. These genes would be an advantage to Jennifer in the face of famine; but in the midst of abundance, they seem like more of a curse. Very low-calorie diets can make matters worse by slowing metabolism and sending our bodies into conservation mode. If we diet enough, our bodies become even more efficient, allowing us to survive on fewer calories. Less commonly, obesity is caused by medications or rare endocrine disorders, such as hypothyroidism, a condition caused by an underactive thyroid, which results in a reduced metabolic rate.

Cultural factors

Like most of us, Jennifer puts a lot of emphasis on social interactions involving food. Whether it is enjoying a family gathering or a night at the movies with friends, food is a fundamental part of the experience. Our society has created an ideal environment for overconsumption. We no longer need to do physical work to get our food. We simply open a refrigerator or freezer and pop a ready-made snack or meal into the microwave. When we are out and about, food beckons us at every turn. Jennifer can't seem to resist stopping for fries or pizza at the mall or running to the corner store for a chocolate bar. We are surrounded by an abundance of food and, not surprisingly, it shows.

The icing on the cake is that this easy access to food goes hand in hand with reduced physical activity. We catch a bus to school or drive to work. Much of the day involves sitting at a desk. In our spare time, we watch television, play video games, or surf the Net. Every convenience possible has been developed to reduce energy expenditure—remote controls, bread machines, electric can openers, elevators, electric mixers, dishwashers, and the list goes on.

Emotional factors

Following a confrontation with her brother, Jennifer often turns to the refrigerator, even when she isn't hungry. Like Jennifer, many people eat to satisfy an emotional hunger rather than a true physical hunger. This often is referred to as emotional eating and is well recognized as a major contributor to overweight. Others use food as a means of constructing walls around themselves to protect them from intimacy or pain. Food never judges, never condemns, and always seems to comfort. These apparent "advantages" are deceiving, as they come at an enormous cost to both physical and emotional well-being.

To add fuel to the fire, society sends a clear message to eat, drink, and be merry—just don't let it go to our hips. If we do happen to accumulate a little excess, we'd better prepare to wage war on those extra pounds or learn to live with the social consequences.

The Cost

The price we pay for the abundance we now enjoy is hard to quantify. Obesity causes a fivefold rise in our risk of type 2 diabetes. Being overweight increases blood pressure, cholesterol levels, triglycerides, and angina, markedly increasing our chances of sudden heart attack or stroke. It also is linked to several types of cancer, including breast, uterine, cervical, ovarian, gallbladder, and colon cancers in women, and rectal, prostate, and colon cancers in men. Excess body weight contributes to our risk of osteoarthritis, sleep apnea (pauses in breathing during sleep), gout (painful swelling in the joints), gallbladder disease, and gallstones.

These health consequences are contributing more to America's rising health care and drug costs than smoking and alcohol abuse. Even more stunning, being obese effectively ages us twenty years in terms of health risk. That puts an obese thirty-year-old in the same risk group as a normal weight fifty-year-old for developing serious medical problems, such as cancer, heart disease, and diabetes.

DETERMINING HEALTHY BODY WEIGHT

Humans come in a wide variety of shapes and sizes. There is no "ideal weight" for a person of a particular height, because our healthiest weight depends on our bone structure, muscle mass, and general body build. So weight charts are of limited value. How do we know if we are overweight or obese? The best way is to determine how much of our body weight is fat. A body fat level greater than 17 percent in men and 27 percent in women indicates being overweight, while a body fat level greater than 25 percent in men and 31 percent in women indicates obesity.

Unfortunately, getting accurate body fat measurements can be a challenge. The most widely used method of determining body fatness is called body mass index (BMI). Our BMI can be calculated using a simple equation or a chart. BMI is recommended for people age twenty to sixty-five, but it has not been considered valid for some people. For example, it does not factor in muscle mass, so very muscular people will have a high BMI but may have low body fat (thus, they appear overweight according to BMI, but are actually very lean). In addition, very short people (less than 5 feet/1.5 m tall) may have a higher BMI than would be expected relative to their size. BMI is not useful for pregnant women or those over the age of sixty-five. To find your BMI, plot your height and weight on the BMI chart on the next page.

What's Jennifer's BMI? Recall that Jennifer is 5 feet, 4 inches (163 cm) tall, and 156 pounds (71 kg). Thus, her BMI is 27—right in the middle of the overweight range. She is about 14 pounds (6.5 kg) heavier than what is considered a "healthy weight" for most people, and 19 pounds (8.6 kg) short of being classified as "obese."

FIGURE 11.1   BODY MASS INDEX (BMI)

	HEIGHT IN INCHES																
WT/ LBS	60	61	62	63	64	65	66	67	68	69	70	71	72	73	74	75	76
100	20	19	18	18	17	17	16	16	15	15	14	14	14	13	13	12	12
105	21	20	19	19	18	17	17	16	16	16	15	15	14	14	13	13	13
110	21	21	20	19	19	18	18	17	17	16	16	15	15	15	14	14	13
115	22	22	21	20	20	19	19	18	17	17	17	16	16	15	15	14	14
120	23	23	22	21	21	20	19	19	18	18	17	17	16	16	15	15	15
125	24	24	23	22	21	21	20	20	19	18	18	17	17	16	16	16	15
130	25	25	24	23	22	22	21	20	20	19	19	18	18	17	17	16	16
135	26	26	25	24	23	22	22	21	21	20	19	19	18	18	17	17	16
140	27	26	26	25	24	23	23	22	21	21	20	20	19	18	18	17	17
145	28	27	27	26	25	24	23	23	22	21	21	20	20	19	19	18	18
150	29	28	27	27	26	25	24	23	23	22	22	21	20	20	19	19	18
155	30	29	28	27	27	26	25	24	24	23	22	22	21	20	20	19	19
160	31	30	29	28	27	27	26	25	24	24	23	22	22	21	21	20	19
165	32	31	30	29	28	27	27	26	25	24	24	23	22	22	21	21	20
170	33	32	31	30	29	28	27	27	26	25	24	24	23	22	22	21	21
175	34	33	32	31	30	29	28	27	27	26	25	24	24	23	22	22	21
180	35	34	33	32	31	30	29	28	27	27	26	25	24	24	23	22	22
185	36	35	34	33	32	31	30	29	28	27	27	26	25	24	24	23	23
190	37	36	35	34	33	32	31	30	29	28	27	26	26	25	24	24	23
195	38	37	36	35	34	33	32	31	30	29	28	28	27	26	25	24	24
200	39	38	37	35	34	33	32	31	30	30	29	28	27	26	26	25	24
205	40	39	37	36	35	34	33	32	31	30	29	29	28	27	26	26	25
210	41	40	38	37	36	35	34	33	32	31	30	29	28	28	27	26	26
215	42	41	39	38	37	36	35	34	33	32	31	30	29	28	28	27	26
220	43	42	40	39	38	37	36	35	34	33	32	31	30	29	28	27	27
225	44	43	41	40	39	37	36	35	34	33	32	31	31	30	29	28	27
230	45	43	42	41	39	38	37	36	35	34	33	32	31	30	30	29	28
235	46	44	43	42	40	39	38	37	36	35	34	33	32	31	31	29	29
240	47	45	44	43	41	40	39	38	36	35	34	33	33	31	31	30	29
245	48	46	45	43	42	41	40	39	37	36	35	34	33	32	32	30	30
250	49	47	46	44	43	42	40	39	38	37	36	35	34	33	32	31	30

BMI less than 19; may indicate underweight

BMI 19–24.9: healthful weight for most people

BMI 25–29.9: indicates overweight

BMI 30 or more; indicates obesity

Note: Overweight is also defined as 10% above healthy weight and obesity as 20% above healthy weight.

THE BATTLE OF THE BULGE

Most people who are overweight at some point become engaged in the usually futile "battle of the bulge." There are thousands of diets, herbal formulas, metabolic stimulants, appetite suppressants, fat blockers, weight loss patches, and other diet aids. The excess fat can be suctioned out or cut off and, if all else fails, our stomachs can be stapled, shrinking them to tiny pouches. Unfortunately, none of these methods has proven to be overly effective, and some even backfire.

Jennifer knows the frustration of diet failure only too well. She has been on one diet after another since the age of twelve. She has tried low-calorie diets, low-carbohydrate diets, the cabbage soup diet, and meal replacement diets. They all worked beautifully—for about a month. Each and every one managed to minimize calories sufficiently to produce weight loss. Then, as old patterns gradually resumed, the weight would creep back, stopping only after an extra 5 pounds (2.3 kilograms) was packed on. She would feel like a complete and utter failure. What Jennifer didn't realize was that her odds of permanent weight loss through dieting were about 5 percent, because approximately 95 percent of all weight-loss methods fail. Why? Because weight-loss diets end. Not too many people are willing to live on protein powders for the rest of their lives or consume ten grapefruits a day.

The fatal flaw of the weight-loss industry is that it is focused on the pursuit of thinness at all costs. It peddles promises of speedy success with miracle cures for obesity. Of course, if a miracle cure for obesity actually existed, the problem would quickly disappear. Yet, the number of overweight people continues to escalate.

What's the answer? It is simple—we must shift our focus from thinness to health.

HEALTHY MIND, HEALTHY BODY

Setting aside the perfect body image and making health a priority instead can be a scary prospect. Most dieters have their sights set on shedding pounds, not on protecting themselves from chronic illness. In fact, good health may appear to have little connection with the goal. Yet, trying to achieve thinness by methods that don't support our health and well-being is like trying to build a house on sand. When we focus solely on thinness, weight-loss efforts usually fail, because the changes we make to shed pounds generally are short-lived.

When health is an integral part of our focus, we make gradual changes that tend to be permanent. This shift in mind-set does not mean we need to settle for being overweight—far from it. When we make choices for health, weight loss naturally occurs in those who carry excess pounds. We eat fewer low fiber foods, such as sweet baked goods and deep-fried foods, and more vegetables and fruits. We watch less television and go biking, hiking, and swimming more often. We spend less time being stressed and more time practicing stress management techniques. Our goal of weight loss will be achieved, but that's not all. We will look great and feel great. Our muscle tone will improve, our endurance will increase, and we'll be more content.

If we review Jennifer's situation, we can see that a few important changes are required for her to reach her health goals. To start, she can dump the dieter's mentality, concentrate on eating foods that are more healthful, and become more physically active. She might enlist her family's support by inviting them to go bowling or jogging. She could encourage her family to also focus more on healthful eating by preparing delicious and nutritious foods for them to share. The following guidelines will support Jennifer, and all of us, in creating a lifestyle that fully supports health and healing.

Prescription for Lifelong Healthy Weight

A healthy lifestyle requires a balance of body, mind, and spirit, and each must be nourished in a way that is mindful of everyone and everything around us. The prescription for lifelong healthy weight involves making health-oriented behavior changes in three key areas:

- ✓ healthful eating
- ✓ active lifestyle
- ✓ positive self-esteem and body image

Healthful eating

1. **Cultivate a healthy relationship with food.** Learn to respond to natural hunger signals. Avoid the temptation to eat when you're not hungry or deprive yourself when you're famished. Take pleasure in eating a wide variety of nourishing foods, but enjoy an occasional indulgence. Make meals a special time—set the table, light a candle, and play some quiet music. Encourage the participation of everyone in your home, and keep the atmosphere cheerful.

2. **Build good food habits.** We all are creatures of habit. We tend to stick with the same routines day after day, whether or not they are healthful. Examine your habits and replace those that undermine your health with better

choices. This doesn't need to happen overnight—one small step at a time will do. For example, switch from 2 percent milk to 1 percent, then to skim milk. You might even consider forgoing the dairy for any of a number of delicious, fortified beverages, such as soymilk, rice milk, or oat milk. If backsliding occurs, don't be consumed with guilt. Instead, work on ways to make new, healthy habits even more enjoyable. Begin the quest by taking these simple steps:

✓ Eat regular meals. Skipping meals can reduce performance and leave us so hungry that we are more apt to gorge at the next meal.

✓ Keep portion sizes moderate. The more food on our plate, the more we end up eating. Overeating causes weight gain, and often a sore stomach as well.

✓ Eat slowly. This not only enables us to better appreciate our food, it can help control the amount we eat and improve digestion.

✓ Eat sitting down, with a proper place setting. Always put food in a dish and sit down to eat. This makes us more conscious of exactly how much we are taking in.

✓ Avoid eating while cooking. Sometimes we eat as much while preparing a meal as we do when the meal is served. If need be, suck on a mint or chew a piece of gum or a fresh herb.

✓ If television is a trigger to overeat, fight it. Limit TV to a few hours a week. When you do watch a show or movie, keep your hands busy with a craft or ironing, or do stretching exercises. A platter of raw veggies is your best TV snack option.

✓ Get hooked on healthy foods when eating out. If tempted, go for fresh fruit, fresh-squeezed juices, an Asian stir-fry, some popcorn (hold the butter), or a frozen yogurt. Steer clear of deep-fried foods.

3. Make healthful food choices. As we shift to a vegetarian diet, whole plant foods should move from the periphery to center stage. A variety of vegetables, legumes, whole grains, fruits, and small amounts of nuts, seeds, and fruit should form the foundation of the diet. Processed foods should be limited, especially those with added fats and sugars. Concentrated sweets, such as chocolate bars, cakes, pies, and candy, are high in calories but low in nutrients. These should not be a regular feature of our diet.

Fat is our most concentrated source of energy. Every tablespoon (15 ml) of fat has 100 calories (two and one-half times more than the same weight of protein or carbohydrate), so go lightly on the fats and oils used in cooking and at the table. Make the fat you do use count nutritionally. Rather than butter on toast, try almond butter. Instead of using sour cream for a dip, pick hummus.

Replace chips with trail mix. (While nuts are high in fat, they provide valuable nutrients.)

A healthful diet is one that is low in saturated fat and cholesterol; rich in fiber, phytochemicals, vitamins, and minerals; and provides ample protein and essential fatty acids. By following the Vegetarian Food Guide on page 193, we will be off to an amazing start in building such a diet. The following tips will help make great choices a breeze in each food group.

Grains: 6 to 11 servings a day

While the recommended number of servings in this group is six to eleven, for some individuals further reducing intake to 4 or 5 servings may be more effective for weight loss. Use mostly intact whole grains such as brown rice, oat groats, barley, quinoa, millet, and kamut berries. If you use breads and cereals, select those made from whole grains; high-fiber foods increase a feeling of fullness. Beware of highly processed items such as snack crackers, commercial granolas, cookies, muffins, cheese breads, garlic breads, croissants, and sweet baked goods. Many derive more than 40 percent of their calories from fat. Make your own low-fat, high-fiber muffins, pancakes, and other baked goods.

Vegetables and Fruits: 5 to 10 servings a day

Vegetables and fruits are our biggest bargains nutritionally and should be featured at every meal. Most are very low in fat and loaded with nutrients. Select cooking methods that don't use added fat—steam, bake, or boil. Avoid deep frying and use little or no fat in stir-fries. Leafy greens are especially important; include at least one or two servings a day. Go easy on the dried fruits—they are a fairly concentrated source of calories, as are avocados. Eat whole fruit instead of just drinking the juice.

Milks and Alternates: 6 to 8 servings a day

The lowest calorie choices in this group are greens, such as broccoli, kale, collards, and Chinese greens. Eat them more often. Fortified soymilk or rice milks also are good options. If using dairy products, select the low-fat or skim varieties of milk, low-fat (1 percent milk fat or less) yogurt, and low-fat cottage cheese (1 percent). Hard cheese is high in fat and should be used sparingly, if at all. (Even many of the "low-fat" cheeses derive over 50 percent of their calories from fat.)

Beans and Alternates: 2 to 4 servings a day

Except for soy and peanuts, most legumes are very low in fat and are ideal sources of protein and calories for the weight-conscious vegetarian. They are rich in protein and complex carbohydrates and give us stamina between meals. Experiment with all kinds of legumes. Sprout lentils (see page 330), stew beans, toss chickpeas with salads, put black beans in soups, add white beans to casseroles, or just eat beans as a side dish. Many veggie "meats," such as veggie burgers and deli slices, are very low in fat and also are excellent choices. Tofu is higher in fat, so keep portions moderate. Nuts and seeds are very high in fat, providing about 175 to 225 calories and about 16 to 20 grams of fat for each ¼-cup (60-ml) serving, so enjoy them in small quantities.

4. **Select beverages with care**. It is amazing how many calories can sneak into the diet in the form of fluids. A 12-ounce (375-ml) serving of lemonade, fruit punch, or soda pop can contain up to 150 calories. A typical milkshake chalks up 350 calories, as does a mere 8 ounces (250 ml) of nonalcoholic egg-nog. Alcoholic beverages can also send calories soaring. Twelve ounces (375 ml) of beer provides 110 to 170 calories, distilled spirits about 110 calories per 1.5 ounces (42 ml), liqueurs 150 to 190 calories per 1.5 ounces (42 ml), and wine about 80 calories per 4 ounces (125 ml). Although black coffee and tea are calorie free, what we add to these beverages is another story. A tall, 12-ounce (375-ml) café mocha with whole milk and whipped cream has close to 350 calories and should be considered "a slice of chocolate cake in a cup." Most of these beverages are filled with "empty calories"—calories with little nutritional value. Drinking four or five calorie-rich beverages a day could easily mean an extra 500 to 1,000 calories.

So what should we drink? Pure water is among our very best bets for fluids. Herbal teas are a tasty alternative. Vegetable and wheat grass juices offer excellent nutrition for minimal calories. Fruit juices, fruit smoothies, and soy, rice, or other grain milks also are good choices, although they are higher in calories.

Active lifestyle

1. **Make exercise a priority**. Physical activity tends not to happen unless it becomes a real priority in our lives. It needs to be looked upon as a necessity, the same as brushing our teeth or going to the bathroom. Our bodies need activity if we are to achieve our health goals. Exercise offers huge advantages

when it comes to weight loss. It increases stamina, energy output, and metabolism. Our goal is an hour of exercise each day, though we may begin slowly with half an hour of exercise every second day. We are most likely to stick with an activity if it is something that we enjoy. It doesn't have to be a grueling workout to provide benefit. Even a brisk walk or low-impact aerobics will do the trick. Visit a friend over a stroll in the park or a game of squash, instead of over coffee and a doughnut.

2. **Make the most of daily activities.** Choose the more physical options in daily activities. Take the stairs instead of the elevator, walk or bicycle instead of driving whenever possible, and use manual tools instead of electric ones (for example, use a manual beater instead of an electric one). Not only will this improve your health, it will make an important contribution to the environment.

3. **Be adventurous.** Take up hiking, biking, canoeing, skating, skiing, rollerblading, tennis, golf, or another challenging sport. Recruit a friend to join you so you can encourage each other to continue.

4. **Don't be a "couch potato."** Be aware of how much time you devote to television, videos, and computer games. Time spent on these pursuits leaves less time for energetic activities, such as playing tennis or going for a bike ride. Gradually replace sedentary activities with more active ones.

Positive self-esteem and body image

1. **Recognize that each of us is far more than the sum of our parts.** Appreciate the tremendous value in all people, regardless of their body size or shape. Be critical of messages that focus on unrealistic thinness or huge muscles. Take the time to pay someone a compliment that has nothing to do with his or her physical beauty, weight, or shape. Enjoy the uniqueness of each person.

2. **Be grateful for your body and all it does for you.** Take a moment to appreciate the unfailing efforts of your body from head to toe. Instead of begrudging a protruding stomach, focus on how huggable it makes you. Rather than moaning about chubby legs, think about the great job your legs do in getting you around.

3. **Don't rely on your scale.** Frequent weighing can be downright depressing. Weight naturally fluctuates, sometimes up to 5 pounds (2.3 kg) in a single day. In addition, muscle weighs more than fat, so with increased exercise, weight may not fluctuate at all, even though fat is lost and muscle is gained. Your clothes will fit better, but the scale won't tell you that. For women, weight

also can vary according to the menstrual cycle. So, we can spare ourselves the misery and self-condemnation associated with ritual weigh-ins. Instead, focus on well-being, energy, and performance.

4. Enjoy life in spite of your body weight. Don't let your shape or size be an excuse to avoid living life to its fullest. Go swimming, buy a new outfit, or visit an old friend. If we wait until we are content with our body weight, life could just pass us by.

5. Take care of your inner being. Great health is the product of both a healthy body and a healthy mind. Making major lifestyle changes can have a profound effect on our social, family, and business interactions. While this can be a very positive experience, it also can bring up uncomfortable issues. Through it all, take time for pampering and self-care. Treat yourself to a massage, join a yoga class, or enjoy a concert. We deserve to be treated with love and respect—and we especially deserve it from ourselves.

How Is Jennifer Doing?

Jennifer has a new attitude. She gave up on weight-loss diets and her ultimate goal of being skinny. Great health is her newfound passion. Instead of rich desserts, she prepares fruit salads, nondairy fruit "ice cream," and grain-based puddings for herself and her family. She uses a variety of new vegetables—as well as legumes, whole grains, and tofu—instead of cheese and eggs for dinner. Jennifer even joined a gym with her mom. Not only do they both feel more energetic, their relationship is closer too. Jennifer's brother no longer bugs her about being vegetarian, as she responds with such lightheartedness that it does not seem worth it anymore. Jennifer feels as though she's gained a new kind of freedom. Weight loss is just a bonus.

For scientific references for this chapter, see
http://www.nutrispeak.com/bvreferences.htm

UNDERWEIGHT AND EATING DISORDERS

There are two challenges of weight and shape that are said to affect vegetarians at somewhat greater rates than nonvegetarians: underweight and eating disorders (specifically anorexia nervosa and bulimia nervosa). Vegetarians, and especially vegans, are underweight slightly more often than nonvegetarians. Being underweight is not a problem that attracts a lot of sympathy in our society. However, gaining a pound can be every bit as difficult for a person who is underweight as losing a pound is for a person who is overweight. Being underweight can be particularly frustrating, as there are far fewer support systems in place.

As many as 50 percent of people suffering from anorexia nervosa or bulimia nervosa are vegetarian. That leads many people to believe that vegetarians must be at high risk for these disorders, or that vegetarian diets may actually contribute to them. While these may seem like logical conclusions, we must realize that most vegetarians with eating disorders developed the eating disorder *before* they became vegetarian. Their goal in making the switch to a vegetarian diet was simple: to legitimize the removal of fatty foods, such as pork chops, burgers, ice cream, and cheese, from their diets. The truth is that vegetarians are not at greater risk for eating disorders. It simply is that many people with eating disorders shun animal products along with all the fat they contain. For more information on underweight and eating disorders, read *Becoming Vegan* by B. Davis and V. Melina (Book Publishing Company; Summertown, TN).

Chapter 12

VEGETARIAN DIPLOMACY

Imagine this. You finally decide to give up meat forever. You had been toying with the idea for some time, but couldn't seem to take the final plunge. Then you attend a lecture that inspires you to take the next step. You feel terrific, as if a burden has been lifted from your shoulders. You race home to tell your wife and kids. You walk into the house and say, "Honey, I have something important to tell you." Your wife looks worried. You blurt it out, "I've decided to become a vegetarian." Her look of concern dissolves as she throws her arms into the air and shouts for joy. "Oh Dan," she says, "this is better than winning the lottery!" She dashes out the back door, beckoning the children to come inside. "Emily, Michael, come quickly! Dad has something to tell you." The children race inside and you break the news to them. They begin jumping up and down wildly and the four of you join hands and dance around in a circle. Then your wife says, "I think you should call your mom and dad right away." You rush into the kitchen, dial the number, and get both your parents on the line before you break the big news to them. Your mother is so overcome with emotion that she can hardly get the words out. "Dan, I have never been more proud of you than I am at this moment." Your father chimes in, "This calls for a celebration—how about this weekend?" On Monday, when you walk into the office, everyone begins cheering. There is a card on your desk that reads, "Congratulations, Dan! Your example of compassion is an inspiration to us all. Your colleagues want to treat you to lunch at the Veggie Garden." The only negative thought that enters your mind is, "Why didn't I make this decision years ago?"

Sadly, this is a more likely story: You race home to tell your wife and kids. You walk into the house and say, "Honey, I have something important to tell you." She looks worried. You blurt it out, "I've decided to become a vegetarian." "I beg your pardon?" she says. "By vegetarian, do you mean that you don't want to eat red meat anymore?" "Well, not exactly," you reply. "I don't want to eat any meat, poultry, or fish anymore." "That's crazy! Are we supposed to cook separate meals every night?" "Oh no," you reply. "Eating vegetarian will be good for all of us, and I am happy to do the cooking. If you and the kids want meat, you can cook it on the side." "Oh right, fried chicken will be just lovely with lentil stew," she says with a note of sarcasm in her voice. "I'll cook normal food," you reply. "What about all of our family favorites and our holiday meals? These are our traditions, Dan," your wife adds. "Don't worry honey, we'll come up with new family favorites, and even better family traditions," you offer. "Thanks, but no thanks," she replies and walks away.

That weekend you make the trek out to your parents' place. Before you take a step in the door, your wife announces, "You aren't going to believe this, but your son has become a vegetarian." Your parents both exclaim in unison, "You're kidding!" Your dad adds, "I hope you don't try to turn your kids into vegetarians. You'll stunt their growth." Your mom chimes in, "I hope you won't be fanatic about it, and at least eat turkey on special occasions." When you arrive at work on Monday, the whole staff seems to know about your new diet. "Hey Dan!" your buddy Ben shouts, "How's about you and me go for some nice, big, juicy steaks for lunch?" You want to fade into the woodwork, but instead you just say, "Very funny," and sit quietly at your desk. Gosh, you think to yourself, people can be such jerks. Yet, somehow, instead of giving up, you strengthen your resolve.

BECOMING VEGETARIAN IN A NONVEGETARIAN WORLD

Perhaps someday the first scenario will become commonplace, but we'd be wise not to hold our breath. Until that time, there are ways we can relate to doubting friends and relatives that will lessen their anguish as well as our own.

Becoming vegetarian in a nonvegetarian world can be both frustrating and empowering at the same time. It is frustrating because we have discovered a profound truth, one that could effectively reduce disease, environmental destruction, and animal suffering. Yet the more we try to share this amazing revelation, the more people resist hearing it. It is empowering because we must draw on our inner strength to stand firm in what we believe, not caving in to social pressures. Thankfully, as each year passes and the number of vegetarians increases, that task becomes a little less intimidating.

Our personal transition and our impact on others depend largely on two things. The first is our awareness of the underlying issues that inspired our change. The second is our example—our choices and our responses to those around us who may oppose or resist our change.

Change presents a unique paradox. It threatens our security, yet it is the one thing we can always count on. Sometimes it is embraced, and other times it is resisted. Much depends on our motivation. When we are inspired by love and compassion, change is more likely to be welcomed and long lasting. When change stems from fear, or from a desire to impress or please others, it often is resented and quickly abandoned. Sometimes we fight change because it seems too overwhelming. When people can't face certain realities, a typical response is to pretend they don't exist and continue with comfortable, old patterns. If we want change to be smooth and enriching, we must be clear about our motivation. When we are solidly rooted in knowledge and truth, our choices become easier, even in the face of ominous obstacles.

Some people are able to make huge changes overnight; however, most adjust more easily when the changes are gradual. For those who are more inclined to make a gradual shift toward becoming vegetarian or vegan, the following suggested steps might be helpful. They are entirely flexible and should be adjusted to suit our individual needs.

Becoming Vegetarian Step by Step

1. Awareness. Our first step in the change process is awareness about our motivation for becoming vegetarian. What factors attract and inspire us? Which hold us back? How will this new way of eating affect our health, family, friends, and colleagues at work? Consider the long-term goals associated with this choice. How would these objectives be affected if we kept eating meat? While our primary motive may be health, or the environment, or concern for animals, as our knowledge increases, these reasons become intertwined. Think about it. Although these may seem like separate issues, they are not. They are deeply connected. For example, if our first motivation is our own health, we soon learn that human health suffers when our environment is poisoned. Factory farming and the production and transportation of animal fodder are among the greatest contributors to environmental destruction and to the pain, suffering, and death of billions of animals every year. Life cannot be compartmentalized. If we make a choice based on our love of life, as our awareness grows, our circle of compassion naturally expands. Books, magazines, newsletters, newspapers, Web sites, lectures, conferences, discussion groups, and courses can enrich and sustain us. (For a few examples, see page 304.)

2. Connections. Talk with family and friends about the changes we are making. In the process, help them to understand the reasons behind these choices. Be open, honest, and, most of all, be compassionate. Share carefully selected reading materials, videos, and Web sites. Invite friends and family to lectures. Honor the perspectives of others and their right to see things differently. Even if we are fortunate enough to have loved ones join us in our journey, their rate of change may be different from our own.

3. Choices. Decide what we are prepared to do at this moment and what will have to wait. Establishing new routines and traditions will help those around us feel safe and connected to us. Typical steps we might take to accomplish our goals are listed below. There is no set amount of time required for each step; this depends on our unique situation. The sequence can be personalized according to our priorities, ethical perspectives, and social commitments. These steps can be switched around and adjusted until the plan feels right. We might take an extended pause or stop at some point along the way.

To eliminate meat, fish, and poultry, we can do the following:

1. Begin by cutting back on animal flesh foods by 50 percent. Perhaps reduce red meat to once a week, chicken to twice a week, and fish to twice a week.

2. Drop red meat completely. Eliminate beef, pork, and lamb.

3. Drop poultry, including chicken, turkey, Cornish hens, duck, and geese.

4. Drop fish. Some people prefer to keep fish until the end, eliminating it after eggs and dairy foods are cut. Others find it easier to drop fish first because dairy products are used so extensively.

To improve overall nutrition, we can do the following:

1. Reduce the "junk foods" in our diet. Eat less fast food, processed snack foods, sodas, and other nutritionally depleted products. Replace refined grains with whole grains. Select lower-fat dairy products and eat smaller portions of animal products.

2. Incorporate more plant foods, such as vegetables, fruits, legumes, whole grains, nuts, and seeds, into our diets. Try new "veggie meats;" explore various kinds of tofu and tempeh. Experiment with vegetarian recipes.

To replace eggs and dairy products, we can do the following:

1. Incorporate dairy and egg substitutes: fortified soymilk, rice milk, or other nondairy milk; nondairy cheeses, ice cream, and yogurt; margarine; and nut and seed butters. Tofu works well as an egg substitute. In addition, there are a number of commercial and homemade egg substitutes for baking (see page 302).

2. Eliminate all visible dairy and eggs. Begin reading labels and start purchasing egg- and dairy-free products.

To replace other animal-based consumer products:

1. We can seek out nonfood items, such as clothing, furniture, cleaning supplies, and personal care products that are not tested on animals or made with animal ingredients.

With careful steps, we build a foundation that can weather the toughest storms. There's no need to waste time and energy feeling guilty about what we have not yet done. Instead, we can delight in what we have accomplished, even if we take only small steps. We can continue to challenge ourselves and find inspiration.

Understanding the Resistance, Objection, and Hostility

It's been said that "today's mighty oak is just yesterday's nut that held its ground." When secure in our own position, we are better able to respond appropriately to others. However, it is imperative that we understand why people condemn, ridicule, or otherwise oppose a change that so obviously promotes kindness, compassion, and life itself. Is it because people are heartless and cruel? Far from it. The vast majority of people are caring, considerate, and inherently good. So why do they respond as they do? It can be boiled down to two factors: personal habit and cultural tradition.

Habits are hard to break. They are easy, familiar, and comfortable. It is immensely painful for people to adopt a set of beliefs that do not fit their actions (or engage in actions that don't fit their beliefs). For example, if they (meat-eaters) consider eating meat to be "bad," they may view themselves as "bad people." In seeing this, we observe the complex framework that must be dismantled for change to occur.

For centuries, tradition has been used to justify numerous atrocities, such as the 400 years of enslavement suffered by Africans in America. Today, this part of our human history is viewed with immeasurable shame and guilt. Now those who assert that all living creatures deserve freedom from torture and suffering are often viewed as extremists. Dr. Albert Schweitzer offers some thought on this position:

> *The time is coming when people will be amazed that the human race existed so long before it recognized that thoughtless injury to life is incompatible with real ethics. Ethics is in its unqualified form extended responsibility with regard to everything that has life.*

We have an unlimited ability to alter our own habits, but to influence others or shift cultural norms is a far greater challenge. We can push the envelope in a number of ways: writing letters, articles, or books; protesting; or even practicing civil disobedience. The most powerful tool of all is our own personal example. Arguing with others about why they choose not to be vegetarian may only stimulate them to come up with more and better counterresponses. However, it is important for us to be aware of the rationale often used to justify the continued consumption of meat, and to be clear within ourselves about how these justifications fall short.

Most Common Reasons for Rejecting the Vegetarian Option

Reason ➜ Nutrition. Many people believe meat is necessary for good health. They know it provides high-quality protein and iron and assume that without meat we will fall short on these nutrients. Some consider vegetarian diets to be all right for other people, but not for themselves. They are convinced that meat makes them more energetic, stronger, or otherwise healthier. Many believe that they must eat meat because of their blood type.

Reality ➜ Humans do not need meat for good health, no matter what their blood type or ethnic origin. Humans are designed to be primarily planteaters, like other primates. However, we are able to adapt to nonvegetarian and vegetarian diets, as evidenced by cultures around the world. Numerous studies have demonstrated that not only are vegetarian diets safe and adequate, they offer significant health advantages. Compared to the general population, vegetarians suffer about half the rates of chronic disease. Studies have demonstrated these health advantages regardless of blood type. If someone feels that a vegetarian diet has compromised their health, chances are that their diet was not appropriately designed. They may have simply eliminated meat and/or dairy products and not replaced these foods with plant foods providing ample protein, iron, zinc, and calcium. Perhaps the root cause was that they had no idea how to transform a cup of lentils or a block of tofu into a delicious meal.

Reason ➜ Food chain champions. Many people believe that humans have a right to eat other animals. They may say something like this: "I am at the top of the food chain, and I think it would be just plain stupid to give up that position. We are naturally hunters, so why try to be anything different."

Reality ➜ While humans may be at the top of the food chain, this should in no way override our responsibility to make moral and ethical choices. We have no justification for causing needless pain and suffering to other thinking, feeling beings. Though we might be better able to justify killing an animal if our survival depended on it, for most people, it does not. We enjoy an abundant food supply that includes sufficient plant-based alternatives and have no need for animal flesh.

Reason ➜ Dominion over animals. Many people believe that humans have a right to eat other animals. They may say something like this: "Humans were given dominion over animals by God. We are clearly given permission to eat animals, so I feel no guilt for doing so."

Reality ➜ While it is true that the Bible states that we have dominion over animals, it does not state that we have a right to use and abuse animals as we wish. Indeed, many believe the very word dominion would be more accurately translated as "stewardship," which implies responsibility and guardianship. Psalms 145:9 states that "The Lord is good to all, and his compassion is over all that he has made." The Bible forbids cruelty toward animals on numerous occasions. Our current means of raising and slaughtering animals used for food contravenes these principles.

Reason ➜ Taste. Some people argue in favor of eating meat on the basis of taste. They may say: "I couldn't ever imagine giving up ham, steak, fried chicken, pork chops, and lobster tails. For what—tofu and beans? I don't think so."

Reality ➜ Taste should not be the only consideration when it comes to food selection. The flavor of meat can be appealing; we can't argue that. Apparently, horses, dogs, or cats taste pretty good to some people, too, but North Americans generally don't eat them. In fact, we may look upon cultures that do eat these animals as being somewhat uncivilized. Why is it wrong to kill a cat for food but not wrong to kill a pig? Pigs are significantly more intelligent than cats and bear many genetic similarities to humans. The only thing that seems to justify this choice is tradition. As humans, we need to take responsibility for what we consume, even when we do not grow, catch, or kill it ourselves. Fortunately, we have numerous delicious vegetarian options to choose from today. We do not need to rely on animals for tasty food.

Reason → Concern for people. Some criticize those who work toward ending the suffering of animals. They ask: "How can you justify spending time and money saving animals when so many people are starving to death, being abused, or being terrorized?"

Reality → Being vegetarian, and especially being an advocate for animals, in no way lessens our concern about the suffering of other people. Reverence for life does not exclude human life. Those who have reverence for life are pushing an agenda of peace, kindness, and compassion for all living beings. If everyone adopted this mentality, abuse and terrorism would cease. Meat eating by affluent populations adds to global hunger problems, because much land and water in developing countries is devoted to livestock production or to raising animal fodder, rather than to growing food staples for local people. Becoming vegetarian allows for much more efficient use of global resources.

Reason → Social situations. Some people agree that being vegetarian is ethically and ecologically sensible, but feel that socially it would be too much of a sacrifice. They believe that it would adversely affect their social interactions and be too much of a burden for family and friends. They couldn't imagine a holiday dinner without turkey or a barbecue without burgers, steaks, ribs, or chicken. What would they order if they went to a fancy restaurant?

Reality → Of all the reasons listed, this one is probably the toughest to counter. We cannot deny a person's feeling, or that becoming vegetarian means some significant social changes. However, becoming vegetarian does not mean that we must sacrifice our relationships with the people we care about. Being vegetarian need not be a burden for others, if we take responsibility for our own needs and are sensitive to the needs of those around us. Vegetarians enjoy holidays, barbecues, and dining out every bit as much as nonvegetarians. Holidays can still include mashed potatoes and gravy, stuffing, sweet potatoes, traditional vegetables, cranberry sauce, and pumpkin pie. Only the centerpiece is different. For vegetarians it may be a giant stuffed squash, a veggie roast, or a tofu "turkey." During barbecue season, vegetarians need not be left out. All sorts of vegetables are wonderful on the grill, as are marinated tofu and many types of veggie "meat." Few restaurants cannot accommodate vegetarians, and today most offer at least a couple of vegetarian options. These days, there are also numerous world-class vegetarian gourmet restaurants everyone can enjoy.

MASTERING THE FINE ART OF DIPLOMACY

If you have men who will exclude any of God's creatures from the shelter of compassion and pity, you will have men who will deal likewise with their fellow men.
— *St. Francis of Assisi*

Diplomacy is the fine art of honoring our own ethical principles and social consciousness without judging, condemning, or otherwise injuring another person. While there will always be situations that trigger less-than-diplomatic responses, such responses generally do little to support our position. It is important to distinguish between being diplomatic and being spineless. Being diplomatic in no way precludes standing firm for what we believe or openly opposing a particular position. It simply means that we do so in a way that does not harm others. True diplomacy is lost if our own values and ethics are not honored. Few of us are born diplomats. Rather, diplomacy is a skill that must be developed and nurtured. The following guidelines are meant to assist in this task.

Guidelines to Getting Along

Be kind, compassionate, and empathetic. Our quest for a kinder, more compassionate world must begin with ourselves. Kindness can be as simple as a smile, lending a hand to someone in need, or lifting someone up with our words. Compassion inspires us to recognize that each person is of value, and it also motivates us to improve our emotional and physical well-being. To be compassionate requires a keen sensitivity to each individual and his or her unique situation. Our ability to be compassionate depends on our capacity to empathize with others and imagine ourselves in their shoes, without losing our sense of self. Extending our kindness and compassion to all living beings sends a powerful message about our ethics.

Respect each person's right to her or his own values and choices. While we will never all agree on issues of ethics, politics, religion, or anything else of consequence, it is important that we respect each other's perspectives. This does not imply that we must applaud everyone's choices and actions, but that we honor the worth and dignity of each human being. Showing respect for people with little status or those we dislike or with whom we disagree is a true reflection of our character. We must treat others the way we would want to be treated. We can begin by listening with our hearts. This involves being attentive, not constantly challenging everything that is said, having appropriate eye contact, and possibly reflecting thoughts and feelings back to the person with whom we are talking. If we disagree, we can say so without judging or belittling the other person. Putting people down does nothing but hurt them, make them resentful, push them away, and strengthen their opposition to us. Recognize that most people try in their own way to make this world a better place. They may donate to charity, volunteer, lead healthy activities for children, or be an advocate for the less fortunate.

Make choices that are consistent with your personal beliefs and values. Our example is the most powerful tool at our disposal. When our actions and behavior are consistent with our words, when we "walk the talk", we demonstrate integrity and earn the trust of others. We can communicate volumes without saying a word. We can inspire others to select more healthful plant-based foods by striving for our own excellent health through wise food choices and regular physical activity. We can encourage people to show greater compassion for animals by treating all animals with love and kindness and not supporting animal abuse in any way. We can demonstrate our commitment to the environment by reducing our use of all material things, buying secondhand items, recycling, and purchasing environmentally friendly products. We can promote nonviolence by choosing to avoid entertainment that supports cruelty, whether it is a circus with animals, a dog race, or violent films. Mahatma Gandhi once said, "Be the change you want to see in the world." Few words have conveyed more meaningful advice.

Do not apologize for your choices. As we respect the choices and beliefs of others, so must we value our own. We all have a right to our own values, and if we want other people to take our position seriously, we must take a clear and strong stand. In our society, where meat is front and center at many social gatherings, vegetarians can feel a little intimidated. Draw courage from those who have set an example in far less tolerant times—people such as Leonardo da Vinci, Albert Schweitzer, George Bernard Shaw, and Ben Franklin. Rather than retreating from social interactions, become more socially involved and use every appropriate opportunity to get others thinking about the traditions that have so crippled our consciousness.

Share information. Often, a major revelation motivates our shift to a vegetarian diet. The information we have acquired is so profound that we want to shout it from the rooftops. While doing this may make people sit up and take notice, it is unlikely to provoke dietary changes. Fortunately, there are much better ways to get our points across. If we are to succeed in influencing family, friends, and colleagues, we need to be sensitive and positive in our message, rather than pushy or critical. We can begin by sharing things in subtle ways. For example, we can bring extra servings of visually appealing and delicious vegetarian foods to work, with copies of the recipes. We can invite friends or colleagues for a wonderful, homemade vegetarian meal, or treat them to lunch at a great vegetarian restaurant. When further efforts seem appropriate, we can share interesting books, magazines, and videos, or invite them to a lecture, conference, or vegetarian cooking class.

Lighten up and laugh more. As vegetarians, we are faced with many grim realities about life and the state of the world. We recognize the atrocities committed against billions of animals every year. Understandably, this can make us angry and even cynical. Yet, if we go through life with a sour and serious view of just about everything, our attitude will only serve as a barrier to creating a kinder, more compassionate world. If our quest is to succeed, we need to lighten up and laugh more. Laughter is the quickest way to shorten the distance between two people. It is necessary to good mental health. It lifts our spirits, eases stress, and brings joy to those around us. Set time aside for laughter—rent a funny movie, see a comedy performance, or get together for fun games with friends. Relax, let loose, and do not feel guilty. Laughter will likely add as many years to our lives as our vegetarian diets.

DIPLOMACY IN ACTION

Whenever we go against the status quo, repercussions can be expected. They may come in the form of criticism, taunting, or teasing; they may involve threats to our relationships or to our work; or they may cause inconvenience or embarrassment. The sticky situations we face as vegetarians can lead to discomfort, sadness, frustration, and anger. In some cases, we feel ill-equipped to handle the challenge. After such an event is over, we may dream up dozens of better responses. How we manage difficult situations can make all the difference in the outcome and our influence on other people. Now that we have covered all the bases regarding what diplomacy is about, let's consider how we can put our knowledge into action. In the following section, we will explore a variety of sensitive situations. We can put ourselves in the place of each person described and think about how we would respond. In each case, a diplomatic solution is provided.

Mixed Marriage

Situation. When you and your partner married twelve years ago, you were both meat eaters. Over the past two years, you have gradually transitioned to a near-vegan diet. While your partner has not objected to this choice for you personally, there is no indication that a switch to a vegetarian diet is anywhere on the horizon for him or her. Your dietary choice has caused several serious disagreements where children and holidays are concerned. Your partner is adamant that the children be given a balanced diet that includes animal products, such as milk, poultry, and fish. You feel strongly that the children should be gradually weaned off these products, especially flesh foods. While you are not opposed to letting them make their own choices when they are away from home, you would prefer that they not eat meat in the house. Currently, your children, ages ten and seven, eat meat at home at least two or three times a week and order meat at restaurants most of the time. Your partner is absolutely firm that holidays include a turkey. You believe that holidays should be about love and compassion and should not include such barbaric traditions. How far should you push the issue of no meat in your home?

Diplomatic solution. Ideally, families share beliefs and values. However, one partner can change his or her core beliefs and values and grow in a direction that is quite separate from the spouse and children. When this happens, it can create a lot of tension and threaten the family's foundation. In this case, you are hoping that your spouse and the children will abide by your wishes and agree to give up meat at home. For a near-vegan, life is more comfortable without meat around, but asking other family members to make this sort of sacrifice goes against one of the basic principles of diplomacy—respecting each person's right to her or his own beliefs and values. You must remember that the vegetarian ethics you have adopted are yours, not your family's. Just as you have a right to your values, so do other family members have an equal right to theirs. Remember that your family's eating habits were formed over many years, with your willing participation. Attempting to suddenly change deeply ingrained habits will result only in frustration and resentment.

If the family is to remain intact, you must simply agree to disagree on these issues. Accept where your spouse and children are and do not attempt to force your beliefs on them. In practical terms, this means that it is unreasonable to expect them not to eat meat in your home unless they volunteer to do so, because it is their home too. However, it is fair to expect that your spouse and children take over the purchase, preparation, and cleanup of these products. You may need separate pots and pans and two main dishes (stuffed squash and turkey) on holiday tables. That said, it does not mean that you should give up trying to influence loved ones. It is very important that everyone clearly understands why you are making these choices. If your family is open to hearing more, you can share magazines, books, and videos. You can bring them to lectures and vegetarian festivals. If they appear very closed to hearing any of this, be patient. Make wonderful vegetarian feasts and get them turned on to vegetarian food. Show appreciation when they shift even a little. Focus on the things you all thoroughly enjoy, and set an example of compassion, kindness, and love.

Teenage Trials

Situation. You have always loved animals and were inwardly attracted to the vegetarian message while growing up. However, you kept silent about it, because meat was always the highlight of family meals, outings, and celebrations. You recall that when you were little, if you were full, your parents would predictably tell you to finish your meat. With increasing independence as a fifteen-year-old teenager, you have drifted to being more and more vegetarian. When your English teacher assigned a project that involved presenting two sides of a debate, you decided to tackle the topic of food animals. You borrowed three books from the city library, and started reading. You didn't get even ten pages into the first book when you vowed never to touch a piece of meat again. As you expected, your parents were not exactly thrilled with the news. They expressed concern about your health, especially your protein intake. The hardest part for you was that they seemed wounded by your words. You recognize that they feel betrayed, as you have rejected established family values. They suggest that perhaps you could be vegetarian at breakfast and lunch and when you aren't home, but they want you to continue to eat regular dinners with the family. How can you make Mom and Dad understand that you do not want to eat meat anymore?

Diplomatic solution. You are concerned about how your parents feel and do not want to hurt them. With this attitude, you are demonstrating the first component of diplomacy—kindness and compassion. This concern will help all of you through this challenging transition. Be careful not to fall into a pattern of being critical or judgmental of their choices. It may be tempting to respond by saying something like, "You just don't get it. I don't want to eat dead animals anymore. It is disgusting and you can't make me do it—ever!" However, this sort of response will serve only to upset your parents more and make them feel attacked. It would be far more effective to establish your position without being critical or condescending.

Begin on a positive note, making it more about you than about them. Tell your parents how much you appreciate them and the many wonderful traditions with which you have been raised. Then gently explain that you do not want to eat any meat at all. Let them know about the many delicious and nutritious veggie "meats" on the market and suggest that you would be happy to eat these foods when meat is served. Think of ways you can help to make your vegetarian diet less of a burden to your family. Offer to help with meals and possibly even to prepare a family meal each week. You could seek out a variety of ethnic dishes that you think they would enjoy. Your parents may love having a night of no cooking and the opportunity to try some new dishes.

Reassure your parents that you love the holiday meals and that adjusting them to include a vegetarian alternative can be very easy. While the main dish is turkey for most people, you can stuff a squash, make a more elaborate tofu-filled creation, buy a Tofurkey (a delicious tofu alternative to turkey), or have some delicious marinated tofu. Almost all of the trimmings can be shared. Let your parents know that your health is important to you and that you will take care to ensure that all your nutritional needs are met, including getting enough protein. Show them this book, and encourage them to read the chapter on protein. Share information with them when you feel they are ready to hear it. Give them time to adjust. Help in any way you can to make your "being different" less of a hassle for the other people in your family. With the right attitude and commitment, your family will soon not only accept but also respect your decision to be a vegetarian.

Holiday Hassles

Situation. Every year you take turns with your sister and parents in hosting the Thanksgiving feast. This will be your first year as a vegetarian host. Your dad has let you know in no uncertain terms that he expects turkey for dinner. Your sister reminds you that it's only once a year and turkey is the primary part of the feast. You don't want to cook a turkey, nor do you want to end up in a huge fight with your family. What should you do?

Diplomatic solution. You first must decide whether or not you are comfortable having turkey in your home. If it is just the cooking of the turkey that is unacceptable to you, there are a few options. You could ask your mom or sister to bring the turkey, or you could opt to purchase one prepared by a caterer. Make your part of the feast extra special. Prepare a gorgeous main dish and go all out with the trimmings. Create wonderful new traditions for your immediate family, and in time you might help your extended family to see that holiday meals can be every bit as fabulous without any meat at all. If you are not willing to have turkey in your home, you will have to graciously ask your parents or sister to host the feast. You can offer to prepare all the trimmings and dessert or offer to host another part of the holiday, such as a brunch or an after skating party in your home. If it is feasible, you might consider treating everyone to a holiday meal at a very special restaurant that offers wonderful vegetarian options.

Rude or Hurtful Comments

Situation. You're part of a small social group. The members of the group all know each other fairly well, and almost everyone knows that you are a vegetarian. One evening, a close friend makes a lighthearted comment about your food choices, and another group member suddenly clues in to the fact that you're a vegetarian. This person had no idea about your food choices, appears quite shocked, and blurts out a less-than-tactful response. "You're a vegetarian? I can't believe it. I hope you're not an animal rights activist too. All they are good for is putting the farmers out of work." The whole group falls silent. What should you say?

Diplomatic solution. In this kind of situation, it is very tempting to completely ignore the person or respond with something just as hurtful. It simply is human nature to become defensive when we are attacked. However, being equally nasty will only further convince this person that you are some sort of fanatic. You can choose to offer a quick, lighthearted response, but it's hard to think of one that does not ooze with sarcasm. Your best option is to reply in a manner that demonstrates confidence, conviction, and respect for others. Say something along these lines: "In answer to your questions, yes, I am a vegetarian, and I do believe in animal rights. I originally became a vegetarian because I had heart disease, and I believe that my diet saved my life. As I learned more, I discovered that vegetarian diets help preserve the environment and reduce animal suffering too. I see my vegetarian diet as being similar to your work at the gospel mission—something I can do to make this world a better place." By responding in this manner, you are demonstrating a level of maturity and sensitivity that the person who was criticizing you failed to show. Instead of a barricade, you have built a bridge.

Bullying or Teasing

Situation. Your eight-year-old son, Jeremy, comes home from school and runs straight to his room. When you go to speak with him, you discover that the relentless teasing by the two class bullies is beginning to escalate. At first, it was just about little things, like poking fun at his lunch. Today, the bullies starting mocking him in the schoolyard and pushing him around. One boy noticed a big spider crawling by and said, "Oh, look at the nice big spider." Then he slowly raised his foot above it and, just as Jeremy screamed, "Nooooo!" he stepped on it. Jeremy, unable to control his emotions, burst into tears. Then the two boys began laughing hysterically. Jeremy was devastated. How can you best help your child to respond effectively to this kind of bullying?

Diplomatic solution. Being bullied can do serious damage to a child's self-esteem. Thus, when children are bullied, they often do everything in their power to hide it. It is a very good sign that your son is willing to share this experience with you. Do whatever you can to keep those lines of communication open. Reassure your child that you will always be there to support, assist, and encourage him, no matter what the situation.

Explain to Jeremy that sometimes bullies are insecure and live in a household with bigger bullies. They may be seeking attention or trying to make themselves seem more important. While this in no way excuses their behavior, it may help your child understand why people behave in such cruel ways. Provide Jeremy with practical advice on how to avoid being bullied and respond effectively when it occurs. Let him know that avoiding encounters with bullies does not mean he is a coward; it means he is being smart. He needs to take precautions not to be alone with these guys. He can steer clear of the places they are likely to be and enlist the support of friends or older siblings. If Jeremy does find himself alone with them, he should leave immediately. If they have already made a rude remark, he should very loudly tell them to stop and then walk away. Teach him not to submit to bullying; bullies love to see people cry, so try to ignore them. If vegetarian lunches seem to be a big source of teasing at school, consider making lunches that do not attract so much attention. Sandwiches using veggie meats, raw vegetables and dip, homemade treats, and fresh fruit all work well.

It is important that Jeremy understands that for the sake of his safety, school authorities need to be aware of the bullying. At no point do the bullies need to know who reported them. The teacher can say it was observed by a supervisor or by other children. One of children's greatest fears is that bullies will beat them up in retaliation. Explain to your son that everyone at the school will make sure this doesn't happen. If the opportunity arises and the situation feels safe, he can speak to the bullies individually about how their behavior makes him feel. This generally is best done in the presence of a teacher or school counselor. Finally, praise your child for his kindness and compassion toward other people and all creatures. Let him know these are outstanding qualities.

Dinner Dilemmas

Situation. You and your partner have been part of a bowling league for two months and really hit it off with another couple. After a great game, they suggest that you should get together outside of the bowling alley and invite you to dinner. These friends have no idea that you are vegetarians. How should you handle the invitation?

Diplomatic solution. While you may be tempted to suggest a non-food-related activity instead, food is so central to socializing that if your friendship is to develop, it is important that you are comfortable eating together. The cardinal rule in such situations is to disclose your dietary requirements right away. Never show up for a dinner invitation assuming that you'll just eat the vegetables and bread. This would be inconsiderate, as the host has prepared the feast in your honor, with a primary objective of pleasing you, the special guests. Meat usually is the focus of the meal for meat eaters, who often purchase expensive cuts of meat, seafood, and other similar extravagances for company. In fact, meat, poultry, seafood, or other animal products could well be a part of every dish. When you tell your friends that you are vegetarian, their response will give a big clue as to how to proceed. If they say, "Oh my goodness, do you eat fish?" you know that preparing a vegetarian meal will be quite a stretch for them. You may want to suggest that they come to your place, or that you go to a restaurant and go back to their place for dessert. If their response is, "No problem," you can relax. However, it still is important to be specific about what you do and don't eat. Offer to help prepare or bring part of the meal. See "Making the Transition to a Vegetarian Diet," page 300, for vegetarian dinner options that are familiar to most nonvegetarians.

Gentle Persuasion

Situation. You have been involved in the church youth league for two years and want to invite your five covolunteers to dinner. While they are well aware that you are vegetarian, most of them view a vegetarian diet as boring and have said so. Some have even made remarks that suggest they actually pity you. You decide that the best way to educate these people would be to surprise them with a wonderful vegetarian feast. When you invite them, one person immediately asks, "Could we make this a potluck? I'd be happy to bring some of my famous chicken Kiev." Everyone quickly chimes in, agreeing that a potluck sounds like a great idea. How should you respond? What sort of menu should you select?

Diplomatic solution. This is one occasion that calls for a lighthearted response. Recognize that everyone is a little nervous about having a vegetarian meal. They likely are imagining little more than a plateful of vegetables. You need to do two things. First, allay their fears. Second, let them know in no uncertain terms that this is not a potluck, and they are not welcome to bring food to your party. You might say something like this: "Absolutely not! This is my treat. Have some faith; I won't let you go hungry. In fact, if you aren't stuffed by the time dinner's over, I'll order pizza!"

Now for the menu. Avoid ingredients with strong flavors that may be an acquired taste, such as cilantro, strong curries, or sea vegetables. Make plenty of food with lots of variety. You may wish to choose an ethnic theme, as many have familiar vegetarian entrées. If you know everyone loves a certain type of ethnic restaurant, such as Greek or Chinese, you may want to stick with one of those cuisines. Alternatively, you can offer vegetarian versions of traditional favorites. Here is a menu that offers plenty of choice. You could try something similar to this, or you may prefer a more simplified version.

Start with a sparkling strawberry and kiwi punch or another light beverage and a tempting appetizer, such as Hazelnut Pâté (page 323) with crackers. Begin the main meal with a flavorful soup, such as Zucchini Chedda Soup (page 319) and fresh bread.

For the entrée, serve a salad and a vegetarian version of a traditional favorite. Go-for-the-Green Salad with Liquid Gold Dressing (pages 328 and 329) and gourmet stuffed pasta would be excellent choices. With the pasta, you might offer two sauces, such as Chunky Red Lentil Tomato Sauce (pages 340–41) and a simple white wine or pesto sauce. If you are especially ambitious, you may want to prepare stuffed portobello mushrooms to serve on the side.

Top off the meal with Lemon Teasecake (pages 354–55) or German Chocolate Cake (page 356). Bon appetit!

Pressure from Within

Situation. It has taken about a year for you to make the complete switch to a vegetarian diet, and the experience has been among the greatest challenges of your life. You got rid of most of your old cookbooks. You gave up foods that you adored, such as barbecued steak, fast-food cheeseburgers, and pepperoni pizza. You even eliminated favorites you always considered healthy, such as roast chicken breast and baked fish. No longer will you order those thick salmon sandwiches at the local lunch hotspot or dig in when your office buddies order a bucket of chicken. Sometimes it is tough, but you persevere. You spend hours trying to figure out what to feed dinner guests and have been chided by your family for not eating "normal" food, especially at Thanksgiving. Yet, despite all the hardships you endure, you feel overwhelmingly positive about the experience. You have shown more willpower in a year than the rest of your life put together.

You have started making friends in the local vegetarian community, even though many of them are more "strict" than you with their diet. Some, such as Kevin, Laura, and Stacy, have been vegetarian for many years. Kevin doesn't use a single drop of dairy or eggs and reads labels to avoid the tiniest speck of casein. He also buys everything organic and eats a lot of raw foods. Laura and Stacy are completely vegan. They avoid any animal products in their clothing, makeup, and cleaning supplies. Just the thought of all this makes your head spin. Still, it is wonderful to be around people who understand the concept of being vegetarian. It builds your confidence and determination to forge ahead.

One day your new vegetarian friends come over to your place over to watch a movie. You dash to the kitchen to put together a few snacks and come out with a bowl of mixed nuts, some chips, and chip dip—ordinary, sour cream–based chip dip. You know some of them won't eat it, but that's okay because it's optional. Kevin says, "Gee whiz, you still eat chip dip?" Laura adds, "Don't you realize that the veal industry is just a by-product of the dairy industry? Buying dairy products is no different than buying beef." Suddenly you feel as though you don't belong, that you will never belong. You're too vegetarian for your family, and not vegetarian enough for your new friends. What could you say to help your friends understand your position?

Diplomatic solution. You have two reasonable options. You could respond in a very lighthearted way and simply say something like, "I am just a baby vegetarian, so please have patience with me." Alternatively, you could use the opportunity to let your friends know how much you need their support rather than their disapproval. Say something like this: "I don't want to spoil the fun, but can I just share something with you? I love hanging out with all of you because I feel connected to you at a very different level than I do with my non-vegetarian friends. You guys have been doing this for a long time, and I get so much strength and inspiration from you that it helps me to keep moving forward. But when you criticize me, it makes me feel like no matter how hard I try, I'll never catch up, and I'll never be good enough." It is important when you share these feelings that you begin by saying something positive.

As we progress on our personal journey, we might be tempted to compare ourselves to other vegetarians to determine how well we are doing. This is a potentially destructive waste of energy. As we get caught up in playing a game of mirror, mirror on the wall, we lose sight of what really matters. No two people are at the exact same stage in their journey. Each of us has unique experiences and different strengths, even though we may have the same ultimate goal of compassion and reverence for life. When we point a finger and judge other people, we sabotage our connection with them and effectively put up a barricade along their path. No one likes to be degraded or ridiculed, particularly when our efforts are sincere and we are doing our best. Instead, we need to be supported, encouraged, and commended, especially by other vegetarians.

Engagement Woes

Situation. You and your fiancé have been engaged for eight months. The wedding is scheduled to take place in just over four months. About six months ago, you made the decision to become a vegetarian. Discussions about the issue have ended in tears on more than one occasion. Your fiancé loves meat and just does not understand the whole "vegetarian thing." You've shared literature and videos, but to no avail. When you discuss the wedding meal, you usually end up in a heated argument. Just yesterday you brought up the subject of children and mentioned that you intend to raise them as vegetarians. Your partner just about lost it. The notion of raising children as vegetarians really hit a nerve. Over the past few weeks you have started to wonder how this marriage will ever work if you can't come to an agreement on these vital issues. Should you break off the engagement?

Diplomatic solution. While no one can tell you what is right for you in such a situation, you are very wise to be questioning the relationship at this point. If you are an ethically committed vegetarian, and your fiancé is a staunch meat eater, your core values are at odds. Shared values are extremely important to lasting relationships, especially when children come into the picture. Chances are that if your becoming vegetarian is the result of concern about animals, you will continue to move toward a more vegan lifestyle. Thus, if you are feeling uneasy now, the gap between you may continue to widen, especially if your fiancé is well informed about the issues but continues to oppose your vegetarian stance. Remember that food is a central part of our social world, especially when it comes to our partners. It is nice to believe that love can overcome anything; however, the reality is that love simply is not enough. You and your partner need professional couples counseling as soon as possible. While your marriage could be successful, it will take considerable work to get it off on the right foot. It is extremely important that your partner completely understands your decision from a deeply personal perspective. It is equally important that you understand why your fiancé is opposed to your vegetarian diet and raising children as vegetarians. Listen without interrupting and without passing judgment. Once your perspectives have been laid out and fully understood, you will need to construct guidelines for your relationship that are acceptable to both of you. Consider everything that might be affected by your differing perspectives, from grocery shopping to cooking, from eating out to how you will raise your children. While you may never completely agree on these issues, you will need to come to a reasonable compromise. If you remain in a gridlock, you may need to seriously consider going your separate ways.

Out to Lunch

Situation. You started a new job only two weeks ago. No one is aware you are a vegetarian. All is going very smoothly until the day everyone decides to go out to lunch to celebrate Barb's promotion. One of your colleagues says, "I know the perfect spot—a wonderful little steakhouse. They specialize in filet mignon and lobster." You were hoping to suggest an Asian restaurant that offers a whole section of vegetarian options, but everyone is so excited about the steak and lobster place that you decide it would be best not to mention it. You reach the restaurant without having voiced your concerns. You feel increasingly uneasy as you scan the menu and notice that there are only about ten items, none of which are vegetarian. Even the salads contain meat or seafood. There are only two soups—clam chowder and French onion, which is likely made with beef broth. What should you do?

Diplomatic solution. You could fake the stomach flu or discreetly eat around the meat, but what would this accomplish? Think about your motivation for not disclosing the fact that you are a vegetarian. Be proud of your choice;

there's no need to hide or apologize for being vegetarian. Instead, scrutinize the menu and see what side dishes might be acceptable or if there is anything that could be made vegetarian. Stir-fries and salads can easily be prepared without added meat. At the very least, there will be baked potatoes and a variety of vegetables. When the waiter arrives, say, without any hint of apology, "I'm vegetarian. I don't eat meat, poultry, or fish. Could you suggest something?" Nine times out of ten, the chef can create a lovely option that isn't listed on the menu. If the waiter is at a loss, suggest something yourself, based on ingredients you see on the menu.

In hindsight, your best bet would have been to let your colleagues know that you are vegetarian when the steakhouse was mentioned. You could simply have asked if anyone knows if there is a vegetarian option. Chances are the steakhouse idea would have been abandoned and your colleagues would have tried to think of an alternative that would work well for everyone. Another plan that generally works well is to call the restaurant ahead of time and discuss your options.

For additional information and suggestions on social situations, see these excellent Web sites:

Grassroots Veganism with Joanne Stepaniak includes an "Ask Joanne" question-and answer-section: www.vegsource.com/joanne/qa/archive.htm

John Robbins' Web site includes an "Ask John" question-and-answer section: www.foodrevolution.org/askjohn/

For scientific references for this chapter, see
http://www.nutrispeak.com/bvreferences.htm

Chapter 13

FROM MARKET TO MEALS

What does the word *change* mean to you? A dictionary defines change as follows: to exchange for or replace; to lay aside, abandon, or leave for another; to switch; to transform. A comedian has said, "Change is inevitable, except from a vending machine." Change is an unavoidable part of life. Although some may view change as a loss, change also brings with it new opportunities. When it comes to changing food habits that we've had since infancy, however, the prospect can be daunting.

Certain concerns might make us question switching to a vegetarian diet. Will the range of foods available to us be more limited? Must we shop only at special stores? Will it cost a lot more? Must we dine at restaurants where none of our friends will want to go? Does vegetarian cooking require a lot of time, expertise, and fancy equipment?

While it is understandable that questions like these would race through our minds, it is reassuring to discover that this particular change can be an extraordinary adventure to a delightful destination. And, for those who aren't quite ready for much of an adventure, the process can be as gradual as we want it to be, unfolding just enough to pique our curiosity. As with any change, we can ease the transition by preparing ourselves well. This chapter will serve as a valuable companion in this journey.

WHERE TO SHOP

Perhaps you are ready to bound out the front door, armed with reusable cloth shopping bags and determined to fill them with wholesome foods that will transform meals into vegetarian masterpieces. Yet where should this expedition begin?

Shopping for vegetarian food can be a bit intimidating if we're not sure what to buy or where to buy it. Perhaps the products we seek are not to be found in the same, familiar supermarket aisles. Shelves are lined with a vast array of products, many touted as nutritional powerhouses—yet are they? If our normal practice is to rush into the store, grab the same few items we always select, and check out as fast as possible, the transformation that has taken place in some sections of the marketplace in recent years may come as a surprise.

Exploring vegetarian foods is an adventure waiting to happen. As we become acquainted with a variety of fruits, vegetables, and whole grains, we will be introduced to marvelous taste sensations. The preparation of delicious, vegetarian recipes (including those in the next chapter) can be a great deal of fun. This can be the foundation of many pleasant evenings shared with one or more friends or family members. Those of us who aren't so keen on cooking will be thrilled with the instant gratification of a veggie burger that rivals our favorite beef burger, veggie Canadian bacon that tastes like "the real thing" and is low in fat, and a divine, dairy-free frozen strawberry dessert. These and many more tasty and convenient items await us in supermarket coolers and freezers. With time, we may find that the quality of breakfast, lunch, and supper surpasses what we'd ever thought possible.

There are many interesting places to discover fresh, wholesome foods. We are likely to come across new options that are very close to home: some amazing little store that we never knew existed or an organic farmer who delivers produce right to our door. Here are a few of the more popular choices.

Supermarkets

The large chains have come a long way in the past five years and many have expanded their organic produce departments, bulk food sections, ethnic options, and natural food selections, including fresh, frozen, and dried vegetarian convenience foods. It may come as a surprise to find that most of the items we need are available in nearby supermarkets. Although most mainstream supermarkets do not carry as many vegetarian or organic product lines as natural food stores, some already have responded to consumer demand. It helps to let local store managers know the specific products we'd like them to order. They are interested in staying in touch with current and potential customers and often are happy to accommodate us. The more demand they have for particular items, the more likely it is they will stock them.

Natural Food Stores

Large natural food stores are becoming more popular and easier to locate. Though some "health food" stores seem to stock nothing but supplements, many specialize in vegetarian and organic foods. They may carry a variety of beans, less-common whole grains, and products made with whole grain flours, such as quinoa, spelt, and kamut. On the shelves and in coolers and freezers we'll find "convenience" foods that are free of hydrogenated vegetable oils, food colors, artificial flavors, preservatives, and other additives. These stores tend to offer bulk foods at a moderate cost, organic produce, hearty baked goods, tofu, soymilks, refrigerated nuts with a good turnover (so they're fresh), soy and dairy yogurts and cheeses, nut butters, and wholesome snacks, such as fat-free tortilla chips and fruit bars. A good natural food store can be a real ally in creating fast, delicious vegetarian meals.

Farmers' Markets

If there are farms nearby, there is likely to be a farmers' market, perhaps even one that sells organic produce. Farmers' markets tend to undercut supermarket prices by 30 percent or more on many items. Most or all of the produce is locally grown, goods are fresh, and the variety is superb, including great greens, such as collards and kale. Some farmers may sell directly to consumers or have "U-pick" options. Some offer consumers an opportunity to buy shares in their farm in exchange for produce. The amount of produce received depends on the number of shares owned. The result can be a nourishing and mutually beneficial connection between our family and our food supply.

Organic Delivery Services

Many communities now offer organic delivery services that provide customers with healthy, high-quality, organically grown fruits and vegetables in a fun and exceptionally convenient way. These services deliver a box of fresh, often locally grown (when possible) produce right to our doorstep. Many such services allow us to custom order the produce we want each week, and some offer additional items such as organic breads, oils, salad dressings, and apple cider.

Buying from such a service not only supports a small local business, it also supports many organic farmers in your area and elsewhere.

Ethnic Shops

Most cities have fascinating ethnic sections that are steeped in the exotic flavors and aromas of foreign places. We can enrich our lives with a regular trip to one of these parts of town. Take a friend and your shopping list, and stop for lunch at a local restaurant—you're sure to find more than one delicious vegetarian option. Larger cities have districts that reflect many different cultures; even on a limited budget, we can almost travel the world!

When we discover a good ethnic store, it's like finding a little treasure chest. Asian stores carry a wonderful selection of tofu, fresh greens, seaweeds (more respectfully known as sea vegetables), seitan (gluten), edamame, and Asian sauces. Some of these cost a fraction of what we would pay at a natural food store or supermarket. Greek stores supply the best tahini in town, as well as a good assortment of chickpeas, lima and white beans, olives, olive oil, Mediterranean herbs, and pita bread. East Indian stores carry a variety of flours, many types of beans, grains, and spice mixes; their curry pastes are great for spicing up vegetable or lentil dishes. Ethnic stores also stock delicious vegetarian convenience foods.

Co-ops

Food co-ops are grocery stores that are owned and often operated by members. This helps to reduce overhead costs and keep food prices fairly reasonable. Members usually can buy in bulk and often enjoy special discounts. Food co-ops generally are health-oriented and offer a wide selection of vegetarian and organic options.

Buying Clubs

A buying club typically includes at least three or four people or families, as most wholesalers require minimum orders of several hundred dollars. We can find the name of a large, local, natural foods wholesaler in the phone book or by asking staff at a health food store. Our discount may be almost as much as the wholesale discount given to stores. Foods are ordered by the case, half case, 25-pound (11.2-kilogram) sack (grains, beans, and flour), or in large containers (for items such as tahini and tamari). Although we'll need to organize some extra storage space and plan our shopping a little differently, the whole process can actually simplify our lives in the long run, as we may need to shop less frequently. The work of placing orders, picking up the food, and distributing items can be shared among club members. A scale for weighing each member's order will be an immense help in dividing the goods. The cost savings often are so impressive that we're hooked in no time.

Bakeries

Discovering a wonderful bakery reawakens our senses in a most delightful way. Although many supermarkets and natural food stores have amazing in-house bakeries, little specialty shops tucked away in the corners of our communities offer some spectacular products. A number specialize in whole grain products, use organic ingredients, or provide options that are free of dairy and eggs. Many ethnic bakeries sell hearty rye and wheat breads, bagels, and tortillas.

If we want to have a hint of bakery aroma wafting through our homes, a bread maker can make it easy. We'll have fresh bread and complete control over the ingredients, which is ideal for those with food allergies. In addition, we can prepare dough in the bread maker and use it to make buns, pizza, cinnamon rolls, and many other treats.

WHAT TO BUY

After we've considered where to shop, we can decide which items we'll need to stock our pantry. Our shopping list will include certain basics for everyday cooking. We might write down breakfast, lunch, and supper ideas for several days or a week. The list on the next page can be photocopied and will help us plan our shopping sprees.

If we are concerned that being vegetarian might limit our options, we'll be happy to discover a whole new world of exciting food choices. There are so many grains, beans, vegetables, fruits, and convenience foods that we could introduce new items every week and never get bored.

FOOD STORAGE TIPS

When we arrive home with loads of wonderful, vegetarian food, we'll need to know how to care for it. There are three primary objectives for storing food:

1. to keep food fresh and appealing;
2. to prevent spoilage, mold, rancidity, or bug infestations;
3. to retain nutrients.

Basic Shopping List

Grain Products

__ Barley
__ Brown rice
__ Bulgur
__ Flours (whole wheat, unbleached, gluten, other)
__ Millet
__ Mixed and ready-to-eat cereals
__ Oatmeal
__ Pasta
__ Popcorn
__ Quinoa
__ Wheat germ
__ Whole grain bread, buns, bagels, crackers

Vegetables and Fruits

__ Fresh greens (broccoli, collards, Chinese/napa cabbage, kale)
__ Seasonal vegetables and fruits
__ Frozen fruit and vegetables
__ Garlic and onions
__ Canned, water-packed fruits
__ Dried fruits (apricots, cranberries, currants, dates, figs, prunes, raisins, others)
__ Fruit and vegetable juices (fresh, frozen, bottled, canned, or in tetra packs)
__ Tomato or pasta sauces, canned tomatoes

Beans, Peas, Lentils, and Related Products

__ Dried legumes (chickpeas, navy, pinto, and kidney beans, lentils, split peas)
__ Canned legumes (chickpeas, pinto, kidney, and baked beans)
__ Tofu, tempeh (plain or seasoned)
__ Prepared bean dishes, such as soups and chili
__ Instant dried legume dishes (hummus, soups, casseroles, refried beans)
__ Meat alternatives, vegetarian patties, soy wieners, veggie slices, sausages
__ Seitan
__ Soy nuts

Nuts, Seeds, and Butters

__ Nut butters
__ Nuts (raw cashews, almonds, walnuts, pecans, filberts, peanuts)
__ Seed butters (tahini, sunflower)
__ Seeds (flax, pumpkin, sesame, sunflower)

Soy and Grain Beverages and Related Products

__ Fortified soy or grain milks
__ Soy yogurt
__ Soy cheese
__ Soy ice cream or other frozen desserts

Dairy Products and Eggs (for lacto-ovo vegetarians)

__ Cow's milk
__ Cheese
__ Eggs
__ Yogurt

Sweeteners

__ Barley malt, rice syrup, maple syrup, agave nectar
__ Blackstrap molasses
__ Dried cane sugar
__ Jams and conserves

Beverages

__ Cereal grain beverages
__ Leaf and herbal teas
__ Organic coffee

Fats and Oils

__ Extra-virgin olive oil
__ Flaxseed oil
__ Mayonnaise or vegan mayonnaise-like spread
__ Nonhydrogenated margarine
__ Nut oils (hazelnut, walnut)
__ Organic canola oil, high-oleic sunflower or safflower oils
__ Toasted sesame oil
__ Vegetable or lecithin spray

Seasonings and Condiments

__ Bragg Liquid Aminos
__ Bottled sauces (teriyaki, barbecue, sweet and sour, other)
__ Cooking wine
__ Ketchup, mustards, and relish
__ Lemon juice
__ Miso
__ Patak's or other curry paste
__ Pickles
__ Tamari or soy sauce
__ Sea vegetables (hijiki, wakame, nori, agar)
__ Vegetable broth powder or cubes or chicken-style seasoning
__ Vegetarian Support Formula nutritional yeast (Red Star brand)
__ Vinegar (rice, wine, balsamic, or apple cider vinegar)

Herbs and Spices

__ Chili powder or hot chile peppers
__ Cinnamon, allspice, nutmeg, cumin, curry
__ Dried herbs (oregano, sage, savory, thyme, rosemary, marjoram)
__ Fresh ginger
__ Fresh herbs (parsley, cilantro, basil)
__ Mixed seasonings (e.g., Spike)
__ Salt and pepper

My additions

_____
_____
_____
_____
_____
_____
_____
_____
_____
_____
_____
_____
_____

Appropriate food storage is especially important when our diet is based on unrefined foods. These foods grow people well; they also grow bugs well! In contrast, items with little nutritional value, such as white sugar, white flour, refined corn oil, and soda pop will keep in the pantry for years, as they are of little interest to pests.

Grains: Whole versus Processed

In their original form, nature gives grains a protective packaging. Intact wheat berries (the whole grains) will keep for about two years in a tightly covered container that is stored in a cool, dry place. However, if we grind the wheat berries into flour, the fats in the germ are exposed to air and can become rancid, reducing the storage time to about two months. Whole grain flour stored in a sealed bag or container that excludes moisture will last three or four months in the freezer; this is why many bread bakers always keep it there. (Before making bread, bring the flour to room temperature.) Some people prefer to grind fresh flour on a regular basis for their Sunday pancakes. Wheat germ, which contains most of the natural oils found in the grain, goes rancid much more quickly than wheat bran, which contains little fat.

Nuts, Seeds, and Their Butters

Whole nuts in the shell are far better keepers than shelled nuts. Nature has carefully designed their hard outer packaging so they will keep for a whole year until the next nut harvest. Once removed from the shell, nuts and seeds should be stored in an airtight container in the refrigerator, where they will last for four months, or freezer, where they will last for a year. Walnuts are unusually vulnerable to rancidity due to their high content of omega-3s; they are best kept in the freezer, or, at the minimum, refrigerated. Other shelled nuts and seeds can be stored unrefrigerated up to two months in containers with lids. Chopping nuts exposes more fat to air and roasting nuts and seeds pushes fat to the surface. Consequently, chopped or roasted nuts and seeds have even shorter shelf lives. Nut and seed butters must always be refrigerated after opening the jar.

Fruits and Vegetables

Fresh fruits and vegetables are very perishable and generally are best stored in the refrigerator. Certain vegetables (such as onions, potatoes, and hard-shell squash) will keep well in a cool, dry place for several weeks. Most fruits and tomatoes can be stored at room temperature for up to a week; however, those that are already very ripe may be best stored in the refrigerator (which stops further ripening). During certain times of the year, local produce is so plentiful that we may want to preserve it to enjoy until the next harvest. The solution is to spend a little time in the kitchen preparing the vegetables and fruits for freezing, canning, drying, or turning into jams, pickles, chutney, salsa, or other goodies to be enjoyed year-round.

Dry Storage of Foods on Pantry Shelves

When we expand our range of grains and beans, we may end up with so many items stuffed into cupboards that it's a challenge to locate ingredients for a given recipe. A little organizing will make food preparation a lot less stressful. If we keep grains, beans, and flours in plastic bags from the store, eventually little critters will find their way into the bags. A simple way to avoid problems is to store foods in Mason jars or other jars with tight-fitting lids. Buy two or three dozen wide-mouth canning jars, label them, and arrange the filled jars on an open shelf or in the pantry. Bulkier items, such as flour, can be kept in larger canisters, plastic buckets with tight-fitting lids, or larger jars. They also can be kept in zippered bags in the refrigerator or freezer. Spices can be stored in small, tightly closed containers, preferably away from the warm stove area.

Refrigerator Storage

Fresh foods are best stored in the refrigerator, as they quickly go rancid at room temperature. The refrigerator tends to dry out produce, so make sure foods are covered. Lettuce and other greens keep especially well in plastic containers with tight-fitting lids. Some people wash leaves, wrap them in a slightly damp, clean tea towel, and place the wrapped greens in a plastic bag. Buy only as much fresh produce as you can use in a week. (Potatoes and garlic should not be refrigerated.)

Freezer Storage

A freezer can be a great asset. It allows us to store precooked beans, to buy or harvest large batches of fruits and vegetables in season and preserve them, and to stock up on perishable bulk foods, such as whole grain flours, wheat germ, seeds, and nuts. We can make dozens of healthy muffins and have them ready to grab and go. (This is an excellent strategy when there are hungry teens in the house.) We can cook huge batches of lentil or bean soups and freeze them in individual or family-sized portions.

TABLE 13.1	FOOD STORAGE		
Food Group	**Store in a Cool, Dry Place**	**Store in the Refrigerator**	**Store in the Freezer**
Grains	Whole grains, dry pasta, crackers, dry cereals	Whole grain flours, fresh pasta	Wheat germ, breads, rolls, muffins (for longer storage)
Vegetables and Fruits	Onions, garlic, potatoes, hard-shell squash, dried fruits, unripe fruits, bananas	Vegetables, fruits, opened containers of juices	Frozen vegetables, fruits, and juices
Beans and Alternates	Dry beans, split peas, lentils, textured soy protein	Tofu, nuts, and seeds and their butters, ground flaxseeds (or in freezer), eggs	Frozen patties, loaves, tempeh, cooked legumes (for longer storage)
Milks and Alternates	Fortified soymilk in Tetra packs, milk powder (nondairy or dairy)	Fortified soymilk and cow's milk, soy or dairy yogurt and cheese	Nondairy and dairy ice creams
Other Foods, Seasonings, and Condiments	Molasses, honey, olive oil, sesame oil, spices, dried herbs	Fresh herbs and ginger, opened jars of cold-pressed oils, condiments, sauces, pure maple syrup	Fresh herbs (freeze in a plastic bag, crumble for instant use)

Foods Kept in Several Places

Tempeh, a soyfood commonly used in Indonesia, often is found in the freezer section of grocery stores. It may be kept in the refrigerator for several days or in the freezer for longer storage.

Dry baker's yeast, if stored in its unopened package (brick or jar), may be kept at room temperature in a dry place until its expiration date. Once the jar or brick is opened, it must be kept airtight and refrigerated. Nutritional yeast can be stored safely in a cool, dry place in an opaque container (light destroys riboflavin).

KITCHEN EQUIPMENT

The following tools allow us to perform kitchen tasks with ease and speed. It's well worth investing in the best quality tools you can afford.

1. Three good-quality knives. The items that will most increase our enjoyment and efficiency in the kitchen are an 8-inch (20-cm) chef's knife that stays sharp and feels good in the hand, a small paring knife, and a high-quality bread knife with a serrated edge.

2. Cutting board. Though wooden boards are aesthetically pleasing and provide excellent performance, plastic boards are easier to clean. The minimum size is 8 x 12 inches (20 x 30.5 cm); for greater chopping pleasure, a 13 x 20-inch (33 x 51-cm) board is a treat.

3. **Mixing bowls**. We need at least three glass, ceramic, or stainless steel bowls of varying sizes. A 14-inch (35.5-centimeter) diameter stainless steel bowl is great for mixing a salad that can last five days. The salad can then be stored in one or more large Tupperware-type, tightly sealed containers. Narrow and deep bowls are especially handy for mixing baked goods.

4. **Nonstick skillet and oil spray**. The winning combo is a nonstick skillet and a refillable oil sprayer. Skillets should have good conducting ability and disperse heat evenly.

5. **Two pots**. At the minimum, get a large pot for soup or pasta and a smaller pot for cooked cereal, sauces, or steamed vegetables. Exact sizes will depend on the number of people in your household.

6. **Stainless steel basket steamer**. This inexpensive gadget fits into almost any size pot and is used to steam vegetables or veggie wieners.

7. **Blender**. Blenders are extremely useful for puréeing dressings, soups, shakes, and smoothies.

8. **Colander or strainer**. These are used to drain liquid from cooked pasta, potatoes, and legumes.

9. **Handheld tools**. The essentials for most cooks are measuring cups and spoons, a wooden spoon, food grater, can opener, vegetable peeler, pancake flipper, rubber spatula, spring-loaded tongs, and perhaps a whisk.

10. **Food processor**. While not essential, a food processor is useful for making hummus and thicker spreads that might burn out the motor of some blenders. It also saves time with chopping.

11. **Juicer**. This can be a fancy machine or a simple stainless steel hand juicer. Look for one with two parts—the top part where the fruit is held and the bottom part that holds the juice.

MAKING THE TRANSITION TO A VEGETARIAN DIET

What's for Dinner?

Most people have eight or nine favorite supper meals they return to again and again. If switching to vegetarian foods seems to be a challenge, you may find you're partway there with three vegetarian meals that you enjoy. Here is a three-step plan that will make the transition simple.

1. Think of three vegetarian meals you already like.

Cooking at home. How about spaghetti with tomato sauce, vegetarian chili, and bean burritos?

Restaurants and take-out meals. Popular favorites are vegetarian pizza, veggie burgers, veggie dogs, Italian pasta dishes, Chinese stir-fries, East Indian curries and samosas, Middle Eastern falafels and tabouli salad, and Mexican bean burritos or tacos.

2. Choose three recipes you can modify at home or at restaurants.

Cooking at home. Split pea soup is just as good without a ham bone. A taco, tortilla, or enchilada is great when made with refried beans or vegetarian "ground round" instead of beef. Fajitas can be made with plain or seasoned firm tofu instead of chicken. There's a scrumptious version of Shepherd's Pie on page 344.

Restaurants and take-out meals. Chinese food can be prepared with tofu or cashews. Japanese nori rolls can be made with tofu. Some nonvegetarian restaurants have extensive all-you-can-eat salad bars that provide abundant, reasonably priced meals.

3. Over the next month or two, try three new recipes or restaurants.

Cooking at home. Look through the Seven Super Simple Suppers on pages 338 to 347. Have fun as you experiment with delightful new flavors and healthful ingredients.

Restaurants and take-out meals. To find new places to go, glance through the phone book, keep your eyes open as you drive around the neighborhood, and ask a few friends about their favorites spots. You're bound to make some very appealing discoveries.

Whether you're a home cook or restaurant diner, when you've found your three hits in each category, you've done it! You'll have your nine delicious vegetarian choices.

Does Vegetarian Eating Require Lots of Time and Cooking Expertise?

For those of us who enjoy cooking, making delicious meals from scratch is a pleasure, but this is not the only route to marvelous meals. Vegetarian convenience items are among the fastest-growing categories in the grocery trade. Look for veggie burgers, dogs, slices, and "ground round"; frozen vegetarian meals, and packaged dinners. Canned beans and soups are handy to keep on the shelf for everyday use, emergencies, or camping trips. All of these enable us to have healthy meals ready to serve in minutes.

Recipes from Breakfast to Dessert

In the next chapter, we take you from breakfast through supper and then to outstanding desserts with some of the tried and true recipes we love best. If you'd like to switch some of your former favorite recipes into more "plant-based" versions, here are substitutions you can make.

TABLE 13.2 INSTEAD OF MEAT, EGG, OR DAIRY: SUBSTITUTION BASICS	
Instead of Meat, Fish, Poultry, or Related Products	**Use These Plant-Based Alternatives**
1 cup (250 ml) meat or chicken stock	1 cup (250 ml) liquid vegetable stock from cubes or powder (see package directions for amounts)
	Bragg Liquid Aminos, tamari, or miso mixed with water (to taste)
1 serving meat, chicken, or fish	Equal weight or volume of veggie "meat," plain or marinated tofu, tempeh, beans, seitan (wheat gluten), gluten-based "meats" from Asian restaurants
	Equal volume of portobello mushrooms
1 cup (250 ml) ground beef	Equal weight or volume of vegetarian "ground round" (such as Yves)
	1/2 cup less 1 tbsp. (110 ml) dry textured soy protein, covered with boiling stock or water, stirred, and soaked for ten minutes (drain, if necessary)
1 tbsp. (15 ml) gelatin	1 tbsp. (15 ml) agar flakes (thickens 1 cup/250 ml liquid)
	1/2 tsp. (2 ml) agar powder (thickens 1 cup/250 ml liquid)
	1 tbsp. (15 ml) veggie gel such as Emes Kosher-Jel, carageenan, or locust bean gum (thickens 2 cups/500 ml liquid)
Instead of Egg	
1 egg	1 tbsp. (15 ml) ground flaxseeds mixed with 3 tbsp. (45 ml) water
(Note that sometimes just leaving out an egg from a muffin or pancake recipe makes very little difference.)	2–4 tbsp. (30–60 ml) soft tofu
	1/4 cup (60 ml) mashed, very ripe banana
	Starch-based egg substitutes (see package directions for amount), such as Ener-G Foods Egg Replacer
	1/8 tsp. (0.5 ml) baking powder added to dry ingredients replaces leavening action of 1 egg or egg white in baking
Instead of Dairy Products	
1 cup (250 ml) cow's milk	1 cup (250 ml) fortified soymilk or rice milk
1 cup (250 ml) buttermilk	1 cup (250 ml) soymilk plus 2 tsp. (10 ml) lemon juice or vinegar
1 cup (250 ml) yogurt	1 cup (250 ml) soy yogurt
1 oz. (25 g) hard cheese	1 oz. (25 g) soy or other nondairy cheese
1 cup (250 ml) cottage cheese (in recipes)	1 cup (250 ml) drained, mashed tofu (medium-firm tofu works well)
1 cup (250 ml) ricotta cheese (as in lasagne)	1 cup (250 ml) drained, mashed tofu (firm works well)
1 cup (250 ml) ice cream	1 cup (250 ml) frozen soy or rice dessert, fruit sherbet, sorbet, or Berry Delicious Ice Dream (recipe, page 359)
1 1/2 cups (375 ml) whipping cream	12 oz. (340 g) package firm silken tofu, 1/4 cup (60 ml) maple syrup, 1 tbsp. (15 ml) lemon juice, and 1 tsp. (5 ml) vanilla, blended
Butter	Olive oil or nonhydrogenated margarine in cooking
	Almond butter or other nut butter as a spread on toast
	Liquid Gold Dressing (page 329) as a topping for baked potatoes

TRAVEL TIPS

The websites that list vegetarian restaurants worldwide are travelers' best friends. Before going anywhere, we can visit one of several good sites. Our favorite is www.vegdining.com. We can click on the destination country or countries, print a comprehensive list of vegetarian restaurants, pack our bags, and know we'll be well nourished. Other sites are www.happycow.net, www.vegeats.com/restaurants, and www.ivu.org/global.

For those who prefer to take along a book rather than surf the Internet, one choice is the *Vegetarian Journal's Guide to Natural Food Restaurants in the U.S. and Canada,* available from the Vegetarian Resource Group at 410-366-8343 (or order online at www.vrg.org/catalog/order.htm). For European travel, check out *Vegetarian Europe* by Alex Bourke (Vegetarian Guides, 2000).

Taking a Few Essentials

Containers of various sizes that have tight-fitting, spillproof lids are travelers' other best friends. These can transport several handy items. One is a serving of a protein-rich food such as hummus, marinated tofu, chickpeas, or curried lentils. Another item to bring could be a little of a favorite salad dressing, or perhaps a serving of fortified soymilk. With these, the rest of a meal may come together fairly easily and be very tasty. Certain vegetarian items—oatmeal, cereals, rice, baked potatoes, salads, vegetables, fruit, and juices—are readily available practically anywhere, including airports, planes, trains, bus depots, and the homes of nonvegetarian friends. If we just have a hearty, protein-rich food, we can end up with an acceptable meal. A favorite salad dressing can taste surprisingly good on bland white rice (as sometimes is necessary with airplane meals) or on a baked potato (salsa and even ketchup are good, too). Fortified soymilk is valuable for those who don't use dairy products, as it's good on cereal and in tea or coffee. Nalgene brand spillproof containers, available at outdoor equipment stores, make transporting foods and beverages a lot simpler!

It's often a good idea to bring along an assortment of nuts, seeds, and dried fruit. Treat yourself to a few of the more exotic ones, such as hazelnuts or cashews, and dried figs, mangoes, cranberries, or cherries.

Air Travel Tips

Airlines are accustomed to plenty of vegetarian meal requests and provide meals that are vegan, lacto-ovo vegetarian, Asian vegetarian, fruit plates, or raw foods. To be reasonably certain of actually getting our choice of meal, it is a good idea to reconfirm the request a day or two ahead of the flight. However, the "meal" may be nothing more than a bagel and a banana, so it is always wise to bring a little something extra, such as a bag of nuts and dried fruits, soy yogurt, or a veggie "meat" sandwich, just in case.

SUPPORT AND INSPIRATION

Support Organizations

In communities across North America and in Britain, Europe, Australia, New Zealand, and many other parts of the world, vegetarian associations arrange potlucks, cooking classes, speaker presentations, and turkey-free Thanksgiving dinners to inspire and nourish others who wish to shift their diets in a healthful, earth-friendly direction.

Festivals and Conferences

Vegetarian festivals provide very pleasant interludes, not to mention outstanding food. A great way to see the world is to attend the World Vegetarian Congress, held in a different country every two years (see www.ivu.org). The Vegetarian Summerfest, held in a beautiful Pennsylvania setting, provides a five-day getaway with well-organized workshops, great speakers, and excellent meals (see www.navs-online.org). EarthSave groups sponsor annual Taste of Health food festivals and dine-outs in many locations (see www.earthsave.org). Vegsource puts on their annual e-Vent in Los Angeles, and FARM has annual animal rights conferences in Washington, D.C., and Los Angeles.

Compassionate Living

Imaginative and enjoyable solutions have been found for people who wish to live more lightly on the planet by being vegetarian. These websites can help tremendously in making sensible choices. We can search these and their many links for information on a multitude of related interests, including cooking schools, summer camps, nonleather shoes, and socially responsible investing.

www.ivu.org   International Vegetarian Union

www.vrg.org   Vegetarian Resource Group

For scientific references for this chapter, see
http://www.nutrispeak.com/bvreferences.htm

Chapter 14

RECIPES

SIMPLE TREASURES

This is a new era in food preparation, and we are all responsible for making healthier food taste really wonderful for those we love.

— *Graham Kerr, chef, author, and TV legend*

Many people, beckoned by the numerous compelling reasons to go vegetarian, face one giant stumbling block—they love their food. They can't even begin to imagine life without barbequed steaks, fried chicken, baked salmon, and Thanksgiving turkey. When they think of vegetarian fare, a pile of beans and brown rice springs to mind. Alas, it seems like far too great a sacrifice. This chapter will shatter the myth that vegetarian food is gastronomically inferior. We will tantalize your taste buds and introduce you to a world of diverse, delicious, and nourishing plant-based meals and snacks.

Some of the recipes included here are extremely easy to prepare, while a few are more complex and gourmet. The ingredients used are widely available from Seattle to Miami. In addition to our own creations (both authors love cooking and taste-testing), we have invited guest chefs to contribute several very special recipes. This has resulted in a wonderful variety of taste sensations and cooking styles. We feature a delectable German Chocolate Cake and its accompanying Coconut Squash Icing as an example of chef Ron Pickarski's genius with food. Ron and his team of expert chefs achieved Gold Medal status in the Culinary Olympics in Germany with an entirely plant-based spread, competing against nonvegetarian, gourmet chefs. Chocolate lovers should definitely try this cake! There's a Lemon Teasecake from Seattle's famous Café Ambrosia. We've shown you what to do with whole grains, kale, and flaxseed oil so your family can enjoy these highly nutritious ingredients. We include some sure-fire winners for family gatherings, potlucks, and parties, and provide a full week of supper menus. There are shakes and smoothies that are equally welcomed by seniors and the hungry hordes after school. Athletes will appreciate Hot Tofu with Cool Greens and Muscle Muffins. The whole family will love African Stew and a vegetarian version of Shepherd's Pie.

Nutritional Analyses of Recipes

In addition to great taste, all of our recipes have been designed with nutrition in mind. Thus, with each recipe you'll find a nutritional analysis. For example, at the bottom corner of the page for Timesaving Tacos (page 342) you'll see the box at right.

Per taco:	
calories	149
protein	4 g
fat	7 g
carbohydrate	20 g
dietary fiber	5 g
calcium	54 mg
iron	1.6 mg
magnesium	28 mg
sodium	302 mg
zinc	2.7 mg
folate	63 mcg
riboflavin	0.1 mg
vitamin B_{12}	0 mcg
vitamin C	14 mg
vitamin E	1.8 mg
omega-3s	0.2 g
% calories from:	
protein	13%
fat	32%
carbohydrate	55%

The nutritional analysis does not include optional ingredients. When two or more choices are given for an ingredient, the analysis is based on the first choice. When there is a range for an amount, the lower amount is used for the analysis.

Below the amounts of protein, fat, carbohydrate, and other nutrients in each serving, we show the percentage of calories that come from protein, fat, and carbohydrate. Note that 35 percent or less *calories* from fat is very different from 35 percent or less of the food's *weight* coming from fat. For example, 2 percent cow's milk indicates that two percent of the weight of this milk comes from fat (89 percent comes from water). Yet 35 percent of the calories in this milk come from fat, along with 25 percent from protein and 40 percent from carbohydrate (primarily the sugar lactose).

For comparison, the pattern suggested for everyone over three years of age to maintain good health and prevent chronic disease is 15 to 35 percent fat, 10 to 20 percent protein, and 50 to 70 percent carbohydrate (see page 55).

Some of the foods we eat—salad dressings, a salad that contains nuts, a favorite entrée, or a dessert—will provide more than 35 percent of calories from fat. These higher-fat items will be balanced by many plant foods—grains, vegetables, fruits, lentils, and beans—that provide 15 percent or less of their calories from fat. All of these contain healthful plant oils and little or no saturated fat. Building our diets around these foods helps us keep a healthy balance. Here are recipes that will feed our bodies and nourish our spirits.

RECIPES FOR HEALTHY EATING

CASHEW FRENCH TOAST

Yield: 6 slices

If you can't imagine French toast without eggs, you are in for a pleasant surprise. This version is easy and delicious. If you are slicing your bread, cut thick slices.

¹/₂ cup	raw cashew pieces	125 ml
1 cup	fortified soymilk	250 ml
¹/₂ teaspoon	vanilla extract	2 ml
1 tablespoon	pure maple syrup	15 ml
up to 2 teaspoons	high-oleic sunflower or safflower oil	up to 10 ml
6 slices	whole grain bread	6 slices

Grind the cashews in a dry blender until they are powdery. Add the soymilk, vanilla, and maple syrup, and blend until smooth. Pour into a shallow bowl or casserole dish. Preheat a heavy skillet (preferably nonstick) over medium heat. If using a nonstick skillet, lightly oil or spray the pan first. If using a cast-iron or other heavy skillet, generously oil the pan first. Dip the bread in the cashew mixture, then place two or three pieces on the skillet (depending on skillet size). Do not overlap the French toast; instead leave a little space between the pieces. Cook until nicely browned, then flip and cook on the other side. Serve hot with Jiffy Fruit Sauce (page 310), maple syrup, or chopped fresh fruit.

Note: A good nonstick skillet works best for this recipe, although any heavy skillet will do. See page 300 for more information on skillets.

Chef's Tip: Choosing Cashews

Cashews can be blended for use in sauces, "uncheeses," French toast, and many other dishes. For these purposes, it is best to use "raw" cashews that have not been roasted, as they are lighter in color and have better thickening power. Technically, these nuts are not truly raw, as they do undergo some heating to remove them from their shell. However, they are not heated further afterward. Cashew pieces often are more reasonably priced than whole cashews and will work just as well in these types of recipes.

Per slice (without oil for frying):	
calories	169
protein	6 g
fat	7 g
carbohydrate	23 g
dietary fiber	2 g
calcium	77 mg
iron	2 mg
magnesium	64 mg
sodium	173 mg
zinc	1.4 mg
folate	32 mcg
riboflavin	0.1 mg
vitamin B$_{12}$	0.5 mcg
vitamin C	0 mg
vitamin E	1.1 mg
omega-3s	0 g
% calories from:	
protein	13%
fat	36%
carbohydrate	51%

BANANA-WALNUT PANCAKES

Yield: 7 (6-inch/15-cm) pancakes

These pancakes are reminiscent of Sunday breakfast at Grandma's house. They are perfect for company or a special occasion.

2 cups	fortified soy, rice, or cow's milk	500 ml
1 tablespoon	ground flaxseeds	15 ml
1½ cups	whole wheat flour	375 ml
2 tablespoons	wheat germ	30 ml
1 tablespoon	natural sugar or other sweetener	15 ml
2 teaspoons	baking powder	10 ml
½ teaspoon	salt	2 ml
⅓ cup	chopped walnuts	85 ml
1	banana, peeled and thinly sliced	1
2 tablespoons	oil (see note)	30 ml

Combine the milk and ground flaxseeds in a large bowl. Combine the flour, wheat germ, sweetener, baking powder, and salt in a medium bowl and mix well. Add the flour mixture to the wet ingredients and stir just until mixed. Fold in the walnuts and banana. Preheat a heavy skillet (preferably nonstick) over medium heat. The pan should be very hot before putting in the batter. Lightly coat the nonstick pan with cooking spray or a few drops of oil. If using a regular skillet, add 1 to 2 teaspoons (5 to 10 ml) additional oil and a little more between each batch. Pour about ½ cup (125 ml) of batter on the heated pan for each pancake. When well browned on one side and bubbles appear on the top surface, turn the pancake over and cook the second side until golden brown. Serve hot with Jiffy Fruit Sauce (page 310), pure maple syrup, or chopped fresh fruit.

Note: For oil, we recommend the use of organic canola, high-oleic sunflower or safflower oil, or melted, nonhydrogenated margarine. If children or teens make this recipe, use ¼ cup (60 ml) of batter for each pancake as smaller pancakes are even easier to turn over.

Per pancake (without oil for frying):	
calories	230
protein	7 g
fat	9 g
carbohydrate	33 g
dietary fiber	5 g
calcium	104 mg
iron	2 mg
magnesium	65 mg
sodium	274 mg
zinc	1.4 mg
folate	19 mcg
riboflavin	0.1 mg
vitamin B12	0.8 mcg
vitamin C	2 mg
vitamin E	4 mg
omega-3s	0.7 g
% calories from:	
protein	12%
fat	34%
carbohydrate	54%

JIFFY FRUIT SAUCE

Yield: 2 cups (500 ml)

*Fruit sauces are a refreshing change from sugary syrups. This simple combination
contains no added sugar and requires no cooking. Raisins provide additional sweetness.*

1	medium banana	1
1	medium orange, peeled and seeded	1
1 to 2 tablespoons	raisins, optional	15 to 30 ml
1 1/2 cups	fresh or frozen berries or sliced fruit (see note)	375 ml

Place the banana, orange, raisins, if using, and one-half of the berries or sliced
fruit (¾ cup/185 ml) in a blender and purée until smooth. Pour into a medium bowl. Stir in the remaining half of the berries or sliced fruit. Serve with
French toast, pancakes, or waffles.

Note: One to two tablespoons (15 to 30 ml) of orange juice concentrate may
be used in place of the orange. For the berries or fruit, try blueberries, raspberries, or peeled, sliced kiwi fruit. You also may wish to experiment and invent
your own blend using your favorite fruits.

Per 1/4 cup (60 ml):	
calories	31
protein	0.4 g
fat	0.2 g
carbohydrate	8 g
dietary fiber	1 g
calcium	9 mg
iron	0.1 mg
magnesium	7 mg
sodium	1 mg
zinc	0.1 mg
folate	9 mcg
riboflavin	0 mg
vitamin B_{12}	0 mcg
vitamin C	12 mg
vitamin E	0.4 mg
omega-3s	0 g
% calories from:	
protein	5%
fat	4%
carbohydrate	91%

MARVELOUS MORNING MUESLI

Yield: 2 cups (500 ml)

This recipe provides an ideal balance among protein, fat, and carbohydrate. It is a nourishing breakfast that can be prepared with ease the night before. A hungry person who eats the whole batch will start the day with 21 grams of protein. Leftovers make a delicious evening snack. You might like to try some of the other grain flakes that are available, such as wheat, barley, kamut, or rice flakes, or a combination.

3/4 cup	rolled oats or other grain flakes	185 ml
2 tablespoons	raisins, currants, or dried cranberries	30 ml
2 tablespoons	chopped walnuts, almonds, or other nuts	30 ml
1/4 teaspoon	cinnamon	1 ml
1 cup	fortified soy, rice, or cow's milk, or fruit juice	250 ml
1	apple, grated or finely chopped	1

Combine the flakes, raisins, nuts, cinnamon, milk, and apple in a medium bowl. Cover and refrigerate for 1 hour or overnight. Alternatively, the apple may be stirred in just before serving. Serve as is or with added milk or juice.

Per 1 cup (250 ml):

calories	333
protein	10 g
fat	9 g
carbohydrate	56 g
dietary fiber	6 g
calcium	192 mg
iron	2.9 mg
magnesium	99 mg
sodium	73 mg
zinc	1.6 mg
folate	77 mcg
riboflavin	0.1 mg
vitamin B_{12}	1.5 mcg
vitamin C	28 mg
vitamin E	3.2 mg
omega-3s	0.7 g
% calories from:	
protein	12%
fat	24%
carbohydrate	64%

BASIC WHOLE GRAIN CEREAL

Yield: 4 to 5 cups (1 to 1.25 L)

This is a great way to begin the adventure of using whole grains. It is satisfying and delicious for breakfast. Leftovers make a nourishing, soothing snack anytime and can be refrigerated and used as a warm cereal or cold pudding for several days.

1 cup	uncooked grain (examples below)	250 ml
4 cups	water	1 L
1/2 teaspoon	salt (less can be used if you prefer)	2 ml
1/2 cup	dried fruit	125 ml
1/2 cup	fortified soy, rice, or cow's milk	125 ml

Place the grain, water, and salt in a heavy pot or the top of a double boiler and bring to a boil. If using a double boiler, place the grain above boiling water and allow to simmer for 2 to 3 hours. If using a pot over direct heat, simmer the grain on a very low setting for 2 to 3 hours, checking occasionally so it does not burn on the bottom. If necessary, add a little water.

Add dried fruit and milk and cook for another 30 minutes. Serve with your choice of milk and perhaps fresh fruit, or Jiffy Fruit Sauce (page 310).

A New World of Whole Grains

Create combinations that are uniquely yours. Equal proportions of barley, kamut berries, and oat groats make a delightful mixture. Use any combination to total the amount of whole grain in the recipe on this or the next page; the mixture might include wheat groats, millet, or brown rice. To boost the protein and mineral content, include quinoa or amaranth. Grains can be pre-rinsed (see page xx). For dried fruit, experiment with raisins, cranberries, chopped apricots, prunes, figs, or dates. Add some or all of the optional ingredients listed in the recipe on the next page. For the nuts and seeds, choose among chopped almonds, walnuts, cashews, hazelnuts, whole or ground flaxseeds, and sesame, pumpkin, or sunflower seeds.

*Analysis based on oat groats, kamut berries, millet (all whole grains), and raisins.

*Per 1 cup (250 ml):	
calories	201
protein	6 g
fat	2 g
carbohydrate	42 g
dietary fiber	4 g
calcium	52 mg
iron	1.7 mg
magnesium	34 mg
sodium	256 mg
zinc	1.2 mg
folate	12 mcg
riboflavin	0.1 mg
vitamin B_{12}	0.3 mcg
vitamin C	1 mg
vitamin E	1 mg
omega-3s	0.1 g
% calories from:	
protein	11%
fat	8%
carbohydrate	81%

YOUR VERY OWN WHOLE GRAIN CEREAL

Yield: 10 cups (2.5 L)

A slow cooker is ideal for preparing whole grains for breakfast. It simmers the cereal gently while you sleep through the night, then it's hot and ready when you awake. This slow method allows even more of the grain's natural sweetness to develop and makes the minerals in it more available. Refrigerate any leftovers for the next day's breakfast, or serve it later in the day, warm or cold, as a creamy pudding for a snack or dessert. The cereal will thicken as it cools, so you may want to add more liquid.

2 cups	uncooked grain	500 ml
8 cups	water	2 L
1 teaspoon	salt (or less if you prefer)	5 ml
1 cup	dried fruit	250 ml
1 cup	fortified soy, rice, or cow's milk	250 ml

Optional Ingredients

1/2 cup	seeds or chopped nuts	125 ml
1/2 cup	shredded dried coconut	125 ml
2 teaspoons	vanilla extract	10 ml
2 tablespoons	pure maple syrup	30 ml
1 teaspoon	cinnamon	5 ml

Place the grain in a sieve and rinse well. Combine the grain, water, and salt in a large slow cooker and cook on low heat for about 8 hours or overnight, until most of the water has been absorbed. Then add dried fruit, milk, and any optional ingredients, and cook for 30 minutes more or longer. If the mixture is too thick, add more water or milk. Serve hot or cold for breakfast with fresh fruit or Jiffy Fruit Sauce (page 310) and your choice of milk.

*Analysis based on oat groats, kamut berries, millet (all whole grains), and raisins.

*Per 1 cup (250 ml):	
calories	201
protein	6 g
fat	2 g
carbohydrate	42 g
dietary fiber	4 g
calcium	52 mg
iron	1.7 mg
magnesium	34 mg
sodium	256 mg
zinc	1.2 mg
folate	12 mcg
riboflavin	0.1 mg
vitamin B$_{12}$	0.3 mcg
vitamin C	1 mg
vitamin E	1 mg
omega-3s	0.1 g
% calories from:	
protein	11%
fat	8%
carbohydrate	81%

SCRAMBLED TOFU

Yield: 3 servings (1¹/2 cups/375 ml)

This dish can be the foundation of a hearty breakfast and is a favorite with vegetarian teens and athletes. Its soft texture makes it appealing for seniors, too. Nutritional yeast and turmeric give this dish a yellow color similar to scrambled eggs. The color of nutritional yeast comes from the bright yellow vitamin riboflavin. Turmeric contains a golden substance called curcumin that inhibits cancer and is an effective anti-inflammatory agent. For bone building, choose tofu that includes calcium on the ingredients list (amounts vary from brand to brand).

1 pound	firm tofu	450 g
2 tablespoons	nutritional yeast flakes	30 ml
1/4 teaspoon	turmeric, optional	1 ml
1/4 teaspoon	salt	1 ml
	pepper	
2 tablespoons	chopped fresh parsley	30 ml
2 teaspoons	olive oil	10 ml
1 cup	sliced mushrooms	250 ml
2 tablespoons	chopped green onion	30 ml
1 or 2	garlic cloves, minced	1 or 2

Drain the tofu well and mash it with a fork (see Chef's Tip, page 328). Stir in the yeast, turmeric, if using, salt, pepper to taste, and parsley. Mix well and set aside. Heat the oil in a heavy pan or cast-iron skillet over medium heat. Add the mushrooms, onion, and garlic and sauté until soft. Add the tofu mixture and stir and cook for 2 to 3 minutes until warmed through. Serve immediately with toast.

Flavor Booster

For even more flavor, add 1 to 2 tablespoons (15 to 30 ml) of tamari or Bragg Liquid Aminos and up to 1 teaspoon (5 ml) of your favorite mixed seasoning (such as Spike or an Italian herb blend).

*Analysis based on Red Star Vegetarian Support Formula nutritional yeast (a source of vitamin B$_{12}$) and calcium-set tofu.

*Per 1/2 cup (125 ml):	
calories	286
protein	28 g
fat	17 g
carbohydrate	12 g
dietary fiber	6 g
calcium	1,045 mg
iron	17 mg
magnesium	102 mg
sodium	221 mg
zinc	4 mg
folate	171 mcg
riboflavin	5 mg
vitamin B$_{12}$	4 mcg
vitamin C	5 mg
vitamin E	0.5 mg
omega-3s	0.9 g
% calories from:	
protein	37%
fat	48%
carbohydrate	15%

QUICK CHOCOLATE SHAKE

Yield: 1¼ cups (310 ml)

This shake is an excellent source of calcium and vitamins B₁₂ and D. It also provides instant energy.

1	banana, fresh or frozen (see Chef's Tip)	1
2 teaspoons	cocoa powder	10 ml
¾ cup	fortified soy, rice, or cow's milk	185 ml

If using a fresh banana, peel it and break into chunks. Place fresh or frozen banana chunks in a blender along with the cocoa and milk. Process until smooth.

Protein Booster

For an extra 10 grams of protein, blend in 2 tablespoons (30 ml) of soy protein powder (soy protein isolate) plus an additional 2 teaspoons (10 ml) of cocoa powder. This shake tastes best when served cold. For a shake that provides 31 grams of protein, try this variation using ¼ cup (60 ml) soy protein powder.

Chef's Tip: Use Frozen Bananas for Thick, Cold Shakes, Smoothies, and Berry Delicious "Ice Cream"!

- Select ripe bananas for freezing as they are much sweeter and have a less starchy aftertaste.
- To prepare bananas for freezing, peel them and leave whole, or break them into chunks. Then place them in plastic bags or airtight containers and freeze.
- A squeeze of fresh lemon juice sprinkled on the bananas will keep them from turning brown.
- Frozen bananas last several weeks, depending on their ripeness and the freezer's temperature.

Analysis based on vanilla soymilk fortified with vitamins B₁₂ and D, riboflavin, and calcium.

*Per recipe:	
calories	175
protein	7 g
fat	3 g
carbohydrate	35 g
dietary fiber	4 g
calcium	222 mg
iron	0.9 mg
magnesium	52 mg
sodium	107 mg
zinc	1.8 mg
folate	24 mcg
riboflavin	0.4 mg
vitamin B₁₂	2.3 mcg
vitamin C	11 mg
vitamin E	0.5 mg
omega-3s	0.1 g
% calories from:	
protein	14%
fat	15%
carbohydrate	71%

SNEAKY DAD'S POWER SMOOTHIE

Yield: 2 servings (3$^1/_2$ cups/875 ml)

This recipe was developed by Louisville lawyer John Borders as a nutrient-dense breakfast or snack for his three children. If you like, any needed supplements may be added to it. Set your young helper beside you on a stool near the blender and begin!

1 cup	calcium-fortified orange juice	250 ml
1 cup	fortified vanilla soymilk	250 ml
1$^1/_2$	frozen bananas (see Chef's Tip, page 315)	1$^1/_2$
1 cup	frozen strawberries	250 ml
1 to 2 tablespoons	ground flaxseeds, or 1 to 2 teaspoons flaxseed oil (5 to 10 ml)	15 to 30 ml
1 tablespoon	nut butter (cashew or almond butter)	15 ml
$^1/_4$	avocado, optional	$^1/_4$

Place the juice, soymilk, bananas, strawberries, flaxseeds, nut butter, and avocado, if using, in a blender, and process until very smooth and creamy. Serve with a straw.

Chef's Tips

#1: You may vary this smoothie recipe in many ways as long you use a 1:1 ratio of total liquids and total frozen fruit. You may double the amount of nut butter or avocado (bringing the calories up to 407), replace the strawberries with pitted cherries, raspberries, or other fresh fruit, or add $^1/_4$ cup (60 ml) cooked carrots.

#2: Roasted nut butters tend to overpower the flavor of the fruit, so raw nut butters are preferable. Experiment with different nut butters to see which your children like best. If you'd like to use peanut butter, try substituting chocolate or carob soymilk for the orange juice.

Nutritional Note

For a child weighing about 30 pounds (14 kilograms), one serving of this smoothie will provide about 25 percent of the day's recommended intake for calories, iron, vitamin A, vitamin D, niacin, and omega-3 fatty acids; 33 percent of the protein, zinc, manganese, riboflavin, thiamin, folate, and fiber; 50 percent of the calcium, phosphorus, and vitamin E; and all of the copper, magnesium, and vitamins B$_6$, B$_{12}$, and C.

Per half recipe:

calories	300
protein	8 g
fat	8 g
carbohydrate	54 g
dietary fiber	6 g
calcium	326 mg
iron	2.5 mg
magnesium	74 mg
sodium	80 mg
zinc	3.0 mg
folate	55 mcg
riboflavin	0.2 mg
vitamin B$_{12}$	1.5 mcg
vitamin C	78 mg
vitamin E	3.2 mg
omega-3s	0.7 g
% calories from:	
protein	10%
fat	22%
carbohydrate	68%

FRUIT SMOOTHIE

Yield: 2 cups (500 ml)

For delicious combinations, try apple juice with blueberries, raspberries, or mango. Made with apple juice and blueberries, this smoothie provides 2 mg of vitamin E and plenty of phytochemicals. With orange juice and strawberries, it's rich in vitamin C. For increased thickness, use frozen fruit. If using room temperature fruits, those who prefer a colder drink can add a few ice cubes before blending (this will also make the smoothie thicker).

1	banana, fresh or frozen (see Chef's Tip, page 315)	1
1 cup	berries or sliced fruit	250 ml
1 cup	fruit juice	250 ml

Peel the banana, break into chunks, and place in a blender along with the fruit and juice. Process until smooth.

Vitamin C Booster

This is the Pink Cadillac of smoothies and is especially refreshing. Use fresh-squeezed orange juice as your base (three oranges will make about 1 cup/250 ml of juice). Replace the banana with 1 cup (250 ml) of sliced mango, and use strawberries for the berries. This provides 132 mg of vitamin C.

Protein Booster

Blend in 2 tablespoons (30 ml) soy protein powder (isolated soy protein) and/or replace the juice with soymilk. Using ¼ cup (60 ml) protein powder will provide 14 grams of protein per 1 cup (250 ml) of smoothie.

Omega-3 Booster

Add 1 teaspoon (5 ml) of flaxseed oil.

*Per 1 cup (250 ml):

calories	135
protein	2 g
fat	0.7 g
carbohydrate	22 g
dietary fiber	4 g
calcium	26 mg
iron	0.6 mg
magnesium	38 mg
sodium	3 mg
zinc	0.3 mg
folate	80 mcg
riboflavin	0.1 mg
vitamin B$_{12}$	0 mcg
vitamin C	101 mg
vitamin E	0.8 mg
omega-3s	0.1 g
% calories from:	
protein	5%
fat	4%
carbohydrate	91%

Analysis based on using orange juice and strawberries.

BLACK BEAN SOUP

Yield: 4 servings (6 cups/1.5 L)

Black beans are a staple in Mexico and Central and South America. They form the basis of wonderful soups, such as this one, as well as stews and salads. A quick vegetable stock can be made from cubes or powder or you can use ready-made. Water can be used instead of stock, though your soup will be less flavorful. If you use a little less liquid, this recipe makes a fine stew. Lime juice added just before serving gives the soup a bright note. This recipe is from Cooking Vegetarian *by V. Melina and J. Forest (John Wiley & Sons; New York, NY).*

1 cup	diced carrots	250 ml
1 cup	diced celery	250 ml
1/2	onion, diced	1/2
1	garlic clove, minced	1
1 tablespoon	olive oil	15 ml
3 cups	cooked or canned black beans	750 ml
4 cups	vegetable stock	1 L
1/4 cup	tomato paste	60 ml
1 1/2 teaspoons	ground cumin	7 ml
1 teaspoon	dried oregano	5 ml
1 teaspoon	dried thyme	5 ml
2 teaspoons	lime juice	10 ml
	salt and pepper	

Combine the carrots, celery, onion, garlic, and oil in a large pot and sauté over medium heat for 5 minutes. Stir in the beans, stock, tomato paste, cumin, oregano, and thyme. Cover and simmer for 20 minutes or until the vegetables are cooked. Just before serving, stir in the lime juice. Add salt and pepper to taste.

Per 1 1/2 cup (375 ml):

calories	256
protein	13 g
fat	4 g
carbohydrate	44 g
dietary fiber	10 g
calcium	131 mg
iron	6 mg
magnesium	90 mg
sodium	217 mg
zinc	1.4 mg
folate	140 mcg
riboflavin	0.2 mg
vitamin B$_{12}$	0 mcg
vitamin C	14 mg
vitamin E	2 mg
omega-3s	0.1 g
% calories from:	
protein	19%
fat	15%
carbohydrate	66%

ZUCCHINI CHEDDA SOUP

Yield: 7 cups (1.75 L)

This marvelous soup is adapted from The Ultimate Uncheese Cookbook *by Joanne Stepaniak (Book Publishing Company; Summertown, TN). It features a rich, tempting broth with lots of delicate zucchini. Cheese lovers adore it!*

3	medium zucchini, diced	3
1	medium onion, diced	1
4 cups	water	1 L
1/2 cup	drained pimento pieces or chopped red bell pepper	125 ml
1/4 cup	tahini	60 ml
1/4 cup	quick-cooking rolled oats	60 ml
3 tablespoons	nutritional yeast flakes	45 ml
1/4 cup	raw cashew pieces (see page 308)	60 ml
2 tablespoons	tamari	30 ml
4 teaspoons	fresh lemon juice	20 ml
1 1/2 teaspoons	dried oregano	7 ml
1 teaspoon	salt	5 ml
2	small cloves garlic, chopped	2
1/8 teaspoon	ground allspice	0.5 ml
1/8 teaspoon	dill seed	0.5 ml
	pepper	

Combine the zucchini, onion, and water in a large pot and bring to a boil. Lower the heat and simmer for 20 to 25 minutes or until the vegetables are very tender. Using a large measuring cup, take out about 1½ cups (375 ml) of the broth, including some of the zucchini and onion, and place in a blender. Add the pimento, tahini, oats, nutritional yeast, cashews, tamari, lemon juice, oregano, salt, garlic, allspice, and dill seed. Process until very smooth. Pour the blended ingredients back into the soup pot with the diced zucchini, onion, and water. Season to taste with pepper. Heat the soup gently, stirring often, until it is slightly thickened and warmed through, about 10 minutes. Do not boil.

Analysis based on Red Star Vegetarian Support Formula nutritional yeast (a source of vitamin B_{12}).

Per 1 cup (250 ml):	
calories	127
protein	6 g
fat	7 g
carbohydrate	12 g
dietary fiber	3 g
calcium	54 mg
iron	2.2 mg
magnesium	49 mg
sodium	634 mg
zinc	1.5 mg
folate	74 mcg
riboflavin	1.8 mg
vitamin B_{12}	1.3 mcg
vitamin C	22 mg
vitamin E	1 mg
omega-3s	0 g
% calories from:	
protein	16%
fat	49%
carbohydrate	35%

MUENSTER CHEEZE

Yield: 2½ cups (625 ml)

This recipe, adapted from The Ultimate Uncheese Cookbook *by Joanne Stepaniak (Book Publishing Company; Summertown, TN), is reminiscent of the German original. The dome-shaped "cheese" can be cut into wedges or slices.*

1½ cups	water	375 ml
⅓ cup	agar flakes	85 ml
	or 2 teaspoons agar powder (10 ml)	
½ cup	raw cashew pieces	125 ml
½ cup	firm silken tofu	125 ml
¼ cup	nutritional yeast flakes	60 ml
¼ cup	fresh lemon juice	60 ml
2 tablespoons	tahini, optional	30 ml
1½ teaspoons	onion powder	7 ml
1 teaspoon	salt	5 ml
½ teaspoon	dry mustard	2 ml
¼ teaspoon	garlic powder	1 ml
¼ teaspoon	ground caraway seeds, optional	1 ml
½ to ¾ cup	canned jalapeño peppers, chopped	125 to 185 ml
½ teaspoon	paprika	2 ml

Lightly oil two nicely shaped, round-bottomed bowls, each able to hold 1½ cups (375 ml). Set aside. Combine the water and agar in a small saucepan and bring to a boil. Reduce the heat and simmer, stirring often, until dissolved, about 5 minutes. Place in a blender along with the cashews, tofu, nutritional yeast, lemon juice, tahini, if using, onion powder, salt, mustard, garlic powder, and caraway seeds. Process until completely smooth. The mixture will be very thick. Stir in the chopped jalapeño peppers immediately after blending. Pour the mixture equally into the prepared bowls and allow it to cool. Cover and chill several hours or overnight. To serve, turn out of the bowls onto serving plates. Sprinkle all over (top and sides) with paprika from a spice shaker. Leftovers may be covered and stored in the refrigerator for several days.

Analysis based on Red Star Vegetarian Support Formula nutritional yeast (a source of vitamin B$_{12}$).

Per ¼ cup (60 ml):	
calories	62
protein	3 g
fat	4 g
carbohydrate	5 g
dietary fiber	1 g
calcium	13 mg
iron	0.7 mg
magnesium	26 mg
sodium	283 mg
zinc	1 mg
folate	46 mcg
riboflavin	1.6 mg
vitamin B$_{12}$	1.2 mcg
vitamin C	5 mg
vitamin E	0.8 mg
omega-3s	0 g
% calories from:	
protein	20%
fat	51%
carbohydrate	29%

Chef's Tip: Agar

Agar, also known as agar-agar, is derived from a type of red seaweed. It is an excellent replacement for gelatin (which is made from the bones and hooves of cattle and horses). Agar is sold at natural food stores in the form of dried white flakes. It also can be found very inexpensively at Asian stores in the form of powder or bars.

Agar must be thoroughly dissolved in liquid and heated for it to gel. Because its gel-forming abilities are powerful, take care to use the amount and type specified in recipes. Even then, there can be some variation from one brand of agar to another. We discovered this by trial and error when we created recipe failures that could double as hockey pucks!

> 1 tablespoon (15 ml) agar flakes will thicken 1 cup (250 ml) liquid
> ¾ teaspoon (4 ml) agar powder will thicken 1 cup (250 ml) liquid

As with gelatin, increased amounts of agar are required with more acidic liquids.

Chef's Tip: Roasting Nuts and Seeds

Roasting nuts and seeds is a wonderful way to bring out their flavor, especially when used in recipes like Hazelnut Paté (page 323). It's essential to watch the timing and check them frequently, however. Nuts and seeds can burn quickly because they contain so little water.

Oven method. Preheat the oven to 350°F (175°C). Place the nuts or seeds on a baking sheet or in a pan and roast for about 5 minutes.

Stove-top method. Place the nuts or seeds in a pan and cook over medium heat for about 5 minutes, stirring occasionally.

Microwave method. Place the nuts in a microwave-safe pan or plate, and roast on medium-low heat for 3 to 4 minutes or on medium-high heat for 1 to 2 minutes.

ANGELIC TOFU SANDWICH FILLING

Yield: 2¹/₂ cups/625 ml (enough for 5 to 6 sandwiches)

How about making a switch from deviled egg sandwiches to "angelic" tofu sandwiches? The flavor similarity is remarkable. Make a batch for lunchbox sandwiches (leftovers can be refrigerated to fill sandwiches the next day). Serve it on a lettuce leaf with raw veggies and a crusty roll on the side. Try it as a spread on crackers or serve it as a dip. Use it to fill a pita pocket along with chopped tomatoes and lettuce or sprouts.

1 pound	firm tofu, drained*	454 g
2 to 3 tablespoons	vegan or other mayonnaise	30 to 45 ml
2 teaspoons	tamari or Bragg Liquid Aminos	10 ml
1 tablespoon	nutritional yeast flakes	15 ml
¹/₄ cup	finely chopped onions	60 ml
¹/₂ cup	finely chopped celery	125 ml
	salt and pepper	

Optional Ingredients

2 teaspoons	prepared mustard, any kind	10 ml
2 tablespoons	finely chopped parsley	30 ml
6	olives, diced	6
¹/₃ cup	diced sweet or dill pickles	85 ml
3 tablespoons	toasted sunflower seeds	45 ml

Place the drained tofu in bowl and mash with a fork or potato masher. Stir in the mayonnaise, using just enough to make the tofu hold together. Add the tamari, nutritional yeast, onions, celery, salt and pepper to taste, and any of the optional ingredients you are using.

*If using water-packed, Chinese-style tofu, you will need to press out the water first. (See Chef's Tip on page 325.)

Analysis based on calcium-set firm tofu and Red Star Vegetarian Support Formula nutritional yeast (a source of vitamin B₁₂).

Per ¹/₂ cup (125 ml):	
calories	152
protein	16 g
fat	9 g
carbohydrate	6 g
dietary fiber	3 g
calcium	627 mg
iron	10 mg
magnesium	58 mg
sodium	183 mg
zinc	1.7 mg
folate	51 mcg
riboflavin	0.9 mg
vitamin B₁₂	0.6 mcg
vitamin C	2 mg
vitamin E	0.1 mg
omega-3s	0.5 g
% calories from:	
protein	38%
fat	48%
carbohydrate	14%

HAZELNUT PÂTÉ

Yield: 2 cups (500 ml)

This spread, from our original edition of Becoming Vegetarian, *won the Best Appetizer of the Show award at North America's largest natural foods show, Natural Products Expo West, held annually in Anaheim, California. It is an innovative way to take advantage of the full flavor of hazelnuts and mushrooms. Serve it on crackers or sliced French bread or use it as a sandwich filling. For festive occasions, form it into a ball on a plate and decorate it with parsley, chives, basil leaves and flowers, or chopped hazelnuts, and surround it with crackers.*

1 teaspoon	olive oil	5 ml
1/2 cup	sliced onions	125 ml
1 cup	sliced mushrooms	250 ml
2	cloves garlic, chopped	2
1 cup	roasted hazelnuts (see Chef's Tip, page 321)	250 ml
1/4 cup	chopped fresh parsley	60 ml
1 tablespoon	tamari or Bragg Liquid Aminos	15 ml
2 teaspoons	nutritional yeast flakes	10 ml
1/4 teaspoon	salt	1 ml
pinch	pepper	pinch
	lemon juice or water	

Heat the oil in a medium skillet. Add the onions and sauté over medium heat until they begin to brown, about 5 minutes. Add the mushrooms and garlic and cook until soft, about 3 minutes. Grind the hazelnuts to a fine powder in a food processor. Add the sautéed mixture to the powdered nuts and process until very smooth, stopping occasionally to scrape down the sides of the processor bowl. Add the parsley, tamari, nutritional yeast, salt, and pepper, and blend well. Add a small amount of lemon juice or water to thin the mixture, if desired.

Variation: Add 1/4 cup (60 ml) of cooked kale or carrots, or 1 tablespoon (15 ml) of chopped black olives to the food processor at the same time as the sautéed mixture.

Analysis based on Red Star Vegetarian Support Formula nutritional yeast, (a source of vitamin B$_{12}$).

Per 2 tablespoons (30 ml):	
calories	61
protein	2 g
fat	5 g
carbohydrate	2 g
dietary fiber	1 g
calcium	13 mg
iron	0.6 mg
magnesium	16 mg
sodium	64 mg
zinc	0.3 mg
folate	16 mcg
riboflavin	0.2 mg
vitamin B$_{12}$	0.1 mcg
vitamin C	2 mg
vitamin E	1 mg
omega-3s	0 g
% calories from:	
protein	10%
fat	75%
carbohydrate	15%

TEN TEMPTING WAYS TO FILL A SANDWICH

Beyond the basic peanut butter sandwich, what can vegetarians take in their lunchboxes or arrange on a pretty sandwich plate? When you begin to search, you'll be delighted by what you discover. The options are never-ending. Here are just a few favorites.

Bread or Roll	Fillings and Veggies	Other Ingredients
Baguette or bagel	Hazelnut pâté (page 323) or store-bought sunflower seed pâté Cucumber slices, onion, sprouts	
Sourdough roll	Veggie burger (hot or cold) Lettuce, tomato, onion	Vegan or other mayonnaise, relish, ketchup, mustard
Russian rye bread	Veggie salami or deli slices Pickles or sauerkraut, onions, lettuce Dijon mustard	Vegan or other mayonnaise
Rice paper wrap	Marinated or flavored tofu strips with or without cooked rice Shredded carrots, cucumber strips, lettuce, sprouts, sunflower seeds, chopped peanuts	Peanut sauce or plum sauce
Whole wheat sub	Veggie ham, turkey, and soy cheese slices Onions, shredded lettuce, cucumber, tomatoes, sprouts	Vegan or other mayonnaise, or mustard

This is just a beginning. There are plenty of flavorful veggie "meats" that make excellent sandwich fillings. You can combine slices to make a hero sandwich or spread a roll with guacamole. A book that contains great sandwich and spread recipes is *The Natural Lunchbox* by J. Brown (Book Publishing Company; Summertown, TN).

Bread or Roll	Fillings and Veggies	Other Ingredients
Crusty roll	Small veggie pepperoni slices Shredded lettuce, black or green olives, tomatoes, onions, sliced green or red pepper	Vegan or other mayonnaise
Multigrain bread	Angelic Tofu Sandwich Filling (page 322) Lettuce, sprouts, tomato slices	Nonhydrogenated margarine
Whole wheat toast	Veggie Canadian bacon and soy cheese slices Tomato and onion slices	Olive oil brushed on outside of bread*
Dried tomato or spinach flour tortilla	Refried beans Roasted cashews and peanuts, sunflower sprouts, avocado slices, shredded carrots, green onions	Salsa
Pita bread	Hummus (homemade or from deli) Diced tomato, onions, sprouts, olives, shredded romaine lettuce	

* Cook sandwich in skillet until browned on both sides.

VEGGIE CLUBHOUSE SANDWICH

Yield: 1 sandwich

For this sandwich, we have suggested the Yves products, as they are fortified with zinc, iron, and vitamin B$_{12}$, though other products will also work. With the wide variety of veggie "meats" available near the produce section in supermarket coolers, sandwich making can be simple. Try vegetarian alternatives for old favorites, such as the clubhouse or BLT (bacon-lettuce-tomato). For those with hearty appetites, this triple-decker is packed with protein, B vitamins, and minerals. It is an appealing combination of colors, textures, and flavors. The veggie bacon can be sautéed to bring out the flavor more, though this step may be omitted as the slices are precooked.

3 slices	whole wheat bread	3
2 tablespoons	vegan or other mayonnaise	30 ml
3 slices	Yves Veggie Turkey	3 slices
1 or 2	lettuce leaves	1 or 2
3 slices	Yves Canadian Veggie Bacon	3
1/2 teaspoon	olive oil, optional	2 ml
4 slices	tomato	4 slices
pinch	salt	pinch
pinch	black pepper	pinch

Toast the bread and spread the mayonnaise on one side of each slice. Place the veggie turkey slices and lettuce on the bottom piece of toast and cover with a second slice of toast. If you wish to cook the veggie bacon, sauté it in oil in a small skillet over medium heat for 30 seconds on each side. (Do not overcook it, as low-fat veggie meats will become too dry.) Place the veggie bacon and tomato on top of the second slice of toast. Sprinkle salt and pepper on the tomato and top with the remaining piece of toast. Cut diagonally into 4 pieces and serve.

Per sandwich:	
calories	457
protein	38 g
fat	12 g
carbohydrate	52 g
dietary fiber	7 g
calcium	140 mg
iron	6 mg
magnesium	82 mg
sodium	1,129 mg
zinc	2 mg
folate	59 mcg
riboflavin	0.2 mg
vitamin B$_{12}$	3 mcg
vitamin C	23 mg
vitamin E	2 mg
omega-3s	0.1 g
% calories from:	
protein	33%
fat	23%
carbohydrate	44%

WORLD'S GREATEST GREENS

Yield: 4 servings (3 cups/750 ml)

Greens such as kale and collards are great calcium sources, but we may not know how to prepare them in appealing ways. This recipe provides a delightful solution! It's so delicious that it's practically addictive. You may use just kale or collards or a combination of both. If you like, you can include 1 cup (250 ml) or so of sharper greens, such as mustard greens or watercress. All of these contain calcium that is well absorbed. Chinese greens are an excellent choice, too.

12 cups	kale or collard greens (2 lb/900 g)	3 L
1 to 2 tablespoons	olive oil	15 to 30 ml
4	cloves garlic, minced	4
2 teaspoons	paprika	10 ml
2 teaspoons	cumin	10 ml
3 cups	chopped fresh parsley, cilantro, or a mixture	750 ml
1/2 teaspoon	tamari	2 ml
1	lemon, cut in wedges or 2 teaspoons fresh lemon juice (10 ml)	1

Remove and discard the stems from the greens, and chop the leaves into strips that are roughly 1 inch (2.5 cm) wide. Cook the greens in a vegetable steamer until soft. Drain well. In large, preheated skillet, combine the oil, garlic, paprika, and cumin and cook over medium heat for 1 to 2 minutes, taking care not to let the garlic get too brown. Add the cooked greens, parsley, and tamari. Stir well to evenly distribute the seasonings. Serve with wedges of fresh lemon. Alternatively, sprinkle with lemon juice just before serving.

Nutritional Note

In addition to all the minerals, folate, riboflavin, vitamins C and E, and omega-3 fatty acids listed at right, a ¾-cup (185-ml) serving provides 13,570 mcg of beta-carotene and 1,838 mcg of vitamin K. This is a delicious alternative to a multivitamin-mineral supplement!

Per ¾ cup (185 ml):	
calories	172
protein	9 g
fat	6 g
carbohydrate	28 g
dietary fiber	6 g
calcium	371 mg
iron	7 mg
magnesium	100 mg
sodium	156 mg
zinc	1.4 mg
folate	135 mcg
riboflavin	0.4 mg
vitamin B_{12}	0 mcg
vitamin C	312 mg
vitamin E	2.5 mg
omega-3s	0.5 g
% calories from:	
protein	18%
fat	25%
carbohydrate	57%

GO-FOR-THE-GREEN SALAD

Yield: 14 cups (3.5 L)

This colorful salad is packed with health-supportive antioxidants and phytochemicals. A serving that includes the almonds and seeds provides 100 mg of calcium; without the nuts and seeds, one serving has 80 mg of calcium. Be creative with your choices of additional vegetables—radishes, cucumbers, snow peas, cauliflower, broccoli, daikon, celery, alfalfa or lentil sprouts, and avocado work very well.

8 cups	bite-size pieces of romaine or leaf lettuce	2 L
4 cups	thinly sliced kale leaves (stems removed)	1 L
2³/₄ cups	broccoli or sunflower sprouts (3 oz./100 g container)	685 ml
1 cup	grated carrots or golden beets	250 ml
1 cup	cherry tomatoes	250 ml
¹/₂ each	sweet red and yellow peppers, sliced	¹/₂ each
¹/₄ cup	pumpkin seeds, optional	60 ml
¹/₄ cup	almonds, raw or toasted, optional	60 ml

Place the lettuce, kale, sprouts, carrots, tomatoes, and sweet peppers in a large salad bowl along with the seeds and almonds, if using. Toss with Liquid Gold Dressing (page 329) or another favorite dressing.

Chef's Tip: How to Press Excess Water from Firm Tofu

When firm tofu is used in certain recipes, such as Scrambled Tofu (page 314) and Angelic Tofu Sandwich Filling (page 322), it should first be pressed to remove excess water. Otherwise, liquid may seep onto the serving plate. To press tofu, first drain it and place the block on a plate or in a shallow bowl. Cover the tofu with a plate or small cutting board and carefully set a weight on top, such as a large can of tomato sauce or a 32-ounce (1-L) Tetra pack of soymilk. Let the tofu rest under this pressure for 15 to 20 minutes. By then, about ½ cup (125 ml) of liquid will have pooled on the bottom plate; this fluid can be discarded. Pat the block of tofu dry with a clean towel, place in a bowl, mash with a fork, and proceed with recipe.

Per 2 cups (500 ml):	
calories	48
protein	3 g
fat	0.6 g
carbohydrate	10 g
dietary fiber	3 g
calcium	86 mg
iron	2 mg
magnesium	27 mg
sodium	30 mg
zinc	0.5 mg
folate	113 mcg
riboflavin	0.2 mg
vitamin B_{12}	0 mcg
vitamin C	100 mg
vitamin E	1.2 mg
omega-3s	0.2 g
% calories from:	
protein	24%
fat	10%
carbohydrate	66%

LIQUID GOLD DRESSING

Yield: 1^1/$_2$ cups (375 ml)

Vesanto developed this dressing for use on salads, baked potatoes, rice, steamed broccoli, and other veggies. We gave it the name "Liquid Gold," and not just because of the color. Two tablespoons (30 ml) provides 5 grams of omega-3 fatty acids (a full day's supply, and then some) along with 40 percent of our B$_{12}$ for the day when it's made with Red Star Vegetarian Support Formula nutritional yeast. This creamy dressing is packed with riboflavin and other B vitamins—plus, it's very tasty. If you add ground flaxseeds, use the larger amount of water, as the dressing will gradually thicken.

^{1}/$_2$ cup	flaxseed oil	125 ml
^{1}/$_3$ to ^{1}/$_2$ cup	water	85 to 125 ml
^{1}/$_3$ cup	lemon juice	85 ml
2 tablespoons	balsamic or raspberry vinegar	30 ml
^{1}/$_4$ cup	tamari or Bragg Liquid Aminos	60 ml
^{1}/$_4$ cup	nutritional yeast flakes	60 ml
2 teaspoons	Dijon mustard	10 ml
1 teaspoon	ground cumin	5 ml
1 tablespoon	ground flaxseeds, optional	15 ml

Place the oil, water, lemon juice, vinegar, tamari, nutritional yeast, mustard, cumin, and flaxseeds, if using, in a blender and process until smooth. The dressing can be kept in a jar with a lid and refrigerated for two weeks.

Green Goddess Dressing

Replace the mustard and cumin with 1 cup (250 ml) of fresh herbs (basil, oregano, and parsley work very well) and 3 cloves of garlic, chopped. Because this variation doesn't contain mustard, the oil and water layers are more likely to separate, so be sure to shake it well before using. (Mustard helps hold emulsions together.)

Per 2 tablespoons (30 ml):	
calories	96
protein	1 g
fat	7 g
carbohydrate	2 g
dietary fiber	0.4 g
calcium	4 mg
iron	0.4 mg
magnesium	6 mg
sodium	180 mg
zinc	0.5 mg
folate	33 mcg
riboflavin	1.3 mg
vitamin B$_{12}$	1 mcg
vitamin C	3 mg
vitamin E	0.2 mg
omega-3s	5 g
% calories from:	
protein	7%
fat	85%
carbohydrate	8%

SIMPLE SPROUTING

The process of sprouting greatly increases the availability of zinc and other minerals in legumes, grains, nuts, and seeds, making it easier for our bodies to absorb these minerals. Sprouts, which are also loaded with vitamins and phytochemicals, add an interesting texture and flavor to salads, sandwiches, and stir-fries. They can be a valuable way to get fresh foods in challenging circumstances, such as northern winters when little local produce is available, or while sailing, or if we live far from produce markets. Campers and people living in remote areas (such as tree planters) can set up sprouting centers. Backpackers and cyclists have even been known to dangle mesh bags of sprouts from their packs! Sprout care is so simple that rinsing them and watching them grow may become a favorite occupation of young children.

Basic care of sprouts involves keeping them moist while providing drainage and air circulation. In the kitchen, place them on a countertop near a sink. Sprouts grow best when they are rinsed often and well drained. In warm weather, they mature more quickly and require frequent rinsing to keep them cool. Hot, direct sunlight can "cook" them; shade is better. To "green" alfalfa sprouts and sunflower greens, a balance of sun and shade works well.

Home sprout growing can be set up with jars, sprout bags, trays, or an automatic sprout grower. With all of these, the method is more or less the same. In the sprouting chart on the next page, we summarize the basic steps for a few dried legumes and raw, unhulled, unsalted seeds with amounts suitable for a 1-quart (1-liter) jar. You may grow your sprouts in wide-neck mason jars, which come in 1-quart (1-liter) and in ½-gallon (2-liter) sizes. Replace the lids with mesh held on with an elastic band, or use special sprouting lids with holes that allow for the necessary air circulation (available at many natural food stores).

Sprouting Summary

In a jar, cover lentils, beans, or seeds with about double the amount of water and soak for the time specified. Drain, rinse, and set the jar upside down at a 45-degree angle (the angle allows air to circulate). Rinse the sprouts at least twice a day by filling the jar with water and allowing it to overflow. Drain and again set it at a 45-degree angle. At harvest, rinse (with alfalfa sprouts, rinse off seed hulls), drain, place in a clean glass jar with a lid that allows air to circulate, and refrigerate. Sprouts will keep for four or five days.

For complete information on sprouting, see *Sprouts: The Miracle Food* by Steve Meyerowitz or *Sprout Garden: Indoor Grower's Guide to Gourmet Sprouts* by M. Braunstein (both from Book Publishing Company; Summertown, TN).

SPROUTING TIMES AND TIPS

Amounts given can be sprouted in a one quart (liter) jar

LENTILS

Amount:	$1/2$ cup (125 ml)
Soaking time:	12 hours
Length at harvest:	$1/4$ to $3/4$ inch (0.6 to 2 cm)
Days until ready:	3 to 5
Tips:	Try regular (green, brown, or gray) dry lentils and the smaller French dry lentils. Grow to either short or longer lengths.

MUNG BEANS

Amount:	$1/4$ cup (60 ml)
Soaking time:	12 hours
Length at harvest:	$1^1/2$ inches (3.8 cm)
Days until ready:	3 to 6
Tips:	The long mung bean sprouts of Chinese cooking are grown away from light, and a small weight is placed above the sprouts so they grow under pressure. This helps them become long. Here we give just the basic sprouting method.

ALFALFA SEEDS

Amount:	2 tablespoons (30 ml)
Soaking time:	4 to 6 hours
Length at harvest:	1 to $1^1/2$ inches (2.5 to 3.8 cm)
Days until ready:	4 to 6
Tips:	To develop chlorophyll and make the sprouts green, place in light 1 to 2 days before harvest.

SPROUTING SUNFLOWER SEEDS

To make sunflower greens, place $1/3$ cup (185 mL) unsalted sunflower seeds that are still in their hulls in a jar. Cover seeds with water and soak for 12 hours. Allow them to drain for another 12 hours using a sprouting lid or mesh on the mouth of the jar. Then scatter the soaked seeds on top of about 1 inch (2.5 centimeters) of topsoil spread on a tray. Over the next week, allow seeds to grow; a room temperature of 65 to 75°F (18 to 24°C) is best. Each day, sprinkle the sprouting seeds with water. To exclude light for the first two days, the tray may be covered with a few clean, damp sheets of paper, or placed in a dark cupboard. For days 3 through 7, the tray is moved to an area with indirect light. After a week, these delicious greens will be 5 to 8 inches (13 to 20 cm) in height. Harvest them with scissors or sharp knife.

COOKING THE BASICS

GREAT GRAINS

A whole world of grains awaits you to add variety and nutrition to your meals. Whole grains may be cooked in many ways: simmered on the stove-top, pressure-cooked, baked, or microwaved. (Below, we feature the standard stove-top method.) Whichever method you choose, be sure to use a pot or dish that is large enough to allow for the expansion of the grain. Millet, barley, and quinoa expand to four times their original size; other grains usually expand two to three times.

Cooking Whole Grains in Under 25 Minutes

Often people who don't use whole grains think they take too long to cook. Most whole grains take about 45 minutes to 1 hour to become tender. However, some small grains, such as quinoa, millet, and whole wheat couscous (which is actually a tiny pasta) can be prepared in 15 to 20 minutes. With larger grains, such as pot barley, brown rice, oat groats, and whole grain berries (rye, wheat, spelt, or kamut), the usual cooking time can be cut in half by pre-soaking the grains for several hours or overnight in about twice as much water as grain. You can then proceed to cook the grain and soaking water together, adding more water depending on which grain you're preparing.

Standard Cooking Method for Grains

To cook grains in the standard stove-top manner, use the amount of water suggested in the grain chart. (A little added salt is optional.) When you are ready to cook the soaked grains, cover and bring to a rapid boil. Stir, cover, and reduce the heat to a simmer. Cook without lifting the lid for approximately the time specified in the chart on the next page. Larger grains take longer than smaller ones. If you use a little less water, the cooking time will be slightly shorter and the texture of the cooked grain will be chewier. With millet, some people prefer to use 4 cups of water for each cup of grain for a creamier result, whereas others prefer the distinct grains produced by using 2 cups of water. If more water is used, the grains will be softer and stickier. Short-grain rice tends to be stickier than medium- or long-grain rice.

General Directions

Whole grains generally need to be washed before they are cooked. Place the grains in a pot, cover with about 2 inches of water, swirl it around, and pour off hulls and bits of debris that float to the surface. Then pour off all water, using a sieve so you don't lose any grains. Combine the rinsed grains with the measured amount of water in a pot with a lid, bring to a boil, cover, reduce the heat, and simmer for the recommended time. If you have hard water, the cooking time will be longer.

For a fluffier product, cook the grain as shown in the chart, then remove the pot from the heat and allow it to sit, covered, for 5 to 15 minutes. This works especially well for millet, quinoa, and bulgur.

It is important to note that cooking times for grains can vary considerably depending on how long the grains have been stored. Older grains will take longer to cook than grains that have been recently harvested.

Cooking Chart for Grains

GRAIN: 1 cup (250 ml)	WATER: cups (ml)	TIME*	YIELD
Amaranth	2 cups (500 ml)	25	2 cups (500 ml)
Barley, pot or pearled	3 cups (750 ml)	45	3$\frac{1}{2}$ cups (875 ml)
Buckwheat groats (kasha)	2 cups (500 ml)	15–20	2$\frac{1}{4}$ cups (560 ml)
Kamut	4 cups (1 L)	90	3$\frac{1}{4}$ cups (810 ml)
Millet	3 cups (750 ml)	25	4 cups (1 L)
Oat groats	3 to 4 cups (750 ml to 1 L)	60	3 cups (750 ml)
Quinoa	2 cups (500 ml)	20	3$\frac{1}{2}$ cups (875 ml)
Rice, brown, any type	2 cups (500 ml)	45	3 cups (750 ml)
Rice, wild	4 cups (1 L)	60	5 cups (1.25 L)
Rye	4 cups (1 L)	60	2$\frac{1}{2}$ cups (625 ml)
Wheat berries	4 cups (1 L)	90	3 cups (750 ml)
Wheat, bulgur	2$\frac{1}{2}$ cups (625 ml)	5–10	2$\frac{1}{2}$ cups (625 ml)
Wheat, cracked	2 cups (500 ml)	30	2$\frac{1}{2}$ cups (625 ml)

*Time = minutes to cook after lowering heat

Perfect Pilaf

Pilafs are quick and easy to make, and they allow freshly cooked or leftover grains to come alive with color, flavor, and nutrition. For example, lightly sauté chopped onion and garlic in a little oil. Add seasonings (choose from the list that follows or use your own ideas) and any combination of cashews, cubes of plain or marinated tofu or tempeh, sliced mushrooms or carrots, fresh or frozen peas, chopped sweet red peppers, or celery. Then stir in the cooked rice or other grain and heat for a few minutes, tossing, to warm through and mix the flavors. Grains that work especially well for pilafs are brown rice, combinations of brown and wild rice, or combinations of barley, wheat berries, and quinoa. Adjust the seasonings to taste. Serve the pilaf on a platter garnished with chopped nuts, cherry tomatoes, or parsley.

Seasoning Ideas

The following list provides seasoning suggestions to achieve particular flavors. Feel free to use any or all of the ingredients in each group.

Asian. Tamari or Bragg Liquid Aminos, sesame seeds, grated ginger, sea vegetable flakes or powder.

Mediterranean. Chopped fresh parsley, diced sweet peppers, basil, marjoram, oregano.

East Indian. Curry powder, garam masala, ground cumin, chopped cilantro, hot or sweet peppers, green onions, orange sections, cashews.

Chef's Tips for Great Grains

Bulgur. Add boiling water, cover, and let stand for 20 to 30 minutes. No cooking is necessary unless the bulgur is very coarse.

Millet. For a wonderful nutty flavor, toast millet in a heavy skillet over medium heat for 2 to 3 minutes before boiling. Millet is a sticky grain, which makes it an excellent choice for use in patties and loaves.

Quinoa. Because quinoa is coated with a very bitter resin, it needs to be rinsed well before cooking. Some brands are prerinsed.

Barley. One of the creamiest of all grains, barley makes a superb replacement for the rice in rice pudding recipes. Delicious!

Kamut or wheat berries. Excess water needs to be drained after cooking.

LEGUME LORE

Beans are such important providers of protein, iron, and zinc that it makes good sense to discover ways to use them that suit your lifestyle. A secret of many vegetarians is to stock the freezer with a variety of cooked beans to use in quick food preparation. These might include chickpeas for hummus or a stir-fry, kidney or pinto beans for a big batch of chili, black beans for soup, and several different beans (lima, pinto, and red) that can be made into a colorful stew or marinated bean salad. Whenever you cook beans (say, once a week), make extra. Then put them in freezer bags or plastic containers in portions to suit the number of people in your household. Lentil, pea, and bean soups also freeze well.

Legumes can be divided into two groups based on their size. Each group requires a different cooking method.

Group 1: Legumes That Do Not Require Presoaking

This group includes the smaller legumes that are about the size of a lentil. Presoaking is not required for them. However, if you have time, presoaking will speed up cooking and increase mineral availability. The cooking times listed are variable. Freshly harvested legumes cook quickly, but very old lentils and beans take much longer. For each cup (250 ml) of lentils or mung beans add 3 cups (750 ml) of water. .

Cooking time (minutes)	
Lentils, red	25–30
Lentils, brown or green	50–60
Mung beans	40–50
Split peas	40–50

Group 2: Legumes That Require Presoaking

This group includes all other beans, such as adzuki, kidney, lima, pinto, garbanzo, white, and black beans. These must be presoaked before cooking. Look through the beans to remove any small stones, then soak the beans overnight for at least 6 hours in at least three times the volume of water. Discard the water and rinse the beans thoroughly. Cover the beans with about 3 inches (7.5 cm) of fresh, unsalted water and boil hard for 1 minute. You may wish to add fennel seeds or kombu (a sea vegetable) to reduce the gas produced during digestion.

Cover and simmer for 1 to 2 hours. The cooked beans should be very tender and so soft that you can mash them with your tongue against the roof of your mouth. Very hard water (i.e, water that is high in minerals) or using beans that have been stored for several years can increase cooking time.

Don't add salt, tomatoes, or other highly acidic foods to beans until after the beans are cooked to the point of being tender. Otherwise, they will not soften properly and will remain difficult to digest. (Herbs and salt-free spices are fine to add, as they do not interfere with the softening process.) When the beans are fully cooked, add any seasonings you like and continue to cook for 10 minutes longer. The cooked beans can be eaten as is or used in recipes.

Cooking Beans in a Slow Cooker

Many people prefer to cook beans all day or overnight in a slow cooker. For every cup (250 ml) of presoaked beans, add 3 cups (750 ml) of fresh water. You may also add bay leaves, peppercorns, or your favorite herbs. Turn on the slow cooker in the morning, cover, and by dinner your beans will be perfect.

Chef's Tip for Reducing Presoaking Time

The long presoaking time of 6 to 10 hours can be shortened by a "quick soak." To do this, bring the beans to a boil, then remove them from the heat, cover, and let them rest for 1 hour. Next, discard the liquid, rinse the beans well, cover them with fresh water, and cook for the recommended time or until tender.

Seven

Super Simple

Suppers

These all-time favorites bring you flavors from around the globe: North America, India, England, Mexico, China, Africa, and Italy

HOT TOFU WITH COOL GREENS

Yield: 2 hearty servings

This is one of Brenda and her husband Paul's very favorite meals. Serve the warm, seasoned tofu on a bed of cool leafy greens (such as ready-to-eat organic salad mix, an assortment of greens with sprouts, or the Go-for-the Greens Salad on page 328). Dress the greens with Liquid Gold Dressing (page 329) or another favorite dressing before putting on the tofu. This meal is reminiscent of a California-style hot chicken salad. Choose extra-firm tofu that is set with calcium, and shred it using the large grid of a vegetable or cheese grater. Herbed tofu is especially delightful. This recipe is very versatile. Feel free to add steamed asparagus, sautéed portobello mushrooms, artichoke hearts, or black olives—or simply let your imagination run wild!

2 teaspoons	olive oil	10 ml
12 ounces	extra-firm tofu, herbed or plain, grated	340 g
2 tablespoons	Bragg Liquid Aminos or tamari	30 ml
1 tablespoon	nutritional yeast flakes	15 ml
2	cloves garlic, minced	2
1/4 teaspoon	dried oregano	1 ml
1/4 teaspoon	dried basil	1 ml
1/4 teaspoon	dried parsley or other herbs	1 ml
	freshly ground pepper	
1/4 cup	raw or toasted almonds	60 ml
8 cups	salad greens	2 L

Heat the olive oil in a large skillet. Add the tofu, Bragg Liquid Aminos, nutritional yeast, garlic, herbs, and pepper. Sauté for about 5 minutes or until the tofu is browned. Heap the salad onto two dinner plates using approximately 4 cups (1 L) of salad per plate. Top each salad with half of the tofu mixture and half of the almonds. Serve immediately with your favorite salad dressing.

Note: If you prefer, substitute 1 to 2 tablespoons (15 to 30 ml) of fresh herbs in place of the dry herbs.

Variations

1. Instead of grating the tofu, cut it in strips about ½ x 2 inches (1.25 x 5 cm). Cook it as directed for the grated tofu.

2. Use pumpkin seeds in place of or in addition to the almonds. For a mix, try using 2 tablespoons (30 ml) of each.

3. Be creative with the seasonings. Replace the Mediterranean-style seasonings with any herbs and spices of your choice.

Per half recipe (without salad or dressing):	
calories	422
protein	34 g
fat	29 g
carbohydrate	13 g
dietary fiber	7 g
calcium*	1,230 mg
iron	18 mg
magnesium	104 mg
sodium	677 mg
zinc	3.3 mg
folate	105 mcg
riboflavin	2.4 mg
vitamin B_{12}	1.6 mcg
vitamin C	1.5 mg
vitamin E	4.5 mg
omega-3s	1.0 g
% calories from:	
protein	30%
fat	58%
carbohydrate	12%

Analysis based on calcium-set firm tofu and Red Star Vegetarian Support Formula nutritional yeast (a source of vitamin B_{12}).
*Calcium content varies considerably between different brands of tofu; check labels.

CHUNKY RED LENTIL TOMATO SAUCE

Yield: about 11 cups (2.75 L)

Red lentils are the fastest cooking of all the legumes, as they cook in 25 to 30 minutes. When vegetables are added, the lentils almost dissolve into the sauce. The flavor of red lentils develops best by simmering them for 1 hour or longer or all day in a slow-cooker. If your family is just getting used to legumes, start with only ½ cup (125 ml) of dry lentils; alternatively, use extra for added protein. "Chunky" refers to the vegetables; you can use those listed here, or substitute others that you have on hand. Serve the sauce with your favorite pasta or spaghetti squash.

4 cups	water	1 L
1 cup	red lentils	250 ml
1	large onion, chopped	1
2 to 3	cloves garlic, minced	2 to 3
1	large carrot, sliced diagonally	1
1	stalk broccoli, stem peeled, chopped	1
1 cup	sliced mushrooms (fresh or canned)	250 ml
½ cup	diced green peppers	125 ml
1	small zucchini, sliced or grated	1
28 ounces	canned tomatoes, whole or diced	796 ml
28 ounces	canned tomato sauce	796 ml
2 tablespoons	fresh basil, or 2 teaspoons/10 ml dried	30 ml
2 tablespoons	fresh oregano, or 2 teaspoons/10 ml dried	30 ml
2 tablespoons	tamari or Bragg Liquid Aminos	30 ml
2 tablespoons	cooking wine, optional	30 ml
2 tablespoons	miso, optional	30 ml

Stove-top method. Place the water and lentils in a large pot, bring to a boil, then reduce the heat, cover, and simmer 20 to 25 minutes or until the lentils are soft. Add a little more water if necessary. Add the onion, garlic, carrot, broccoli, mushrooms, green peppers, zucchini, tomatoes, tomato sauce, basil, oregano, tamari, and wine, if using. Bring to boil, then cover, lower the heat, and simmer the sauce for about 1 hour. If using miso, place it in a small bowl; add about ½ cup (125 ml) of the sauce, stir to make a smooth paste, then stir the paste into the sauce.

Slow-cooker method. Place all of the ingredients in slow-cooker. Cook on low for 6 to 8 hours or on high for about 4 hours.

Variations

1. For an extra-fast sauce, use canned or precooked lentils and vegetables. Steam the carrots and broccoli for about 10 minutes. Sauté the onions, mushrooms, peppers, and garlic in 1 tablespoon (15 ml) of olive oil until tender, about 7 minutes. Combine the tomatoes, tomato sauce, cooked vegetables, lentils, optional ingredients, and seasonings in a large pot and simmer for about 20 minutes.

2. Try other vegetables in this recipe. Some good choices are chopped cauliflower, asparagus pieces, sweet peppers, celery, spinach, or kale.

Chef's Tip: Amount of Spaghetti Per Person

It can be a challenge to figure out how much spaghetti to cook per person. One estimate that may be useful is to grasp an amount of dry (10-inch/25-cm) spaghetti noodles that is the diameter of a 25-cent piece, and cook this much for each person. This is about 4 ounces (113 g) of dry pasta and makes a hearty serving of 2 cups (500 ml) per person when cooked.

Per 1 cup (250 ml):	
calories	125
protein	7 g
fat	0.3 g
carbohydrate	26 g
dietary fiber	6 g
calcium*	61 mg
iron	2.3 mg
magnesium	51 mg
sodium*	703 mg
zinc	1.1 mg
folate	105 mcg
riboflavin	0.2 mg
vitamin B$_{12}$	0 mcg
vitamin C	38 mg
vitamin E	1.6 mg
omega-3s	0 g
% calories from:	
protein	22%
fat	2%
carbohydrate	76%

*Sodium is lower if the amounts in the canned tomatoes and tomato sauce are low.

Timesaving Tacos

Yield: 10 tacos (serves 3 to 5 people)

For an instant meal, one of the fastest, nutritionally balanced combinations is the well-loved taco. Just warm the shells and beans, heat the optional Mexican Ground Round, chop the veggies, and set out the colorful fillings in pretty bowls. Let people assemble their own tacos to suit their individual preferences. If you prefer burritos, replace the taco shells with soft tortillas.

12 ounces	Yves Veggie Mexican Ground Round, optional	340 g
2 teaspoons	olive oil, optional	10 ml
14 ounces	canned refried beans	398 ml
1	ripe avocado, mashed or chopped	1
2 teaspoons	fresh lemon juice	10 ml
10	corn taco shells, warmed in oven or microwave	10
2 cups	shredded lettuce	500 ml
2	large ripe tomatoes, chopped	2
1	large carrot, grated	1
3	green onions, thinly sliced	3
1 cup	salsa or taco sauce	250 ml
1/2 cup	sliced pitted olives, optional	125 ml
1 cup	grated soy or cheddar cheese, optional	250 ml

If using the veggie ground round, sauté it in the olive oil on medium heat until lightly browned, about 5 minutes. Meanwhile, warm the refried beans in a small saucepan, vegetable steamer, or microwave. If too thick, add 1 tablespoon (15 ml) of salsa or taco sauce. Mash the avocado and stir in the lemon juice. Place the veggie ground round, taco shells, beans, avocado, lettuce, tomato, carrot, green onions, salsa, olives, and cheese in serving bowls on the table.

Per taco:	
calories	149
protein	4 g
fat	7 g
carbohydrate	20 g
dietary fiber	5 g
calcium	54 mg
iron	1.6 mg
magnesium	28 mg
sodium	302 mg
zinc	2.7 mg
folate	63 mcg
riboflavin	0.1 mg
vitamin B_{12}	0 mcg
vitamin C	14 mg
vitamin E	1.8 mg
omega-3s	0.2 g
% calories from:	
protein	13%
fat	32%
carbohydrate	55%

AFRICAN STEW

Yield: about 4 servings (6 cups/1.5 L)

Peanut butter makes a wonderful, creamy sauce for this nutrition-packed stew that is likely to become a family favorite. Vegetable stock may be made from cubes or powder or purchased ready-made. Lemon juice adds a lively nuance to the flavor. Season the stew with a dash of hot pepper sauce, fiery chipotle sauce, or Vietnamese chili sauce. This recipe is from Cooking Vegetarian *by V. Melina and J. Forest (John Wiley & Sons, New York, NY).*

4 cups	vegetable stock or water	1 L
1	onion, chopped	1
2 cups	peeled, diced yams or sweet potatoes	500 ml
1 cup	cooked or canned chickpeas	250 ml
1 cup	brown rice	250 ml
$1/4$ teaspoon	salt	1 ml
$1/4$ cup	peanut butter	60 ml
2 cups	chopped collards or kale	500 ml
2 tablespoons	fresh lemon juice	30 ml
$1/2$ teaspoon	black pepper	2 ml
1 tablespoon	tamari or Bragg Liquid Aminos	15 ml
	chili sauce	

Heat 2 tablespoons (30 ml) of the stock in a large pot. Add the onion and sauté over medium heat for 5 minutes, adding more stock if necessary. Add the remaining stock, yams, chickpeas, rice, and salt; simmer for 45 minutes. In small bowl, blend the peanut butter with ½ cup (125 ml) of liquid from the stew to make a smooth paste. Stir into the stew along with the collards and cook for 5 minutes. Stir in the lemon juice, pepper, and tamari; add chili sauce to taste. Adjust seasonings.

Per 1 cup (250 ml):	
calories	295
protein	9 g
fat	7 g
carbohydrate	51 g
dietary fiber	7 g
calcium	62 mg
iron	2 mg
magnesium	92 mg
sodium	233 mg
zinc	1.6 mg
folate	97 mcg
riboflavin	0.1 mg
vitamin B$_{12}$	0 mcg
vitamin C	17 mg
vitamin E	2.4 mg
omega-3s	0.1 g
% calories from:	
protein	12%
fat	21%
carbohydrate	67%

SHEPHERD'S PIE

Yield: 8 servings (10 cups/2.5 L)

This classic comfort food may stir fond memories from childhood. It has a dark, rich, meaty-flavored bottom layer followed by a layer of bright yellow corn. Then the whole casserole is covered with a smooth topping of mashed potatoes. To give it a pleasant texture, we used a combination of creamed and whole kernel corn. We suggest using white rather than black pepper because black pepper adds speckles to mashed potatoes. Of course, if you don't mind this appearance, black pepper will do fine, too. Look for vegetarian Worcestershire sauce at your natural food store. One good brand is The Wizard's from Edward & Sons Trading Co.

Potato Topping

8	large russet potatoes, peeled (4 pounds/1.8 kg)	8
3 to 4 tablespoons	olive oil	45 to 60 ml
1/2 cup	fortified soymilk	125 ml
1/2 teaspoon	salt	2 ml
1/4 teaspoon	white or black pepper	1 ml
1/4 teaspoon	paprika	1 ml

Preheat the oven to 350°F (180°C). Spray or lightly oil a 9 x 13-inch (23 x 33-cm) casserole dish and set it aside.

Cut each potato into thirds and cook in boiling water until tender. Drain well, add the oil, soymilk, salt, and pepper, and mash until fluffy. Set aside.

Pie Mixture

1 tablespoon	olive oil	15 ml
2²/₃ cups	diced onions	665 ml
6	cloves garlic, minced	6
1¹/₂ cups	chopped celery	375 ml
12 ounces	Yves Veggie Ground Round	340 g
2 tablespoons + 2 teaspoons	vegetarian Worcestershire sauce	40 ml
2 tablespoons	tamari or Bragg Liquid Aminos	30 ml
1 teaspoon	salt, optional	5 ml
1¹/₂ teaspoons	dried tarragon	7 ml
1 teaspoon	dried thyme	5 ml
¹/₂ teaspoon	black pepper	2 ml
14 ounces	canned creamed corn	398 ml
14 ounces	canned whole kernel corn, drained or 1¹/₂ cups (375 ml) frozen corn kernels, thawed	398 ml

Heat the oil in a skillet, add the onion, garlic, and celery, and sauté over medium-high heat until soft. Turn off the heat. Crumble the veggie ground round and add it to the skillet along with the Worcestershire sauce, tamari, salt, if using, tarragon, thyme, and pepper. Mix thoroughly and transfer to the prepared casserole dish. Spread the mixture evenly. Combine the creamed corn and corn kernels and spread evenly over the veggie ground round mixture. Evenly spread the mashed potato topping over the corn. Sprinkle the top with paprika and bake until heated through, about 20 minutes.

Per 1 cup (250 ml):	
calories	262
protein	6 g
fat	6 g
carbohydrate	48 g
dietary fiber	5 g
calcium	56 mg
iron	1.9 mg
magnesium	54 mg
sodium	627 mg
zinc	1.4 mg
folate	51 mcg
riboflavin	0.1 mg
vitamin B$_{12}$	0.2 mcg
vitamin C	37 mg
vitamin E	1.2 mg
omega-3s	0.1 g
% calories from:	
protein	9%
fat	20%
carbohydrate	71%

CASHEW AND VEGETABLE STIR-FRY

Yield: 2 moderate servings (4 cups/1 L)

To give appealing textures in a stir-fry, the denser vegetables are added at the beginning for longer cooking, and the more tender, leafy vegetables are put in at the end. Serve the stir-fry over brown rice. The recipe can be easily doubled.

Sauce

2 tablespoons	cashew butter or peanut butter	30 ml
1 to 2 tablespoons	Chinese or other chili garlic sauce	15 to 30 ml
1 tablespoon	tamari or Bragg Liquid Aminos	15 ml
1 tablespoon	water	15 ml

Stir-Fry

1/4 cup	cashew nuts	60 ml
1 to 2 teaspoons	olive oil	5 to 10 ml
1	large red, yellow, or white onion, sliced	1
1	large carrot, sliced diagonally	1
1 cup	broccoli florets, chopped	250 ml
1	red pepper, diced	1
1 cup	chopped bok choy or Chinese cabbage	250 ml
1 cup	snow pea pods	250 ml

Combine the cashew butter, chili garlic sauce, tamari, and water in a small bowl, and stir to make a smooth paste. If you wish, toast the cashew nuts lightly in a small frying pan or the oven for a few minutes. (See Chef's Tip, page 321.) Heat the oil in a wok or pan, add the onion, and cook over high heat until it begins to brown, about 3 minutes. Add the carrot and cook for 1 minute; add the broccoli and cook for another 30 seconds; then add the red pepper, bok choy, and snow peas, and cook just long enough to heat through. Add the sauce, stir to combine, sprinkle with the cashews, and serve over rice.

Per 1/2 recipe without rice:	
calories	312
protein	11 g
fat	19 g
carbohydrate	30 g
dietary fiber	8 g
calcium	157 mg
iron	4.8 mg
magnesium	134 mg
sodium	889 mg
zinc	2.5 mg
folate	122 mcg
riboflavin	0.3 mg
vitamin B_{12}	0 mcg
vitamin C	147 mg
vitamin E	4 mg
omega-3s	0.2 g
% calories from:	
protein	14%
fat	50%
carbohydrate	36%

EASIEST-EVER CURRIED LENTILS

Yield: 4 servings (6 cups/1.5 L)

This recipe is a favorite with Vesanto because it's so simple. The hands-on preparation takes about 5 minutes; then it simply cooks for another 45 minutes. Salt is added near the end of the cooking time; if added earlier, it can prevent the lentils from softening properly. The texture and nutrition are best with brown, green, or small French lentils. However, the quick method in variation 4 uses red lentils and is ready in 25 minutes. Patak's brand of curry paste is suggested because it has superb flavor; even the mild variety is plenty hot enough for most tastes. Serve this dish with rice and a salad. Leftovers will keep in the refrigerator for four days; they also freeze well.

5 cups	water	1.25 L
2 cups	brown, green, or French lentils	500 ml
2	medium (or 1 large) onions, chopped	2
1 to 3 tablespoons	Patak's Mild Curry Paste	15 to 45 ml
2 tablespoons	tamari or Bragg Liquid Aminos or 1 teaspoon (5 ml) salt	30 ml

Combine the water, lentils, onions, curry paste, and tamari in a large pot. Mix and bring to a boil. Cover, reduce the heat, and simmer until the lentils are soft enough to mash on the roof of your mouth with your tongue, about 45 minutes. If desired, add more curry paste and tamari.

Variations

1. Add some chopped raw cauliflower at the same time as the lentils or, if you like your cauliflower a little crunchy, after 25 minutes of cooking.
2. Stir in cooked vegetables, such as cauliflower or broccoli, near the end of the cooking time.
3. Add diced raw tomato to the final dish as a garnish.
4. For even faster cooking, use red lentils and simmer for 20 minutes.
5. For a soupier consistency, use more water.

Per 1 cup (250 ml):	
calories	256
protein	19 g
fat	2 g
carbohydrate	42 g
dietary fiber	21 g
calcium	55 mg
iron	6 mg
magnesium	75 mg
sodium	350 mg
zinc	2.4 mg
folate	279 mcg
riboflavin	0.2 mg
vitamin B$_{12}$	0 mcg
vitamin C	8 mg
vitamin E	0.5 mg
omega-3s	0.2 g
% calories from:	
protein	29%
fat	8%
carbohydrate	63%

MUSCLE MUFFINS

Yield: 12 muffins

These muffins are quite different from cake-type muffins; they're heartier and more satisfying and nutritious. Made with soy protein, each muffin provides 8 grams of protein, 3.5 mg of iron, and 143 mg of calcium. Store them in individual plastic bags in your freezer to grab for a mid-morning snack, hiking treat, or a boost after the gym.

1 cup	whole wheat flour	250 ml
1 cup	unbleached flour	250 ml
1/2 cup	soy protein powder, optional	125 ml
1 tablespoon	baking powder	15 ml
1 teaspoon	baking soda	5 ml
1 teaspoon	cinnamon	5 ml
2	frozen or fresh ripe bananas	2
3/4 cup	fortified soymilk	185 ml
1/4 cup	vegetable oil	60 ml
1/4 cup	blackstrap molasses	60 ml
1/4 cup	pure maple syrup	60 ml
2 teaspoons	apple cider vinegar	10 ml
1 cup	raisins or chopped dates	250 ml

Preheat the oven to 350°F (180°C). Lightly oil or spray a 12-cup muffin tin. Place the flours, protein powder, baking powder, soda, and cinnamon in a large bowl and stir to combine. In a smaller bowl, mash the bananas, then stir in the soymilk, oil, molasses, syrup, and vinegar. (If you prefer, you can purée these in a blender.) Add the wet ingredients to the dry ingredients, stir until just blended, and then stir in the raisins. Fill the muffin tins and bake for 30 to 35 minutes or until done. You can tell the muffins are done when they pull away from the sides of the tin, and when the dent made by a finger pressed in the center of a muffin pops up again to its original shape.

Variations

1. Add ½ cup (125 ml) of chopped walnuts or pecans.
2. Replace the mashed bananas with 2 apples, cored and grated.

Per muffin:	
calories	226
protein	8 g
fat	5 g
carbohydrate	39 g
dietary fiber	3 g
calcium	143 mg
iron	3.5 mg
magnesium	54 mg
sodium	216 mg
zinc	1.5 mg
folate	38 mcg
riboflavin	0.2 mg
vitamin B_{12}	0.5 mcg
vitamin C	5 mg
vitamin E	1.3 mg
omega-3s	0.4 g
% calories from:	
protein	14%
fat	20%
carbohydrate	66%

Nutty Date Cookies

Yield: 2 dozen large cookies

These cookies were developed in Brenda's kitchen and were originally featured in Defeating Diabetes by B. Davis, T. Barnard, and B. Bloomfield (Book Publishing Comapny; Summertown, TN). They are delicious enough for the country fair—no one would even suspect they are free of sugar, butter, and eggs! The only sweetener used is cooked dates, yet they are very sweet. In place of canola oil, you may use another high-monounsaturated-fat oil, such as high-oleic sunflower or safflower oil, if desired. Instead of eggs, flaxseeds are used as a binder. Be sure to use fresh walnuts so they don't have any bitter aftertaste. For a low-fat version of this recipe, see variation 1. Enjoy!

2 cups	packed pitted dates	500 ml
1/2 cup	water	125 ml
1 tablespoon	fresh lemon juice	15 ml
1/2 cup	canola oil	125 ml
1/4 cup	soymilk	60 ml
1 teaspoon	vanilla extract	5 ml
1 tablespoon	ground flaxseeds	15 ml
1 cup	whole wheat flour	250 ml
2 teaspoons	baking powder	10 ml
1/2 teaspoon	baking soda	2 ml
1/2 teaspoon	salt	2 ml
1 cup	walnut halves	250 ml

Preheat the oven to 325°F (160°C). Oil a cookie sheet and set it aside.

Combine the dates and water in a small saucepan and bring to a boil. Cover, reduce the heat, and simmer until the dates are soft, about 5 minutes. Remove from the heat and mash (a potato masher works well).

Combine the lemon juice, oil, soymilk, vanilla, ground flaxseeds, and mashed dates in a large bowl. In a small bowl or 2-cup (500-ml) measuring cup, combine the flour, baking powder, baking soda, and salt. Pour the dry ingredients into the wet ingredients and stir to mix (take care not to overmix). Fold in the walnuts.

Drop with a tablespoon onto the prepared cookie sheet. Bake 20 to 25 minutes or until nicely browned. Remove from the oven and cool on a wire rack or on the pan. Store in an airtight container.

Variations

1. **Low-fat variation** with only 4 grams of fat per cookie: Grate 1 large apple, or use ½ cup (125 ml) applesauce, and stir it into the date mixture before adding the flour. Decrease the oil to ¼ cup (60 ml), and decrease the walnuts to ½ cup (125 ml).

2. **For Nutty Cranberry Cookies** add ½ cup (125 ml) dried cranberries, and use pecan halves instead of walnut halves.

Chef's Tip: Ground Flaxseed Egg Replacer

This flaxseed egg substitute works well to replace an egg or two in pancakes, muffins, and most cakes and cookies. It is easy to prepare your own ground flaxseeds: just place ½ cup (125 ml) of whole flaxseeds in a dry blender and process for about 1 minute until all the seeds are ground into a coarse powder. If you prefer a finer powder, blend until the desired consistency is reached. Ground flaxseeds can be stored for several months in a jar in the refrigerator or freezer; they will retain their omega-3s either way. When stored in the freezer, ground flaxseeds will remain powdery and do not need to be thawed before using. In recipes, use the proportions listed below as a replacement for one egg.

1 tablespoon	ground flaxseeds	15 ml
3 tablespoon	water	45 ml

Combine the ground flaxseeds and water in a bowl and mix well. When thick, add to the wet ingredients of your recipe.

Per cookie:	
calories	129
protein	1.8 g
fat	8 g
carbohydrate	16 g
dietary fiber	2 g
calcium	39 mg
iron	0.7 mg
magnesium	33 mg
sodium	132 mg
zinc	0.7 mg
folate	9 mcg
riboflavin	0 mg
vitamin B_{12}	0 mcg
vitamin C	0 mg
vitamin E	12 mg
omega-3s	0.2 g
% calories from:	
protein	5%
fat	50%
carbohydrate	45%

CHOCOLATE MINT NUT BARS

Yield: 21 small bars

These wonderful, energy-packed chocolate candies are super simple to make. Be creative—almost anything goes! Make a double batch for the holidays, as they keep beautifully. To make these even more like fudge or candy, reduce the cereal to 1 cup (250 ml). You can replace the chocolate with 2.5 ounces (70 g) of carob chips, if desired.

$^1/_2$ cup	syrup (corn, rice, or barley malt syrup)	125 ml
$^1/_4$ cup	tahini or other seed or nut butter	60 ml
$2^1/_2$ ounces	semisweet baking chocolate ($2^1/_2$ squares)	70 g
$^1/_4$ teaspoon	mint extract	1 ml
1 cup	flaked cereal	250 ml
1 cup	puffed cereal	250 ml
$^1/_2$ cup	chopped walnuts or other unsalted nuts	125 ml

Lightly oil a 4 x 9-inch (10 x 23-cm) loaf pan and set it aside. Combine the syrup, tahini, and chocolate in a medium saucepan. Place over medium-low heat, stirring frequently, until the chocolate melts and the mixture begins to bubble. Remove from the heat and add the mint extract. Stir in the cereal and nuts and mix until they are evenly coated with the chocolate mixture. Pack the mixture into the prepared loaf pan, refrigerate for 30 minutes or until set, and cut into squares. Store in the refrigerator.

Note: This recipe can be doubled. Just use an 8 x 8-inch (20 x 20-cm) pan for the larger batch.

Nutrition Boosters

Calcium booster. Use almonds and almond butter.

Zinc booster. Use cashews and cashew butter.

Omega-3 booster. Use walnuts and flaked cereal that contains flaxseeds.

Protein and pocketbook booster. Use peanuts and peanut butter.

Cory's Cranberry Squares

Replace the mint extract with 1 teaspoon (5 ml) vanilla extract. Use a total of only 1 cup of cereal. Instead of flaked or puffed cereal, toasted oats may be used. Add ⅔ cup (165 ml) of dried cranberries and, if desired, ¼ cup (60 ml) of dried, unsweetened coconut at the same time the cereal and nuts are added.

Chocolate Mint Nut Balls

Both the mint and cranberry squares can be rolled into balls. Spread ⅓ cup (85 ml) of fine, unsweetened coconut onto a plate or wide, shallow bowl. Take a spoonful of the chocolate mixture, form it into a ball about 1 inch (2.5 cm) in diameter, and roll the ball in the coconut. Store in the refrigerator until used. These freeze well. (Yield: about 21 to 24 balls)

Chef's Tip: Toasting Rolled Oats

Rolled oats can be toasted in the microwave on high for 2 minutes, in a skillet on medium heat for 5 minutes, or in the oven at 350°F (180°C) for 10 to 15 minutes.

Per bar:	
calories	87
protein	1 g
fat	4 g
carbohydrate	11 g
dietary fiber	1 g
calcium	7 mg
iron	0.4 mg
magnesium	7 mg
sodium	11 mg
zinc	0.2 mg
folate	6 mcg
riboflavin	0 mg
vitamin B_{12}	0 mcg
vitamin C	0 mg
vitamin E	0.2 mg
omega-3s	0.3 g
% calories from:	
protein	7%
fat	43%
carbohydrate	50%

LEMON TEASECAKE

Yield: 10 servings

This is one of the scrumptious desserts at Seattle's gourmet vegetarian restaurant, Café Ambrosia, and was developed by executive chef and owner Francis Janes. With a revolving international menu, Café Ambrosia is an absolute must for those who wish to experience innovative, organic, vegetarian fine dining. People with food allergies will be delighted to find that both the crust and filling in this dessert are free of eggs, dairy, wheat, and soy. Choose Meyer lemons when in season, as they are sweeter and milder than the Eureka and Lisbon varieties common to most produce departments. Meyer lemons are available from November through March in specialty food stores.

Oatmeal Cinnamon Crust

1 cup	rolled oats	250 ml
1/2 cup	brown rice flour	125 ml
1/2 cup	ground walnuts	125 ml
1 teaspoon	cinnamon	5 ml
1/2 teaspoon	sea salt	2 ml
1 teaspoon	vanilla extract	5 ml
3 tablespoons	pure maple syrup	45 ml
1/4 cup	canola oil	60 ml

Filling

1/2 cup	millet	125 ml
2 1/2 cups	water	625 ml
1/2 cup	raw cashews	125 ml
1/3 cup	fresh lemon juice	85 ml
1/3 cup	pure maple syrup	85 ml
2 teaspoons	vanilla extract	10 ml
1 teaspoon	lemon extract	5 ml

Topping

8 ounces	cherry or other fruit preserves	250 ml
2	kiwi fruit, peeled, sliced thin into rounds	2
	or other sliced fruit or berries for decoration	

To make the crust

Preheat the oven to 350°F (180°C). Combine the oats, flour, walnuts, cinnamon, and salt in a large bowl and mix well. In a smaller bowl or measuring cup, combine the vanilla, maple syrup, and oil and stir well. Pour into the dry ingredients and mix thoroughly. Press firmly into an 8- or 9-inch (20-cm) springform pan. Bake until lightly browned, about 15 minutes. Cool at least 30 minutes before filling.

To make the filling

Combine the millet and water in a medium saucepan and bring to a boil. Cover tightly and simmer over low heat until the water is completely absorbed and the millet is soft, about 30 minutes. While the millet is cooking, place the cashews, lemon juice, maple syrup, and extracts in a blender. Process on high speed for 3 minutes or until perfectly smooth. If necessary, scrape down the sides of the blender jar with a spatula and process for another minute. Add the warm millet and process on high speed until creamy, about 3 minutes longer. Pour into the cooled crust.

Cool the filling and crust at room temperature for 1 hour. Place plastic wrap over the surface to prevent excess cracking. Place in the refrigerator and chill for at least 4 hours before serving. Teasecake will keep for about three days in the refrigerator.

To make the topping

Place the fruit preserves in a small saucepan and stir over medium-low heat until barely melted. Spread this topping evenly over the chilled and set filling. When ready to serve, garnish with slices of kiwi fruit or any combination of sliced fruit and/or berries.

Per slice ($^1/_{10}$ of cake):	
calories	360
protein	5 g
fat	14 g
carbohydrate	57 g
dietary fiber	3 g
calcium	41 mg
iron	2.2 mg
magnesium	49 mg
sodium	131 mg
zinc	1.6 mg
folate	31 mcg
riboflavin	0.1 mg
vitamin B_{12}	0 mcg
vitamin C	22 mg
vitamin E	2 mg
omega-3s	1.1 g
% calories from:	
protein	6%
fat	33%
carbohydrate	61%

GERMAN CHOCOLATE CAKE

Yield: 16 servings

The recipes of chef Ron Pickarski are designed to support personal health and the health of the natural environment while tantalizing the most sophisticated taste buds. They truly are amazing! You will find his books Eco-Cuisine *and* Friendly Foods *(both from Ten Speed Press), video, and vegan products at www.eco-cuisine.com. Ron is a seven-time Culinary Olympics medal winner whose dishes range from the everyday to the elegant. This superb cake with Coconut Squash Icing is a great way to introduce people to the delights of vegan cuisine. It is a celebratory way of getting our day's supply of omega-3 fatty acids from the walnuts and canola oil!*

1¹/₂ cups	unbleached sugar (such as Sucanat) or brown sugar	375 ml
1¹/₂ cups	unbleached white flour	375 ml
1¹/₂ cups	whole wheat flour	375 ml
³/₄ cup	cocoa or carob powder	185 ml
2 teaspoons	baking soda	10 ml
¹/₂ teaspoon	salt	2 ml
2 cups	water	500 ml
¹/₂ cup	pure maple syrup	125 ml
6 tablespoons	canola oil	90 ml
2 tablespoons	apple cider vinegar	30 ml
2 teaspoons	vanilla extract	10 m

Preheat the oven to 350°F (180°C). Lightly oil and flour 2 (9-inch/23-cm) round cake pans (springform pans are ideal) and set aside.

Combine the sugar, flours, cocoa, soda, and salt in a large bowl and mix well. In another bowl, combine the water, maple syrup, oil, vinegar, and vanilla extract. Pour into the dry ingredients and mix well. Pour the batter into the prepared cake pans and bake until a toothpick inserted into the center comes out dry, about 30 minutes. Cool completely. Turn one layer onto a serving plate so that bottom is facing up. Spread one-third of the Coconut Squash Cake Icing (recipe follows) onto the surface. Place the other layer on top of the icing and spread the remaining icing on top. (The layers of icing will be thick.) Do not ice the sides.

COCONUT SQUASH CAKE ICING

Yield: 6 cups

2 cups	almond milk	500 ml
1/4 cup	coconut milk	60 ml
1 cup	dried unsweetened coconut	250 ml
3 tablespoons	arrowroot powder	45 ml
3 tablespoons	cool water	45 ml
1 cup	unbleached sugar (such as Sucanat) or brown sugar	250 ml
1/2 teaspoon	vanilla extract	2 ml
1/2 cup	steamed and peeled butternut squash	125 ml
2 cups	chopped walnuts, ground to a medium-coarse meal	500 ml

Combine the almond milk, coconut milk, and dried coconut in a medium saucepan and bring to a simmer over medium heat. Meanwhile, dissolve the arrowroot in the cool water. Remove the saucepan from heat, add the arrowroot mixture, and stir vigorously with a whisk until thickened. Stir in the sugar and vanilla, then transfer the mixture to a blender. Add the squash and walnuts and blend until smooth. Chill for 1 hour before using.

Per slice (1/16 cake) with Coconut Squash Cake Icing:

calories	452
protein	6 g
fat	20 g
carbohydrate	67 g
dietary fiber	5 g
calcium	94 mg
iron	3 mg
magnesium	78 mg
sodium	270 mg
zinc	1.6 mg
folate	23 mcg
riboflavin	0.1 mg
vitamin B_{12}	0 mcg
vitamin C	1 mg
vitamin E	3.4 mg
omega-3s	1.8 g
% calories from:	
protein	6%
fat	38%
carbohydrate	56%

SUPER SIMPLE CHOCOLATE ICING

Yield: 3$\frac{1}{2}$ cups

This classic chocolate icing is a simple alternative to using Ron Pickarski's gourmet Coconut Squash Cake Icing on the German Chocolate Cake (page 356). It is perfect for a birthday cake and can be decorated in the traditional way with writing, grated chocolate, coconut, nuts, or sprinkles, and candles. Put any decorations on before the icing sets, especially if you want to decorate the sides of the cake.

3 cups	confectioners' sugar	750 ml
$\frac{1}{4}$ cup	cocoa powder	60 ml
2 tablespoons	nonhydrogenated margarine	30 ml
3 tablespoons	fortified soymilk or other milk	45 ml
1 teaspoon	vanilla extract	5 ml

Combine the confectioners' sugar and cocoa powder in a medium bowl. Stir in the margarine, soymilk, and vanilla. Beat until smooth and creamy. If the icing is too thick, add another tablespoon (15 ml) or so of soymilk until the desired consistency is reached. Spread about one-third of the icing on the first layer of the German Chocolate Cake (page 356). Place the second layer on top. Spread another one-third of the icing on the top layer, and the final one-third on the sides of the cake (or you may use one-half of the icing between the layers and one-half on top). Decorate immediately.

Per slice ($\frac{1}{16}$ cake) with Super Simple Chocolate Icing:	
calories	316
protein	4 g
fat	7 g
carbohydrate	63 g
dietary fiber	3 g
calcium	37 mg
iron	2 mg
magnesium	47 mg
sodium	260 mg
zinc	1.1 mg
folate	6 mcg
riboflavin	0.1 mg
vitamin B$_{12}$	0 mcg
vitamin C	0 mg
vitamin E	2 mg
omega-3s	0.5 g
% calories from:	
protein	5%
fat	20%
carbohydrate	75%

BERRY DELICIOUS ICE DREAM

Yield: 3 servings (3 cups/750 ml)

This creamy, sweet "ice cream" is sure to be a favorite with those who want to avoid dairy products, fat, or excess calories. You won't be disappointed; it is bursting with real fruit flavor. Put it in fancy sherbet glasses and serve it to your guests for a refreshing summer treat.

3	frozen bananas (See Chef's Tip, page 315)	3
1 cup	frozen berries (such as raspberries, strawberries, or blueberries)	250 ml
1 cup	fortified soymilk (vanilla or plain) or vanilla soy or dairy yogurt	250 ml
2 tablespoons	frozen juice concentrate (orange, citrus blend, peach, or mango)	30 ml

Place the frozen bananas, berries, soymilk, and frozen juice concentrate in a blender or food processor. Blend on high speed until completely smooth. Serve immediately in bowls or in cups with a spoon. Top with nuts or fresh berries, if desired.

Note: A sturdy blender is ideal for this recipe, although many food processors will work well too. If your blender struggles to blend the mixture, it will help to partially thaw the fruit first, especially the strawberries.

Variation

Replace some or all of the berries with other frozen fruit, such as peaches, kiwi, mango, or melon.

Per 1 cup (250 ml):	
calories	200
protein	4 g
fat	2 g
carbohydrate	45 g
dietary fiber	6 g
calcium	126 mg
iron	1.3 mg
magnesium	67 mg
sodium	51 mg
zinc	0.6 mg
folate	73 mcg
riboflavin	0.2 mg
vitamin B_{12}	1 mcg
vitamin C	37 mg
vitamin E	0.6 mg
omega-3s	0.1 g
% calories from:	
protein	8%
fat	9%
carbohydrate	83%

APPENDIX

DIETARY REFERENCE INTAKES FOR VITAMINS AND MINERALS

TABLE 15.1 DIETARY REFERENCE INTAKES FOR VITAMINS*

Life Stage/ Age	Vitamin A (mcg)	Vitamin C (mg)	Vitamin D (mcg)	Vitamin E (mg)	Vitamin K (mcg)	Thiamin (mg)	Riboflavin (mg)	Niacin (mg)	Vitamin B_6 (mg)	Folate (mcg)	Vit B_{12} (mcg)	Pantothenic Acid (mg)	Biotin (mcg)	Choline (mcg)
Infants														
0–6 months	400	40	5	4	2.0	0.2	0.3	2	0.1	65	0.4	1.7	5	125
7–12 months	500	50	5	5	2.5	0.3	0.4	4	0.3	80	0.5	1.8	6	150
Children														
1–3 years	**300**	**15**	5	**6**	30	**0.5**	**0.5**	**6**	**0.5**	**150**	**0.9**	2	8	200
4–8 years	**400**	**25**	5	**7**	55	**0.6**	**0.6**	**8**	**0.6**	**200**	**1.2**	3	12	250
Males														
9–13 years	**600**	**45**	5	**11**	60	**0.9**	**0.9**	**12**	**1.0**	**300**	**1.8**	4	20	375
14–18 years	**900**	**75**	5	**15**	75	**1.2**	**1.3**	**16**	**1.3**	**400**	**2.4**	5	25	550
19–30 years	**900**	**90**	5	**15**	120	**1.2**	**1.3**	**16**	**1.3**	**400**	**2.4**	5	30	550
31–50 years	**900**	**90**	5	**15**	120	**1.2**	**1.3**	**16**	**1.3**	**400**	**2.4**	5	30	550
51–70 years	**900**	**90**	10	**15**	120	**1.2**	**1.3**	**16**	**1.7**	**400**	**2.4**	5	30	550
>70 years	**900**	**90**	15	**15**	120	**1.2**	**1.3**	**16**	**1.7**	**400**	**2.4**	5	30	550
Females														
9–13 years	**600**	**45**	5	**11**	60	**0.9**	**0.9**	**12**	**1.0**	**300**	**1.8**	4	20	375
14–18 years	**700**	**65**	5	**15**	75	**1.0**	**1.0**	**14**	**1.2**	**400**	**2.4**	5	25	400
19–30 years	**700**	**75**	5	**15**	90	**1.1**	**1.1**	**14**	**1.3**	**400**	**2.4**	5	30	425
31–50 years	**700**	**75**	5	**15**	90	**1.1**	**1.1**	**14**	**1.3**	**400**	**2.4**	5	30	425
51–70 years	**700**	**75**	10	**15**	90	**1.1**	**1.1**	**14**	**1.5**	**400**	**2.4**	5	30	425
>70 years	**700**	**75**	15	**15**	90	**1.1**	**1.1**	**14**	**1.5**	**400**	**2.4**	5	30	425
Pregnancy														
≤18 years	**750**	**80**	5	**15**	75	**1.4**	**1.4**	**18**	**1.9**	**600**	**2.6**	6	30	450
19–30 years	**770**	**85**	5	**15**	90	**1.4**	**1.4**	**18**	**1.9**	**600**	**2.6**	6	30	450
31–50 years	**770**	**85**	5	**15**	90	**1.4**	**1.4**	**18**	**1.9**	**600**	**2.6**	6	30	450
Lactation														
≤18 years	**1,200**	**115**	5	**19**	75	**1.4**	**1.6**	**17**	**2.0**	**500**	**2.8**	7	35	550
19–30 years	**1,300**	**120**	5	**19**	90	**1.4**	**1.6**	**17**	**2.0**	**500**	**2.8**	7	35	550
31–50 years	**1,300**	**120**	5	**19**	90	**1.4**	**1.6**	**17**	**2.0**	**500**	**2.8**	7	35	550

* Recommended dietary allowances (RDAs) are in **bold type** and adequate intakes (AIs) are in regular type. Both RDA and AI can be used as goals for individual intake. Source: Food and Nutrition Board, the Institute of Nutrition, National Academy of Sciences. All Dietary Reference Intake reports can be accessed free at www.nap.edu (search for "Dietary Reference Intakes" and several books will be shown—all can be opened online and read free of charge).

TABLE 15.2 DIETARY REFERENCE INTAKES FOR MINERALS*

Life stage/age	Calcium mg	Chromium mcg	Copper mcg	Fluoride mg	Iodine mcg	Iron mg	Magnesium mg	Manganese mg	Molybdenum mcg	Phosphorus mg	Selenium mcg	Zinc mg
Infants												
0–6 months	210	0.2	200	0.01	110	0.27	30	0.003	2	100	15	2
7–12 months	270	5.5	220	0.5	130	11	75	0.6	3	275	20	3
Children												
1–3 years	500	11	340	0.7	90	7	80	1.2	17	460	20	3
4–8 years	800	15	440	1	90	10	130	1.5	22	500	30	5
Males												
9–13 years	1,300	25	700	2	120	8	240	1.9	34	1,250	40	8
14–18 years	1,300	35	890	3	150	11	410	2.2	43	1,250	55	11
19–30 years	1,000	35	900	4	150	8	400	2.3	45	700	55	11
31–50 years	1,000	35	900	4	150	8	420	2.3	45	700	55	11
51–70 years	1,200	30	900	4	150	8	420	2.3	45	700	55	11
>70 years	1,200	30	900	4	150	8	420	2.3	45	700	55	11
Females												
9–13 years	1,300	21	700	2	120	8	240	1.6	34	1,250	40	8
14–18 years	1,300	24	890	3	150	15	360	1.6	43	1,250	55	9
19–30 years	1,000	25	900	3	150	18	310	1.8	45	700	55	8
31–50 years	1,000	25	900	3	150	18	320	1.8	45	700	55	8
51–70 years	1,200	20	900	3	150	8	320	1.8	45	700	55	8
>70 years	1,200	20	900	3	150	8	320	1.8	45	700	55	8
Pregnancy												
≤18 years	1,300	29	1,000	3	220	27	400	2.0	50	1,250	60	13
19–30 years	1,000	30	1,000	3	220	27	350	2.0	50	700	60	11
31–50 years	1,000	30	1,000	3	220	27	360	2.0	50	700	60	11
Lactation												
≤18 years	1,300	44	1,300	3	290	10	360	2.6	50	1,250	70	14
19–30 years	1,000	45	1,300	3	290	9	310	2.6	50	700	70	12
31–50 years	1,000	45	1,300	3	290	9	320	2.6	50	700	70	12

* Recommended dietary allowances (RDAs) are in **bold type** and adequate intakes (AIs) are in regular type. Both RDA and AI can be used as goals for individual intake.
Source: Food and Nutrition Board, the Institute of Nutrition, National Academy of Sciences. All Dietary Reference Intake reports can be accessed free at www.nap.edu
(search for "Dietary Reference Intakes" and several books will be shown—all can be opened online and read free of charge).

INDEX

Tables, figures, and recipe titles are shown in italic.

C

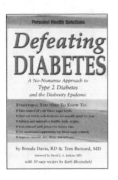